Issues and Perspectives
in The Korean Peace Process

ISSUES AND PERSPECTIVES IN THE KOREAN PEACE PROCESS

UNDERSTANDING OF THE KOREAN PEACE PROCESS

DIPLOMATIC APPROACH TO THE KOREAN PEACE PROCESS

IMPLEMENTATION AND EXECUTION OF THE KOREAN PEACE PROCESS

FUTURE OF THE KOREAN PEACE PROCESS

THE KOREAN ASSOCIATION OF INTERNATIONAL STUDIES
SANG-HWAN LEE / SCOTT GATES

HU:iNE

This work was supported by the Korea Foundation and the result of the KAIS(Korean Association of International Studies)-PRIO(Peace Research Institute Oslo) joint academic conference on the Korean peace process.

Preface

This book seeks to bring about a greater understanding of Korean peace process by exploring past and present policy toward North Korea since the 1990s. The Korean peace process was initiated in order to resolve the inter-Korean conflict and denuclearize North Korea. In 1998, South Korean President Kim Dae-jung announced a Sunshine Policy towards North Korea and an Inter-Korean summit was held in 2000. In 2006, North Korea conducted its first nuclear test. A second inter-Korean summit was held in 2007. In 2017 South Korean President Moon Jae-in returned to the Sunshine Policy. A summit between Moon and Kim took place in the South Korean zone of the Joint Security Area, and they signed the Panmunjom Declaration pledging to work towards a permanent peace to the Korean peninsula and the complete denuclearization of Korea.

President Trump met with North Korean leader Kim on June 12, 2018, in the first summit in Singapore. They signed a joint statement, agreeing to reaffirmation of the denuclearization of the Korean Peninsula, security guarantees for North Korea, recovery of soldiers' remains, and follow-up high-level talks. President Trump met with Kim Jong-un of North Korea on February 27, 2019, in the second summit in Hanoi, Vietnam. The summit was cut short without any agreement. On June 30, 2019, Trump of the US and Moon of South Korea met with Kim of North Korea at the DMZ. At the brief meeting both US and North Korea agreed to resume denuclearization talks, ended in deadlock at the Hanoi Summit. North Korea, nonetheless, continued short–range missile tests in 2019. All the nations around the Korean peninsula demand a regional security system for peace and stability in Northeast Asia. A possible solution is to develop the US-included regional security regime.

This book deals with four main subjects—Understanding of the Korean Peace Process, Diplomatic Approach to the Korean Peace Process, Implementation and Execution of the Korean Peace Process, and Future of the Korean Peace Process. The search for historical lessons is a perpetual one that is fraught with conflicting judgments. Ignoring such lesson, however, tempts far greater perils. The American philosopher George Santayana mentioned, "Those who cannot remember the past are condemned to repeat it." The insights inspires and sustains this book. As readers will discover, past is prologue in many aspects of inter-Korean relations and great powers' foreign policies toward two Koreas.

Acknowledgments

This book is truly a group effort. It is the result of the KAIS(Korean Association of International Studies)-PRIO(Peace Research Institute Oslo) joint academic conference on the Korean peace process hosted by the KAIS and supported by the KF(Korea Foundation). We appreciate the help of the external reviewers who provided invaluable guidance throughout the texts. We also thank to Professor Youngwan Kim who managed the details of the KF project and assisted in the editorial process, and to Hankuk University of Foreign Studies Knowledge Contents & Press for helping in publishing this book. Finally, we are deeply grateful to President Geun Lee of the Korea Foundation for supporting the KAIS to publish this book.

Table of contents

Preface 5

Introduction

Chapter 1 The Korean Peace Process in the Context of Conflicts in the Global and Regional Orders
Sang-Hwan Lee · Scott Gates 9

Understanding of the Korean Peace Process

Chapter 2 The Direction of the Korean Peninsula's Peace from the Perspective of Peace Studies
Soo Hwan Hwang 29

Chapter 3 South Korea's Tasks on the Peace Process & Unification Policy
Sukhoon Hong 52

Diplomatic Approach to the Korean Peace Process

Chapter 4 How Commitment Problems Affect the Prospects for Peace in the Korean Peninsula
Scott Gates · Havard Mokleiv Nygård 75

Chapter 5 A Systematic Analysis of the Trump Foreign Policy:
Implications for Northeast Asia and the Korean Peninsula
Dongsoo Kim 104

Chapter 6 The Impact of U.S.-China Power Competition on the Korean Peace Process
Wonjae Hwang 124

Chapter 7 **Sunrise, Sunset:**
The Rise and Fall of Inter-Korean Economic Relations
Inhan Kim 142

Implementation and Execution of the Korean Peace Process

Chapter 8 **Political Oppression, Human Rights, and UN Targeted Sanctions:**
A Case of North Korea
Jiyoun Park · Hyun Jin Choi 167

Chapter 9 **Bridge between South and North Korea:**
Analysis of South Korean Aid to North Korea for Peace in the Korean Peninsula
Youngwan Kim · Jaeyoung Hur · Jiyoun Park 191

Chapter 10 **What Do We Know and Do Not Know?:**
Attitudes Toward North Korea and Unification
Jaeyoung Hur · Sanghoon Park 214

Chapter 11 **Japan and South Korea:**
Can they get along by overcoming the challenges?
Atsushi Tago 242

Future of the Korean Peace Process

Chapter 12 **Be Careful What You Wish For:**
Security Challenges Facing the Korean Peninsula During a Potential Unification Process
Mason Richey · Daewon Ohn · Jangho Kim · Jae Jeok Park 267

Chapter 13 **Challenges and Opportunities of the '*Korean Peace Process*' in the Moon Jae-in Government:**
Lessons from '*NAPCI*' in the Park Geun-hye Government
Eunmi Choi 299

Authors' Bios 326

Chapter 1. Introduction

The Korean Peace Process in the Context of Conflicts in the Global and Regional Orders

Sang-Hwan Lee (Hankuk University of Foreign Studies)
Scott Gates (University of Oslo and Peace Research Institute Oslo(PRIO))

COVID-19 may one day be recorded in history as the origin of the Neo-Cold War between the US and China. A new global order has emerged in the wake of the virus's spread, characterized by de-globalization and digitalization of the global community. COVID-19 has accelerated the de-globalization trends in domestic and global societies and deviations from shared values have resulted in a Neo-Cold War Order. The Neo-Cold War is a product of the US-China hegemonic struggles in the post-cold war period in association with China's rapid economic and military growth. Their value clashes further have riven the relationship.

The shift from a world of globalized and open societies to an international order based on de-globalization and closed societies concerns us. A valuable lesson COVID-19 taught us is that communitarian cooperation and open societies guarantee an optimistic future in the global order.

The rise of China affects not only US hegemony but constitutes a more immediate regional power transition with Japan in northeast Asia and plays a critical role in shaping the peace process in the Korean peninsula. Indeed, to understand the Korean peace process, we must consider these three different layers of politics, in the Korean Peninsula, Northeast Asia, and the global order. All three layers will be examined through the lens of power transition theory. The rise of China profoundly shapes all of these relations.

The Global Order: From US Preponderance to Sino–US Competition

[China as a dissatisfied challenger]

For almost two decades, the most significant feature of the global balance of power has been the steady rise of Chinese economic and military strength, as well as the spread of its soft power. Indeed, the most important, and persistent, issue relating to the rise of China is whether China is willing and able to take over as the lone superpower (Lee & Kim 2016).

Given China's capabilities and intentions, China cannot initiate the power transition for the time being. The US still maintains supremacy in terms of military capabilities, usage of IT technologies, and physical quality of life. China will take another couple of decades at the very least to develop its capabilities to reach parity with the US. China also faces fundamental difficulties in eliciting a power transition away from the US, because the US is a different type of hegemonic power than any previous rising state has faced. Representing Western civilization, the current international order led by the US is easy to integrate into, but difficult to deconstruct. In this light, China's power transition, and taking over as global hegemon seems hardly possible for the time being (Lee & Kim 2016).

There have been many differing analyses concerning a potential power transition from the US to China. Chinese analysts have argued that current US power is on the decline; that the US-led unipolar system is unambiguously creeping towards an end and making room for a multipolar system; and that the current international order may be under a radical shift. Some have highlighted the US' neglect of its soft power and its subsequent loss of legitimacy as a leader in the international arena (Lam, 2010; Lampton, 2010; and Saunders, 2010). Reviewing changes in Chinese perceptions of US power and the future international order, American China experts have suggested that the major source of the current Sino-American confrontation is the serious Chinese miscalculation, stemming from the combination of its diplomatic overconfidence and its internal insecurity (Nye, 2010; Glaser and Morris, 2009).

Notably, given the growing diversity within the Chinese academia and society, some Chinese scholars have cautiously and rationally warned against drawing premature conclusions. Generally positioned in the higher echelons of academia and representing the majority opinion, these scholars have argued that no conspicuous rationale suggests that the US is falling in an irrecoverable setback and have also ruled out the possibility of a fundamental change to the global balance of power. Given the current international environment, they insist, no state has been able to constitute a comprehensive challenge against the US, and the current international power structure of "one superpower and many great powers" will continue for the foreseeable future. Admitting that there is no decline in US power and no fundamental changes in the global structure, these scholars have drawn a conclusion that China should avoid becoming embroiled in the central maelstrom of global politics and prioritize, instead, managing its own domestic affairs (Lam 2010).

Critical to US and China relations and the prospects of a power transition is the degree of satisfaction with the current global system exhibited by China. System satisfaction can be understood in terms of bilateral coordination, cooperation, and recognition between the US and China. We draw on a prominent study that employs content analysis of articles appearing in Chosun Ilbo (a prominent South Korean newspaper) from the period 2003 to 2013 (H. Kim, 2014). A total of 348 articles regarding US-China relations were classified in terms of conflict (210 cases), cooperation (98 cases) and other (40 cases). Note that there have been twice as many conflict cases as cooperation cases for the period.

Conflict over economic issues has primarily related to exchange rates, energy, and trade. Exchange rate problems concern currency valuation, where the US has been more offensive and China more defensive. They have often reproached each other but avoided catastrophe. In contrast, as the US trade deficit resulting from Chinese import penetration has expanded, economic relations have been more conflictual, especially during the Trump administration. Notably, in spite of these tensions, the two powers have successfully managed crises through strategic dialogue.

Security relations between the US and China relate to North Korea, military training, and territorial disputes. Their views on how to deal with the North Korean nuclear tests and missile launches differ substantially. In addition, several conflicts concerning military training of US allies and territorial disputes in East Asia have flared, but the conflicts have been managed.

The two countries, nevertheless, have narrowed the differences between their views. According to Pew Research, there have been ups and downs in conflictive and cooperative events; and sometimes they occur together. In sum, China cannot yet be categorized as a dissatisfied great power willing to challenge the US globally as a hegemon in the terms described by the power transition theory (Lee & Kim 2016).

The Regional Order: From Power Parity between China and Japan(+US) to Sino-Japanese(+US) Competition [China as a dissatisfied challenger]

Bilateral security arrangements of northeast Asia remain the lynch pin of security relations in the region. The region is extremely diverse in its politics, economics, and culture; strongly nationalistic in its outlook; and China, Russia, the US, and Japan are great powers with their own differing interests and strategies, giving the region a very different character to that of Europe. Northeast Asian security depends on a hub-and-spokes network of bilateral arrangements centered on the US. This security order, forged in the aftermath of the civil wars of China and Korea, has endured for more than sixty years. As the East-West confrontation of the Cold War came to its end, the strategic and political environment in northeast Asia changed, but to a much lesser extent than in the Europe Atlantic region. In Europe, shared political values, economic interests, and cultural roots helped to underpin a peace mechanism. Similar circumstances have never existed in northeast Asia, and a sense of common security interest cannot be created artificially under the currently prevailing policies of confrontation and polarization (Lee & Kim 2016).

In contrast to the global level, the rise of China has been more conspicuously felt in the East Asia region in general and in the Northeast Asian region in particular. China has been more assertive in challenging the traditional American influence over the region. Taking advantage of its economic vitality, China wants to be seen by its East Asian neighboring states as a more attractive and reliable partner to cooperate with. China also pursues securing more emotional and moral support from the East Asian states by projecting it's a more refined and beneficial image to them (Li, 2008; 2009).

With the increase of Chinese economic clout in the region, more specifically the strategic leverage that the Chinese enjoy due to their economic influence, China has, arguably, risen to become another pole in northeast Asia. Although the Chinese have downsized their armed forces in numbers, the reduction in numbers has been offset by qualitative improvements. As the trend in China's defense spending shows, a massive modernization program has been undertaken. China's renewed military doctrine (blue-water navy and other power projection capabilities), and recent statements and actions in the South China Sea, including their efforts to revise the territorial status quo through an enlargement strategy, support this argument (Lee & Kim 2016).

The structure of the global order may be unipolar, but the Northeast Asian regional order exhibits a bipolar structure in which China and Japan—together with the US—are competing for a larger share of the balance of influence (revisionist vs. maintenance of the status quo). China also draws considerable strength from the size of its territory and population, as well as from its cultural cohesion and history. China's humiliation by the great powers during the 'century of humiliation' underlies its goal of building a powerful, modern state – a goal which preceded the 'four modernizations' as defined by the reformers under Deng Xiaoping, as well as the ascendancy of the Communist Party in 1949. Considering that China traditionally has been a regional great power, China's attempt to throw her weight around in northeast Asia is normal and expected (Lee & Kim 2016).

This is particularly true for Japan. To Japan, China is a legitimate geo-strategic threat. The Japanese see growing Chinese influence on its neighbors as well as its growing military capabilities as a prime threat to its national interests. The disputed islands of Senkaku, Chinese military activities in the South China Sea, historical legacies, and competition for a leading role in East Asian security and economic architecture all add to Japanese sense of insecurity. Japanese efforts to strengthen its alliance with the US and renew its defense guidelines can be seen as reactions to the effects of a more assertive China (Lee & Kim 2016).

Power transition from Japan to China is ongoing in Northeast Asia. China is ahead of Japan in military and economic capabilities. Moreover, consider Chinese satisfaction with the current regional system. Regional system satisfaction can be understood by bilateral recognitions between China and Japan. Turning again to the content analysis results from Chosun Ilbo (H. Kim, 2014), a total of 207 articles involving Japan and China were classified into conflict (142 cases), cooperation (60 cases) and others (5 cases). Since 2010, bilateral confrontations between China and Japan frequently occurred concerning territorial disputes, economic issues, and Japanese historical legacy and failure to admit past wrongs. The number of conflict cases is far greater than that of cooperation cases. Several conflicts concerning the East China Sea Gas development have been tense (Lee

& Kim 2016). The main issues regarding China–Japan security relations relate to North Korea and territorial disputes. Japan and China differ considerably with respect to North Korean nuclear weapons and missile development. China–Japan relations have been especially conflictual since 2010.

China can be described as a dissatisfied great power willing to challenge Japan, in spite of its alliance with the US. China's unhindered economic growth as well as a more assertive foreign policy, have made northeast Asian states reconsider their relations with the growing China and simultaneously with other major powers in the region. Rapid growth often produces social and international turmoil, because accommodation is tricky, and because China is rising in a fluid regional environment lacking most of the elements that can mitigate conflict. Indeed, the future of Northeast Asian international politics seems especially problematic.

America's post World War II dominance in northeast Asia, though justified as a deterrent to Soviet ambitions, had an equally important function of keeping apart the traditional regional rivals—Japan and China. Tokyo and Beijing are aware that America's retrenchment would weaken the buffer that stands between them and that there is no apparent successor to play this role. The Americans realize that a substantial weakening of their military position in South Korea would be taken in Tokyo as a sign of US withdrawal from Asia and would encourage an independent rearmament of Japan. Even without any reason for the speculation of American military withdrawal from the region, Japanese "normalization" is under consideration (Lee & Kim 2016). The US should decide what kind of diplomatic stance it will take to minimize the tension between China and Japan (Lee, 2015). The future of the Northeast Asian regional and global orders depends upon the directions of the US-led countermeasures to China, which takes a status quo policy in the global order and a revisionist policy in the regional order.

At least for the short-term, as long as the Communist Party remains in power, China will most likely to be preoccupied with the task of maintaining political stability while generating economic development. Having said that, it is not what China is doing now that is confounding policymakers in Tokyo and Washington, but what it might do in ten, twenty or fifty years later on. Given continued economic growth over the long run, there is no reason whatsoever to believe that China will be satisfied with the current American network of alliances, nor the US Dollar dominated economic system, in this region. The power shift from Japan to China in northeast Asia might well be the bridge that allows China to gain access to a power transition game on the global level (Lee & Kim 2016).

China cannot be evaluated yet as a challenger threatening the hegemonic status of the U.S. in the global order. It accepts the current system as an axis of the G2 at this time. China does not appear to be a genuine dissatisfied challenger pressing for a global power transition. Instead, China focuses much more attention towards its relative rise with respect to Japan in the regional order and is pursuing a status of regional hegemon. If this process is left unchecked by the US, we may see instability in the regional order overwhelming stability in the global order.

The Korean Peace Process: Power Parity between South Korea(+US) and North Korea [North Korea as a dissatisfied challenger]

The Korean peace process was initiated in order to resolve the inter-Korean conflict and denuclearize North Korea. In 1998, South Korean President Kim Dae-jung announced a Sunshine Policy towards North Korea and an Inter-Korean summit was held in 2000. In 2006, North Korea conducted its first nuclear test. A second inter-Korean summit was held in 2007. In 2017, South Korean President Moon Jae-in returned to the Sunshine Policy. A summit between Moon and Kim took place in the South Korean zone of the Joint Security Area, and they signed the Panmunjom Declaration pledging to work towards a permanent peace to the Korean peninsula and the complete denuclearization of Korea. Both leaders also agreed to reopen a jointly operated liaison office in Kaesong since the South had shut down in February 2016 after a North Korean nuclear test.

President Trump met with North Korean leader Kim on June 12, 2018, in the first summit in Singapore. They signed a joint statement, agreeing to reaffirmation of the denuclearization of the Korean Peninsula, security guarantees for North Korea, recovery of soldiers' remains, and follow-up high-level talks. Also, President Trump announced that the US would suspend provocative joint military exercises with South Korea. In Pyongyang, both Moon and Kim announced the 'Pyongyang Joint Declaration of September 2018'. North Korea agreed to dismantle its nuclear program in the presence of international experts if the U.S. took reciprocal action. Moon gave a speech to a North

Korean audience at the Arirang Festival on 19 September. President Trump met with Kim Jong-un of North Korea on February 27, 2019, in the second summit in Hanoi, Vietnam. The summit was cut short without any agreement. On June 30, 2019, Trump of the US and Moon of South Korea met with Kim of North Korea at the DMZ. Donald Trump shortly crossed the border into North Korea and then came back to South Korea. At the brief meeting, both the US and North Korea agreed to resume denuclearization talks, ended in deadlock at the Hanoi Summit. North Korea, nonetheless, continued short–range missile tests in 2019. The US and South Korea participated in joint military drills in August.

On 23 September 2019, both Trump and Moon announced support for continuing negotiations at the 74th UN General Assembly session in New York. In June 2020, North Korea demolished the inter-Korean liaison office in Kaesong. In September 2020, Moon and Kim exchanged friendly letters about COVID-19 and the flood damages of typhoons. President Moon addressed at the UN General Assembly in September and called for a 'permanent peace regime' in Korea. In November, the South Korean defense ministry reaffirmed its commitment to the peace process in an ASEAN security meeting. Peace efforts continue despite setbacks.

All the nations around the Korean peninsula demand a regional security system for peace and stability in Northeast Asia. A possible solution is to develop the US-included regional security regime. Japan also pursues military cooperation with the US and South Korea and extends it by integrating China and Russia into a regional security regime. Russia has abandoned the intention of catching up to the US. It emphasizes its role in maintaining the peace and stability of Northeast Asia as an influential regional power.

Two main limitations, nevertheless, work against the establishment of a regional security regime. First is a competing structure emphasizing 'relative interest' in terms of the neo-realist self-help perspective. When the regional nations, in the case of China and Japan, consider relative interest first in international relations, the possibility of cooperation is not high. Second is the concern about Japan's return to military power, which makes the establishment of the regional regime difficult. These two obstacles need to be overcome for regime construction.

What is the best way to achieve the security regime in Northeast Asia? To achieve the regional security regime, we need to solve these obstacles. To reduce the militarily competing structure stressing relative interest between China and Japan, a peace agreement or arms control treaty between them is desirable. This is a precondition for building up the regional security regime. To overcome the emotionally charged problems relating to historical Japanese transgressions, the regional nations should strengthen economic interdependence and enhance socio-cultural exchanges.

In addition, the security alliance with the United States must adapt to the changing Northeast Asian security situation. US military presence is very important for regional stability and South Korean security interests. If South Korea is concerned about the military power of neighboring countries or unspecified threats in the future, it is essential to maintain the US-South Korea alliance and the presence of US Forces in South Korea. The military alliance with the US should be maintained in some form.

In South Korea, a debate has emerged whereby the current global order has been reshuffled into two competing groups including a "shared values first network" and a "shared interests first network". The world is either a bipolar system under a multipolar system or a G2 structure under a G20 structure. Such a dichotomy presents South Korea with a difficult time addressing the dilemma of choosing a side between the US and China. The dichotomy, however, is too stark. Reform of the security relations between South Korea and the US can allow them to avoid the dilemma. The USFK must alter its image from anti-communist, anti-Soviet, and anti-North Korean to a peace-keeping frame. The relocation of the USFK should be based on a defensive strategy adapted to new weapons systems. To achieve regional security cooperation, an engagement policy with North Korea must be maintained, but contingent on reciprocity. Diplomatic pressure with a goal that North Korea abandons its nuclear weapons in exchange for economic incentives and a soft landing. The stabilization of North Korea is a precondition for the security regime.

This book deals with four main subjects—Understanding of the Korean Peace Process, Diplomatic Approach to the Korean Peace Process, Implementation and Execution of the Korean Peace Process, and Future of the Korean Peace Process. The first part covers two research papers, "The Direction of the Korean Peninsula's Peace from the Perspective of Peace Studies" and "South Korea's Tasks on the Peace Process & Unification Policy". Part two contains "How Commitment Problems Affect the

Prospects for Peace on the Korean Peninsula", "A Systematic Analysis of the Trump Foreign Policy: Implications for Northeast Asia and the Korean Peninsula", "The Impact of US-China Competition on the Korean Peace Process", and "Sunrise, Sunset: The Rise and Fall of Inter-Korean Economic Relations". The third part includes four chapters, "Political Oppression, Human Rights, and UN Targeted Sanctions: A Case of North Korea", "Bridge between South and North Korea: Analysis of South Korean Aid to North Korea for Peace in the Korean Peninsula", "What Do We Know and Do Not Know?: Attitudes toward North Korea and Unification", "Japan and South Korea: Can they get along by overcoming the challenges?" Part IV presents two research papers—"Be Careful What You Wish For: Security Challenges Facing the Korean Peninsula During a Potential Unification Process" and "Challenges and Opportunities of the 'Korean Peace Process' in the Moon Jae-in Government: Lessons from 'NAPCI' in the Park Geun-hye Government".

The summaries of each chapter are as follows:

Part I. Understanding of the Korean Peace Process

Chapter 2. The Direction of the Korean Peninsula's Peace from the Perspective of Peace Studies

Soo Hwan Hwang (Kangwon Institute for Unification Studies, Kangwon National University)

Abstract: The looming possibilities for the Korean peninsula's permanent peace began to appear through the North-South summit and the US-NK summit in 2018. Especially, the three rounds of the North-South summit contributed to forming trust between the North and the South and developing a foundation for peace. This paper analyzed the prerequisites to achieve peace in the Korean Peninsula from the perspective of peace studies. In the perspective of peace studies, unification by peace, realization of human security, and overcoming the division toward everyday peace have to be achieved. In other words, the path towards the Korean Peninsula's peace should be considered as the long-term process including not only political and military factors, but also positive peace where everyday peace can be realized. Furthermore, the Korean Peninsula's peace must be understood as the concept which encompasses institutional factors such as norms, principles, rules, procedures and the tangible improvement of the relationship based on the change of trust and awareness.

Chapter 3. South Korea's Tasks on the Peace Process & Unification Policy

Sukhoon Hong (Korea Institute for National Unification)

Abstract: Entering 2018, the South Korean government's policy of dialogue and cooperation toward North Korea and North Korea's shift in national strategy brought about rapid changes in the political landscape of the Korean peninsula. The inter-Korean relations entered a new phase after three inter-Korean summits, including the Panmunjeom Declaration and the Pyongyang Joint Declaration, during the Moon Jae-in administration. Despite the administration's emphasis on the settlement of peace and pursuit of peaceful unification based on engagement policy on North Korea, the reality is that the North Korean nuclear issue and other international factors such as U.S.-China confrontation hinder the South Korean government's policy on North Korean and unification. Hence, this chapter analyzes domestic factors including inter-Korean relations and the North Korean nuclear issues, international factors surrounding the Korean Peninsula such as the U.S.-China relations, and tasks for the Moon Jae-in administration for the settlement of peace and unification.

Part II. Diplomatic Approaches to the Korean Peace Process

Chapter 4. How Commitment Problems Affect the Prospects for Peace on the Korean Peninsula

Scott Gates (University of Oslo and Peace Research Institute Oslo (PRIO)), Håvard Mokleiv Nygård (Peace Research Institute Oslo (PRIO))

Abstract: The Korean peninsula is fraught with tension. We analyze three aspects of the commitment problem, incomplete information, preemptive war, and preventative war as they apply to the conflict between North Korea and the USA (along with South Korea) employing the bargaining theory of war. In doing this, we also extend the bargaining theory of war to an asymmetric conflict. First, how the USA regards the costs of a war with North Korea is uncertain. A couple of years ago the Trump administration seemed to discount the costs of North Korean counter-strike on Seoul, if they were to 'give North Korea a bloody nose'. We find that this incomplete information problem is destabilizing and could lead to war. Second, the USA has made military advances capable of taking out much of North Korea's counter-strike capability. Such a weapon would provide the USA with an incentive to launch a first-strike attack. Preemptive war could be a possibility, but with asymmetric capabilities, if the USA does not launch a first-strike, the opportunities for mutually advantageous bargain remain. Third, we examine the growing nuclear capability of North Korea over time. Their relative capability is rising viz-a-viz the USA. They cannot credibly commit to an agreement today, given their better bargaining position in the future. This creates an incentive for the USA to launch a preventive war sooner rather than later, while they retain a strong military advantage. Again, with asymmetric capabilities, while the bargaining range decreases, it nonetheless persists. The biggest threat of war between North Korea and the USA concerns the situation of a rising power and two-sided incomplete information. Such a situation may reflect reality.

Chapter 5. A Systematic Analysis of the Trump Foreign Policy: Implications for Northeast Asia and the Korean Peninsula

Dongsoo Kim (Pukyong National University)

Abstract: Donald Trump was elected as 45th U.S. President in 2016. The conventional understa nding of President Trump when his administration started in early 2017 was that he had a unique personality as a politician, and therefore, the U.S. under his leadership would pursue different foreign policy goals and strategies to achieve them, distinct from his predecessors. Against this background, this study aims to address such questions as "Is he really different from his predecessors?" or "Will U.S. foreign policies under Trump be totally different from those of the past?" Especially, this study will analyze Trump's foreign policy orientations, utilizing dimensions of foreign policy analysis: security, prosperity, and community values. Based on the analysis of the fundamentals of the Trump administration's foreign policy, this study will also discuss its policy toward Northeast Asia, especially the Korean peninsula.

Chapter 6. The Impact of US-China Competition on the Korean Peace Process

Wonjae Hwang (University of Tennessee)

Abstract: This paper examines the impact of the ongoing U.S.-China power competition on the Korean Peace Process. Based on the discussion of power transition theory and hedging strategy, this paper evaluates how the great power competition may affect the prospect of the initiative particularly with respect to the goal of creating a new economic community on the Korean Peninsula. As a way to minimize the risk of being entrapped by the great power competition and pursue the goals specified in the Korean Peace Process, this paper argues that South Korea needs to adopt a strategy of multilateral engagement with other middle powers.

Chapter 7. Sunrise, Sunset: The Rise and Fall of Inter-Korean Economic Relations

Inhan Kim (Ewha Womans University)

Abstract: What explains the dramatic rise and fall of inter-Korean economic relations over the past two decades? The conventional explanation has been differences in the beliefs of political leaders. That is, liberal presidents such as Kim Dae-jung and Roh Moo-hyun pursued engagement policies with a firm belief that growing economic interdependence with North Korea would help it come out of isolation and moderate its foreign policy, while the conservative next two leaders were skeptical. Examining almost two decades of economic cooperation between the two Koreas, this paper asserts that the fate of inter-Korean economic relations has depended not just on the political leaders' beliefs but also on two external forces: Pyongyang's response to engagement efforts from Seoul and support from Washington. Throughout the sunshine period, the two Koreas were able to expand economic ties both in scope and quantity as both Pyongyang and Washington responded favorably to Seoul's sunshine policies. In contrast, economic cooperation shrank in scope and the overall volume of exchange fluctuated during—but not because of—the conservatives' rule in Seoul as Pyongyang rejected Seoul's proposals and instead accelerated its nuclear armament. This study projects poor prospects for Seoul's recent efforts to revive economic cooperation with Pyongyang.

Part III. Implementation and Execution of the Korean Peace Process

Chapter 8. Political Oppression, Human Rights, and UN Targeted Sanctions: A Case of North Korea

Jiyoun Park (Jeonbuk National University), Hyun Jin Choi (Kyung Hee University)

Abstract: Why do some UN targeted sanctions (or 'smart' sanctions) cause collateral damage to the general population, while others minimize it? We suggest the scope and the effectiveness of smart sanctions, and the political institutions of target countries are critical determinants of sanctions' adverse effects on human rights. Leaders targeted by sanctions with a broad scope will have a greater incentive to oppress people to ward off potential support for challengers. The degree to which they can carry out successful oppression, however, hinges upon the effectiveness of sanctions implementation. Furthermore, we expect that authoritarian systems are more likely to encourage oppression than other ones. We conduct a quantitative analysis of 56 UN-imposed smart sanction episodes. Our study reveals sanctions with a broad scope that are less effective result in deteriorated human rights conditions especially in authoritarian countries. However, we find when sanctions with a narrow scope work effectively, they do not hurt innocent citizens. We illustrate the workings of our theory with an example of North Korea under smart sanctions (2006-2019).

Chapter 9. Bridge between South and North Korea: Analysis of South Korean Aid to North Korea for Peace in the Korean Peninsula

Youngwan Kim (Hankuk University of Foreign Studies), Jaeyoung Hur (Yonsei University), Jiyoun Park (Jeonbuk National University)

Abstract: This study suggests new approaches to conceptualize South Korean aid to North Korea as equivalent to Official Development Assistance (ODA) by looking at its historical background and present situation, as well as related laws. We review the characteristics and development of South Korean aid to North Korea, compare it to ODA, and suggest an innovative way of conceptualizing it as ODA. In particular, we assert that if South Korean aid to North Korea is considered ODA, South Korea would be able to effectively assist North Korea and become a more influential and responsible donor in international society. In addition, it will motivate two Koreas to work together for peace in the Korean peninsula.

Chapter 10. What Do We Know and Do Not Know?: Attitudes toward North Korea and Unification

Jaeyoung Hur (Yonsei University), Sanghoon Park (University of South Carolina)

Abstract: This article examines whether existing explanations of South Korean attitudes regarding North Korea and Korean unification adequately explain changes after the declaration at Panmunjom on April 27, 2018. This study uses the National Consciousness Survey Data to estimate these shifts in attitude. Our results show that South Korean attitudes shifted following the Panmunjom Declaration for Peace,

Prosperity, and Unification of the Korean Peninsula. We show that existing explanations for generational effects do not explain the national attitude shifts on unification; our study demonstrates that a wide divergence exists between younger and the older generations, and younger generations are more likely to display a negative attitude toward North Korea and unification even after the Declaration. We also show that the prospects of unification evoke different attitudes across generations. Our results imply that the Panmunjom Declaration is a prominent political event, but it is necessary to analyze it without overestimating it.

Chapter 11. Japan and South Korea: Can they get along by overcoming the challenges?

Atsushi Tago (Waseda University and Peace Research Institute Oslo (PRIO))

Abstract: Japan and South Korea have been facing varieties of bilateral issues. Those challenges between the two democracies in East Asia indeed prevent further regional cooperation like East Asian Community, and they could jeopardize the regional and potentially global peace and security. Nevertheless, an optimistic view over the two countries might not be dead (yet). Japan and South Korea co-hosted the FIFA World Cup in 2002. Also, there has been a new development of DCA (defense cooperation agreement) between the two countries, while it has been under serious pressure of withdrawal of the commitment on both sides. As a major alliance partner of the United States of America, Japan and South Korea could have been a strong ally with each other in theory. This study, based on those two competing views, will uncover why the two countries tend to overtly fight with each other. Also, this study will seek to answer how the two countries can stop engaging in such a negative interaction and make some practical cooperation to stabilize peace and security in East Asia.

Part IV. Future of the Korean Peace Process

Chapter 12. Be Careful What You Wish For: Security Challenges Facing the Korean Peninsula During a Potential Unification Process

Mason Richey (Hankuk University of Foreign Studies), Daewon Ohn (Hankuk University of Foreign Studies), Jangho Kim (Hankuk University of Foreign Studies), Jae Jeok Park (Hankuk University of Foreign Studies)

Abstract: There is a lacuna in the literature analyzing the mid-term (6-24 months) period after a DPRK contingency that results in the Pyongyang regime's relatively sudden and unmanaged fall. This chapter helps fill that gap, particularly with respect to security issues that would challenge Korean unification efforts during such a period. Following an Introduction, Section I first makes the case for a DPRK contingency being the most plausible end to the Pyongyang regime. Assuming the scenarios from Section I, Section II addresses the question of what critical issues a unifying Korea will face over the mid-term, and how dealing with these challenges will condition the type of end-state that a unified Korea will embody. In particular, we examine three challenges: (a) mid-term security provision related to potential weapons proliferation, cyber-security, organized criminality, and human security; (b) the foundations of institution-building through measures dealing with issues of transitional justice, disputed land title claims, and generating broad domestic stakeholder buy-in in a unifying Korea; (c) the disposition of Korea's strategic alignment in Northeast Asia that will have undergone a major alteration of the regional system. Section III concludes with policy recommendations concerning what efforts should be made now to prepare for the situations described in Sections I and II.

Chapter 13. Challenges and Opportunities of the 'Korean Peace Process' in the Moon Jae-in Government: Lessons from 'NAPCI' in the Park Geun-hye Government

Eunmi Choi (The Asan Institute for Policy Studies)

Abstract: The 'Korean Peace Process' is the Moon Jae-in government's policy toward North Korea for resolving conflicts and confrontation which has been prevalent on the Korean Peninsula for a long period time and to realize denuclearization. The North Korean nuclear issue was still difficult to solve. In spite of several historic meetings, North Korea and the U.S. eventually failed to reach an agreement on denuclearization. In this study, first, I examine the progress and current situations of the Korean Peace Process. Second, I analyze the advantages and limitations of the (neo-)functional approach by comparing them with the examples of previous governments, especially focusing on the Northeast Asia Peace and Cooperation Initiative in the Park Geun-hye government, which is the very model of the application of the neo-functional approach to solve the North Korean issue, and explore its effectiveness and limitations. Third, I research the challenges and opportunities of the Korean Peace Process, and then give my insight on the Korean Peace Process and the way forward. As a result of this study, it has proved functionalist approach would be difficult to reach an eventual solution to the North Korean nuclear issue, even though it could help to ease tensions on the Korean Peninsula and in Northeast Asia.

Reference

Glaser, Bonnie S. and Lyle Morris. 2009. "Chinese Perceptions of U.S. Decline and Power." China Brief, Vol. 9(14).

Kim, Hyunkyu. 2014. "The Rise of China and the World Order in the 21st century: Triangular Structure of China, the US and Japan in the view of Multi-layered Power Transition Theory. Master's Thesis, Hankuk University of Foreign Studies, Seoul, Republic of Korea.

Lam, Willy. 2010. "Beijing Seeks Paradigm Shift in Geopolitics." China Brief, Vol. 10(5).

Lampton, David. 2010. "Power Constrained: Sources of Mutual Strategic Suspicion in US-China Relations." NBR Analysis, No. 93.

Lee, Sang-Hwan. 2015. "Global and Regional Orders in the 21st century in terms of Multi-layered Power Transition Theory: The Cases of US-China and China-Japan Relations." International Area Studies Review, Vol. 18(3).

Lee, Sang-Hwan and Jangho Kim. 2016. "Regionalization of Power Transition: Sino-Japanese Relationship and its Implications to the Global Balance of Power." Paper to be presented at the 57th International Studies Association Annual Conference,

Li, Mingjiang. 2009. "Domestic Sources of China's Soft Power Approach." China Security, Vol. 5(2).

___________. 2008. "China Debates Soft Power." Chinese Journal of International Politics, Vol. 2(2).

Nye, Joseph S. 2010. "The Future of American Power: Dominance and Decline in Perspective." Foreign Affairs, Vol. 89(6).

Saunders, Phillip C. 2010. "Will China's Dream turn into America's Nightmare?" China Brief, Vol. 10(7).

Understanding of the Korean Peace Process

Chapter 2.
The Direction of the Korean Peninsula's Peace from the Perspective of Peace Studies
Soo Hwan Hwang
(Kangwon Institute for Unification Studies, Kangwon National University)

Chapter 3.
South Korea's Tasks on the Peace Process & Unification Policy
Sukhoon Hong
(Korea Institute for National Unification)

Chapter 2

The Direction of the Korean Peninsula's Peace from the Perspective of Peace Studies[1]

Soo Hwan Hwang
(Kangwon Institute for Unification Studies, Kangwon National University)

Abstract

The looming possibilities for the Korean peninsula's permanent peace began to appear through the North-South summit and the US-NK summit in 2018. Especially, the three rounds of the North-South summit contributed to forming trust between the North and the South and developing a foundation for peace. This paper analyzed the prerequisites to achieve peace in the Korean Peninsula from the perspective of peace studies. In the perspective of peace studies, unification by peace, realization of human security, and overcoming the division toward everyday peace have to be achieved. In other words, the path towards the Korean Peninsula's peace should be considered as the long-term process including not only political and military factors, but also positive peace where everyday peace can be realized. Furthermore, the Korean Peninsula's peace must be understood as the concept which encompasses institutional factors such as norms, principles, rules, procedures and the tangible improvement of the relationship based on the change of trust and awareness.

Keywords: Peace, Peace Studies, Positive Peace, Everyday Peace, Korean Peninsula

---

1 This paper is a translated version of Hwang Soo Hwan's "The Direction of the Korean Peninsula's Peace from the Perspective of Peace Studies" published in 2019 (The Journal of Peace Studies Vol. 20 No. 1).

I. Introduction

In 2018, some significant historic turns took place on the Korean peninsula concerning foreign policy and security. Through the Panmunjom Declaration for Peace, Prosperity, and Unification of the Korean Peninsula on April 27, 2018 and the Pyongyang Joint Declaration of September on September 19, 2018, South Korea and North Korea agreed to work together to achieve permanent peace on the Korean peninsula. In addition, the United States and North Korea signed a joint statement, agreeing to renewing peaceful relations and achieving the denuclearization of the Korean peninsula, in the 2018 North Korea-United States Singapore Summit on June 12, 2018. Through three times of inter-Korean summit talks and the Singapore Summit in 2018, a glimmer of hope was observed in easing the half-century military tensions and confrontations on the Korean peninsula.

Moon Jae-in, President of the Republic of Korea, declared, "I propose before the 80 million Korean people that we should completely end the past 70 years of hostility and take a big stride of peace to become one again" at the Mass Games in Pyongyang on September 19, 2018.[2] Also, in the new year's address in 2019,[3] Kim Jong-un, Chairman of the State Affairs Commission of the Democratic People's Republic of Korea, remarked that a peaceful mood had been created between the two Koreas. The 2018 Inter-Korean summit played a significant role in improving ties between the South and the North, laying the groundwork for realizing peace and prosperity on the Korean peninsula. Also, tensions between Washington and Pyongyang, which escalated by a series of missile and nuclear tests on North Korean soil in late 2017, turned into a peaceful mood in 2018.[4]

However, the 2019 North Korea-United States Hanoi Summit on February 28, 2019, which was expected to be a watershed moment in resolving the North Korean

2 JoongAng Daily, Sept. 19, 2018. "President Moon Declared Emergence of New Era in Front of 150,000 Pyongyang People"

3 Choson Sinbo, Jan. 1, 2019. During the new year's address, Kim Jong-un, Chairman of the State Affairs Commission of the Democratic People's Republic of Korea, said, "I am highly satisfied to have seen a remarkable progress in terms of the two Koreas' relations within a short time period, transforming distrust and confrontation into trust and harmony."

4 During the mid-term election rally held on September 27, 2018, Donald Trump, President of the United States, said, "He wrote me beautiful letters, and they're great letters. I was really being tough and so was he. And we would go back and forth. And then we fell in love."

nuclear issue and normalizing relations between the two countries, was cut short with no agreement. The U.S. asked North Korea to permanently dismantle nuclear facilities in Yongbyon as well as other nuclear reactors, but the North asked for the relaxing of the United Nations sanctions, which eventually led to a failed agreement. Due to the Hanoi Summit debacle, the expectations for peace and prosperity on the Korean peninsula since 2018 have declined. In 2018 alone, drastic changes led by external and internal factors in Korea were evaluated to have contributed to achieving peace on the Korean peninsula, but the failed second summit talk between the U.S. and North Korea in 2019 once again proved that there is still a long way to go before achieving sustainable peace.

Under these circumstances, it is questionable whether North Korea's normalized relations with South Korea and the U.S. may lead to the achievement of genuine peace on the Korean peninsula. If tensions in politics, diplomacy, and military are eased in conjunction with the normalization of relations, could peace on the Korean peninsula truly be achieved? It is still not certain whether reduced tensions led by normalized relations at a state level could contribute to addressing various internal conflicts and problems caused by state-level confrontations and building lasting peace in the end. Against this backdrop, this paper will carefully examine the complexity and ambiguity of the concept "peace" in relation to the aforementioned issues and identify the degree of peace to build "genuine peace" on the Korean peninsula from the perspective of peace studies. The direction of the Korean peninsula's peace from the perspective of peace studies will be examined from a growing peaceful mood on the Korean peninsula in 2018.

II. What is Peace?

Peace is defined as "a state of tranquility and harmony."[5] It literally means a state of concord or tranquility without wars or conflicts. However, the definition of peace differed for a long time according to the worldviews and social implications of the

5 Encyclopedia of Political Science, "21st Political Science Encyclopedia 2" (Seoul: Academia Research, 2002), p. 2520.

Eastern and Western worlds. Peace, which was borrowed from Latin pax, meant "absence of war," whereas "eir-ene" from ancient Greece, "shalom" from Hebrew, and "shanti" from ancient India were defined as peace with a focus on "justice" and "harmony." Since the ancient times, the meaning of peace has been equivalent to that of "relaxation" or "harmony and peace" in China. In particular, "relaxation" was used as a term encompassing "absence of war," "justice," and "harmony."[6]

Table 1. Concept of Peace among Different Cultures

source : Ishida(1969), 135

	will of God justice	prosperity	order	tranquility of mind
Ancient Judaism	Shâlôm			
Greece		Eirene		
Rome			Pax	
China(Japan)			ho p'ing/p'ing ho(heiwa)	
India				Šânti

Source: Masatsugu Matsuo, "Concept of Peace in Peace Studies–A Short Historical Sketch" in Peace Studies and Peace Discourse in Education edited by Vladimir Zelicheko, et al. IPSHU English research Report 20, (2007), p.15.

Historically, conceptual differences existed depending on the scope and conditions of peace. As for the traditional definition of peace in international relations, Alighieri Dante took an international approach to peace by publicizing the "Theory of the Empire," a world government theory, for the first time. He stated that the absence of the highest legal authority had led to a series of conflicts, urging the need for a world government as well as a world empire. He claimed that peace can be achieved when several countries are integrated into an empire reigned by an emperor.[7] In the medieval times, peace had a religious and social meaning with the implications of love and protection[8] by being categorized into either "true peace" or "false peace" based on justice.

6 Kim Hak-sung, "Modern Peace Theory and Conditions for Peace," Lee Woo-young et al., "Harmony, Cooperation, Prosperity, and Reunification" (Seoul: Hanul Academy, 2005), 13.
7 Choi Sang-yong, "Peace's Political Perspective" (Seoul: Nanam, 1997), 89-92.
8 Kim Hak-jae, "Origin of Panmunjom System: Korean War and Peace Planning of Liberalism" (Seoul: Humanitas, 2015), 52-53.

Approaching the modern times, it was perceived that peace among countries could be achieved through power, rule and order. Niccolo Machiavelli insisted that peace could be achieved only by power.

Thomas Hobbes also asserted that the ways to achieve peace and eliminate the fear of wars were by reinforcing power for the sake of a nation's survival or suppressing enemies through wars. On the contrary, Hugo Grotius claimed that peace could be achieved through international laws by way of preventing conflicts among nations and promoting legal orders in the international community. Based on the enlightenment of political order, Immanuel Kant underscored that perpetual peace could be achieved when the world unites.[9]

In particular, Kant admitted in "Perpetual Peace: A Philosophical Sketch" that perpetual peace led by peace treaties, which include six preliminary articles, three confirmed articles, secret articles and the guarantee of perpetual peace, was not an empty ideology but an agenda necessary to achieve its goal on a gradual basis.[10] Jean Jacques Rousseau defined peace by contrasting the state of peace with that of war. As peace is related to terms, such as relaxation, union, harmony, favor, and affection, the destruction of peace is not directly associated with wars.[11] As the infringement of relaxation and the loss of affection are not the immediate causes of war, Rousseau used the term peace in a broader sense by including justice, not the absence of wars.[12]

In Modern Europe, peace had a secular meaning and was understood as the absence of wars. Considering that wars mostly took place at a state level, the term peace was seen in a new light in the global community, which had emerged along with

---

9 Ha Youngsun, "21st Century Peace Studies" (Seoul: Pulbit, 2002), 19-21.; Kim Hak-sung, "Theoretical Approach on Peace System on Korean Peninsula-Comparative Studies on Realism, Liberalism, and Constructionism" (Seoul: Korea Institute for National Unification, 2000), 13.

10 Kant, Immanuel, *Zum ewigen Frieden. Ein philosophischer Entwurf*. Königsberg: Friedrich Nicolovius, (1796): Translated by Lee Han-gu, "Permanent Peace Theory (Revised)" (Paju: Seogwangsa, 2008), 13-90.

11 Jean-Jacques Rousseau, "The State of War, Summary and critique of The Abb de Saint-Pierre's project for Perpetual Peace," In *Reading Rousseau in the Nuclear Age*, Translated by Grace G. Roosevelt. Philadelphia: Temple University Press, (1990), 194; Kim Yong-min, "Rousseau's Perspectives on International Relations and Thoughts on Peace" (Sejong Institute, National Strategy, Vol. 12, No. 1, 2006), 16.

12 Kim Yong-min, "Rousseau's Perspectives on International Relations and Thoughts on Peace," 16-17.

modern states. The institutionalization of international law in Europe at the time is a clear example. Viewing peace as the absence of wars dominated Modern Europe until the end of World War II.[13] After World War II, due to the Cold War between the United States and the Soviet Union, many nations maintained the balance of power or alliance geopolitically, or promoted peace with the prevention of wars based on the theory of democratic peace. After the Cold War, due largely to diverse ethnic conflicts, civil wars spiraled into a long-term warfare. Not only that, long-term civil wars led to many forms of violence among different ethnicities and religions. Consequently, the definition of peace transformed from being negative and narrow to positive—pursuing individual freedom by keeping violence and deprivation in check. Together with a negative meaning—"a state without wars" or "a state without violence"—a positive meaning, peaceful efforts to eradicate the root causes that threaten human security even without wars or conflicts, was defined.

Johan Galtung categorized peace into "positive peace" and "negative peace."[14] He defined negative peace as "a state without physical violence at an individual level," whereas defined positive peace as "a state without structural violence, such as poverty, chaos, and discrimination, at a socio-economic level." Galtung stated that as long as peace remains at a negative level—a state without wars or conflicts—genuine peace cannot be achieved. Namely, positive peace is the best defense to prevent violence, and negative peace may collapse or remain unattainable if positive peace is not considered.[15] Observed from the people living in conflict-ridden areas, including the Middle East and Africa, pursuing positive peace single-mindedly seem unrealistic.[16] Considering that the two Koreas are still at war, it seems very challenging to eliminate positive, structural violence like diseases, poverty, and oppression.

Linda Rennie Forcey defined negative peace as "unstable peace," which is susceptible to factors that could lead to conflicts or wars anytime depending on the

---

13 Kim Hak-sung, "Theoretical Approach on Peace System on Korean Peninsula-Comparative Studies on Realism, Liberalism, and Constructionism,"13-14.

14 Galtung, Johan, "Violence, Peace, and Peace Research," *Journal of Peace Research*. 6 (3) (1969), 167-191.

15 Jung Joo-jin, "Eyes Seeing Peace" (Seoul: Gaema Gowon, 2015), 26.

16 Lim Hyun-jin & Gong Seuk-ki, "Twisted Globalization: Finding Alternatives by Korea" (Paju: Nanam, 2014), 121.

Table 2. Historic Categorization of Peace

	Social, Religious Peace	Hobb's Peace Nation's Peace	Kant's Peace Liberal Peace	Sally/Durkheim's Peace Social & Aligned Peace
Background	Medieval society	British civil war (1642-51) European Wars of Religion (1524-1648)	French Revolution (1789) Napoleon War (1803-15)	Chaos in the late 19th century World War I (1914-18)
Definition	Love & protection, just order	Nation's peace	Universal obligations of enlightenment and rationality	Social demands consist of individuals
Conditions	Voluntary agreement, mutual alliance, harmonious order	Powerful nation's peace	Republicanism, obligation of international law, utilitarian free trade	Objective science, alliance with labor division, society-anti-government
Priorities and Pursuits	Justice, love, tranquility	Internal security	Overcoming absolutism, achieving permanent peace	Social advancement and alliance based on science
Means for International Peace	-	War, agreement among countries, deterrence, and balance of power	International law, international alliance	The world federation of nations, international law, and alliance with labor division

Source: Kim Hak-jae, "Origin of Panmunjom System: Korean War and Peace Planning of Liberalism" (Seoul: Humanitas, 2015), p.60.

situation.[17] To achieve both "positive peace" and "genuine peace," an improved world order should be established by reinforcing social justice. Positive peace is a state when all the potential threats leading to conflicts are reduced; thereby raising the need for social justice that puts everyone at ease.

Peace can also be categorized into "stable or unstable peace" rather than "negative or positive peace." Kenneth Boulding divided peace into "stable" or "unstable" depending on the state of peace from a long-term perspective. Stable peace is defined as a "situation that is not taken seriously because of low chances of war."[18] Alexander George

17 Linda Rennie Forcey, *Peace: Meanings, Politics*, Strategies. New York: Praeger, (1989), 6.
18 Kenneth E. Boulding, *Stable Peace*, Austin: University of Texas Press, (1978): Lee Sang-geun, "Definition of Stable Peace and Possibility of Application to Korean Peninsula"

claimed that peace is a relationship in which none of the parties involved in conflicts uses military power or threats, defining stable peace similar to Boulding.[19] Lee Sang-geun defined stable peace as "a state that does not use military power or threats as a means of resolving conflicts among states and conflicts within a state."[20] As such, stable peace is perceived as maintaining a long-standing, peaceful relationship while reducing the chances of war based on the principle of mutual respect among the countries concerned. In contrast, unstable peace is defined as "a state of considering the use of military power or threats to address conflicts among states or conflicts within a state even without the occurrence of war."[21] If small-scale military confrontations or preparations for such clashes are considered, unstable peace implies the state of neither war nor stable peace. To put it differently, unstable peace means suspending hostile actions temporarily by preventing wars by deterrence, regulations, and agreements, including armistice, non-aggression pact, and arms control.[22]

Song Dae-sung perceives peace as either "genuine peace" or "pseudo-peace."[23] Genuine peace is generally defined as follows: First, it is a state of universally valid peace without wars or military clashes. Second, the purpose of pursuing peace should be purely peace. Third, peace should be achieved on the basis of trust among the relevant countries. Fourth, initiatives and business ideas devised for the purpose of achieving peace need to be transparent and mutually verifiable. Fifth, commitments made and agreements signed with regards to peace should be put into practice. Meanwhile, pseudo-peace emerges when conditions for achieving genuine peace are not met. It surfaces when the concept of peace transforms from universal to idiosyncratic, or when peace is used for achieving certain goals beyond peace. Also, pseudo-peace is generated when peace is pursued

---

(Korean Political Science Review, Vol. 49, No. 1, 2015), 138.

19 Alexander George's definition on stable peace was re-quoted by re-referencing Kacowicz and Bar-Siman-Tov's articles. Arie M., Yaacov Kacowicz & Bar-Siman-Tov, Ole Elgstrom, and Magnus Jerneck, eds, *Stable Peace Among Nations*. Lanham, Md.: Rowman & Littlefield Publishers, (2000), 17-18.

20 Lee Sang-geun, "Definition of Stable Peace and Possibility of Application to Korean Peninsula," 145.

21 Lee Sang-geun, "Definition of Stable Peace and Possibility of Application to Korean Peninsula," 138-145.

22 Moon Jeong-in, "Kim Dae-jung Government and Peace System on Korean Peninsula" (Sejong Institute, National Strategy, Vol. 5, No. 2, 1999), 140.

23 Song Dae-sung, "International Cases of Establishing Peace System Based on Korean Peninsula, Middle East, and Northern Island" (Seoul: Sejong Institute, 2000), 11.

without mutual trust; the grounds for peace lack transparency and accurate verification; and empty words without actions run rampant.

Depending on how peace is defined and perceived, the approaches and means of promoting peace could differ, resulting in the expansion of its scope. The conventional meaning of peace is in contrast to that of war; therefore, a state without war is perceived as a state of peace. It is similar to treating someone without any illnesses as being healthy. If people posit that the opposite of war is peace, it can only be narrowly defined. In modern society, peace has been viewed broadly as an absence of war and a solution to eliminating all forms of violence that put the lives of humans in harm's way. Therefore, it is hard to tell whether peace is the ultimate goal or is used merely for achieving national interests. In general, it is difficult to distinguish which state is seen as "at peace" and how peace can be achieved. Approaches are taken differently depending on how peace is defined. Peace is typically placed at the opposite end of the war, but if peace is defined in parallel with other human values and ideals, such as justice, happiness, and freedom, peace can be defined differently. The prerequisites for peace are easy to understand in theory, but in reality, it becomes harder to define because a perfect form of peace is nearly impossible.

III. What is Peace Studies?

Peace studies is a social science field that finds ways to promote peace by eradicating and preventing violence. It is an interdisciplinary studies ranging from social science to human science and natural science. It is also sub-categorized into peace research, peace education, and peace movement. It is an interdisciplinary effort aiming at the prevention, de-escalation, and resolution of conflicts by peaceful means, thereby promoting peace among all parties involved.[24] International relations focuses on the prevention and resolution of conflicts, whereas human science explores the areas of peace education and peace movement. Taking World War I and II as a lesson in the early 20th century, peace studies used all possible means to prevent conflicts and achieve peace. After World War II, peace studies was eventually recognized as one of the studies.

---

24 Seo Bo-hyuk, "Research on Korean Peace Studies" (Seoul: Pakyoungsa, 2019), 311-312.

Peace studies in the 20th century mainly covered conflict resolutions among countries as well as the management and maintenance of international relations and orders. Raymond Aron defined international relations studies as the "studies of peace and war,"[25] implying that peace studies is closely linked with or almost equivalent to war studies. At the time, armed conflicts among countries were seen as the biggest threat to peace. Therefore, peace studies in the 20th century had developed in close connection with security studies, which was based on each country's sovereignty protection and territorial integrity.[26] From the perspective of relatively weak powers, such as South Korea and North Korea, peace studies without self-protection was considered insecure. As invasion deterrence is similar to the protection of national security, security has been at the core of peace studies. Noting that the ideological clashes during the Cold War had a tremendous impact worldwide, each nation's security had become naturally associated with regime security or bloc security, resulting in the development of both peace and security studies.[27]

Due to the expansion of anti-war movements around the world stemming from the Vietnam War in the late 1960s, the so-called "critical peace studies" was established in Northern Europe. Also, with the rise of the Third World issues, a range of fields involving development, poverty, and inequality were dissected from the viewpoint of peace studies. Ever since, food, ocean, environment, and human rights had been included in peace studies. Moreover, as opposed to nuclear weapons and wars, peace studies had focused on resolving various conflicts by non-violent interventions, restrictions and non-aggressive defenses. As a result, peace studies in the 20th century was defined as an "interdisciplinary area exploring and teaching the causes of war and violence and the conditions for peace in a systematic way."[28]

With the end of the Cold War, the threats of war had reduced dramatically on a global scale, thereby putting the fate of peace studies in jeopardy. Nevertheless, due

---

25 Jung In-heung et al. "Encyclopedia of Political Science" (Seoul: Pakyoungsa, 1983), 1642.

26 Institute for Peace and Unification Studies Seoul National University, "What is Peace Human Science?," 18.

27 Kim Myung-seob, "Current Status and Prospects of Peace Studies," Ha Young-sun et al., "21st Century Peace Studies" (Seoul: Pulbit, 2002)

28 C.M. Stephenson, "Peace studies, overview", L. R. Kurtz ed. *Encyclopedia of Violence, Peace, & Conflict* (2ed.) (Amsterdam: London: Elsevier, 2008).

Fields of Peace Studies		Political Science	Sociology	Psychology	Anthropology	Economics	History	Literature / Language	Philosophy	Religion	Arts	Physics	Biology	Chemistry
Reasons of War														
	Competition	×		×	×	×	×	×	×		×			
	Invasion	×	×	×	×		×	×	×	×	×		×	×
	Weapon/ technology	×		×	×		×				×	×	×	×
	Ideology/ culture	×	×		×		×	×		×	×			
	Socio, economic, political structure	×	×		×	×	×		×					
Conditions for Peace														
	Human's basic desire	×		×	×	×			×				×	
	Human rights	×	×	×	×	×	×	×	×	×	×			
	Fairness	×	×	×	×	×	×	×	×	×	×			
	Peaceful conflict resolution process	×	×	×	×	×	×		×	×				
		Social science					Human science					Natural science		
		Traditional sub-academic disciplines												

Source: C.M. Stephenson, "Peace Studies, Overview," L. R. Kurtz ed. Encyclopedia of Violence, Peace, & Conflict (2ed.), Amsterdam: London: Elsevier, 2008); Institute for Peace and Unification Studies Seoul National University, "What is Peace Human Science?" (Seoul: Acanet, 2013), p.15. revised and re-referenced.

to incessant occurrence of conflicts engaging tribes, religions, identity conflicts, and cultural oppression, peace studies came to be examined from a different angle. In 1992, the United Nations declared, "An Agenda for Peace," outlining actions for prevention, peacemaking, peace-keeping, and peace-building. In 1998, the United Nations also adopted a resolution on the issues of peace culture, sustainable economic development, respect for all human rights, gender equality, democratic participation, tolerance and alliance, participatory dialogue and freedom of speech, and international peace and security, which became the major agenda for peace studies.

Peace studies in the 21st century was seen differently due to a series of conflicts, such as the Kosovo War in 1998, the September 11 attacks in 2001, and the Fukushima nuclear disaster in 2011. As more and more actors took a convergent, complex approach in addressing transnational issues—ethnic conflicts, refugees, terrorism, environment, climate change, and natural disaster—peace studies was adopted based on the convergence of social science and natural science, and social science and human science.[29] However, peace studies was still downplayed as a sub-academic discipline of the mainstream academic domain. Most importantly, peace studies in the 21st century is not placed in contrast to military security studies, but it has developed into a value-driven, ecological studies for the purpose of enriching human lives and achieving universal values.

IV. How is Peace Built?

The law of circulation exists when it comes to peace-building. Peace is not built solely by fulfilling certain goals, but progresses over the course of seeking changes. In other words, peace is built while maintaining it and pursuing reconstruction in war-torn communities. Therefore, peace-building is dynamic, not static. Peace-building needs changes from diverse backgrounds and viewpoints as well as vision and design to achieve long-term goals. The vision and design with regards to the changing process is helpful in

29 Institute for Peace and Unification Studies Seoul National University, "What is Peace Human Science?," 31.

identifying the methods and conditions for peace-building.

Conflict is based on relationship; therefore, its feature is periodic and fragmentary. Periodic means that conflict based on relationship entails continuity. Fragmentary means the rise and fall of conflicts embroiled in controversial issues. When assessing conflicts, the long-term context and the current status of such conflicts should be considered altogether. Figure 1. demonstrates the periodic features of peace-building caused by the periodic cycle of conflicts. Each cycle consists of constant context of relationship and dynamics of specific incidents.

Joyce Hocker and William Wilmot put forth the following three goals in conflict conversion and peace-building.[30] First, "prospective goal" is a definite goal set even before the beginning stage of addressing specific conflicts. Second, "transactive goal" is a goal that becomes more definite in the midst of addressing conflicts. Third, "retrospective goal" is a goal that makes people continue to see certain conflicts in retrospect even if the clashes happened a long time ago. Such goals are closely linked to identify the process of peace-building, approaches to understanding peace, and efforts to promote peace.[31] If agreements or treaties are signed over the course of building peace, they can act as an impetus for the resolution of conflicts and a result of an active and effective decision-making process.

Considering that Boulding defined stable peace as "a mere absence of war," stable peace does not necessarily equal lack of conflicts because a complete, perfect form of peace has never existed. Stable peace does not mean positive peace, which was defined by Galtung, but it means the stable management of negative peace. To secure stable peace, a constant process of reaching consensus is crucial among the parties concerned. In an effort to maintain stable peace continually, conflicts and confrontations should be resolved by the signing of peace agreements. True, this approach is no panacea to achieving peace, but how the related parties perceive and understand peace is the key to maintaining peace.

A state of peace shows no or minimal differences among the members involved,

---

30 Hocker, Joyce and William Wilmot, *Interpersonal Conflict*, Madison, Wis: Brown and Benchmark, (1995), 57-63.; John Paul Lederach, Translated by Kim Dongjin, "How Peace is Made?" (Seoul: Humanitas, 2012), 190.

31 John Paul Lederach, Translated by Kim Dongjin, "How Peace is Made?" (Seoul: Humanitas, 2012), 190-191.

but a state of conflict demonstrates big differences among the related members. Therefore, the process of achieving peace comes down to reducing the differences among members under a certain framework. The approaches to narrowing differences within a system and securing peace are diverse. Also, peace is achieved by multiple factors, such as ethnicity, citizenship, elite leadership, religions, cultural differences, and government system.

Gary Cox asserts that building a peace system is critical to achieving peace; thus, a consensus among the parties involved is important. He claims that the following five conditions are needed to promote peace.[32] First, a voluntary consensus is needed among the parties involved. As coercion and compulsory consensus can lead to heightened conflicts, a peace system should be built voluntarily. Second, common areas of interests should be shared among the related parties. Third, a peace system should be established based on the knowledge and mutual understanding acquired by active participation of the parties involved. In other words, matters related to peace should be discussed carefully through mutual understanding, problem-spotting, and active discussions. Fourth, matters agreed among the parties involved must be put into practice. Without full support or practical actions from the related parties, it becomes virtually difficult to build a peace system. Fifth, the agreements on building a peace system should contribute to implementing joint expressions, joint projects, and joint practices in the future. Joint expressions include conventions, declarations, agreements, and treaties. Joint projects are exclusively designed for securing peace and promoting national interests. Joint practices can increase efficiency by the voluntary consensus of participants.

Cox categories the types of achieving peace as follows[33]: First, it is the "nonviolent resistance movement." It was a peace movement advocated by Mahatma Gandhi in India, which was then under the rule of the British Empire, to seek independence and achieve peace. Instead of implementing armed and violent resistance, the movement aimed at minimizing differences and seeking truth though a self-denunciated method.[34] Through communal dialogues, similarities and differences of the related parties were

---

32 Gary Cox, The Ways of Peace: A Philosophy of Peace as Action, New York: Paulist Press, (1986), 130.

33 Cox, "The Ways of Peace," 132-133.

34 Song Dae-sung, Acquisition of Peace on Korean Peninsula (Paju: Hanul Academy, 2005), 43.

examined carefully and peace was achieved while persuading the counterparts based on a non-violent approach. Second, it is the "Quaker Process of Consensus." Quakers belong to a historically Christian denomination, united by their belief in addressing conflicts and achieving peace within the community. When there are differences, they constantly pray according to their religious beliefs and practice a life of absolute peace based on their absolute obedience for God to resolve confrontations and maintain peace.[35] Depending on the same religious faith, they resolve differences and conflicts within the community and seek peace by a common decision-making process. Third, it is the "Process of Principled Negotiation." This process is established to resolve internal conflicts among those with vastly different opinions by way of proving the validity based on participants' principled negotiation. Principled negotiation is established on the basis of domestic and international laws. There are several approaches to resolving conflicts: exchange of ideas, selecting the ideas with relative advantage, or selection of memorandum.[36] To seek consensus among the parties involved in conflicts, resilience is a must to adjust each party's principled negotiation.

However, this method differs among the parties engaged regarding its scope and interpretation. Also, when seeking consensus through compromise, other issues in need of agreement should be discussed to fill the losses. However, Cox's approach to achieving peace is just for resolving conflicts among the parties involved, but not for building sustainable peace by the acts of forgiveness and reconciliation.

Johan Galtung suggests the following four approaches in transforming structural conflicts to a state of peace.[37] First, "confrontation" is about selecting a contentious issue and placing it for confrontation, thereby shedding light on the goals and issues at hand. Second, "struggle" is about overcoming suppressions and exploitations. Nonviolent means are desperately needed for conflict resolution and peace-building because violence begets contradiction. Third, it is "decoupling." Decoupling is a process of disconnecting the structural links from suppressors and exploiters. Gandhi's "non-cooperative movement" and "non-violent civil disobedience movement" are good examples. Fourth,

35 Cox, "The Ways of Peace," 135-137.

36 Cox, "The Ways of Peace", 135; Song Dae-sung, Acquisition of Peace on Korean Peninsula, 46-47 re-referenced.

37 Johan Galtung, Translated by Kang Dong-il et al., "Peace by Peaceful Means" (Seoul: Duelneuk, 2000), 212-213.

it is "recoupling." Recoupling seeks a horizontal structure; thus, it pursues human rights over oppression, equality over exploitation, autonomy over infiltration, integration over division, alliance over separation, and participation over differentiation. Recoupling is known to contribute to establishing a comprehensive, but less violent structure.

Managing and resolving conflicts are particularly important on the Korean peninsula, which has long been embroiled in conflicts together with structural complexity. Namely, the two Koreas might as well consider promoting peace through conflict management.[38] Conflict management is a sustainable solution to achieving permanent peace. Most importantly, peace should be viewed as a way of understanding the process, not the result. As if there are twists and turns in people's expectations on peace on the Korean peninsula, successes and failures take place all the time. Therefore, it is even more important to consider mutual trust, all relevant parties, continued discussions and resolution efforts on key agenda, peaceful means and approaches, and so forth to achieve peace from a procedural perspective. With the signing of peace agreements, coexistence and stability among the parties engaged in conflicts are achieved, but peace agreements do not necessarily guarantee lasting peace. Even if agreements are signed among the countries with conflicts to achieve peace, the processes involving management, maintenance, and implementation are critical. The process of achieving peace requires a series of arduous tasks loaded with constant, enduring efforts. Peace has always been one of the goals pursued by humanbeings, but our history and reality tell a different story.[39]

---

38 Conflict management is made up of conflict avoidance, conflict prevention, conflict suppression, conflict regulation, conflict settlement, and conflict resolution. C. R. Mitchell, *The Structure of International Conflict*, New York: St. Martin's Press, (1981), 253-279.

39 Kim Hak-sung, "Modern Peace Theory and Conditions for Peace," 11.

Ⅴ. Perspective of Peace Studies on Peace on Korean Peninsula

1. Reunification Led by Peace

To transition from "a state of armistice" to "a state of peace" on the Korean peninsula, the three processes—peace-making, peace-keeping, and peace-building—are needed. Peace-making is the transition of conflicts. To build confidence between the two Koreas in politics and military, "a state of military tensions" should be converted to "a state of peaceful coexistence" by military negotiations and dialogues. Peace-keeping means keeping armed collisions between the South and the North in check. It is an effort made to maintain "a state of peace" by preventing the occurrence of accidental armed collisions, limiting the arrangement of aggressive weapons, and reducing arms. Peace-building is a process of building and maintaining a permanent peace system through the signing of peace agreements to maintain a sustainable state of peace.[40] Permanent peace on the Korean peninsula is possible when the causes of war are eliminated. It implies that the threats of war are reduced structurally through one unified nation. Reunification efforts should be made to achieve "a state of peace." If other forms of conflicts and violence take place through reunification, "genuine reunification" and "peace" can be far from realizing. From the perspective of peace studies, reunification is defined as a long-term process involving peace-making, peace-keeping, and peace-building, which ultimately brings a society destroyed by confrontations and violence back to normal.

2. Achieving Human Life

Peace studies in the 21st century calls for a change in the definition of national security. It urges a comprehensive transformation from the perception on the ultimate goal of national security to its use of means, placing the desire for peace at the core to live a more humane life.[41] Therefore, from the perspective of peace studies, a peace system on the Korean peninsula means breaking away from a period of political, military

---

40 Jo Sung-yeul, "Resolution of Korean Peninsula Issues and Three-stage Peace Theory Based on Positive Peace Theory" (Journal of Northeast Asia Research, Vol 30, No. 1, 2015) 37.

41 Park Eui-kyung, "Recommendations for Sustainable Peace" (Korean Journal of International Studies, Vol. 54, No. 4, 2014), 348-360.

confrontations and conflicts and convert to a state of having a safe, humane life in various areas. As national security underscores the importance of preserving human life with a little focus on people's daily lives and behaviors in real-life; national security does not necessarily lead to the promotion of peace from the viewpoint of peace studies.

Peace system is not built primarily to ease military tensions, but to sustain human life. Human life is seen as the realization of human security. It is about managing the seven categories of threats associated with human security—economic security, food security, health security, environmental security, personal security, community security, and political security—introduced in the 1994 Human Development Report (HBR) by the United Nations Development Programme (UNDP).[42] By eliminating some passive thoughts, such as the declaration of the end of war or the signing of peace agreements, and creating an environment where people from the two Koreas live an improved human life, "a genuine peace" can come to fruition. In addition to the threats of war and terrorism, other ensuing threats, involving poverty, hunger, diseases, inequality, and discrimination, should be addressed to achieve peace.

3. Overcoming System of Division

It is important to address violence resulting from the division of the two Koreas and exacerbated by violent events, structures, and discourses.[43] In particular, a multitude of oppressions on human rights conducted within the system of division should be addressed. Violent situations triggered by the division are deeply ingrained in Korean society, making it difficult to root out all at once. As exercising coercive, mandatory power while eradicating and integrating the system of division begets other forms of violence, the approach is not desirable from the perspective of peace studies. To address the issue of violence led by division, an integrated leadership that mediates conflicts and heals trauma is required.[44] Namely, in the process of handling the system of division, it is necessary to build sustainable peace by acts of forgiveness and reconciliation.

---

42 Human Development Report 1994, http://hdr.undp.org/sites/default/files/reports/255/hdr_1994_en_complete_nostats.pdf (Searched Date: Nov 25, 2018).

43 Kim Byung-ro, Seo Bo-hyuk, "Violence of Division: Militarization of Korean Peninsula from the Perspective of Peace Studies" (Paju: Acanet, 2016).

44 Kim Byung-ro, Seo Bo-hyuk, (2016), 62-63.

4. Peace in People's Daily Lives

The threats of war have declined since 2018 due to eased tensions among countries neighboring the Korean peninsula, but it is all the more important to maintain peace in our daily lives instead of eliminating the threats from the perspective of peace studies. From a historical perspective, peace to date was not "a state of true peace," but "a state of armistice" in which actual military activities had been suspended for years. Considering that the absence of war has not meant peace in the history of mankind, the absence of war does not lead to permanent peace, but peace in the livelihoods of people.[45] Conflicts that occur in people's daily lives are natural happenings; therefore, any forms of war or violence are not acceptable under any circumstances. As a solution to address conflicts and confrontations, the likelihood of war should be out of people's minds.

Instead, such conflicts and clashes need to be tackled in a peaceful way from the perspective of peace studies.[46] Lasting peace on the Korean peninsula is possible on the condition that structural factors threatening conflicts are removed instead of maintaining the existing system. According to Galtung, structural violence takes place because of unjust social conditions; therefore, eliminating the occasions that deprive of people's opportunities is needed for maintaining peace. As structural violence is perceived differently by individuals, it cannot be defined as a single term, making it even more difficult for the two Koreas to achieve peace.[47] The Constitution of South Korea defines that the freedom of individual people can be restricted for the purpose of national security.[48] It is paradoxical to some extent that national security essential for peace can limit people's freedom—the very purpose of promoting peace.[49]

45 Park Eui-kyung, "Recommendations for Sustainable Peace," 350.

46 Park Eui-kyung, "Recommendations for Sustainable Peace," 352.

47 Shin Jong-hyun, "Structural Violence and Peace Research: Johan Galtung's Conceptualization," Lee Ho-jae, "Peace Theory on Korean Peninsula" (Seoul: Bobmunsa, 1989), 169-183.

48 Constitution of the Republic of Korea, Article 37 (2): the freedoms and rights of citizens may be restricted by Act only when necessary for national security, the maintenance of law and order or for public welfare. Even when such restriction is imposed, no essential aspect of the freedom or right shall be violated.

49 Park Eui-kyung, "Recommendations for Sustainable Peace," 348.

VI. Conclusion

While holding three times of inter-Korean summit and one time of North Korea-U.S. summit in 2018, the expectations that half-century-long tensions and conflicts on the Korean peninsula might come to an end were heightened. However, as the second North Korea-U.S. summit, held on February 27 and 28 in 2019, ended without reaching an agreement, it raised people's understanding that achieving peace on the Korean peninsula is not an easy task. People once again realized that peace is not "a mere result," but can be achieved through arduous, continued efforts. Regarding the current landscape in global politics, the peacebuilding process on the Korean peninsula is assumed to take enormous time and effort. Therefore, peace on the Korean peninsula should be taken as a process of reducing and eliminating "a state of tension" through the institutionalization of peace instead of a result in which "a state of peace" is entirely built. The peace system cannot be established simply through the signing of peace agreements, but through a rigorous healing process of all parties involved from a socio-psychological perspective.

From the perspective of peace studies, reduced tensions in politics, diplomacy, and military through normalized relations among countries is a necessary condition, not a sufficient condition to maintaining peace. In other words, complex, structural issues generated through conflicts among countries as well as internal contradictions should be addressed to achieve "genuine peace" from the viewpoint of peace studies.

Peace on the Korean peninsula is achieved by political and military factors—the signing of peace agreements, resolution of North Korea's nuclear weapons program, military trust-building between the two Koreas, enhanced cooperation, institutionalization of dialogue, improved relations between the U.S. and North Korea as well as Japan and North Korea—as well as peace in people's daily lives in the long run. Peace in people's daily lives encompasses both nations-based peace and peace led by individual people. Enhanced relations among countries is similar to the achievement of negative peace, but achieving the universal values of humans equals the promotion of positive peace. From the perspective of peace studies, reunification of the Korean peninsula can be achieved through peace led by individuals, not nations. Beyond that, overcoming the system of division is possible along with personal and collective acts of forgiveness and reconciliation to bring about positive peace in people's everyday lives. After all, the direction of peace on the Korean peninsula from the perspective of peace studies should be understood as a set of institutional systems, including standards, principles, rules, and procedures. Also, based on the shift of trust and perception, it should be taken as a concept consists of structural and practical changes both internally and externally.

The Moon Jae-in Administration's efforts to achieve peace on the Korean peninsula is significant in that the South Korean government had exerted great efforts to keep the dialogue alive with North Korea and the United States alike in 2018. However, from the perspective of peace studies, it is important to note that some government policies to address domestic issues caused by the division of the two Koreas should go hand in hand with the global efforts to resolve issues among the relevant countries. As the definition of peace is used not only to strengthen security centered on nations, but also to enhance the universal values and lives of all humanbeings, it is recommendable for the South Korean government to keep the two elements in mind when making peacebuilding efforts and policies on the Korean peninsula.

Reference

Kim Myung-seob, "Current Status and Prospects of Peace Studies," Ha Young-sun et al., "21st Century Peace Studies" (Seoul: Pulbit, 2002)

Kim Byung-ro, Seo Bo-hyuk, "Violence of Division: Militarization of Korean Peninsula from the Perspective of Peace Studies" (Paju: Acanet, 2016)

Kim Yong-min, "Rousseau's Perspectives on International Relations and Thoughts on Peace" (Sejong Institute, National Strategy, Vol. 12, No. 1, 2006)

Kim Hak-sung, "Modern Peace Theory and Conditions for Peace," Lee Woo-young et al., "Harmony, Cooperation, Prosperity, and Reunification" (Seoul: Hanul Academy, 2005)

Kim Hak-sung, "Theoretical Approach on Peace System on Korean Peninsula-Comparative Studies on Realism, Liberalism, and Constructionism" (Seoul: Korea Institute for National Unification, 2000)

Kim Hak-jae, "Origin of Panmunjom System: Korean War and Peace Planning of Liberalism" (Seoul: Humanitas, 2015)

Moon Jeong-in, "Kim Dae-jung Government and Peace System on Korean Peninsula" (Sejong Institute, National Strategy, Vol. 5, No. 2, 1999)

Park Eui-kyung, "Recommendations for Sustainable Peace" (Korean Journal of International Studies, Vol. 54, No. 4, 2014)

Seo Bo-hyuk, "Reorganization of Reunification Issues from Perspective of Peace Studies" (Korean Culture, Vol 63, 2017)

Seo Bo-hyuk, "Research on Korean Peace Studies" (Seoul: Pakyoungsa, 2019)

Institute for Peace and Unification Studies Seoul National University, "What is Peace Human Science?" (Seoul: Acanet, 2013)

Song Dae-sung, "International Cases of Establishing Peace System Based on Korean Peninsula, Middle East, and Northern Island" (Seoul: Sejong Institute, 2000)

Song Dae-sung, "Achievement of Peace on Korean Peninsula" (Paju: Hanul Academy, 2005)

Shin Jong-hyun, "Structural Violence and Peace Research: Johan Galtung's Conceptualization," Lee Ho-jae, "Peace Theory on Korean Peninsula" (Seoul: Bobmunsa, 1989)

Johan Galtung, Translated by Kang Dong-il et al., "Peace by Peaceful Means" (Seoul: Duelneuk, 2000)

Lee Sang-geun, "Definition of Stable Peace and Possibility of Application to Korean Peninsula" (Korean Political Science Review, Vol. 49, No. 1, 2015)

Lim Hyun-jin, Gong Seuk-ki, "Twisted Globalization: Finding Alternatives by Korea" (Paju: Nanam, 2014)

Jung In-heung et al. "Encyclopedia of Political Science" (Seoul: Pakyoungsa, 1983)

Jung Joo-jin, "Eyes Seeing Peace" (Seoul: Gaema Gowon, 2015)

Encyclopedia of Political Science, "21st Political Science Encyclopedia 2" (Seoul: Academia Research,

2002)
Jo Sung-yeul, "Resolution of Korean Peninsula Issues and Three-stage Peace Theory Based on Positive Peace Theory" (Journal of Northeast Asia Research, Vol 30, No. 1, 2015)
John Paul Lederach, Translated by Kim Dongjin, "How Peace is Made?" (Seoul: Humanitas, 2012)
Choi Sang-yong, "Peace's Political Perspective" (Seoul: Nanam, 1997)
Ha Youngsun, "21st Century Peace Studies" (Seoul: Pulbit, 2002)
Boulding, Kenneth E. "Twelve Friendly Quarrels with Johan Galtung," Journal of Peace Research. 14(1) (1977)
Boulding, Kenneth E. Stable Peace. Austin: University of Texas Press, 1978
Cox, Gary. The Ways of Peace: A Philosophy of Peace as Action. New York: Paulist Press, 1986
Darby, John and Roger MacGinty, eds, The Management of Peace Processes. Houndmills: Macmillan Press Ltd, 2000
Forcey, Linda Rennie. Peace: Meanings, Politics, Strategies. New York: Praeger, 1989
Galtung, Johan, "Violence, Peace, and Peace Research." Journal of Peace Research. 6(3) (1969)
Hocker, Joyce and William Wilmot, Interpersonal Conflict. Madison, Wis: Brown and Benchmark, 1995
Kacowicz, Arie M,.Yaacov & Bar-Siman-Tov, Ole Elgstrom, and Magnus Jerneck, eds, Stable Peace Among Nations. Lanham, Md.: Rowman & Littlefield Publishers, 2000
Kant, Immanuel, Zum ewigen Frieden. Ein philosophischer Entwurf. Königsberg: Friedrich Nicolovius, 1796; Translated by Lee Han-gu, "Permanent Peace Theory (Revised)" (Paju: Seogwangsa, 2008)
Mitchell, C. R. The Structure of International Conflict. New York: St. Martin's Press, 1981.
Rousseau, Jean-Jacques "The State of War, Summary and critique of The Abb de Saint-Pieere's project for Perpetual Peace," In Reading Rousseau in the Nuclear Age, Translated by Grace G. Roosevelt. Philadelphia: Temple University Press, 1990.
Stephenson, C.M. "Peace studies, overview", L. R. Kurtz ed. Encyclopedia of Violence, Peace, & Conflict (2ed.). (Amsterdam: London: Elsevier, 2008).
Choson Sinbo, Jan 1, 2019
Korean Central News Agency, Nov. 2, 2018
JoongAng Daily, Sept 19, 2018
Human Development Report, 1994
http://hdr.undp.org/sites/default/files/reports/255/hdr_1994_en_complete_nostats.pdf
(Searched Date: Nov 25, 2018).

Chapter 3

South Korea's Tasks on the Peace Process & Unification Policy

Sukhoon Hong
(Korea Institute for National Unification)[1]

Abstract

Entering 2018, the South Korean government's policy of dialogue and cooperation toward North Korea and North Korea's shift in national strategy brought about rapid changes in the political landscape of the Korean peninsula. The inter-Korean relations entered a new phase after three inter-Korean summits, including the Panmunjeom Declaration and the Pyongyang Joint Declaration, during the Moon Jae-in administration. Despite the administration's emphasis on the settlement of peace and pursuit of peaceful unification based on engagement policy on North Korea, the reality is that the North Korean nuclear issue and other international factors such as U.S.-China confrontation hinder the South Korean government's policy on North Korean and unification. Hence, this chapter analyzes domestic factors including inter-Korean relations and the North Korean nuclear issues, international factors surrounding the Korean Peninsula such as the U.S.-China relations, and tasks for the Moon Jae-in administration for the settlement of peace and unification.

Keywords: South Korea's Unification Policy, the Peace Pross on the Korean Peninsula, North Korea's Nuclear Policy, Peace Paradigm, the US and China Relations

1 Research Fellow, KINU(hongsh626@gmail.com)

Ⅰ. Introduction

Entering 2018, the South Korean government's policy of dialogue and cooperation toward North Korea and North Korea's shift in national strategy brought about rapid changes in the political landscape of the Korean peninsula. The inter-Korean relations entered a new phase after three inter-Korean summits, including the Panmunjeom Declaration and the Pyongyang Joint Declaration, during the Moon Jae-in administration. In the Panmunjeom Declaration, the leaders of the two Koreas agreed on agendas related to inter-Korean cooperation and exchanges; and Panmunjeom Declaration, Pyongyang Joint Declaration, and the Agreement on the Implementation of the Historic Panmunjeom Declaration in the Military Domain have raised expectations for inter-Korean cooperation and exchanges in all domains. Moreover, Pyongyang, with Seoul claiming the driver's seat on Korean Peninsular affairs, resumed talks with Washington on denuclearization and the agenda seemed to progress precipitously with the June 12 summit.

Nevertheless, since the collapse of the summit in Hanoi in February 2019, talks have been halted, even social and cultural exchanges have lacked progress, and the issues such as denuclearizing North Korea and establishing a peace regime on the Korean Peninsula have been in troubled waters. In addition, the Korean Peninsula in the second half of 2020 has been at a standstill with the pandemic escalating U.S-China tensions and North Korea's explosion of the inter-Korean liaison office in Kaesong, on the pretense of the anti-regime flyers from the South. On top of this, the new U.S. administration's policy on East Asia and the Korean Peninsula emerges as the crucial factor regarding the Korean Peninsula affairs in 2021.

Since its inauguration in May 2017, the Moon administration has set five goals under the vision of 'A Nation of the People, a Just Republic of Korea' - 'a Government of the People', 'an Economy Pursuing Mutual Prosperity', 'a Nation Taking Responsibility for Each Individual', 'Well-balanced Development across Every Region', and 'a Peaceful and Prosperous Korean Peninsula'. President Moon introduced the concept of 'new Korean Peninsula regime' and elaborated the government's initiative on peace on the Korean peninsula in his address on March First Independence Movement Day in 2019. He coined the term 'new Korean Peninsula regime' as a plan for a new Korean peninsula with 'peace economy' and 'peaceful cooperation'. Also, marking the third anniversary of his administration on May 10, 2020, President Moon, mentioning the significance of human security, broadened discussion on 'community of life' covering the two Koreas, Northeast Asia, ASEAN, and the rest of the world and stressed that the whole world should strive toward a peace community.

Despite the administration's emphasis on the settlement of peace and pursuit of peaceful unification based on engagement policy on North Korea, the reality is that the North Korean nuclear issue and other international factors such as U.S.-China confrontation hinder the South Korean government's policy on North Korean and unification. Hence, this chapter analyzes domestic factors including inter-Korean relations and the North Korean nuclear issues, international factors surrounding the Korean Peninsula such as the U.S.-China relations, and tasks for the Moon Jae-in administration for the settlement of peace and unification.

II. Policy on Korean Unification and a 'Peace Paradigm'[2]

1. Two Koreas' Unification Policy

In the face of the North Korean nuclear issue and the U.S.-China competition for hegemony, South Korea has a national mandate to settle peace and achieve Korean unification. Besides, the integration of two Koreas signals 'the end of a new Cold War' – an acute conflict in Northeast Asia – and will hugely contribute to world peace. The analysis of the political situation surrounding the peninsula amid the changing international environment and the evolution of North Korea's nuclear policy should be perceived as a layout to achieve 'peace and prosperity on the Korean Peninsula'. As a start, the chapter compares previous unification policies of two Koreas and examines hands-on tasks.

Generally, Korean unification refers to the institutional integration between

2 Sukhoon Hong, "The Moon Jae-In Government's Peace & Unification Policy: Focus on the North Korean Nuclear Policy and the Relations between the US and China" (in Korean), The Journal of Peace Studies 19(1), Chapter 2.

the two Koreas. As institutional integration cannot be easily distinguished with the integration of values, the conceptual definition varies.[3] Previously, South and North Korea both claimed political legitimacy over the other and engaged in discourses on their version of institutional unification.

In terms of unification policy, the South Korean government has pursued peaceful unification based on values of liberal democracy and a gradual, phased approach towards it, regardless of the administrations. The South Korean government's strategy on peaceful unification is 'achieving a unified country with a peaceful soft-landing, carrying out with a South Korea-led process, being based on superiority of power, raising awareness for unification and national homogeneity, encouraging North Korea to change in a preferable direction, and garnering international support and cooperation.'[4]

As the Iron Curtain fell, the South Korean government pursued an aggressive engagement policy toward its northern neighbor, founded on its relative advantage in strength and international status, and its unification policy is built on from 'Korean National Community Unification Formula' (September 11, 1989). Seoul has designed the 'Three-phased Unification Formula for Building a Korean National Community' in 1994 and successive administrations have followed this policy orientation.

This discourse intends to lay the theoretical grounds from functionalism in the past, neo-functionalism, and arms control theory, to establish an apolitical 'national community' through gradual exchanges and cooperation with a touch of sociological approach, and to ultimately achieve a 'single political community' – the political unification as a unified state. In the process, the two Koreas will establish a 'Korean Commonwealth' – a provisional unified regime where the two Koreas embrace peace and development.[5] 'Unification Formula for Building a Korean National Community' takes three steps from 'reconciliation and cooperation' to 'Korean Commonwealth' to 'a

---

3 Juhwa Park et al., 2016 Survey of Inter-Korea Integration (in Korean) (Seoul: Korea Institute for National Unification, 2016).

4 p.10, Sukhoon Hong et al., Seeking a Unification Strategy Based on the Changed Conditions for Unification After the North Korea's 4th and 5th Nuclear Tests and Ways to Spread the Public Consensus on Unification (in Korean), (Seoul: Korea Institute for National Unification, 2017)

5 The South Korean government deliberately threw the term 'commonwealth' instead of 'confederation' as it had posited a loose union in mind like the British Commonwealth.: p.15, Ibid.

unified nation-state.' Ever since this has been the South Korean official narrative.[6]

With regards to North Korea's approach to institutional integration, it aims to complete the construction and revolution of communism on the whole of the Korean Peninsula, asserting national self-determination. At the 15th anniversary of Liberation Day on August 15, 1960, Pyongyang first suggested a transitional inter-Korean 'confederation' – while the two each preserve their own systems and institutions. In 1973, it put forth the 'Confederal Republic of Koryo' and in 1980, proposed a 'Formula for Creating a Democratic Confederal Republic of Koryo' – a complete confederation beyond a transitional confederation.[7]

However, North Korea focused on coexistence with South Korea due to the collapse of the communist bloc and economic hardships in the 1990s and advocated a loose confederation of 'one people, one state, two systems, and two governments' in 1991. Even in the 2000s, it forwarded an idea of institutional integration – confederation at a low level based on retaining the existing influence and authority.

Previous unification strategies of the two Koreas concentrated on 'institutional integration'. Nevertheless, weakening ideological confrontations and the advent of a global economy due to the collapse of the Cold War regime and the spread of capitalism respectively, social integration has become ever more important. Past South Korean administrations have also centered on system integration and received realistic criticisms – that it does not guarantee practical effects and public persuasion as its unification discourse was built on the rationales of unification. Moreover, it has been argued that pre-existed unification discourse, viewing unification as completion, failed to grasp the necessity of socio-cultural integration and the diversity suited in the times of the 21st century. In spite of numerous efforts to advance inter-Korean relations and achieve unification, it has been understood that South Korean administrations have not set a mark in strategic tasks for the settlement of peace on the Korean Peninsula such as peaceful resolution to the North Korean nuclear issue, the national reconciliation and restoration of homogeneity through inter-Korean exchanges and cooperation, and incentive for North Korea to open to the international community. In addition, North

6 Further details are available in pp.103-130, Ibid.

7 p.146. Institute for Unification Education, Understanding North Korea 2017 (in Korean). (Seoul: Institute for Unification Education, 2017)

Korea's nuclear and missile development escalated alert levels on the peninsula and the competitive structure surrounding the peninsula has even jeopardized peaceful coexistence.

2. Peace Paradigm Shift for Korean Unification

As previous unification policies of South and North Korea focused on institutional integration based on legitimacy, it is essential to newly fathom the reality that the two Koreas face. There are several limitations to the politically and institutionally focused mindset in the Cold War era and the institutional unification led by political elites. It is necessary to revisit the concept of focusing on institutional integration driven by a race for legitimacy. The post-Cold War world has seen globalization deepened with the development of IT and individualism prioritized. Therefore, it is high time to consider institutional unification and a socio-cultural approach for unification policy.

Concerning inter-Korean integration from a sociocultural perspective, Chung and Song defined, 'South and North Korean people coming to an agreement on common values of society through mutual communication and understanding. Choi stated, 'the whole constituents building a single political community as well as feeling homogeneity after overcoming heterogeneity with a sense of uniformity among all members in all domains such as economy, society, and culture'.[8] As long as Korean unification focuses on unifying political systems, the society is projected to witness relentless social unrest and confusion of values and norms when unified.

That is, the unification strategy centered on politics, institutions, and state as a unitary actor needs readjustment. It is vital to devise a unification strategy driven by the people rather than the state or the institution. Also, it is crucial to transform the security paradigm in the Cold War era to a peace paradigm. Peace Studies has stretched its scope to ecological peace, peace culture, multiculturalism, diversity since the end of the Cold War. Johan Galtung wrote of direct, structural, and cultural violence, and direct,

8 p.4 Juhwa Park et al., 2016 Survey of Inter-Korea Integration; p.222, Eun Mee Jeong and Younghoon Song, "North Koreans` Attitude towards Unification and Social Inclusiveness for North Koreans in South Korea" (in Korean), The Journal of Unification Affairs 24(1); pp.286-7, Sunjong Choi, "Unification and integration concerning the Korean reunification -In matters of the German reunification" (in Korean), Journal of Korean Unification Culture and Arts 15.

structural, and cultural peace and restructuring the Korean unification issue from the perspective of Peace Studies, the reality of the peninsula requires systemic consideration of regional specificity and global universality.[9] This is because war logic for peace demands too much sacrifice.

Obviously, security assumes the utmost priority when a country establishes foreign policy goals.[10] As national security is the most fundamental matter, this is not to say that Korea should neglect security. Rather, since national security is the basic constant in national policy, this is to say that it should not be politically manipulated. In terms of national security, military security should be prioritized over others and strengthening deterrence by bolstering national defense capabilities solidifies the grounds for negative peace (prevention of war). However, such a paradigm cannot fundamentally ameliorate the current Cold War-type inter-Korean relations. Only positive peace can establish a perpetual peace regime on the peninsula.

'Positive peace paradigm' requires the structural establishment of a peace regime between the two Koreas, rather than military strength. In other words, Korean unification should not only focus on existing institutional and military perspective but also pursue social and normative integration simultaneously.[11] The shift in peace paradigm is a task to seek a peace regime on the Korean peninsula, even developing further as a blueprint for a peace regime in Northeast Asia.

Lastly, the Moon Jae-in administration's policies on North Korea and unification calls for public consultation and understanding to formulate and implement them. South Korean society has matured with the development of democracy. Unification strategy and strategy on North Korea is no longer sustainable to be driven by political elites. South Korea vastly differs from the North in terms of policy formulation and implementation as it reflects public opinion. Noting James Fearon's domestic audience cost theory, the North Korean population has no say in the foreign policy making

9 p.21 Bo-hyuk Suh, "Reconstructing Reunification Issues from the Perspective of Peace Studies" (in Korean), Journal of Koreanology 63.

10 Dr. Chittick illustrates U.S. foreign policy decision making process with three foreign policy goals of security, identity, and economic prosperity in mind. p.17 William O. Chittick, American Foreign Policy: a Framework for Analysis (Washington, D.C.: CQ Press, 2006),

11 Johan Galtung differentiates 'negative peace: as the absence of direct violence' from 'positive peace: as the absence of structural violence' and explains them both.

process. Generally, dictatorial states such as North Korea do not take public opinion into account and the political elites have a dominant share in the decision-making structure.[12]

Jessica Weeks, analyzing the extent of audience cost's influence, domestic political factor, in policymaking of authoritarian states, evaluated audience cost of political elites, albeit limited, has effects in China. Nevertheless, she views that audience cost has no place in the decision-making structure of North Korea - an autocratic regime. That is, it could be assumed that the perception and policy preference of North Korea's political leadership decides foreign policy. Eventually, for North Korea to have a more rational decision-making structure, she points that it needs a pragmatic liberal approach of 'spread of democracy'.[13]

As for South Korea, a country with Western-style democracy, audience costs are incurred in national policy. In other words, the South Korean government inevitably pays domestic audience cost in the decision-making process for policies on North Korea and unification. While a democratic system considers international factors, domestic factors such as public opinion have relatively significant sway in the decision-making process. Seoul, taking the domestic audience cost theory into account, should engage with the public and make common grounds. Also, being a representative democracy, the legislative branch - the ruling party and the opposition - should formulate sustainable policies based on debates and consultations.

---

12 According to James Fearon, when national leaders fail to react successfully to foreign signals or suffer defeat in a war, he/she has to pay domestic audience costs. Leaders in democracy has to take responsibility for their decisions for the next elections. Generally, this theory claims that audience costs applies to leaders in the democratic world but not to dictators. James Fearon, "Domestic Political Audiences and the Escalation of International Disputes." American Political Science Review, Vol. 88, Issue 3. (1994).

13 Jessica L. P. Weeks, Dictators at War and Peace, (Ithaca and London: Cornell University Press, 2014); Sukhoon Hong and Yongwoo Na. "The Acceleration of North Korea's Nuclear Capability and the Searching for South Korea's New Policy toward North Korea: Evolution of North Korea's Offensive Nuke Strategy and South Korea's Response Strategy"(in Korean) National Security and Strategy 17(3)

III. Deadlock in DPRK–U.S. Denuclearization Talks and Intensifying U.S.–China Strategy Confrontation

1. Stalling DPRK–U.S. Denuclearization Talks and Increasing Uncertainty in Inter–Korean Relations

Since some moves initiated the improvement of inter-Korean relations thanks to PyeongChang Winter Olympics in 2018, enlarging mood of peace, created by Panmunjeom Declaration in April and Pyongyang Joint Declaration in September of the same year, led to mitigating military tensions between the two Koreas. The two leaders agreed to transform the demilitarized zone (DMZ) to a peace zone in the Panmunjeom Declaration, marking a significant step toward a peace regime. In September, they agreed to implement the terms agreed in previous inter-Korean summits and establish west coast joint special economic zone and an east coast joint special tourism zone, expanding inter-Korean economic cooperation.

Nonetheless, until recently, the inter-Korean economic cooperation has not made a milestone. After the breakdown in Hanoi in February 2019, North Korea and the U.S. have been at loggerheads and Pyongyang has taken a hawkish stance with Seoul as well. As North Korea's denuclearization process and the sanctions on North Korea are at a standstill, economic cooperation projects that the two leaders agreed have not begun and hostility and distrust between the two Korean have increased. On the other hand, the Trump administration has not changed its position on denuclearization talks. It negotiates with the North Korean regime on the condition that North Korea completely dismantles nuclear facilities in Yongbyon, adheres to additional measures that the U.S. wants, and follows a roadmap for denuclearization. In other words, the U.S. can only meet North Korea's demands for the removal of sanctions and security assurances for the regime when North Korea's steps toward denuclearization are noticeable. That is, Pyongyang should actively take measures that satisfy the U.S. As President-elect Joe Biden is expected to take a 'bottom-up' approach with precise responses at the working-level, meaningful bilateral talks will resume only when the two countries find a common ground in the negotiations.

Instead of the traditional New Year's address, North Korea issued the 'Report on the 5th Plenary Meeting of the 7th Central Committee of the Workers' Party of

Korea' addressing the impending issues that North Korea faces along with the changes in national strategy ('a new way'). This hints at a 'frontal breakthrough' considering that the sanctions will remain for long - pursuing an aggressive military policy in the future. Especially, the report blamed the U.S. 'hostile policy toward the DPRK' for the difficulties in denuclearization negotiations and the uncertainty surrounding the Korean peninsula and claimed the negotiation strategy toward the U.S. as 'lifting sanctions first, and then resuming negotiations on denuclearization'. Furthermore, it indicated that the U.S. actions will determine whether North Korea bolsters its nuclear capabilities or not while maintaining firm nuclear deterrence - alluding that North Korea will take a hardline policy on the international community and South Korea unless the negotiations with the U.S. make progress.

Adding to this, North Korea's diatribe and hardline stance caused by anti-regime flyers have acted as a new variable. Since Kim Yo-jong issued a statement on June 4, the North Korean authorities have aggravated its relations with the South, destroying the 'inter-Korean Liaison Office' in Kaesong on June 16. With economic sanctions in place due to the stalemate in denuclearization talks, North Korea's aggressiveness toward the outside world has worsened the security environment of the Korean Peninsula, as the inter-Korean relations strained. While there is a hiatus in the security environment because of the pandemic, the political landscape surrounding the peninsula is highly likely to experience turmoil due to the North Korean nuclear issue and sanctions on North Korea among others.

However, North Korea has left some room for negotiations with the U.S. when U.S. Special Representative for North Korea Stephen Biegun visited South Korea on July 7. On July 10, while downplaying the possibility of a third DPRK-U.S. summit, First Vice Department Director Kim Yo-jong expressed that this was her 'personal thoughts' and stated that Chairman Kim 'wishes to President Trump that he would certainly achieve great successes in his work', stressing the friendship between Chairman Kim and President Trump. (Rodong Sinmun, July 10, 2020) And at the end of her statement, she hinted that she may be a special envoy to the U.S. or lead the negotiations with the U.S. by expressing her intent to personally obtain the DVD of U.S. Independence Day celebrations. Additionally, Chairman Kim Jong-un supposedly showed some leeway to reconcile with the South through the conciliatory message to the South in his address at the parade commemorating the 75th anniversary of the establishment of the Workers' Party of Korea on October 10, 2020.

2. The International Factor of U.S–China Relations and the Korean Peninsula

Sino-U.S. struggle for hegemony takes the form of the U.S. offensive followed by China's response. Especially, the Trump administration. inaugurated in 2017, proclaimed isolationism and aims to prevent China's economic rise and regional dominance. This entails the intention to maintain U.S.-led international economic order, and secure global dominance through cooperation with its allies. On the contrary, China has manifested its determination not to back down against the U.S. through stretching its economic influence in the region. While U.S-China strategic confrontation unfolds in economic domains such as trade, currency, technology, and intellectual property, it tends to focus on geopolitical security confrontation in East Asia.

Joe Biden's victory will crucially swing the U.S. policy on Korean Peninsula. The new administration is predicted to return to multilateralism. He condemned that President Trump's 'America first' policy made 'American alone' and implied that he will embrace internationalism in foreign policy. (ABC, October 15). In his victory speech on November 8, President-elect Biden mentioned the U.S. leadership in global affairs, restoration of traditional cooperation with NATO and other allies including South Korea and Japan. He also hinted that the U.S. will hugely alter the Trump administration's approach in pending security and foreign policy affairs with South Korea and relations with North Korea such as the North Korean nuclear issue. The Biden administration's foreign policy will be summarized as the spread of democracy, stronger alliances, economic diplomacy, restoration of global leadership.[14]

Under the slogans of 'a new type of great power relations' and 'Chinese dream', China has aspired to construct a stronger China, develop as a maritime power, and pose an aggressive stance in territorial issues with its neighbors. China's pursuit as a regional hegemon also has considerable implications for the Korean Peninsula. The question then

14 "[Contribution] U.S. President-Elect Biden's Policy on the Korean Peninsula," (in Korean) Maeil Sinmun, November 9, 2020.

becomes what is the Xi leadership's policy orientation on the U.S. President Xi plans to establish 'a new type of great power relations'. President Xi views U.S. military alliances in the Asia-Pacific as a key factor in Sino-U.S. relations. Also, he opposed the U.S. having responsibilities with allies in the East China Sea and the South China Sea. This is the initial concept of 'a new type of great power relations' that President Xi reiterates over and over. As much as proclaiming a strong China, President Xi strongly opposes wider U.S. military presence in the Asia-Pacific - foreshadowing security friction with the U.S.

Most of all, the Trump administration failed to notice the seriousness of COVID-19 in the early days – a late response to the pandemic, the suggestion of injecting disinfectants, etc. - and responded tepidly only seeking opportunities to exude confidence in its system and 'America First' policy. Without an adequate response to a global crisis, the U.S. global leadership has hit a crisis. The post-WWII U.S.-led international order has rapidly exacerbated. Beijing moved in swiftly and aptly to fill in the leadership vacuum. President Xi desires to position China as the global leader with this pandemic as an opportunity. A hegemon needs overwhelming national strength, respectable leadership, and domestic public support. While the U.S. has robust national capabilities to provide international public goods to the world, its leadership and public opinion have left question marks. Leadership entails recognition and cooperation with others. Being an exemplary model, it should maintain a consensus-based multilateral order. Trump's America First narrative and the idea of peace through strength have weakened these two factors.

The ROK-U.S. alliance has faced some fresh challenges. Unlike the past, the stationing cost of U.S. soldiers, the transfer of wartime operational control, and the intelligence pact (General Security of Military Information Agreement, GSOMIA) between South Korea and Japan have been bones of contention. China may drive a wedge between the bilateral relations, strengthening ties and coordination on the North Korean nuclear issue with South Korea. When Seoul and Tokyo engaged in a fierce argument over the extension of GSOMIA last year, Washington expressed the hope to broaden its alliance with Seoul to cover the Indo-Pacific; and Seoul shied away from replying. Until recently, the two sides have had differences over the defense cost-sharing, unlikely to be resolved anytime soon.

In sum, U.S.-China rivalry in Northeast Asia is likely to intensify in the future.

The strategic confrontation does not stop at areas of politics, military, and security, and rather spilled over to all fronts, such as economy and trade. The escalating tensions and confrontation will be the largest determinant of the Northeast Asian order for some time to come. Accordingly, South Korea is likely to face a foreign policy dilemma - to choose one side or the other.

Ⅳ. Peace Process on the Korean Peninsula and Sustainable Inter-Korean Cooperation

1. The Moon Jae-in Administration's Peace Process on the Korean Peninsula

The Moon Jae-in administration's North Korea policy is aimed at defusing military tensions and establishing peace on the peninsula through inter-Korean exchanges and cooperation - achieving three different types of peace: 'security peace', 'market peace', and 'democratic peace'.[15] The administration endorsed a peace-first approach to discourse on North Korea and unification. In the Third Basic Plan on Development of Inter-Korean Relations announced by the Ministry of Unification in 2018, the government set goals such as the resolution to the North Korean nuclear issue, settlement of perpetual peace, sustainable development of inter-Korean relations, and implementation of a new economic community on the Korean Peninsula. Furthermore, the Moon Jae-in administration clearly stated that it will prioritize mutual co-existence based on "three noes'" - no pursuit of North Korean regime collapse, unification by absorption, and unification by force.

President Moon announced the declaration on a 'new Korean Peninsula peace regime' on February 25, 2019. The 'new Korean Peninsula peace regime' is construed as an initiative to establish a lasting peace regime based on the community of sustainable peace and cooperation and economic cooperation built by a peace economy. The birth

15 p.16, Seong-Ryoul Cho, "Moon Jae-in government's Challenge on North Korean Policy: Visions for Denuclearizing North Korea and Peace Regime-building on Korean Peninsula" (in Korean), Unification Policy Studies 26(1).

Figure 1. Moon Jae-in's Policy on the Korean Peninsula at a Glance

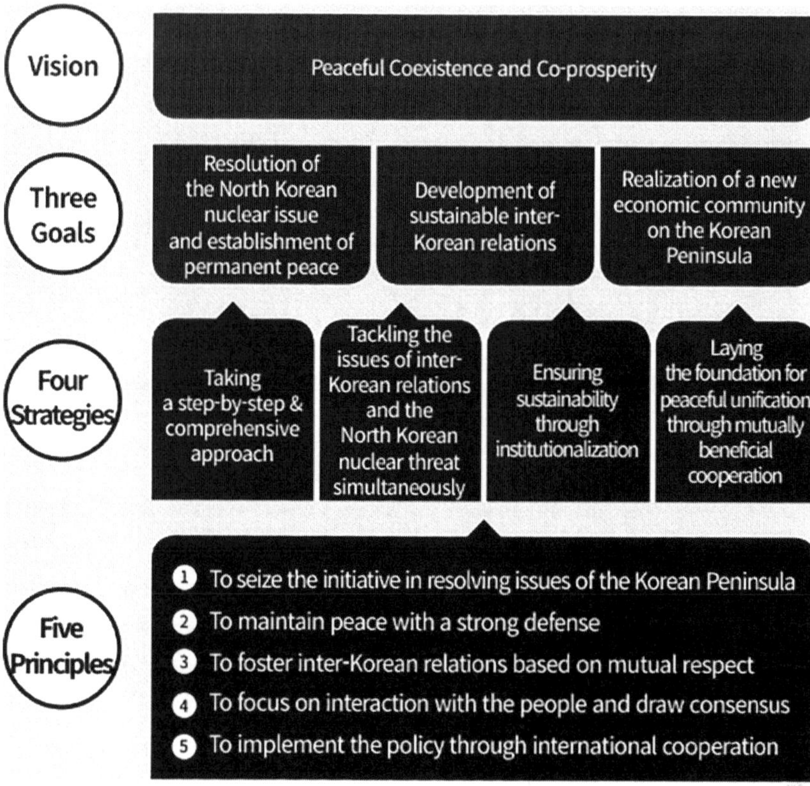

Source: Moon Jae-in's Policy on the Korean Peninsula: A Korean Peninsula of Peace and Prosperity, November 2017, Ministry of Unification, p. 11.

of the concept begins with the critical viewpoint that the South Korean government failed to have a specific design of security strategy amid the absence of a grand strategy. President Moon proclaimed the new regime on the Peninsula as a blueprint for a century to come. The goal is to establish a nuclear-free, peace regime, a new security order in Northeast Asia, sustainable inter-Korean cooperation, and peace economy. The starting point of the new Korean Peninsula regime is establishing a nuclear-free and peace regime and resolving military hostility may be the starting point to shape an order of peace and cooperation on the Korean Peninsula. The new Korean Peninsula regime will also contribute to establishing a new security cooperation architecture in Northeast Asia. The

ASEAN Regional Forum (ARF) is an example to follow, and this will drive forward the nonnuclear security regime for the complete denuclearization of the peninsula.

As for the goal of 'A Peaceful and Prosperous Korean Peninsula, the government's national goal in the security domain, the government specified 'Ensuring Strong National Security and Dependable Defense', 'Fostering Inter-Korean Reconciliation and Cooperation as well as Denuclearization of the Korean Peninsula', and 'Reinforcing International Cooperation through Diplomacy' among others as implementation strategies. President Moon elaborated the government's initiative for peace on the Korean peninsula and announced the vision for the peninsula in the addresses commemorating the 100th anniversary of March 1 Independence Movement Day and the 74th anniversary of the Liberation Day, and the address at the 74th UN General Assembly, to name a few.

The South Korean government strives to establish a peace regime on the peninsula and foster peace and cooperation in Northeast Asia through cooperative and balanced diplomacy. Particularly, the government has endeavored to implement the New Northern Policy and New Southern Policy, proclaimed respectively when President Moon visited Russia in September 2017 and Southeast Asia in November of the same year. To this end, it has developed discussions on a community of peace and cooperation in Northeast Asia.

Moreover, Seoul has made efforts to maintain close coordination with Washington at every level to make progress in inter-Korean dialogue and DPRK-U.S. dialogue in a virtuous cycle. It has drawn constructive cooperation with Beijing, Tokyo, and Moscow - enhancing strategic communications with them. Also, the South Korean government has made efforts in multiple channels to strengthen the international community's understanding of its policy on the Korean Peninsula and galvanize support, using various bilateral and multilateral diplomatic events. As a result, numerous events such as ARF, the East Asia Summit (EAS), ASEAN Plus Three Summit, and Asia-Europe Meeting (ASEM), have included expressions of active cooperation and support for the government's policy on the peninsula in the concluding statements. The South Korean government has vigorously pursued to diversify its diplomacy partners, shoring up multilateral cooperation to supplement the shortfalls of bilateral diplomacy as well as making efforts to widen its diplomatic frontiers by increasing cooperation partners at the global stage.

2. Sustainable Inter-Korean Exchanges and Cooperation through a Community of Life

In his address at the March 1 Independence Movement Day event in 2020, President Moon emphasized the possible cooperation with North Korea on public health against contagious diseases; and in his special address to mark his third day in office on May 10, 2020, he furthered the discussion on a 'community of life' to the two Koreas, Northeast Asia, Asia, and the world, laying emphasis on human security and highlighted the need for the world to move toward a community of peace. In fact, the two Koreas agreed, 'The two sides agreed to strengthen cooperation in the areas of prevention of epidemics, public health and medical care, including emergency measures to prevent the influx and spread of contagious diseases.' (Article 2, clause 4) regardless of the political environment - COVID-19 being the imminent threat calling for cooperation.

President Moon's keyword in his address on 75th Korea's Liberation Day was 'people' and 'life and safety'. Underlining that 'Only when everyone is living well can we say that genuine liberation has been achieved', he elucidated 'The spirit that permeates the core of the Korean New Deal is also people-centered mutual benefit.' To recover a community for life, inter-Korean cooperation is a necessary value. Even though the inter-Korean relations and DPRK-U.S. relations have been in deadlock caused by the failure of the Hanoi summit and the explosion of the inter-Korean liaison office, the president showed his determination to engage in inter-Korean cooperation for the life and safety of the people.

COVID-19 forced countries to protect their citizens' lives above all else. These diseases know no borders, spreading proportionally to the global connectedness. Also, COVID-19 has paralyzed states as this has become an issue of international politics, economy, and society, beyond a public health problem. The North Korean authorities have spared no efforts to prevent the intrusion of the virus, requested protective equipment from UNICEF and the IFRC has been granted exemption to provide these supplies from the UN Sanctions Committee on North Korea. Moreover, when the two Koreas' joint disaster relief efforts achieve success, this could provide momentum to pursue cooperation in the tourism sector and exchanges, even garnering international support for the peace regime on the peninsula.

Beginning from the cooperation on disaster relief, the two Koreas should advance bilateral economic cooperation. Previously, the administration initiated in a joint investigation to connect and modernize roads and railways and had a groundbreaking ceremony, and proceeded with cooperation in health quarantine, public health, and environment to prevent the spread of contagious diseases, to restore ecology, and to protect forestry. It also laid the foundation to resolve the humanitarian issues as it carried out 'reunion of separated families' in 2018 and agreed with North Korea to open a permanent venue to enable reunion of separated families in Mount Kumgang, as well as holding video meetings, regularizing reunions, carrying out visits to hometowns for those who have been displaced since the Korean War and verifying survival of separated families. It has engaged in exchanges and cooperation with the North in sports, making efforts for a joint team at the Tokyo Olympics and joint bid for 2032 Olympics and holding events such as 'inter-Korean workers' football match' and 'international youth football tournament' along with other fields such as religion, NGOs, media, and education through visits and contacts.[16]

The establishment of a peace zone in DMZ is one of the tasks in policy on North Korea to expand the discussion on the community of life and exchanges and cooperation with North Korea. In his remarks at the UN General Assembly on September 24, 2019, President Moon accentuated the 'three principles to resolve the Korean Peninsula issue' ('zero tolerance for war', 'mutual security guarantee', and 'co-prosperity') and proposed an international peace zone in the DMZ.[17] He has resolutely suggested the idea of transforming the DMZ as a sustainable peace zone - at this year's New Year's address. Furthermore, he promised to commit to inter-Korean agreements including cooperation in quarantine and common management of rivers flowing on both sides.

V. Conclusion

The North Korean nuclear issue has loomed as a core variable in determining the political landscape surrounding the Korean Peninsula. First, security peace is important

16 pp. 12-13. Ministry of Unification, 2020 Unification White Paper (in Korean), (Seoul, Ministry of Unification, 2020),

17 p. 13. Ibid.

to realize passive peace on the peninsula. Without the guarantee to peacefully resolve the North Korean nuclear issue, peace on the peninsula and East Asia is a remote possibility. However, a security guarantee cannot solely bring peace and unification. Hence, it is imperative to pursue active peace at the same time. Active peace on the peninsula demands the peace paradigm to expand, beyond the security paradigm. 'Active peace', an absence of structural violence, needs to be reflected in South Korea's policy on North Korea and unification, developing to 'peace paradigm'.

In the security domain, the alliance with the U.S. and the economic, strategic partnership with China should be deepened. Additionally, the South Korean government should pursue the New Economic Map Initiative for the Korean Peninsula in association with China's Belt and Road Initiative and Russia's New Eastern Policy and common architecture for peace and cooperation in East Asia, including ASEAN. It should strive for a 'Northeast Asian peace regime' enhancing relations with North Korea as well as other neighbors, focusing on pragmatic and economic areas. Linked with the peace paradigm, this will have a significant meaning as it provides an opportunity to transform into a perpetual peace paradigm in which people co-exist through mutual economic benefits and cultural exchanges.

In reality, institutional unification and radical measures for unification have limits and unification policy needs both short- and long-term approaches simultaneously. Emphasizing that the discussions on peaceful unification involve psychological integration of the inter-Korean community, it is needless to say that the concept of unification stretches to encompass social and cultural integration, beyond institutional integration. Most of all, the South Korean government's policy on North Korea and unification requires public consultation and understanding in the policy formulation and implementation process.

Amid the changing international environment, sustainable inter-Korean cooperation and peace process on the Korean Peninsula are crucial tasks. Seoul should endeavor to resolve the North Korean nuclear issue rationally, pushing for DPRK-U.S. denuclearization talks, to establish a peace regime on the peninsula. Besides, cooperation with neighbors including Washington and Beijing is essential and above all, it should prepare for improvement of inter-Korean relations and unification through sustainable inter-Korean exchanges and cooperation.

Finally, Korean unification should be based on peaceful means. Thus, it is necessary to contemplate the most appropriate approach to peaceful unification, abandoning the idea of war. In the end, both South and North Koreans should be able to enjoy peaceful coexistence and prosperity. To this end, it is mandatory to foster a social and national atmosphere so as to entice North Korea to adopt reform and opening-up measures. From a framework of 'peace paradigm', peace and unification will only be possible under a long-term strategy, proceeding with social and normative understanding and integration while the system centered on "democratic peace" and universal "human rights" and social constituents with common interests are guaranteed.

References

Park, Juhwa et al., *2016 Survey of Inter-Korea Integration* (in Korean). Seoul: Korea Institute for National Unification, 2016.

Suh, Bo-hyuk, "Reconstructing Reunification Issues from the Perspective of Peace Studies" (in Korean), *Journal of Koreanology* 63. pp.33-64.

Republic of Korea Defence Intelligence Command. North Korean Forces and Division. Daejon: ROK Army Press, 2019.

Chung, Sungyoon. "Assessing North Korea's Nuclear Capabilities" (in Korean). *KINU Unification Plus* 2(3). 2016.

Jeung, Young-Tae et al. *North Korea's Nuclear Strategy and South Korea's Responsive Strategies* (in Korean). Seoul: Korea Institute for National Unification, 2014.

Jeong, Eun Mee and Younghoon Song. "North Koreans` Attitude towards Unification and Social Inclusiveness for North Koreans in South Korea" (in Korean), *The Journal of Unification Affairs* 24(1).

Choi, Sunjong. "Unification and integration concerning the Korean reunification -In matters of the German reunification" (in Korean), *Journal of Korean Unification Culture and Arts* 15, pp. 283-310.

Institute for Unification Education, *Understanding North Korea* 2017 (in Korean). Seoul: Institute for Unification Education, 2017.

KINU North Korean Studies Division, "Analysis of 2017 North Korea's New Year's Day Speech and Prospect for its Internal and External Policy", *KINU Online Series* 17-01. 2017.

Hong, Min. "Comprehensive Assessment of the North Korean Affairs after the Byungjin line of Simultaneous Development of Economic and Nuclear Development" (in Korean). Eleventh KINU Unification Forum. Seoul: Korea Institute for National Unification, 2015.

Hong, Sukhoon. "China's Policy Orientation and Strategy on North Korea: Perceptions and Policy Preferences of the Chinese Leadership" (in Korean). *The Journal of Political Science and Communication* 17(1), pp. 123-145.

Hong, Sukhoon. "Dictators' War and Peace" (in Korean). *KINU Unification Plus* 1(3). 2015.

Hong, Sukhoon et al., *Seeking a Unification Strategy Based on the Changed Conditions for Unification After the North Korea's 4th and 5th Nuclear Tests and Ways to Spread the Public Consensus on Unification* (in Korean), Seoul: Korea Institute for National Unification, 2017.

Sukhoon Hong and Yongwoo Na. "The Acceleration of North Korea's Nuclear Capability and the Searching for South Korea's New Policy toward North Korea: Evolution of North Korea's Offensive Nuke Strategy and South Korea's Response Strategy"(in Korean) *National Security and Strategy* 17(3), pp. 103-130.

______, "Analysis of North Korea's New Year Address in 2014" *Analysis of Unification*

Environment 2014.

Chosun Ilbo, July 3, 2017 Issue.
Korea Central News Agency, October 30, 2015.
JoongAng Ilbo, October 24, 2017.
Herald Business, January 6, 2014.
Rodong Sinmun. July 5, 2017.
Rodong Sinmun November 29, 2017.
Rodong Sinmun August 1, 2008 – March 31, 2017.

The Washington Post, December 27, 2017.
McMaster, H.R. and Cohn G. D. "America First Doesn't Mean America Alone" *Wall Street Journal*, May 3, 2017.

Chittick, William, O. *American Foreign Policy: a Framework for Analysis*. Washington, D.C.: CQ Press, 2006.
Fearon, James "Domestic Political Audiences and the Escalation of International Disputes." *American Political Science Review* 88(3) (1994), 577-592.
Habermas, Jurden. *The Theory of Communication Action, Volume One: Reason and the Rationalization of Society*. translated by Thomas A. McCarthy. Boston: Beacon Press, 1984.
Hong, S. and Cho, Y. "DPRK's Policy Priorities toward the US: What impact does North Korea's foreign policy on its Strategic Choices?" *The Journal of Peace Studies* 17(6) (2016), 115-137.
Hong, S. and Cho, Y. "Consistent pattern of DPRK's policy on ROK: What Shapes North Korea's foreign policy? *International Area Studies Review* 20(1) (2017), 57-75.
Jervis, Robert. *Perception and Misperception in International Politics*. Princeton: Princeton University Press, 1976.
Nye, Joseph S. and Welch, David A. *Understanding Global Conflict and Cooperation*, 9th Edition. Pearson, 2013.
Krippendorff, K. 2004. *Content Analysis: An Introduction to its Methodology*. California: Sage Publications, 2004.
Waltz, Kenneth N. *Man, the State, and War: A Theoretical Analysis*. Columbia University Press, 1959.
Weeks, J. *Dictators at War and Peace*. Cornell University Press: Ithaca and London, 2014.

The White House, *National Security Strategy of the United States of America*, December 2017, accessed December 28, 2017. https://www.whitehouse.gov/wp-content/uploads/2017/12/NSS-Final-12-18-2017-0905.pdf.

Diplomatic Approach to the Korean Peace Process

Chapter 4.
How Commitment Problems Affect the Prospects for Peace in the Korean Peninsula
Scott Gates (Peace Research Institute Oslo (PRIO), (University of Oslo))
Havard Mokleiv Nygård (Peace Research Institute Oslo (PRIO))

Chapter 5.
A Systematic Analysis of the Trump Foreign Policy:
Implications for Northeast Asia and the Korean Peninsula
Dongsoo Kim
(Pukyong National University)

Chapter 6.
The Impact of U.S.-China Competition on the Korean Peace Process
Wonjae Hwang
(University of Tennessee)

Chapter 7.
Sunrise, Sunset:
The Rise and Fall of Inter-Korean Economic Relations
Inhan Kim
(Ewha Womans University)

Chapter 4

How Commitment Problems Affect the Prospects for Peace in the Korean Peninsula

Scott Gates (Peace Research Institute Oslo (PRIO), (University of Oslo))
Havard Mokleiv Nygård (Peace Research Institute Oslo (PRIO))

Abstract

The Korean peninsula is fraught with tension. We analyze three aspects of the commitment problem, incomplete information, preemptive war, and preventative war as they apply to the conflict between North Korea and the USA (along with South Korea) employing the bargaining theory of war. In doing this, we also extend the bargaining theory of war to an asymmetric conflict. First, how the USA regards the costs of a war with North Korea is uncertain. A couple of years ago the Trump administration seemed to discount the costs of North Korean counter-strike on Seoul, if they were to 'give North Korea a bloody nose'. We find that this incomplete information problem is destabilizing and could lead to war. Second, the USA has made military advances capable of taking out much of North Korea's counter-strike capability. Such a weapon would provide the USA with an incentive to launch a first-strike attack. Preemptive war could be a possibility, but with asymmetric capabilities, if the USA does not launch a first-strike, the opportunities for mutually advantageous bargain remain. Third, we examine the growing nuclear capability of North Korea over time. Their relative capability is rising viz-a-viz the USA. They cannot credibly commit to an agreement today, given their better bargaining position in the future. This creates an incentive for the USA to launch a preventive war sooner rather than later, while they retain a strong military advantage. Again, with asymmetric capabilities, while the bargaining range decreases, it nonetheless persists. The biggest threat of war between North Korea and the USA concerns the situation of a rising power and two-sided incomplete information. Such a situation may reflect reality.

Keywords: North Korea, nuclear war, commitment problems, preemptive war, preventive war, bargaining theory of war

I. Introduction

Despite possessing overwhelming military capability, for decades the United States of America has been unable to coerce the Democratic Republic of Korea to abandon its efforts to build a nuclear arsenal. Indeed, in recent years, Pyongyang has developed its nuclear capabilities to such an extent that their arsenal serves as a potent source of leverage against the USA (Tan and Park, 2020). The asymmetric nature of the contest has not deterred North Korea from developing nuclear capabilities.

North Korea is now likely to possess sufficient military capacity to launch a nuclear attack. South Korea is most vulnerable, but so are other US allies, such as Japan. Further development of an ICBM missile, the Hwasong-14 is estimated to have a range of 10,400 kilometers, which if true would mean that US cities from Los Angeles to Denver are within striking range (Kristensen and Norris, 2018; Wright, 2017).

Much fuss has been made of the erratic nature of North Korean leaders, Kim Jong-il and Kim Jong-un. We shall not follow this line of reasoning. Our analysis treats the US and North Korea as rational agents. Drawing on game theoretic models and more particularly the bargaining theory of war, we analyze the prospects for war between these two countries. Problems relating to credible commitment and incomplete information make any bargain between the US and North Korea inherently unstable. We do not need to look to find craziness or signs of insanity, even with fully rational actors, our findings are unsettling.

This chapter addresses the question: How do commitment problems affect the prospects for peace in the Korean Peninsula? We proceed by providing an overview of the bargaining theory of war and the meaning of the commitment problem in an asymmetric contest. The theory is explicated by using the example of the contest between North Korea and the USA. We begin our analysis of a complete information game, which shows that under such conditions, war is not rational. Instead of war, with complete information, we should see nations find mutually beneficial negotiated settlements. We then turn to an analysis of incomplete information and show how this can lead to war even with rational actors. This analysis is followed with a discussion of two types of commitment problems, preemptive war and preventive war. Preemptive war is a situation arising from one power having a first-strike advantage. Most analyses of preemptive war involve relatively balanced powers. Here we extend this analysis to an asymmetric dyad. Preventive war takes place when one power's capability is rising sharply relative the other, which creates an incentive to start a war now rather than wait, since the rising power will be able to drive a harder bargain in the future than now. We also discuss the prospects for bargains that entail forfeiting fighting capacity of one power. Given the denuclearization nature of the negotiations, the USA and North Korea face this type of commitment problem. We end with a discussion of the prospects for peace between North Korea and the United States.

II. Bargaining theory of war

Bargaining theory focuses our attention to the inherently strategic nature of war. War is costly. Yet, we still have war and the threat of war. The bargaining theory of war allows us to explain why states use the inefficient mechanism of war to settle disagreements and why negotiated settlements fail. Most importantly, it highlights the problems of credible commitment and asymmetric information that lead countries with conflicts of interest to go to war.

Our starting point is the critical insight that war is *ex post* inefficient and therefore belligerents should be able to find a 'deal', a bargain, that satisfies them enough to avoid a costly war (Fearon, 1995; Blainey, 1988; Powell, 2006). Wars are extremely costly. Yet, of course, wars do happen. War is thus a failure of bargaining, producing an inefficient outcome that all parties should try to avoid.

The standard setup of the Bargaining Theory of War, credited to James Fearon and his doctoral advisor, Robert Powell, depicts two actors — in most cases, states — that are in dispute over an issue of fixed value (e.g., territory, trade, human rights, nuclear weapons development, or some other issue which can be bargained) (Fearon, 1995; Powell, 1999; Kydd, 2018). In this chapter we will focus on the conflict between North Korea and the USA. Our analytical focus is on North Korean nuclear weapons and their effect on the relative fighting capability of the two countries and the nature of bargained outcomes between the two countries.

III. War and the commitment problem

Drawing on the bargaining theory of war, we focus on two strands of explanations in particular that have been advanced to explain war. First, even though war is inefficient *ex post*, war can occur in a rational strategic interplay if there is incomplete information (Fearon, 1995; Kydd, 2002). Second, war may also occur between two parties, whether they are states or non-state actors (such as a rebel group), if the parties cannot credibly commit to an agreement. This is called the commitment problem. Three broad variants of the commitment problem have been described and discussed at length in the literature: (1) incomplete information about the costs of war, 2) preemptive war and offensive advantages, (3) preventive war as a commitment problem (Fearon, 1995; Powell, 2002, 1999). We discuss all three in more detail below and analyze the conflict between North Korea and the United States in light of these. The asymmetric nature of their military capabilities sheds additional insights into the bargaining theory of war.

1. War and information

In a given conflict, the belligerents will be uncertain about any number of critical issues relating to the war. The parties will be unsure about what the other wants to achieve, what their capabilities are, their resolve and about what the actual cost of the war will be. Here we focus in particular on the latter: the cost of the war. As discussed above, we limit our analysis to the dyadic conflict between the US and North Korea. This is a simplifying assumption, but it also leads us to highlight some key dynamics relating to information. In particular, even though the main fault line is between the US and North Korea, it is arguably South Korea that will bear the brunt of the costs of the war. Indeed, most war game scenarios expect any conflict between the US and North Korea to include an utterly devastating artillery bombardment of Seoul, and attack that in itself could incur hundreds of thousands of deaths (see e.g. Parachini et al., 2020).

Even if we would expect the US and North Korea, on their own, to have a reasonably good idea of how costly the war will be to them, the fact that South Korea will bear so many of the costs provides an additional complication. The US itself is likely to bear a small proportion of the costs. A key question for North Korea thus becomes how willing, or unwilling, the US will be in accepting costs on the South Korean side.

Moreover, this willingness is likely to change across administrations. North Korean uncertainty about the type of US administration they are facing here becomes important for understanding the prospects for peace.

In the first step, however, we abstract away from this and focus on an incomplete information version of the interaction. See Figure 1. Here there is, crucially, no uncertainty about the costs of the war – be it to the US or North Korea, or to South Korea. In this, the USA and North Korea contest an issue space $X = [0,1]$ where 0 is the USA's preferred point and 1 North Korea's ideal point. Let x denote the share of the issue space controlled by the USA. Note that we have placed x relatively far to the right, reflecting asymmetric capabilities.

Figure 1: Issue Space for North Korea and the USA

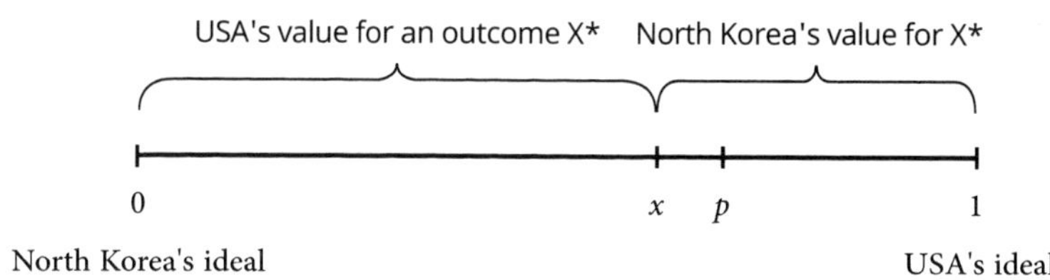

In a typical complete information scenario, the question of the probability of winning is key. Under complete information, this is known. So, in our case, let us, for the sake of simplicity, assume that if the states fight a war, it is common knowledge that North Korea wins with probability $p = 0.3$, and the US with $1 - p = 0.7$. This 7:3 ratio is probably unrealistic, North Korea is much weaker, but it allows us nonetheless to explicate the asymmetric nature of the contest. We further assume that a war always has one victor and that the victor secures the entire prize. Wars, however, are, as discussed, always costly. In this simple example, let us assume that the US's costs of war are $C_{uS} = 0.3$ and North Korea's costs of war are $C_{NK} = 0.2$. This leads the expected utility of war for North Korea to be:

$$EU^{W}_{NK} = (p \cdot UW^{V}_{NK} + (1 - p) \cdot UW^{D}_{NK}) - C_{NK} = (0.3 \cdot 1 + (1 - 0.3) \cdot 0) - 0.2 = 0.3 -$$

0.2=0.1

And for the US the expected utility of war is:

$$EU_{US}^{W} = (p \cdot + UW_{US}^{D} + (1 - p) \cdot UW_{US}^{V}) - C_{US} = (0.3 \cdot 0 + 0.7 \cdot 1 - 0.3 = 0.7 - 0.3 = 0.4$$

The escalatory sequence in such a game can be summed up in three stylized moved. First, North Korea makes a demand x^* – i.e. 'grabs' some issue space. This may be a single demand or a mix of many demands. Next, the US decides to reject or accept the demand. Following this, North Korea decides to attack or not attack. If we assume that the initial distribution is $x0 = 0$, then this leads to the game tree shown in 2.

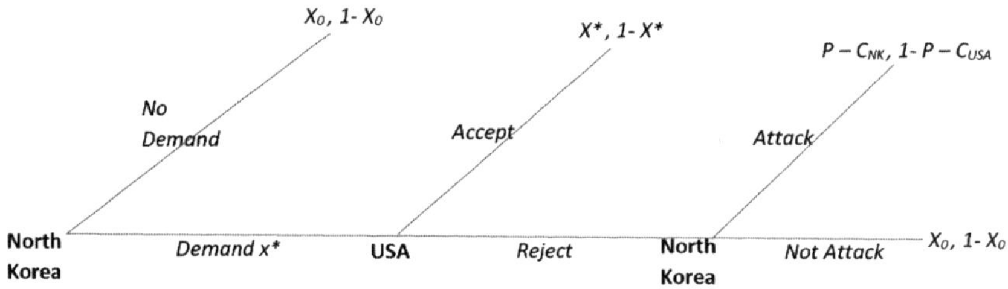

Figure 2: Complete information game tree

We solve the game in Figure 2 by backwards induction to solve for the subgame perfect equilibria (SPE). At the last node, node 3, North Korea attacks if $EU_{NK}^{W} > x_0$, i.e. North Korea attacks if the expected utility of war is larger than the status quo distribution. In our example, there is indeed a war, North Korea attacks since 0.1 > 0. At the second node, focus is instead on the conditions under which the US accepts x^*. The US knows $EU_{NK}^{W} = 0.1 > x_0$, meaning they know that North Korea is willing to attack. The USA then accepts if $1 - x^* > EU_{US}^{W}$ and rejects otherwise. Again, in our example: USA accepts if $1 - x^* > 0.40 \rightarrow x^* < 0.60$. Knowing this, what will North Korea demand at the first node? If North Korea demands $x^* = 0.7$, the US prefers war to accepting the demand. If, instead, North Korea demands $x^* = 0.5$, the US prefers accepting the demand to war. This leads to the following sub-game perfect equilibrium: North Korea demands $x^* = 0.5$, and the US accepts this. North Korea can do even better by demanding the highest possible demand x^* that satisfies $(1 - x^*) > (1 - p) - c_{NK} = 0.7 - 0.3$. North Korea's utility will then be $U_{NK} = 1 - x^*$ and the US's $U_{US} = x^*$. If North Korea can decide x^* freely, the SPE is that North Korea demands $x^* = 0.599$, and the US accepts.

2. Bargaining space

Figure 3: Complete Information Game: Bargaining Space

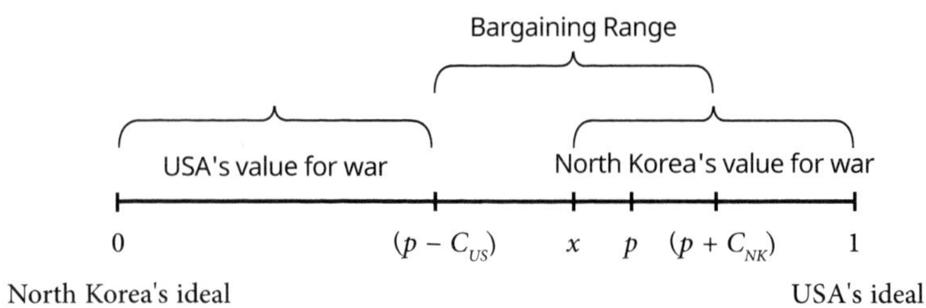

This exercise usefully focuses our attention on the bargaining space. More particularly, we ask, what is the range of outcomes that both North Korea and the US could agree on? Generally, for an efficient bargain to exist some assumptions need to be in place. First, there needs to be complete information: The states know that there is a true probability p that state A wins. This entails that even if the US and North Korea have conflicting estimates of this probability they will know that an agreement exists that both will prefer to war, since a true probability *exists*. Next, we assume that both the US and North Korea are risk-averse or risk-neutral. In practical terms, this means they will weakly prefer a certain 70 – 30 split to a 70% – 30% chance of winning all or losing everything. Note that with risk-averseness, a bargaining range exists even without war costs. Lastly, we assume that a continuous range of peaceful settlements (from 0 to 1) exists. This means that it is possible for the parties to divide the issue, or issues, in dispute. The bargaining space is shown in Figure 3, mathematically it covers the range in between the two parties' expected cost of war. Again, this highlights the centrality of the cost. Under complete information, however, there are limits to our ability to understand its role in the conflict between North Korea and the US. We therefore next relax this assumption and start to analyze an incomplete information version of this interaction.

IV. Incomplete information and war

To better understand the role of costs of war, or more precisely beliefs about such costs, in the interaction between the US and North Korea, we now turn to an incomplete information version of the game sketched above. The core difference in this incomplete information environment is Figure 4: Incomplete information game tree that the US and North Korea now may have different opinions about their own and the other's relative power or over *capabilities*. This, in turn, fundamentally affects their beliefs about e.g. the magnitude of p. Formally, this means that North Korea has 'private information' regarding p. Note that we here focus on rational reasons for why the parties may hold different beliefs about p, but in theory and in practice disagreements over p may also have non-rational explanations. In addition to beliefs about capabilities or about p, the US and North Korea may also have different opinions about their respective *willingness* or *resolve* to fight. This is usually modeled as uncertainty about the *cost* parameters C_{NK} and C_{USA}. This is our primary focus here.

To lead us into this, assume that North Korea is uncertain about the USA's costs of war C_{US}. A first step is then to build a model of this uncertainty. We handle this formally by letting North Korea be uncertain about what kind of 'type' the US is. The US can in this either be a 'hawkish' type that is willing to risk more costs, and thus the US's costs for war are low, than a more 'dovish' US type would, for which the costs are high. Formally this entails that North Korea believes the United States has high costs of war: C^H_{US} with probability h and low costs of war: C^L_{US} with probability $1 - h$. Given this, North Korea can choose between demanding $x^* = 0.5$ and $x^* = 0.7$. Assume further the following parameters: that: $C^L_{US} = 0.3$ and $C^H_{US} = 0.5$, $C_{NK} = 0.2$, and $x_0 = 0$. With these parameters we can now draw the extensive form incomplete information game tree see in Figure 4.

Figure 4: Incomplete information game tree

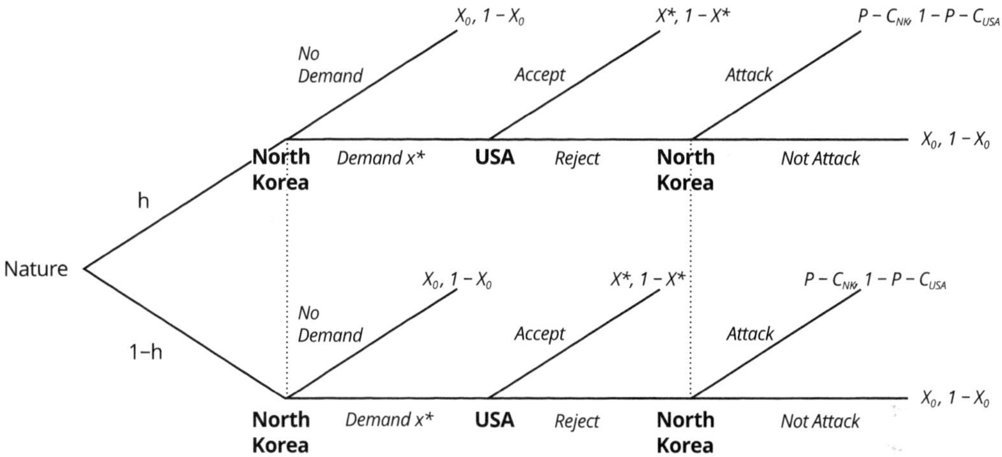

As above, we solve the game via backwards induction. At the ultimate node, node 3, North Korea attacks if $EU^{W}_{NK} > x_0$. This will be the case when $C_{NK} = 0.2$ and $p = 0.3$. At node 2, if the US will accept the offer depends on its type and the US will accept the offer x^* under the following conditions. If US is a low-cost type, North Korea accepts if $x^* < 0.60$ (as above). The USA will then accept if $x^* = 0.5$ and reject if $x^* = 0.7$. If, in contrast, the USA is high-cost, the picture is different. For this scenario the expected utility of war for a high-costs US is:

$$EU^{W}_{US}(H) = (p \cdot UW^{D}_{US} + (1-p) \cdot UW^{V}_{US}) - c^{H}_{US} = 0.3 \cdot 0 + 0.7 \cdot 1 - 0.3 = 0.7 - 0.5 = 0.2 \quad (1)$$

Under this scenario, the US accepts if $1 - x^* < 1 - 0.2 \rightarrow x^* < 0.8$. A high-cost US will accept if $x^* = 0.5$ *and* if $x^* = 0.7$. At the starting node the key question is what North Korea will demand. This demand, in turn, depends on what kind of type North Korea thinks the US is. If North Korea knew the US was a low-cost type it would demand $x^* = 0.5$, the highest demand the US would accept. If, in contrast, they knew that the US was a high-cost type, they would demand $x^* = 0.7$, the highest demand the US would accept. The expected utility of demanding $x^* = 0.5$ is $EU^{0.5} = h \cdot 0.5 + (1-h) \cdot 0.5 = 0.5$. The expected utility of demanding $x^* = 0.7$, in contrast, is $EU^{0.7} = h \cdot 0.7 + (1-h) \cdot 0.1 = 0.1$

$+ 0.6h$. North Korea demands $x^* = 0.7$ if $EU^{0.7} > EU^{0.5} \rightarrow 0.1 + 0.6h > 0.5 \rightarrow h > ⅔$. This leads to the condition that if $h > ⅔$ North Korea demands $x^* = 0.7$, otherwise it demands $x^* = 0.5$. This leads to the following equilibrium outcomes. If $h < ⅔$ and the USA is high-cost: (the North Korea demands $x^* = 0.5$, the USA accepts), giving each the payoffs: (0.5, 0.5). If $h < ⅔$ and the USA is low-cost: (North Korea demands $x^* = 0.5$, the USA accepts), and again the payoffs: (0.5, 0.5). If and the USA is high-cost: (North Korea demands $x^* = 0.7$, the USA accepts), yielding the payoffs: (0.7, 0.3). Lastly, if $h > ⅔$ and the US is low-cost: (North Korea demands $x^* = 0.7$, the USA rejects and North Korea attacks). In this war scenario the payoffs are (0.1, 0.4).

The above analysis shows how war between the US and North Korea may be an equilibrium outcome under incomplete information. This, however, naturally leads to the question of why incomplete information occurs in the first place? One reason could, simply, be that incomplete information arises because of irrationality. And indeed, truly rational agents with similar information should have identical beliefs. We therefore focus on the basis of these beliefs. Note that the US does better if $h < ⅔$. If the US could choose h it would choose a low h no matter what type it is. In other words, the US has an inherent incentive to exaggerate resolve and keep information private. North Korea, in turn, should expect this. Because of this, any pre-conflict statements are of no value – North Korea will simply discount messages from the US. This feature of incomplete information entails that both the US and North Korea have strong incentives to exaggerate their capabilities or resolve in order to obtain a better deal. Or, alternatively, to underplay capabilities or resolve in order to gain a, later, military advantages or to avoid being perceived as overly aggressive. This creates a dangerous and potentially volatile situation where games of bluffing could set in motion an escalatory chain of events that eventually spirals out of control and leads to full blown war.

The democratic peace is often explained by norms or institutions increasing the costs of war for the adversaries. Fearon (1994) suggests that domestic audience costs and the superior ability of democratic regimes of making costly and credible signals are a mechanism explaining the democratic peace. Such supposedly more credible signals can also be sent by democratic regimes like the US towards non-democratic regimes like North Korea. But it is not a given that increasing the costs of war easily remove the possibility of war. Indeed, increasing costs may or may not reduce the risk of war.

Is it then possible for the US and North Korea to send credible signals to each other in a way that may affect the risk of war? In other words, what kind of 'costly signals' exist that could be used as effective signalling devices. Past research has suggested that the parties attempt to inform their opponent about what is private information such that the other understands this is not a bluff (Kydd, 2018). To be effective, any such 'signals' must be costly so that a state with less resolve does not wish to send it. In this, a state may be able to send a signal that leads to a separating equilibrium convincing the opponent that they are of a particular type.

Figure 5: Bargaining space under incomplete information

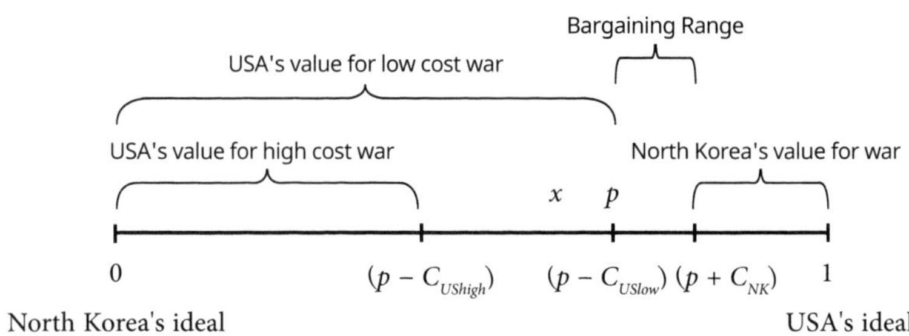

How the USA regards the costs of a war with North Korea is uncertain. Debates within the Trump administration enhanced uncertainty. Early in 2018, the Trump administration seemed to discount the costs of North Korean counter-strike on Seoul, if they were to 'give North Korea a bloody nose'. U.S. officials debated whether it was possible to mount a limited military strike against North Korean nuclear sites without igniting an all-out war on the Korean Peninsula. The limited strike would target a North Korean facility as punishment for one of the country's nuclear or missile tests.

The 'bloody nose', would serve as a signal of willingness to retaliate and to credibly go to war. Tweets, after all, are cheap. Indeed, such protests in game theory are called 'cheap talk'. A limited attack on North Korea would constitute a costly signal. Such a drastic step lets North Korea know that its threats are not a bluff.

The debate did not stop there. The idea of giving North Korea a 'bloody nose' could prove to be very costly. Escalation to full out war would be a real possibility. North Korea would presumably retaliate. The possibility of massive casualties in South Korea or on American bases in Japan would be likely. The response from some advocates of the 'bloody nose' attack was to dismiss the costs of a strike on Seoul or the capability of North Korea to launch such a counter-attack. Such a public debate sent a signal that the cost of war for the USA might not be as high as it had been for previous presidential administrations. The signal regarding the costs of war, creates an incomplete information problem like the one we presented above in Figures 4 and 5 and in our discussion about if $h > 2/3$ and the US is low-cost, whereby North Korea demands $x^* = 0.7$, the USA rejects and North Korea attacks. We find that this incomplete information problem is destabilizing and could lead to war.

We have not modeled it here, but in addition to uncertainty about the costs of war, incomplete information about p, the prospects for victory in a war, may also produce uncertainty. Bluffing plays a big role as states try to get the other side to think it is more powerful than it really is. This in theory should give them more bargaining power and a better negotiated settlement. The problem is what if an actual signal of strength is viewed as a bluff. Calling your opponent's bluff could be catastrophic. Costly signalling is one way to differentiate cheap talk bluffs from true signals of strength.

In the interaction between North Korea and the US, the parties clearly engage in a lot of such signalling. On the side of the US, potential credible signals include troop movements – both increases to signal resolve and draw-downs to signal peaceful intentions – changes to the sanction's regime, or the regular joint US-South Korea military exercises. In the past, the US has also made a show out of flying strategic bombers that could carry nuclear weapons, such as the B-2, over South Korean territory. On the North Korean side, signals include ballistic missile tests, military drills, or, to ease tensions, to expand production or the scope of the Kaesong industrial region. Most of these examples are costly signals.

The signalling can be presumed to be designed to lessen the degree of incomplete information. Nonetheless, we cannot dismiss the possibility of some signals as a form of bluffing. Given incomplete information environments, this should be expected. For example, North Korea may parade a huge new missile, such as the Hwasong-XX, but we really do not know its true capabilities. Ultimately, incomplete information creates an environment of uncertainty, which is destabilizing and reduces the prospects for a bargained solution to the conflict.

V. Preemptive war

There are two main rationalist approaches to the inefficiency puzzle inherent in war. The purely informational problem exists when states fight because of asymmetric information, as discussed in the section above. If there were complete information, no one would fight. By contrast, a pure commitment problem exists when states possess complete information and still fight. Indeed, when a state would rather fight than accommodate, war is the result. This is the essence of the commitment problem (Powell, 2006).

The first type of commitment problem relates to first-strike advantage and preemptive war. Preemptive war occurs when one side attacks to forestall what it sees as an impending attack. A first-strike advantage tempts a state to attack first to preemptively damage their target's war-making capacity and tilt the balance of power in their favor, as in the example of Pearl Harbor or North Korea's surprise attack that started the Korean War (Beard and Strayhorn, 2018). As Fearon (1995) notes, the logic of the first-strike advantage as a commitment problem is like the gunslinger, the advantage lies in firing first. In this sense, the first-strike advantage that we examine is when a successful attack would inflict large, disproportionate losses on the defender. A 'bloody nose' limited attack, although literally a 'first-strike', does not describe what is meant by a first-strike advantage. The ability to destroy the enemy's fighting capability with a first-strike attack is what induces the problem of preemptive war.

Presently, in the contest between North Korea and the United States, it is the Americans that possesses a considerable first-strike advantage. Indeed, the US nuclear arsenal 'is being transformed into a force that has the unambiguous characteristics of being optimized for surprise attacks ... and for fighting and winning nuclear wars' (Kristensen, McKinzie and Postol, 2017). North Korea could launch a first-strike against Seoul, but the USA would respond with an overwhelming second-strike that would totally destroy North Korea.

This analysis will focus on the USA's first-strike advantage. This is where there is a commitment problem. Our analysis is useful in two ways. First, it is directly relevant to understanding the nature of the contest between the USA and North Korea. Second, our analysis extends the bargaining theory of war. Most applications of the bargaining theory of war involve two relatively balanced powers, e.g. the USA and the Russia (or in the past, the USSR) or India and Pakistan. In some ways, the contest between two relatively balanced powers cannot be generalized to an asymmetric situation.

Preemptive war and first-strike advantage

The logic of the commitment problem can be shown using game theory. Drawing from Fearon (1995), let p_f be the probability that the USA wins a war if the USA attacks; p_s the probability that the USA wins if the USA strikes second or defends; and p the chance that the USA wins if both states mobilize and attack at the same time. An offensive advantage exists when $p_f > p > p_s$.

Assuming that both states are risk-neutral, the preferred bargained outcome for the USA must be $x > p_f - C_{US}$ in order for it to prefer not to attack. Similarly, for North Korea, $1 - x > 1 - p_s - C_{NK}$ for it to prefer the bargained outcome x. Both sides prefer to not fight provided that $p_f - C_{US} < p_s + C_{NK}$, which produces a bargaining range $(P_f - C_{US}, p_s + C_{NK})$.

These values are evident in Figure 6.

Figure 6: The Bargaining Space, First Strike Advantage, and Preemptive War

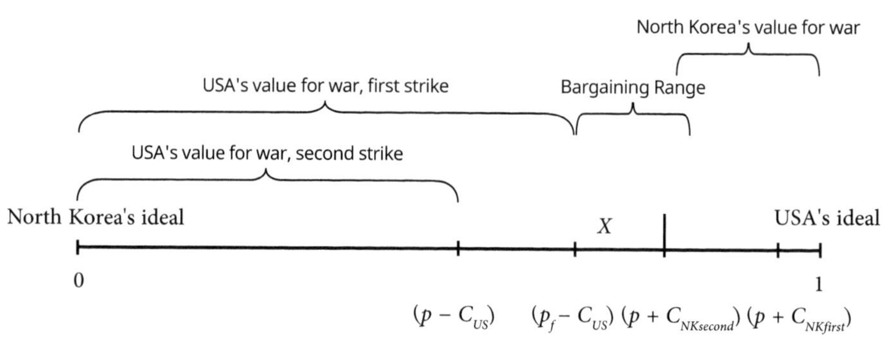

where p_f is the USA's probability of winning if P strikes first; p_s is USA's probability of winning if it strikes first, $p_f > p_s$; costs C_{USA}, C_{NK} are as they were above in the incomplete and complete information games seen in Figures 3 and 5.

Look again at Figure 6 and compare it to Figure 3, what happened to the bargaining space?

It has been diminished considerably. These results reflect what Fearon (1995, 402-404) shows – that the 'de facto' bargaining range disappears, if the first-strike advantage is big enough. Keep in mind that as p_f increases above p, and p_s decreases below it, the bargaining range shrinks. Thus, we see that first-strike advantages narrow the de facto bargaining range, while second-strike (or defensive) advantages increase it.

When $p_f - c_P > p_s + c_I$ or $p_f - p_s > c_P + c_I$, that is when the value of winning the war with a first strike subtracting the costs of war is greater than the value of the other power launching a second strike accounting for costs or when the difference between the value of a first strike minus the second strike is greater than the difference in the costs of war for both sides, the bargaining range is empty and no self-enforcing peaceful outcomes exist.

Still, bargains exist that both sides would prefer to war, since both states cannot enjoy the advantage of going first, agreements that both sides prefer to fighting are always available in principle. The problem is that these bargains are not enforceable. The two parties cannot *credibly commit* to the bargain when first-strike advantages exist. This is a problem facing the US and North Korea.

We have good reason to focus on the diminished bargaining range and not its elimination. Indeed, as noted by Fearon (1995), 'Rather than completely eliminating enforceable bargains and so causing war, it seems more plausible that first-strike and offensive advantages exacerbate other causes of war by narrowing the bargaining range' (Fearon, 1995). Shrinking the bargaining range is troublesome.

One point that should be made in our analysis. Most research on first-strike advantage has featured more or less balanced powers. This is certainly the nature of the models developed by Fearon (1995); Powell (2006) and Kydd (2002). Indeed, according to Powell (2006), a key way that a first-strike advantage undermines potential bargained agreements is by creating shifts in the distribution of power. 'When a state decides to bargain rather than attack, it is also deciding not to exploit the advantages to striking first. This decision effectively shifts the distribution of power in the adversary's favor by giving it the opportunity to exploit the advantage to striking first, and this shift can lead to war ...'(Powell, 2006). This situation, however, does not describe the situation that USA finds itself. The first-strike advantage can be considered to be exclusively the USA's. When the

USA does not exploit its advantage, it does not necessarily shift the opportunity to North Korea to strike first. The USA still possesses preponderant second-strike capabilities. The USA has not explicitly ruled out the option of a first-strike attack, but one can presume that the norm of no first-use is operative. The effect of this unwillingness to exploit a first-strike advantage serves to keep the bargaining range a bit wider.

VI. Preventive war

The second type of commitment problem relates to preventive war, which we subsume under the condition of bargaining over issues that affect future bargaining power. Commitment problems arise when anticipated shifts in the distribution of power cause relatively more powerful states to go to war in order to prevent a decrease in their future bargaining power. In contrast, the rising state may prefer to avoid war by committing to not exercise its future bargaining power with a negotiated settlement (Krainin et al., 2017). North Korea's acquisition and development of nuclear weapons and missile technology fit this category. Given North Korea's rise, the USA cannot credibly commit that it will not engage in a preventive war. North Korea in this scenario will not agree to a bargain now, when it views a future bargain to be more advantageous.

1. Infinitely repeated games

We now present the asymmetric bargaining game in normal form (Gibbons, 1997: 136–7); and replace with cardinal utilities p = 0.7 and $c_{NK} = c_{US}$ = 0.2. We assume that the USA chooses a point towards the middle of the bargaining range but reflecting asymmetric payoffs, as the offered $x1$; i.e. $x1$ = 0.7. This means North Korea would receive 0.3 if it sticks to the bargain.

This game may be repeated an infinite number of times. A discount factor δ models how players value payoffs in the present more than payoffs in the future. The discount factor is the value in present payoff units of one payoff unit to be received one period from the present; $0 \leq \delta \leq 1$. There are two interpretations of the discount factor: (1) Given that the utility is certain: the extent to which consumption today is valued over consumption next year, e.g. 1 million paid out now compared to 1.1 million paid out

Figure 7: Static Choices

		USA	
		Stick to bargain	Fight
North Korea	Stick to bargain	$x_1, 1 - x_1$	$p - c_p, 1 - p - c_I$
	Fight	$p - c_p, 1 - p - c_I$	$p - c_p, 1 - p - c_I$

		USA	
		Stick to bargain	Fight
North Korea	Stick to bargain	0.7, 0.3	0.5, 0.1
	Fight	0.5, 0.1	0.5, 0.1

in a year. (2) Uncertainty regarding whether the situation/game will persist, e.g. death, change of president, etc.

The iterations (or periods) are labeled $t = 0,1,2,3,...$. If the payoff u_0 at $t = 0$ is u, the payoff u_1 at $t = 1$ is $u \cdot \delta$. If the payoff is repeated an infinite number of times, the total payoff:

$$\Sigma_t(u_t) = \Sigma_{t=0}^{\infty}(u\delta^t) = u + u\delta + u\delta^2 + u\delta^3 + ... + u\delta^t = u_t / (1 - \delta)$$

If both parties choose to stick to the bargain forever, North Korea will obtain: $U_{NK} = \Sigma_{t=0}^{\infty}(0.3\delta^t) = 0.3 / (1 - \delta)$. Under such conditions, the United States will receive a payoff of:

$$U_{US} = \Sigma_{t=0}^{\infty}(0.7\delta^t) = 0.7 / (1 - \delta)$$

If one of the parties breaks the bargain in period 0, North Korea will obtain: $= U_{NK}^{W} = \Sigma_{t=0}^{\infty}(0.1\delta^t) = 0.1 / (1 - \delta)$. For the USA, the payoff for war will be: $U_{US}^{W} = \Sigma_{t=0}^{\infty}(0.5\delta^t) = 0.5 / (1 - \delta)$. With these payoffs neither party will ever break the bargain in the future. It simply will not pay. For example, if $\delta = 0.9$, the utility for war for the USA is: $U_{US}^{W} = 0.5/(1-0.9) = 5$, while the utility for sticking to the bargain would be: $U_{US}^{P} = 0.7 / (1 - 0.9) = 7$; for North Korea, the respective payoffs for war and peace would be: $U_{NK}^{W} = 0.1/(1 - 0.9) = 1$ and $U_{NK}^{P} = 0.3 / (1 - 0.9) = 3$. For all discount values, neither party has an incentive to break the agreement and peace will endure. This is the logic of the complete information game, but now with discounting and repeated play.

2. The rising power - North Korea advances its capabilities

Now consider, what if: (i) the probability of winning a war may be altered in the future, and (ii) winning a war may prevent this? Assume that $1 - p$ changes to 0.4 at time $t = 1$ (the second period), such that $p = 0.6$ and not 0.7. The midpoint x_2 to the bargaining range is then 0.5. In other words, we assume that North Korea continues to develop its nuclear and missile capabilities relative to the USA. Asymmetry persists, but the degree of asymmetry decreases.

The result is evident in Figure 8.

Figure 8: Increasing North Korea's relative capabilities

		USA	
		Stick to bargain	Fight
North Korea	Stick to bargain	0.6, 0.4	0.4, 0.2
	Fight	0.4, 0.2	0.6, 0.2

If both parties choose to stick to the first-period bargain in all future rounds of the game, North Korea will obtain: $\sum_{t=0}^{\infty}(0.4\delta^t) = 0.4 / (1 - \delta)$ as before. If $\delta = 0.9$: $U_{NK}^{P} = 0.4/(1 - 0.9) = 0.4 / 0.1 = 4$. The USA will in turn receive the following payoff: $\sum_{t=0}^{\infty}(0.6\delta^t) = 0.6 / (1 - \delta)$ as before. If $\delta = 0.9$: $U_{US}^{P} = 0.6 / (1 - 0.9) = 0.6 / 0.1 = 6$.

Given the increase in North Korea's capabilities, in the second period ($t = 1$), North Korea will have an incentive to offer/demand a new distribution $x_2 = 0.4$. The discounted payoff from period $t = 1$ for North Korea will be: $\sum_{t=0}^{\infty}(0.4\delta^t) = 0.4 / (1 - \delta)$. For the USA: $\sum_{t=0}^{\infty}(0.6\delta^t) = 0.6 / (1 - \delta)$.

Seen from the first period, the discounted cumulative payoffs for sticking to the bargain are:

$$U_{NK}^{P} = 0.3 + \delta(\textstyle\sum_{t=0}^{\infty}(0.4\delta^t) = 0.3 + \delta(0.4 / (1 - \delta));$$
$$U_{US}^{P} = 0.7 + \delta(\textstyle\sum_{t=0}^{\infty}(0.6\delta^t) = 0.7 + \delta(0.6 / (1 - \delta));$$
$$\text{If } \delta = 0.9\text{: } U_{NK}^{P} = 0.3 + 0.4(0.9/0.1) = 0.3 + 3.6 = 3.9;$$
$$\text{If } \delta = 0.9\text{: } U_{US}^{P} = 0.7 + 0.6(0.9/0.1) = 0.7 + 5.4 = 6.1.$$

These are the payoffs if both countries keep to their bargain at $t = 1$. The result of the increase in North Korean capabilities is that the utility to the USA for sticking to the bargain decreases relative to the outcome shown in Figure 7. The USA loses (from an outcome of 7 to 6.1) and North Korea gains (from 3 to 3.9).

Can North Korea get the USA to accept this new bargain? It cannot. North Korea cannot credibly threaten war. Seen from the first period, the discounted cumulative payoffs for sticking to the bargain in the first round and fighting in the second period are:

$$U^{W}_{NK} = 0.3 + \delta(\textstyle\sum_{t=0}^{\infty}((0.4 - 0.2)\delta^{t}) = 0.3 + \delta(0.2 / 1 - \delta), \text{ and}$$
$$\text{if } \delta = 0.9\text{: } U^{P}_{NK} = 0.3 + (0.4 - 0.2)(0.9 / 0.1) = 0.3 + 1.8 = 2.1.$$

Comparing the utility of sticking to the bargain and receiving a discounted payoff of 3 is greater than starting a war and getting 2.1. It will not pay for North Korea to break the bargain at $t = 1$ given these payoffs.

3. Implications of rising to parity

What happens if North Korea were to rise in capability so that it was equal in strength to the United States. Of course, this is a totally unrealistic presumption, but it pays to examine such a situation to analyze the scope conditions of a rising power and credible commitment.

Figure 9: Increasing North Korea's relative capabilities

		USA	
		Stick to bargain	Fight
North Korea	Stick to bargain	0.5, 0.5	0.3, 0.3
	Fight	0.3, 0.3	0.3, 0.3

With this rise to parity, can North Korea get the USA to accept a new bargain? Seen from the first period, the discounted cumulative payoffs for sticking to the bargain in the first round and fighting in the second period for North Korea are:

$U^W_{NK} = 0.3 + \delta(\sum^{\infty}_{t=0}((0.5 - 0.2)\delta^t) = 0.3 + \delta((0.5 - 0.2) / (1 - \delta))$, and
If $\delta = 0.9$: $U^W_{NK} = 0.3 + (0.3)(0.9 / 0.1) = 0.3 + 2.7 = 3.0$

The utility of sticking to the bargain and receiving a discounted payoff of 3 is the same as the payoff from starting a war. If North Korea were to rise to American levels of military capability, it would be indifferent between breaking the bargain or sticking to the bargain at $t = 1$ given these payoffs.

If North Korea were to start a war after achieving parity, in the second period ($t = 1$), the USA would obtain: $U^W_{US} = 0.7 + \delta(\sum^{\infty}_{t}=0((0.5 - 0.2)\delta^t) = 0.7 + \delta((0.3 - 0.2) / (1 - \delta))$, and if $\delta = 0.9$: $U^W_{US} = 0.7 +(0.3)(0.9 / 1) = 0.7 + 2.7 = 3.4$. Given this, it will not pay for the USA to choose to fight at $t = 0$ and for all subsequent periods, since $3.4 > 3.0$. It would be in the USA's interest to agree to the new bargain of 0.5 and 0.5 for each side in the second round.

In order for the USA to find it in its interest to fight a preventive war, North Korea would have to transcend American capabilities.[1] Given the degree to which the two powers are asymmetric, such a rise in capabilities is unlikely.

Under conditions in which North Korea were to become ascendant, the problem of preventive war would arise. Because North Korea would not be able to commit to never renege on the negotiated outcome. Note that both parties are worse off without an agreement. Here, the preventive war is assumed to last indefinitely. Similar conclusions can also be sustained if war is assumed to last for a shorter period. Such analysis often modeled with a random draw of capabilities or resolve in every iteration – p is a stochastic variable, see Fearon (2004) on the duration of civil wars.

In a situation of asymmetry, preventive war is unlikely. Nonetheless, the prospect of a rising power does present a challenging problem. In the next section, we examine how the bargaining range is affected by the rising capability of an asymmetrically weaker state.

---

1 Given our numerical example with δ =0.9, North Korean capabilities would have to be greater than $0.5\overline{4}$, and for the USA, $p < .4\overline{5}$, before it would pay for the USA to engage in war with North Korea.

4. The Dynamic Bargaining Range

We return to our bargaining range figures to show how a rising power affects the bargaining range. Figure 10 shows the effect of a rising power in a dynamic environment on the bargaining space. Our figure follows from Spaniel (2019). Figure 10 shows the bargaining range between $p_{NK}+C_{NK}$ and $p_{US}-C_{US}$ under a static equilibrium. Although given US preponderant capabilities, the bargaining range is reasonably large. When we take into account that North Korea is rapidly developing both its nuclear stockpile, missile technology, and associated military capabilities, then the bargaining range falls between $p_{US} - C_{US}$ and $p'_{NK} + C_{NK} - \frac{(1-\delta)k}{\delta}$. The value of North Korea's increased capability p^0 minus the cost of war $C_{NK}(p'_{NK} + C_{NK})$. The value of building in a period of time is $(1 - \delta)$ discounted by δ, which can be expressed as $(\frac{(1-\delta)}{\delta})$. The discounted dynamic payoff for North Korea is thus $(\frac{(1-\delta)}{\delta})(p'_{NK} + C_{NK})$.

Figure 10: The dynamic bargaining range with a rising power

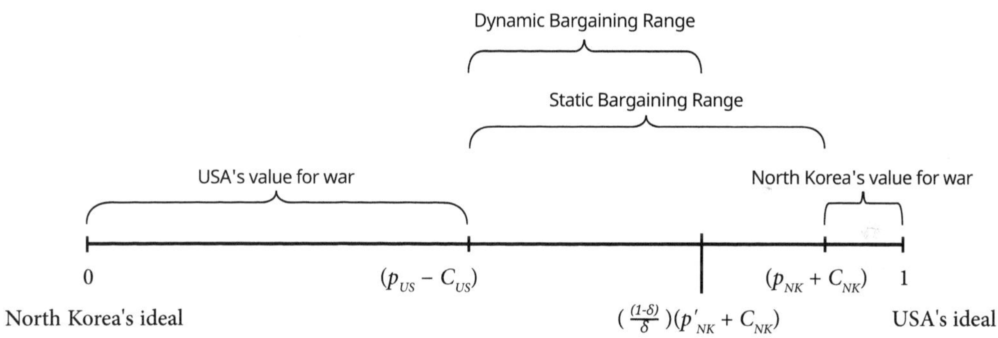

Figure 10 shows the static bargaining range, which is fairly large. This is the space between the zones designating North Korea's value for war and the USA's value for war. The size of the static bargaining range is determined by p and the costs of war for both states, C_{NK} and C_{US}. Given the nature of North Korea's military development and increasing relative capabilities, the dynamic bargaining zone takes into account the new capabilities of North Korea, p^0_{NK} as well as the costs of war, C_{NK}, for North Korea and the present value discounted for future iterations of the game. The dynamic bargaining range as represented here is substantially smaller than the static bargaining range. North Korea's rising capabilities decrease the scope for reaching a negotiated settlement. As North Korea develops relative to the USA, the dynamic bargaining range will continue to decrease.

The logic of preventive war

Preventive war occurs despite the parties' agreement about relative power and resolve. The declining state does not attack because it fears being attacked in the future, but since it fears peace, it will have to accept that the rival has grown stronger in the future. Iraq serves as an example. The 1991 war occurred to prevent Iraq from increasing its bargaining leverage in oil supply issues.

The lack of trust between the states is not due to uncertainty about future motivations (i.e. resolve) but is due to uncertainty about future relative power. The commitment problem may be undermined if the determinants of military power can reliably be transferred between states. A rising state has an incentive to limit the sources of its new strength (e.g. Japan throughout the post-World War II period). Indeed, stability is not a reflection of the balance of power, but rather it reflects the balance of power *and* the balance of power in a future world without the agreement. Given a lack of sufficiently attractive offers, rising states will pursue costly actions so as to improve their bargaining power. Using backwards induction, more powerful states will offer concessions to the rising state, and thereby extracting the inefficient cost of building their military capability. 'Consequently, potential power acts as an "invisible fist" in international relations' (Spaniel, 2019, 190).

Given the asymmetric nature of the contest between North Korea and the USA, this logic does not apply. See Figure 10. We should only expect to see a preventive war, if $(\frac{(1-\delta)}{\delta})(p'_{NK} + C_{NK}) > p_{US} + C_{US}$ in the second round, whereby no bargaining range would exist. One can see how this would work by looking at Figure 10, as $(\frac{(1-\delta)}{\delta})(p'_{NK} + C_{NK})$ is shifted further and further to the left, the dynamic bargaining range becomes smaller and smaller until it disappears. This is not a condition we should expect to see with regard to North Korea. The asymmetry between the powers is too vast.

VII. The problem of bargaining over military power

The objects over which states bargain are frequently the sources of military power themselves. This describes the situation between North Korea and the USA. The focus of negotiations is nuclear weapons. With regard to the contest between the USA and North Korea, nuclear weapons are the main factor that shapes the relative military capability of North Korea. Given the nature of the negotiations, the outcome of a bargain would almost certainly therefore affect the outcome of future bargains.

From a North Korean perspective, we could model this as a repeated game, whereby the USA is the stronger party, and that every negotiated outcome increases p by a small amount. Eventually, North Korea's per-period utility approaches zero as its bargaining power would weaken after each bargain. North Korea may then prefer the costly lottery of war in the first period. The alternative is to not accept any bargain and draw out the negotiation process. This indeed seems to describe what is going on between North Korea and the United States. This conclusion resembles Chadefaux (2011, 161) argument that a rising state will gain more by innovating at an acceptable rate and thereby taking advantage of its stronger bargaining power in the future. If a rising power advances too quickly, it may trigger a preventive war. As such, this reflects Schelling (1966) and his observations about 'salami tactics'.

The historical evidence points towards North Korea's behavior of deceit and delay. North Korea has remained for the most part intransigent, unwilling to yield in the quest to develop advanced nuclear capability. Prior to North Korea's development of nuclear weapons technology, the 1994 Agreed Framework was intended to have traded their nuclear war program in exchange for normalized relations and light-water nuclear power plants. The agreement failed. Two explanations are offered by Spaniel (2019, 120). The most common explanation is that North Korea violated the agreement and continued to work on uranium enrichment. The alternative explanation is that Republicans in the US Congress thought that they could obtain compliance at a lower cost and blocked critical funding for the agreement (Martin, 2002; Chinoy, 2010). Indeed, the nuclear power plant was delayed as a result of inadequate funding. The funds were not released until 2002, arriving far too late for the planned groundbreaking in 2003 (Spaniel, 2019). Subsequently, President George W. Bush terminated the agreement later in 2003. Continued efforts by the Obama administration led to nothing. Trump met with Kim Jong-un three times, once in the DMZ, in Singapore, and in Hanoi. The tone of the meetings was positive. The meetings generated considerable hope. Unfortunately, no agreement was reached. North Korea continues to develop its nuclear and missile capabilities.

The problem is nicely summarized by Tan and Park (2020, 206): 'Due to its politics of over-attention in viewing US preponderance, there is no conceivable measure the US can offer that can plausibly assuage Kim Jong Un's fears. Conversely, so long as Kim Jong Un remains committed to viewing his nuclear program as an "insurance policy" to ensure regime survival, there is little prospect of Washington willing to accept the *fait accompli* of North Korea's status as a de facto nuclear power. Such calculations are likely to remain in place for the foreseeable future.'

1. Information and a rising power

Incomplete information is a powerful explanation for war. The true probability of victory and the true costs of fighting are often unknown. Without this information, negotiators in a crisis face an extremely difficult problem in assessing the other side's bargaining range.

Figure 11 shows the bargaining game with one-sided incomplete information.

Figure 11: Incomplete information and a rising power

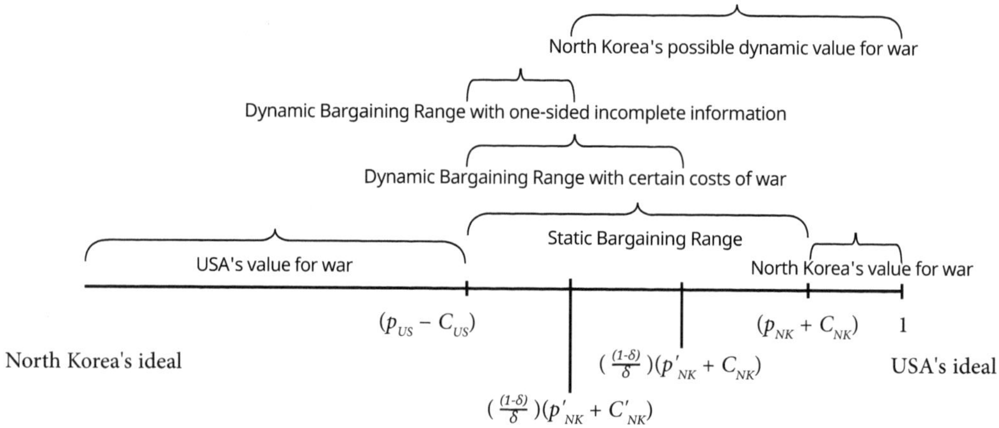

This is derived from Figure 10. What we have added is a new dynamic cost value for North Korea, C'_{NK}. This shifts North Korea's value for war to the left to $(\frac{(1\text{-}\delta)}{\delta})(p'_{NK} + C'_{NK})$ from $(\frac{(1\text{-}\delta)}{\delta})(p'_{NK} + C_{NK})$. This decreases the range of the dynamic bargaining range considerably. This is evident in Figure 11, comparing the green and black braces. In this game, the USA does not know whether the costs of war to North Korea are C_{NK} or C^{0}_{NK}. The uncertainty increases North Korea's bargaining power.

2. Incomplete information and preventive war

In Figure 12, we examine a two-sided incomplete information game. All the important values from Figure 11 appear in Figure 12. In addition, we have added $p_{US} - C'_{US}$. North Korea does not know whether the USA faces a cost of C_{US} or C'_{US}. The United States does not know whether North Korea's cost of war are C_{NK} or C'_{NK}. If both powers would experience low costs of war, the bargaining range would disappear. (In Figure 12, the utility to the USA for war, $p_{US} - C'_{US}$, is ever so slightly to the right of $(\frac{(1\text{-}\delta)}{\delta})(p'_{NK} + C'_{NK})$. This means that the values for war for the two states overlap.) Given that the USA knows when it faces high or low war costs, the situation when there is no bargaining range, makes preventive war a possibility. Whereby the USA would attack sooner rather than later, since North Korea will possess a stronger bargaining position the longer the USA waits.

The combination of incomplete information and the preventive war commitment

Figure 12: Incomplete information and preventive war

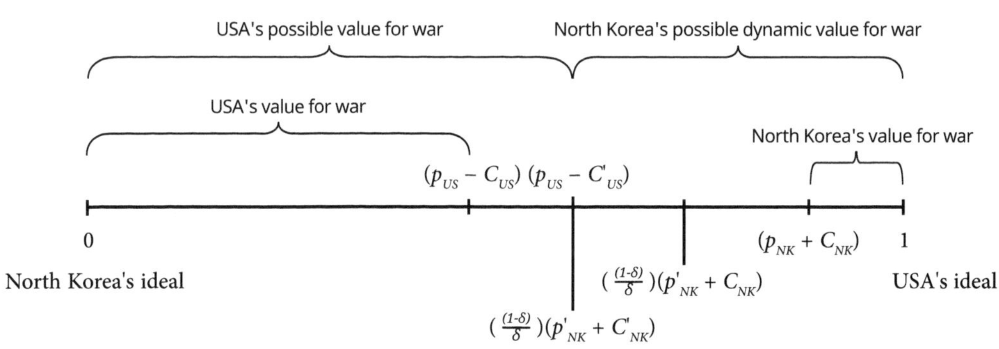

problem serve to make war a definite possibility even for rational agents. Not knowing the opponent's minimally acceptable bargaining demands can cause each state to pursue unacceptable negotiating strategies. Incomplete information makes the situation more dangerous.

Incomplete information could serve the more powerful state. If, for example, North Korea is unsure whether the USA would experience high wars costs or low, a high-cost USA could bluff that it is a low-cost type. The risk is that the rising state may call the bluff and continue to build its nuclear capabilities. Generally, strong states are more likely to start a war and weak states to acquiesce. At a global level, the outcome is inefficient, producing too many unnecessary wars and too much nuclear weapons proliferation.

VIII. Conclusion

Our analysis has featured three explanations as to how war between rational actors could occur despite the high costs of fighting. Our analytical focus has been on nuclear bargaining between the United States and North Korea. We have examined incomplete information problems and commitment problems relating to first strike advantage and preemptive war. Information problems regarding the costs of conflict, respective military capabilities, and resolve are extremely relevant to the conflict between North Korea and the United States.

Asymmetry, in contrast, strongly affects both the commitment problems. While each problem potentially reduces the bargaining range for a negotiated settlement, neither problem generates war. When two powers are more proportional in capability, the problems of preemptive and preventive war are potent. In an asymmetric environment, the first-strike advantage is contingent upon the power possessing this capability will be using it. If the superior power elects to not use the first-strike advantage, the bargaining range is not affected and there is no temptation for preemptive war. In the case of preventive war, as long as the rising power does not overtake the superior power, extremely unlikely under asymmetric conditions, a bargaining range will remain, which serves to preclude the temptation for a preventive war.

When we consider information problems in combination with a rising power, the preventive war commitment problem becomes a possibility. If there is uncertainty about both parties' costs of war, the dynamic bargaining range could disappear. In the case of the USA and North Korea, doubts about the costs of war, especially for the USA, are what make this problem tenable.

The central problem regards the negotiation of North Korea's military capability. The Americans are viewed as an existential enemy, threatening the very existence of the regime. Asymmetry compels North Korea to continue to develop its nuclear weapons capabilities. It serves an 'insurance policy' securing a future for the regime. For the USA, accepting a nuclear North Korea is not an option. Views regarding the unreliability of the rogue state and the stability of the Great Leader make this politically untenable in Washington. The prospects for striking a denuclearization agreement remain remote.

The prospects are high for continued instability between the USA and North Korea. Information problems make war possible, but other conditions make war unlikely. Commitment problems narrow the bargaining range, but some space for negotiated settlement theoretically remains. The central problem is that the main aspect of negotiation, nuclear weapons, is unlikely to be bargained away. The nuclear crisis in the Korean peninsula will persist.

References

Beard, Steven and Joshua A Strayhorn. 2018. "When Will States Strike First? Battlefield Advantages and Rationalist War." *International Studies Quarterly* 62(1):42–53.

Blainey, Geoffrey. 1988. *The Causes of War*. New York: The Free Press.

Chadefaux, Thomas. 2011. "Bargaining over Power: When do shifts in power lead to war." *International Theory* 3:228.

Chinoy, Mike. 2010. *Meltdown: the inside story of the North Korean nuclear crisis*. St. Martin's Press.

Fearon, James D. 1994. "Domestic Political Audiences and the Escalation of International Disputes." *American Political Science Review* 88(3):577–592.

Fearon, James D. 1995. "Rationalist explanations for war." *International organization* 49(3):379–379.

Fearon, James D. 2004. "Why Do Some Civil Wars Last So Much Longer Than Others?" *Journal of Peace Research* 41(3):275–301.

Hassner, Ron E. 2009. *War on Sacred Grounds*. Cornell: Cornell University Press.

Krainin, Colin et al. 2017. "Preventive War as a Result of Long Term Shifts in Power." *Political Science Research and Methods* 5(1):103–21.

Kristensen, Hans M, Matthew McKinzie and Theodore A Postol. 2017. "How US nuclear force modernization is undermining strategic stability: The burst-height compensating super-fuze." *Bulletin of the Atomic Scientists* 1.

Kristensen, Hans M and Robert S Norris. 2018. "North Korean nuclear capabilities, 2018." Bulletin of the Atomic Scientists 74(1):41–51.

Kydd, Andrew. 2002. Game Theory and Security Studies: The Art of Shaker Modeling. In *Cases, Numbers, Models: International Relations Research Methods*, ed. Detlef F. Sprinz and Yael Wolinsky. Ann Arbor: University of Michigan Press pp. 370–395.

Kydd, Andrew H. 2018. *International Relations Theory: The Game-Theoretic Approach*. Cambridge: Cambridge University Press.

Martin, Curtis H. 2002. "Rewarding North Korea: Theoretical perspectives on the 1994 agreed framework." *Journal of Peace Research* 39(1):51–68.

Parachini, John V, Scott W Harold, Gian Gentile, Derek Grossman, Leah H Kim, Logan Ma, Michael J Mazarr and Linda Robinson. 2020. North Korean Decision-making: Economic Opening, Conventional Deterrence Breakdown, and Nuclear Use. Technical report RAND Corporation, Santa Monica Santa Monica United States.

Powell, Robert. 1999. *In the Shadow of Power*. Princeton: Princeton University Press.

Powell, Robert. 2002. "The Bargaining Model of War." *Annual Review of Political Science* 5:1–30.

Powell, Robert. 2006. "War as a Commitment Problem." *International Organization* 60:169– 189.

Schelling, Thomas. 1966. *Arms and Influence*. New Haven: Yale University Press.

Spaniel, William. 2019. *Bargaining over the bomb: the successes and failures of nuclear negotiations.* Cambridge University Press.

Tan, Erwin and Jae Jeok Park. 2020. "The US-North Korean asymmetrical security dilemma: Past the point of nuclear no return?" *International Area Studies Review* p. 2233865920918508.

Wright, David. 2017. "North Korean ICBM Appears Able to Reach Major US Cities." *Union of Concerned Scientists, All Things Nuclear Blog*, July 28.

Chapter 5

A Systematic Analysis of the Trump Foreign Policy: Implications for Northeast Asia and the Korean Peninsula[1]

Dongsoo Kim
(Pukyong National University)

Abstract

Donald Trump was elected as 45th U.S. President in 2016. The conventional understanding of President Trump when his administration started in early 2017 was that he had a unique personality as a politician, and therefore, the U.S. under his leadership would pursue different foreign policy goals and strategies to achieve them, distinct from his predecessors. Against this background, this study aims to address such questions as "Is he really different from his predecessors?" or "Will U.S. foreign policies under Trump be totally different from those of the past?" Especially, this study will analyze Trump's foreign policy orientations, utilizing dimensions of foreign policy analysis: security, prosperity, and community values. Based on the analysis of the fundamentals of the Trump administration's foreign policy, this study will also discuss its policy toward Northeast Asia, especially the Korean peninsula.

Keywords: Trump, U.S. Foreign Policy, Korean Peninsula, Northeast Asia

1 This is an updated and revised version of the original paper, which was published at *The Korean Journal of Security Affairs*, Vol.23, No.1 (2018).

I. Introduction

In November 2016 Donald Trump was elected as the 45th president of the United States. Because the majority prediction of the election result was President another Clinton, the real election result was absolutely shocking to a lot of people not just inside of the U.S. but also throughout the world. Indeed, before and during the phase of the election campaign, primarily because of his peculiar behaviors, Trump was not considered as the real candidate for president of the U.S., who was supposed to be the leader of the global community to fight against global threats such as terrorism or economic crisis. In contrast, the candidate Clinton was regarded as the right person to achieve the goal by the global community since she indicated interventionism along with strong willingness to handle global affairs.

Anyhow Trump was elected as U.S. president and now he is close to the end of his first term. The conventional understanding of President Trump when his administration started in 2017 was that he had a unique personality as a politician, and therefore, the U.S. under his leadership would pursue different foreign policy goals and strategies to achieve them, distinct from his predecessors. Indeed, in an article, the election of Trump was described as the end of "the Age of Great Expectations and the Great Void,"[2] meaning significant changes in U.S. foreign policy goals and behavior. His campaign catch-phrases such as "America First" or "Making American Great Again" were commonly read as important signs to indicate the possibility of big changes in American foreign policy at least during his tenure. Furthermore, many of the experts in international relations (IR) and foreign policy even began to worry about the future of global stability, which was mostly maintained by the U.S.-led order for the past decades.

As his first term approaches conclusion, it is now a good time to ask questions like "Is he really different from his predecessors?", "Is U.S. foreign policies under Trump different from those of the past?". Taking one step further, it may be asked, "Are the foreign policies that he pledged really abnormal?" These are the questions that this study will try to address with a systematic analysis of his foreign policy. Especially, this study will

2 Andrew J. Bacevich, "The Age of Great Expectations and the Great Void: History after the End of History." Available at http://americanempireproject.com/blog/the-age-of-great-expectations-and-the-great-void/ (accessed on Oct. 27, 2017).

analyze Trump foreign policy orientations, utilizing dimensions of foreign policy analysis: security, prosperity, and community values. Based on the analysis of the fundamentals of Trump administration's foreign policy, I will also discuss its policy toward Northeast Asia, especially the Korean peninsula.

The rest of this paper is organized as follows. The next section will review important previous analyses on Trump foreign policy. In the following section, I will present a theoretical framework to systematically analyze Trump foreign policy, which will be followed by an actual analysis. In the final section, I will summarize the key findings of this study and discuss their implications to Northeast Asian security, more specifically, the Korean peninsula.

II. Previous Analyses of Trump Foreign Policy

The most widely shared idea about Trump foreign policy is that he is much different from his predecessors in terms of U.S. foreign policy goals and strategies. Indeed, based on the analyses of what he said during the campaign and afterwards, there is a considerable agreement that Trump will pursue changes that go well beyond the normal range of policy change from one administration to another. They point out that Trump "has espoused foreign policy views radically different from those of his predecessors,"[3] or that he "radically defined the American national interest as understood since World War II."[4] While scholars and experts do not uniformly agree with their characterization of U.S. foreign policy under Trump, they commonly predict that Trump administration will significantly undermine the stable liberal world order, which has been effectively led by the U.S. for the past several decades. In a word, the majority perspective of existing analyses on Trump foreign policy is that it is significantly different from those

3 Robert Jervis, "President Trump and IR Theory," ISSF Policy Series, January 2, 2017. Available at https://issforum.org/roundtables/policy/1-5b-jervis (accessed on Oct. 9, 2017).

4 Charles Krauthammer, "Trump's Foreign Policy Revolutions," *The Washington Post*, Jan. 26, 2017. Available at https://www.washingtonpost.com/opinions/global-opinions/trumps-foreign-policy-revolution/2017/01/26/c69268a6-e402-11e6-ba11-63c4b4fb5a63_story.html?utm_term=.1a3006c31b05 (accessed on Oct. 9, 2017).

of previous administrations and therefore the U.S.-centered world order is also subject to change as well.

The second line of analyses on Trump foreign policy is to link it with IR theory, especially realism. Indeed, many critics argue that Trump foreign policy is only a gathering of inconsistent, impetuous, and fragmented ideas on foreign policy rather than a coherent doctrine.[5] The supporters of Trump tend to advocate his ideas on foreign policy, connecting them to the realist doctrine of IR theory, as a rejoinder to the critics. While Trump ideas do not always align with the conventional academic understanding of realism, they claim, the essential part of his ideas correspond with realism to a great extent. The campaign catch-phrase like 'Make America Great Again' or 'America First' reminds realism of IR theory. Furthermore, his frequent use of the word 'power' is another indication that his idea is in the line of the realist doctrine. Not only his supporters but critics like Wright assert that Trump embraces "antiquated notions of power that haven't been prevalent since prior to World War II."[6] Realists are basically skeptical of the value of international institutions, and view interstate alignments as merely conditional means to achieve strategic goals coupled with the distribution of power in international politics. In pointing out the elements of realism in Trump foreign policy, Walt notes that "his commonsense observation that key U.S. allies are free-riding, his recognition that open-ended 'nation building' exercises are foolish, and he believes that U.S. foreign policy should first and foremost serve the U.S. national interest."[7]

Another interpretation of Trump foreign policy is to treat it as a representation of isolationism.[8] During the campaign and around his inauguration, Trump frequently indicated elements of the isolationist approach, which suggests that the U.S. will

---

5 Don Zakheim, "Trump Must Be Stopped," *The National Interest*, Mar. 5, 2016. Available at http://nationalinterest.org/feature/trump-must-be-stopped-15408 (accessed on Oct. 10, 2017).

6 Thomas Wright, "Trump's 19th Century Foreign Policy," *Politico*, Jan. 20, 2017. Available at http://www.politico.com/magazine/story/2016/01/donald-trump-foreign-policy-213546 (accessed on Oct. 10, 2017).

7 Stephen M. Walt, "Could There Be a Peace of Trumphalia?" *Foreign Policy* (Nov. 14, 2016). Available at http://foreignpolicy.com/2016/11/14/could-there-be-a-peace-of-trumphalia (accessed on Oct. 13, 2017).

8 Sunhee Lee, Joongwan Kim and Hanbeom Jeong, "The Nature of U.S. Isolationism in U.S. Foreign Policy Viewed in the Trump Phenomenon," *Journal of Korean Political and Diplomatic History*, Vol. 38, No. 1 (Aug. 2016), pp. 281-314.

minimize intervention in foreign affairs and focus on domestic issues, especially the economy. This line of analyses claims that although he does not agree, Trump is close to isolationist in the sense that he opposes to the most of the already signed and ratified free trade agreement of the U.S. When it comes to security issues, his tendency toward isolationism has become more evident, when he criticized multilateral security institutions like the United Nations and NATO as 'obsolete.' According to the critics, therefore, Trump is a very dangerous leader because he seems ready to abandon the security-related multilateral institutions, which has been a significant pillar to support U.S. grand strategy for a long time.[9]

While the aforementioned analyses provide useful insights on foreign policy of Trump administration, they are neither systematic nor complete analyses. They are more inclined to focus on particular aspects of Trump foreign policy, neglecting other important characteristics. Thus, this study intends to provide more systematic analysis of Trump foreign policy, based on the framework of foreign policy analysis, which combines major theories of international relations and basic human needs.

III. Analytical Framework

Foreign policy is defined as "a guide to actions taken beyond the boundaries of the state to further the goals of the state."[10] In other words, foreign policy is a policy that intends to achieve goals of the state. If a policy is defined as "a set of behaviors used to obtain a desired result," a policymaker selects a particular method to achieve a particular objective in a particular situation."[11] Objectives and methods of foreign policy should be discussed based not just on major theories of international relations such as realism, liberalism, and constructivism but also basic human needs.[12] Based on the theories of international relations and discussion on basic human needs, foreign policy goals of states

---

9 Bruce W. Jentleson, "Global Governance, the United Nations, and the Challenge of Trumping Trump," *Global Governance*, Vol. 23 (2017), pp. 143-149.

10 David Kinsella, Bruce Russett and Harvey Starr, *World Politics: The Menu for Choice*, 10th ed. (Wadsworth, 2013), p. 99.

11 William O. Chittick, *American Foreign Policy* (Washington, DC: CQ Press, 2006), p .4.

12 David C. McClelland, *Human Motivation* (Cambridge: Cambridge University Press, 1987).

are said to include such values as security, prosperity, and community.

Community values are based on constructivism in international relations theory and social affiliation in human needs. The main concern here is with the community to which individual foreign policy actor feels most strongly committed when making foreign policy choices. If the actor stresses the unifying values and goals of equality, universality, and generality, then the actor will identify with a more inclusive community. Such a view is referred to as 'cosmopolitan.' If the actor emphasizes the individualistic values and goals of liberty, freedom and independence, then the actor will identify with a more exclusive community. Such a view is often referred to as 'communitarian.' Therefore, the community domain, when defined in terms of values and goals, ranges from unification, at one extreme, to independence, at the other extreme.

It is also important to describe each of the three domains in terms of its methods as well as goals because the activation of goals involves means as well as ends. On the one hand, foreign policy actors who most value a unified community tend to act on a multilateral basis, attempting to coordinate their actions with the other parties involved or even to avoid acting altogether without support from allies. By contrast, a unilateral policy is more easily recognized, because it is produced by a state that determines for itself what it wants to do. Thus the primary dimension for community is multilateral-unilateral.

Security values are based on realism in international relations and power in human needs. The goal dimension underlying security is based on actor's perception of different levels and kinds of threats. If a state (actor) perceives a high level of threat, it usually wants to put itself in a position of control that would provide something similar with absolute security. If a state actor perceives a lower level of threat, it may be satisfied with the relative security that comes from a more balanced situation. Therefore, foreign policy actors pursue goals in the security category that vary from domination, at one extreme, to accommodation, at the other extreme.

An actor's choice of security goals affects its preferences for methods. If a foreign policy actor such as a state feels that to be secure it must dominate others, it will be more prepared to use or threaten force to achieve its goal. Coercion implies one state's willingness to compel another state to do something against its will. It will involve the threat or use of military force, but economic measures are possible as well. If a state perceives that true security depends on mutual consent, then it will favor non-coercive methods. Such methods might entail negotiation or persuasion. Thus the primary differences in security measures among actors for security ranges from the coercive to non-coercive dimension.

Lastly, along with community and security, economic prosperity is often considered as an important interest by foreign policy actors. The primary dimension for prosperity values is based on the state's confidence in its own culture and economy. Generally speaking, the greater the state's confidence in its own culture and economy, the more open its foreign policy. The confident state perceives itself, if not superior, at least secure with respect to others and welcomes open relationships with other states, because it expects to benefit from them. By contrast, the less confident a state is, the more pessimistic it is about enhancing its prosperity by opening itself to outside influences. Therefore, the underlying value in the prosperity category is well-being: either trying to get more, or just trying to preserve what one has.

Like indicated earlier, an actor's prosperity goals influence the methods it prefers for achieving them. Foreign policy actors that seek wealth and maximum benefits will be proactive, such actors generally believe that their purposes are best served by participating actively in the international exchange of goods, people, and ideas. Actors concerned mainly with meeting basic needs and minimizing the costs of participating in the international system will be reactive. They will be cautious and even defensive when it comes to international exchanges. Thus, the primary dimension for prosperity is proactive at one end and reactive at the other.

All three dimensions discussed above-community, security, and prosperity- are incorporated in Table 1.

Table 1. Essential Elements of the Three Foreign Policy Approaches including Primary Dimensions

Approaches	Motive	Value Orientation	Value continuum "Dimension
Realism/Neorealism	Power	Security	Coercive - Non-coercive
Liberalism/Neoliberalism	Profit or Achievement	Economic prosperity	Proactive - Reactive
Idealism/Constructivism	Social affiliation	Community	Multilateral - Unilateral

Source: Chittick (2006), p.29

IV. Analysis of Foreign Policy of Trump Administration

Based on the framework suggested above, it is possible to characterize foreign policy of each administration. In other words, foreign policy of each administration can be analyzed along the multilateral-unilateral dimension in community domain, coercive-non-coercive dimension in security domain, and proactive-reactive domain in prosperity domain. Foreign policy of the Trump administration can be similarly analyzed in this way.

Before directly analyzing Trump administration's foreign policy, it is also necessary to discuss key characteristics of previous administrations in order to understand whether or not and to what extent Trump administration is different from the previous ones. Therefore, the conventional U.S. foreign policy principles of previous administrations, especially after the end of the Cold War, will be discussed first.

1. The Conventional U.S. Foreign Policy Principles.

After the end of World War II, the most fundamental principle of the U.S. grand strategy has been based upon 'liberal hegemony,' which suggests that the U.S. aims to construct the liberal order of the world through diverse measure including building multilateral institutions on security and economy, spreading democracy and capitalism, and utilizing formidable military power in every corner of the world.[13] While the U.S.-led order was in serious competition against the Soviet-led communists, it was further strengthened after the end of the Cold War in the late 1980s and the early 1990s. In the post-Cold War era, the U.S. has enjoyed the unprecedented 'uni-polarity,' as opposed to bi-polarity or multi-polarity, and therefore is given a huge opportunity to build a 'new world order' under U.S. leadership with no serious challenges. 'The End of History' was just a written declaration of the triumph of the U.S.-led 'liberal hegemony' to the global community.[14]

The ideal of 'liberal hegemony' was differently implemented by different presidents since the end of the Cold War. President Clinton pursued the same goal with a particular

13 Barry Posen, *Restraint: A New Foundation for U.S. Grand Strategy* (Ithaca: Cornell University Press, 2014).

14 Francis Fukuyama, *The End of History and the Last Man* (New York: Harmondsworth, 1992).

strategy named 'engagement and enlargement,' which implied the enlargement of liberal democracy camp throughout the world and the engagement of the former communist countries with the global society. Clinton especially preferred multilateral ways of achieving the U.S. foreign policy goals, i.e. signing Kyoto protocol and strengthening of security alliance systems. Clinton did not hesitate to intervene in international affairs whenever possible in the pursuit of American ideals throughout the world. He was also deeply involved in dealing with issues like non-proliferation, terrorism, cyber security, environment, economic integration, and so on.[15] Literally, he was an advocate of 'internationalism' of U.S. foreign policy.

The subsequent George W. Bush administration was quite different from the previous Clinton administration in terms of the ways of handling global affairs. While 'liberal hegemony' principle was also the strong foundation of the Bush administration's foreign policy, it was pursued in more unilateral, as opposed to multilateral, as military, as opposed to diplomatic, ways. This dramatic change from the Clinton style to the G.W. Bush style was originated not only from their different political orientation but also from the shocking 9/11 terror, which was regarded as a 'blowback' against the U.S.-led liberal order of the world and a stimulus to change its policy toward the world. However, the Bush administration even strengthened the U.S.-centered unilateralism and militarism against the Islamic societies. Nonetheless, there is no doubt that the so-called 'Bush Doctrine' was in the same line of 'liberal hegemony' with the Clinton administration.

As a response to the 'Bush Doctrine,' which was considered as excessive expansion, the Obama administration is characterized as restraints and caution. Obama stated in 2013 that "I am more mindful, probably than most, of not only our incredible strengths and capabilities, but also our limitations,"[16] and added a year later 'Since World War II, some of our most costly mistakes came not from our restraint but from our willingness to rush into military adventures without thinking through the consequences, without building international support and legitimacy for our nation, without leveling with the

15 The White House, "The Clinton-Presidency: A Foreign Policy for the Global Age." Available at https://clintonwhitehouse5.archives.gov/WH/Accomplishments/eightyears-10.html (accessed on Jun. 29, 2017).

16 Franklin Foer and Chris Hughes, "Barack Obama Is Not Pleased," *New Republic*, Jan. 27, 2013. Available at https://newrepublic.com/article/112190/obama-interview-2013-sit-down-president (accessed on Jun. 30, 2017).

American people about sacrifices required."[17] In other words, the Obama administration pursued a more cautious approach in handling international issues, mainly because of increasing antagonism and alleged failure of the 'Bush Doctrine.' In this context, the so called 'Obama Doctrine' is understood as 'pragmatic internationalism' suggesting that while the administration pursued internationalism, intervention in global affairs was cautious, selective , and pragmatic.[18] However, there is no denying that Obama's foreign policy was also in the same line of 'liberal hegemony,' although his style was more cautious and practical than Clinton or G.W. Bush.

2. Characterization of Trump Foreign Policy

Trump shows significant differences from his predecessors mentioned above in foreign policy goals and strategies. In a word, it can be described in a word as 'distance from liberal hegemony.' As a successful businessman and an outsider from the Washington politics, he showed different behaviors and strategies from the mainstream politicians of Washington, DC during the campaign period and also in his presidency. With the understanding that he is different from his predecessor in terms of background and behaviors, his different foreign policy goals and strategies can be analyzed utilizing the analytical framework explained above.

Firstly, when it comes to the community domain, the Trump administration pursues the goal of independence and individualistic values over cosmopolitan values. Thus, the administration tends to rely on unilateral than multilateral method. At many different times and places, Trump repeatedly mentioned that the existing multilateral institutions undermined the U.S. interests. He already ordered a withdrawal from the TPP (Trans-Pacific Partnership) and often criticized other multilateral and bilateral institutions that are believed to have supported U.S. hegemony for a long time such as NATO and NAFTA. And most recently, in the amid of COVID-19 pandemic, he announced that the US would withdraw from the World Health Organization, claiming

17 U.S.News, "Obama's Foreign Policy Flop" (May 29, 2014). Available at https://www.usnews.com/opinion/blogs/world-report/2014/05/29/obama-west-point-speech-fails-to-outline-convincing-foreign-policy-strategy (Accessed on Jun., 30, 2017).

18 John G. Ikenberry, "Obama's Pragmatic Internationalism," *The American Interest*, Vol. 9, No. 5. Available at https://www.the-american-interest.com/2014/04/08/obamas-pragmatic-internationalism (accessed on Oct. 18, 2017).

that it was in favor of China.

Trump's unilateralism is well expressed in his campaign slogan, "Make America Great Again," which was based upon the perception that America had been deteriorating for the past decades both economically and militarily. Indeed, he claims that the internationalism that was pursued by the previous administrations made the current decline of America and therefore, the U.S. needs to abandon its foreign policy principle, 'liberal hegemony.' In the same line, he argued, the U.S. should abandon its role as 'world police,' needs to be more realistic in foreign relations, and pursues better self-interest. 'America First' principle of the Trump administration's foreign policy indicates that the administration is "committed to a foreign policy focused on American interests and American national interests."[19] When it comes to military affairs, the 'America First' foreign policy principle suggests that the U.S. will not hesitate to rely on the use of military forces when necessary to defeat ISIS and other terrorist groups, which is a huge threat to the U.S. security. The administration believes that "the world would be more peaceful and prosperous with a stronger and more respected America."[20] In other words, the 'America First' principle in military issues suggests that the Trump administration will focus its use on the critical American interests, instead of conventional American ideals such as democracy, human rights, openness, or engagement.

The principle is more evidently expressed in economic issues. Trump demonstrates clear objections to the multilateral trade negotiations such as Trans-Pacific Partnership (TPP), North Atlantic Free Trade Agreement (NAFTA), and some bilateral free trade agreements, because these deals, he believes, have brought more costs than benefits to American economy. He made it clear that the U.S. would not hesitate to re-negotiate the seemingly failed trade deals. The White House states that "with tough and fair agreement, international trade can be used to grow our economy, return millions of jobs to America's shores, and revitalize our nation's suffering communities."[21]

Secondly, when it comes to security domain, the Trump administration seeks the goal of domination over accommodation, which entails the method of coercion. Trump

19 The White House, "America First Foreign Policy." Available at https://www.whitehouse.gov/america-first-foreign-policy (accessed on July 1, 2017).
20 The White House, ibid.
21 The White House, ibid.

often indicated his preference on the coercive measures to realize American interests. He made it clear that 'Peace through Strength' would be the first principle in handling diverse issues, which resembles Ronald Reagan's security policy. For that purpose, he suggests a dramatic increase in defense budget for the purpose of strengthening the U.S. military forces, domestic and abroad.[22] 'Peace through strength' principle is articulated in the strategies in diverse security issues including terrorism by ISIS, the Iran nuclear deal, Russia, the rise of China, etc.[23] Not surprisingly, his staff has been filled with experts who prefers hawkish, as opposed to dovish, policies including James Mattis, Herbert McMaster, Rex Tillerson, Mike Pompeo, Peter Navarro, and so on. In many different places, Trump obviously shows his preference toward 'power,' the realist principle, rather than the liberal ideals like democracy, human rights, multilateralism, international institutions, etc.

Lastly, when it comes to prosperity domain, the Trump administration pursues the reactive and isolationist approach rather than the proactive and globalist approach. Indeed, 'isolationism' is another word that describes the essence of Trump foreign policy. The 'America First' principle aforementioned also cannot be separated from the isolationist approach. Although he said "I don't believe isolationist policy. I believe in fair policy,"[24] he is close to isolationist in the sense that he opposed to the most of the already signed and ratified free trade agreement of the U.S. He denies the ideals of neo-liberalism, globalization, and free trade, which had been a very important part of U.S. foreign economic policy. Rather than proactively seeking for U.S. economic interest in the global market, he intends to protect pre-existing economic benefits of U.S. citizens, especially workers of labor class, who were considered as the foundation for his success in the election. Trump and the labor class agree that jobs in America were removed greatly because of the possibly 'unfair' free trade agreements. Therefore, it is not surprising to see

22 One of the interesting points in his principle of 'Peace through Strength' is that he emphasizes the fair sharing of defense burden among allies like NATO, Japan, and South Korea (Navarro 2016), indicating that his principle in economic issues is also applied in security issues.

23 Peter Navarro, "America will be great again through a strong military and economy," *The National Interest* (March 31, 2016). Available at http://nationalinterest.org/feature/the-trump-doctrine-peace-through-strength-15631 (Accessed on July 2, 2017).

24 *The Washington Times*, "Donald Trump: I Don't Believe in Isolationist Policy," Mar. 17, 2017. Available at http://www.washingtontimes.com/news/2017/mar/17/donald-trump-i-dont-believe-isolationist-policy/ (accessed on Oct. 20, 2017).

that the Trump administration seeks protectionist policy in trade over free trade.

In sum, U.S. foreign policy under Trump is different from those of his predecessors. While the grand strategy of 'liberal hegemony,' which was maintained by several administrations for the past decades since the end of the World War II, the Trump administration pursues the 'America First' principle, the 'Peace through Strength' policy, and the 'Isolationist' approach. It seems apparent that his preference is on the individualistic, dominative, and tangible short-term economic interests over global, accommodative, and long-term political interests. Furthermore, according to the analysis above, he prefers unilateralism over multilateralism, coercive over non-coercive measures, and reactive over proactive methods.

Having understood that Trump is different from his predecessors in terms of foreign policy goals and strategies, it is also important to recognize that his policy is not beyond the range of legitimate policy choices. In other words, Trump is a rational foreign policy decision-maker whose calculation of cost and benefits operates within a rational framework, although his way of calculation is more or less different from those of previous leaders. His choices of unilateralism over multilateralism, coercive measures over non-coercive measures, and reactive method over proactive method are all based upon his unique characteristics, but within the range of the analytical framework discussed earlier.

Furthermore, some of his key principles are the results of his correct reading of what the American public wants. The isolationist approach is a good example of this analysis. Indeed, the isolationist approach was somehow implied in the Obama foreign policy when he indicated the 'cautious and selective' intervention in international affairs. Obama's policy on the one hand reflected the U.S. public's sense of fatigue in the excessive intervention outside their own countries for longtime, i.e. Iraq and Afghanistan. On the other hand, it was also influenced by the economic downturn of the U.S. that provoked the global financial crisis in 2008. The isolationist approach of the Trump administration is also based upon the similar perception of the U.S. public to a great extent. According to a poll, the U.S. public showed strong support for the change of U.S. foreign policy and the isolationist approach. In this poll, 57% of respondents expressed support for the isolationist approach and only 37% showed opposition to the policy.[25]

---

25 Sunhee Lee, Joongwan Kim, and Hanbeom Jeong, "The Nature of U.S. Isolationism and

Trump just correctly read what the voters wanted and utilized it for his success.

Not just the domestic political environment but also global structural condition contributed to the election of Trump. Since the end of the Cold War, the U.S-led liberal ideology was the dominant order of the global politics and economy for a few decades. The liberal ideology made globalization popular and contributed to the spread of democracy, free trade, and neo-liberal economic policies. However, this big wave of globalization and neo-liberalism has faced strong backlash represented by anti-globalization, anti-immigration, and anti-free trade, and so on. The anti-immigration and anti-Islam atmosphere in Europe provoked the United Kingdom's decision to withdraw from the European Union in June, 2016. Although the so-called 'Brexit (British Exit) was shocking to the rest of the world, it was a prelude to another stunning instance across the Atlantic Ocean. The election of Trump should be understood in the same context with 'Brexit' in the sense that both of them are reflections of the strong liberal states to negate neo-liberal order of the world and to strengthen nationalism. Consequently, considering the domestic and global conditions, the success of Trump in the election is not surprising at all. Instead, it should be noted, the election of Trump was predictable in the context of anti-free trade, anti-immigration, and anti-globalization. The U.S. voters have chosen their jobs and domestic economic rise over the U.S. grand strategy of 'liberal hegemony.'

V. Conclusion: Implications for Northeast Asia and the Korean Peninsula

The analysis of this study suggests that Trump administration's foreign policy is somewhat different from those of previous administrations. While his predecessors pursued the strategy of 'liberal hegemony,' Trump intends to maintain 'distance' from the principle. Instead, he places greater emphasis on unilateralism over multilateralism, coercive measures over non-coercive measures, and isolationist approach over globalism.

Its Prospect in U.S. Foreign Policy Viewed in the Trump Phenomenon," *Journal of Korean Political Diplomatic History*, Vol. 38, No. 1, pp. 283.

However, it is also noted that Trump is a rational decision-maker and therefore Trump's foreign policy operates within a rational framework to maximize national interests, although his calculation of cost and benefits is different from his predecessors to some extent.

Based on the analysis of the characteristics of the Trump administration, it is possible to discuss its policy toward a particular area like Northeast Asia or the Korean Peninsula. Indeed, the strategic importance of Northeast Asia to the U.S. has been dramatically increasing since the end of the Cold War mainly because of the rise of China. The U.S. policy toward Northeast Asia during the Obama administration was well expressed in its 'Pivot to Asia' or 'Rebalancing' policy.[26] Hillary Clinton, the secretary of state then, claimed that the U.S. strategic focus should be placed on Asia, especially Northeast Asia, instead of the North Atlantic area, or Europe or the middle-east. In other words, she suggested, while the U.S. focused on the Atlantic area and the middle-east for several decades, its strategic focus for the next century should be concerned about how to handle Northeast Asia, particularly China.

The rise of China has been fast particularly since the financial crisis of the late 2000s and the country is now considered as the only potential challenger to the hegemonic status of the U.S. Therefore, it is not surprising that the Obama administration strengthened its cautious approach toward this area. The main U.S. policy toward China during the Obama administration was to engage the country in the global affairs as an equivalent partner and thus to provoke positive evaluation of the current world order. While Trump shows somewhat different perception toward the global affairs and the U.S.'s status in the world from Obama, they share similar one toward China. Trump also believes that China can be a threat to U.S. interest in both economy and security. However, his approach to handle China is quite different depending on issues.

When it comes to security issues, the Trump administration pursues a more cautious approach toward China. Indeed, in the sense that Trump and Xi Jinping share the necessity of co-existence of China and the U.S., neither side provokes the other by acting unnecessarily aggressive. Therefore, the U.S. policy toward China under Trump

26 For detailed information, see Hillary Clinton, "America's Pacific Century," *Foreign Policy* (Nov., 2011). Available at http://foreignpolicy.com/2011/10/11/americas-pacific-century/ (accessed on Oct. 21, 2017).

can be characterized as 'check and balance' in a cautious way. Reportedly no serious security related issues has come up between the U.S. and China. For example, Trump agreed to honor the so-called 'One China' policy, which is the most important foreign policy principle of China.[27] In their meeting, Trump repeatedly asked Xi Jinping to pressure North Korea to abandon its nuclear and long-range missile programs,[28] but he never directly touched upon any security-sensitive issue concerning China.

However, the Sino-US relation during Trump and Xi Jinping has not been always stable since the inauguration of the Trump administration. As indicated in the previous section, Trump has shown the realist propensity and made it clear that 'Peace through Strength' is one of his foreign policy principle, which suggests that he would not be reluctant to get involved in disputes with other countries if necessary, although the probability is low. Indeed, there were also instances that indicated the rough relations between Trump and Xi, for example, over the Taiwan issues, the North Korea issues, and so on. It is necessary to remember that the two administrations failed to produce any joint statement after the summit meeting in April 2017. In sum, when it comes to security, the Trump administration has been cautious in relations with China. Although it is possible that the two administrations get involved in some troubles over some issues, it is not likely to be escalated to a kind of serious disputes.

Unlike security area, when it comes to economic issues, the Trump administration is more aggressive in defending U.S. interest. The different approaches in the security and economic issues are understandable, considering that Trump himself is a successful businessman rather than a traditional politician. He has cultivated greater confidence in himself about economic issues than in security issues and not surprisingly he is unlikely to be hesitant to preserve the national economic interest, especially the interest of the working class, who is believed to the significant part of the voters who voted for him in the election.

Especially in relations with China, the Trump administrations has not been

---

27 BBC news, "Trump agrees to honour 'One China' policy despite threats" (Feb. 10, 2017). Available at http://www.bbc.com/news/world-asia-china-38927891 (accessed on July 13, 2017).

28 CNN, "Trump urges action on North Korea in meeting with China's Xi" (July 8, 2017). Available at http://edition.cnn.com/2017/07/08/politics/north-korea-trump-xi/index.htm, (accessed on July 13, 2017)

reluctant to show its aggressiveness. In 2018 and 2019, the U.S. and China had been in the severe conflict in trade issues, which is so called 'trade war.' After several negotiations, they seemed to reach potential agreements on trade issues. However, the trade war is now changed to 'technology war,' where the U.S. impose a wide range of restrictions on the China based technology companies including Hwawei, Tiktok, and WeChat. The U.S. seems to intend to curb the growth of the technology power of China because it can a serious threat to the technology based U.S. economy. In a word, in the area of economy, the U.S. and China are directly colliding.

Based on the analysis of the Trump administration above, it is also possible to discuss its policy toward the Korean peninsula. When the U.S. policy toward the Korean peninsula is divided into its North Korean and South Korean policy, undoubtedly the more difficult one is its North Korean policy in the sense that North Korea is a long-time enemy of the U.S. Even worse, North Korea is believed to have recently developed its capability to strike the U.S. with nuclear weapons (or very close to the capability). In other words, North Korea is now considered as an imminent threat to the U.S. security. The problem is the judgment on whether North Korea has passed the threshold that the U.S. has established. The previous Obama administration's judgment was that North Korea was still within the boundary of their control and therefore the U.S. policy toward North Korea was rather slow and easy. Its policy toward North Korea was named 'strategic patience,' which suggested that they would strategically wait until North Korea would change or collapse, but they would not move first to change it. Whatever it was called, the policy was regarded as almost no policy toward North Korea because the administration did nothing to make something happen. Indeed, with the exclusion of the option of the use of military force, the U.S. did not have many choices but to wait. Especially considering the strong ambition of North Korea to become a nuclear power.

The Trump administration has also been hesitant to use military power in the Korean peninsula because they understand that the use of coercion using military force in the Korean peninsula would entail too much cost not only for South Korea but also for the U.S. as well. Instead, in 2018 the Trump administration made a series of peace talk with North Korea until it came to an end at the Hanoi summit in February 2019. Since then the U.S. and North Korea have never involved in serious talk for denuclearization and peace treaty in the Korean Peninsula. Furthermore, it is unlikely that the talks will resume in near future. The U.S. has to deal with so many issues before they turn their attention to North Korea.

The Trump administration's policy toward South Korea is rather easier to predict. South Korea and the U.S. have no reason to disturb its strong military alliance, especially in the current environment under which the threat from North Korea is significantly increasing. The strong and stable relations in the security area between the countries will continue as long as they share a common enemy, North Korea. Their economic relations will be somewhat different. That is, Trump is very stubborn in preserving the U.S. economic interest even in the relation with allies like Japan and South Korea. In sum, the formula of 'cautious approach in security area' but 'aggressive one in the economic area is also applied in the Korean peninsula as well.

References

Bacevich, Andrew J. 2017. "The Age of Great Expectations and the Great Void: History after 'The End of History.' Available at http://americanempireproject.com/blog/the-age-of-great-expectations-and-the-great-void/ (accessed on Oct. 27, 2017).

BBC news, "Trump agrees to honour 'One China' policy despite threats" (Feb. 10, 2017). Available at http://www.bbc.com/news/world-asia-china-38927891 (accessed on July 13, 2017).

Chittick, William O. *American Foreign Policy* (Washington, D.C.: CQ Press, 2006).

Clinton, Hillary. "America's Pacific Century," *Foreign Policy* (2011 Nov.). Available at http://foreignpolicy.com/2011/10/11/americas-pacific-century/ (accessed on Oct. 21, 2017).

CNN, "Trump urges action on North Korea in meeting with China's Xi" (July 8, 2017). Available at http://edition.cnn.com/2017/07/08/politics/north-korea-trump-xi/index.html (accessed on July 13, 2017).

Foer, Franklin and Chris Hughes. "Barack Obama Is Not Pleased," *New Republic* (Jan. 27, 2013). Available at https://newrepublic.com/article/112190/obama-interview-2013-sit-down-president (accessed on Jun. 30, 2017).

Fukuyama Francis. *The End of History and the Last Man* (New York: Harmondsworth, 1992).

Ikenberry, John G. "Obama's Pragmatic Internationalism." *The American Interest*, Vol.9, No.5 (2014). Available at https://www.the-american-interest.com/2014/04/08/obamas-pragmatic-internationalism (accessed on Oct. 18, 2017).

Kinsella, David, Bruce Russett, and Harvey Starr. *World Politics: The Menu for Choice*, 10th ed. (New York: Wadsworth, 2013).

Krauthammer, Charles. "Trump's Foreign Policy Revolutions," *The Washington Post* (Jan. 26, 2017). Available at https://www.washingtonpost.com/opinions/global-opinions/trumps-foreign-policy-revolution/2017/01/26/c69268a6-e402-11e6-ba11-63c4b4fb5a63_story.html?utm_term=.1a3006c31b05 (accessed on Oct. 9, 2017).

Jentleson, Bruce W. "Global Governance, the United Nations, and the Challenge of Trumping Trump," *Global Governance*, Vol. 23 (2017), pp.143-149.

Jervis, Robert. "President Trump and IR Theory," ISSF Policy Series (Jan. 2, 2017). Available at https://issforum.org/roundtables/policy/1-5b-jervis (accessed on Oct. 9, 2017).

Lee, Sunhee, Joongwan Kim, Hanbeom Jeong. "The Nature of U.S. Isolationism and Its Prospect in US Foreign Policy Viewed in the Trump Phenomenon," *Journal of Korean Political and Diplomatic History*, Vol. 38, No. 1 (Aug. 2016), pp. 281-314.

McClelland, David C. *Human Motivation* (Cambridge: Cambridge University Press, 1987).

Navarro, Peter. "America will be great again through a strong military and economy," *The National Interest* (March 31, 2016). Available at http://nationalinterest.org/feature/the-trump-doctrine-peace-through-strength-15631 (accessed on July 2, 2017).

Posen, Barry R. *Restraint: A New Foundation for U.S. Grand Strategy* (Ithaca: Cornell University Press, 2014).

The Washington Times, "Donald Trump: I Don't Believe in Isolationist Policy" (Mar. 17, 2017). Available at http://www.washingtontimes.com/news/2017/mar/17/ donald-trump-i-dont-believe-isolationist-policy/ (accessed on Oct. 20, 2017).

The White House, "America First Foreign Policy." Available at https://www.whitehouse.gov/america-first-foreign-policy (accessed on July 1, 2017).

The White House, "The Clinton-Presidency: A Foreign Policy for the Global Age. Available at https://clintonwhitehouse5.archives.gov/WH/Accomplishments/eightyears-10.html. (accessed on Jun. 29, 2017).

U.S.News, "Obama's Foreign Policy Flop" (May 29, 2014). Available at https://www.usnews.com/opinion/blogs/world-report/2014/05/29/obama-west-point-speech-fails-to-outline-convincing-foreign-policy-strategy. (accessed on Jun. 30, 2017).

Walt, Stephen M. "Could There Be a Peace of Trumphalia?" *Foreign Policy*, (Nov. 14, 2016). Available at http://foreignpolicy.com/2016/11/14/could-there-be-a-peace-of-trumphalia (accessed on Oct. 13, 2017).

Wright, Thomas. "Trump's 19th Century Foreign Policy," *Politico* (Jan. 20, 2017). Available at http://www.politico.com/magazine/story/2016/01/donald-trump-foreign-policy-213546 (accessed on Oct. 10, 2017).

Zakheim, Don. "Trump Must Be Stopped," The National Interest, Mar. 5, 2017. Available at http://nationalinterest.org/feature/trump-must-be-stopped-15408 (accessed on Oct. 10, 2017).

Chapter 6

The Impact of U.S.–China Power Competition on the Korean Peace Process

Wonjae Hwang
(University of Tennessee)

Abstract

This paper examines the impact of the ongoing U.S.-China power competition on the Korean Peace Process. Based on the discussion of power transition theory and hedging strategy, this paper evaluates how the great power competition may affect the prospect of the initiative particularly with respect to the goal of creating a new economic community on the Korean Peninsula. As a way to minimize the risk of being entrapped by the great power competition and pursue the goals specified in the Korean Peace Process, this paper argues that South Korea needs to adopt a strategy of multilateral engagement with other middle powers.

Keywords: the Korean Peace Process, U.S–China Power Competition, Economic Community, Middle Power

Ⅰ. Introduction

How does the ongoing power competition between the U.S. and China affect the prospect of the Korean Peace Process? The Korean Peace Process initiated by South Korean President Moon Jae-in in July 2017 has three goals: denuclearization and peace building on the peninsula, sustainable development of inter-Korean relations, and the creation of a new economic community on the peninsula (Ministry of Culture, Sports and Tourism 2020). After the introduction of the initiative, the world has observed positive movements on the peninsula including a series of summits between South and North Korea and between the U.S. and North Korea. Increased diplomatic and cultural exchanges have also occurred between South and North Korea. In the Panmunjom Declaration in April 2018, leaders from the two Koreas agreed to work towards a peaceful reunification in the future. Later in June 2018, in a historic summit meeting between Kim Jong-un and Donald Trump held in Singapore, the two leaders signed a joint statement, making commitments to work together for the achievements of denuclearization of the Korean Peninsula, security guarantees for North Korea, and peaceful bilateral relations along with other agreements specified in the statement.

Despite significant advancements in dialogue and cooperation in recent years, however, the peace process initiative is far away from success yet to achieve the goals. One of the difficulties facing the initiative is the U.S.-China power competition. The ongoing power competition has caused troubles to South Korea, its economy, and foreign policy. South Korea has been under pressure to take a side between the two great powers over contentious issues. However, South Korea, as a strong economic partner to China and a security ally to the U.S., has difficulties in taking a side with either. The power competition also poses a threat to the stability of regional politics and economy and deteriorates the prospect of the Korean Peace Process. To achieve the goals announced in the initiative, South Korea needs to effectively respond to the power competition and its challenges. In this regard, this paper examines the nature of the power competition and its impact on the prospect of the initiative. Crises often come with opportunities. If properly managed, the power competition may generate environments that serve well for the purpose of the Korean Peace Process particularly with respect to the creation of a new economic community on the Korean Peninsula. By utilizing an engagement strategy with other middle powers and multilateral institutions, South Korea can promote multilateral economic cooperation surrounding the peninsula.

II. The U.S.–China Power Competition and Middle Power Strategy

1. Great Power Competition and Middle Powers

The ongoing power competition between the U.S. and China can be understood in multiple different ways. Some may view it as a diversionary foreign policy significantly motivated by domestic political reasons that the Trump administration or the Chinese leadership may have. Others may argue that the power competition is driven mainly by geopolitical or geo-economic interests such as economic preeminence, high technology and economic security (Roberts et al. 2019). Probably, the most popular theory that many scholars and experts employ to account for the nature of the competition is power transition theory. According to the theory, a rising power that is not satisfied with the status quo is likely to challenge the existing dominant state. The dominant state is not likely to allow a regional hegemon to challenge its global leadership, either. Such motivations and fears that both powers may have against each other can lead them to fall into the Thucydides trap (Allison 2017), resulting in a preventive or hegemonic war.

Although this theory is widely cited by scholars, discussion about middle powers and their strategic behavior in the time of great power competition or power transition is relatively limited. This is mainly because middle powers are viewed as buffer states between great powers or primarily subordinate states to them. In fact, the prospect of stability and peace on the Korean Peninsula is likely to be subjugated by the ongoing power struggle between the U.S. and China to a great extent.

As a response to the great power competition, South Korea cannot take a side with one of them easily by adopting balancing or bandwagoning strategy. Balancing is a foreign policy strategy to align against prevailing threats or a rising power. By joining the threatened and aligning with a weaker side in a dispute, other states can bring power into balance and reduce their vulnerability to the threats and demands from a stronger side (Bueno de Mesquita 2000; Waltz 1979). In contrast, bandwagoning is a strategy employed by states that align themselves with a stronger side. When states find themselves in a weak position and a strong side can take what it wants by force anyway, states can join the threatening and a stronger side in a dispute as a survival strategy (Mearsheimer 2001). Since both the U.S. and China are critical partners to South Korea in various aspects, however, the opportunity costs that South Korea has to pay by taking either balancing or bandwagoning strategy could be very significant. Moreover, in the time of power transition, it is extremely difficult to predict how the power competition will unfold. In this regard, hedging, a third strategic choice located between balancing and bandwagoning, is often considered as an effective strategy for South Korea to optimize its national interests.

2. Hedging Strategy

Hedging has been utilized by states as a strategy to reduce security risk by implementing seemly contradictory policies in one or multiple dimensions. For example, in the face of evolving Sino-U.S. rivalry in East Asia, Japan has adopted a hedging strategy by economically engaging China and strengthening its military tie with the U.S. By using this dual engagement strategy, Japan intends to hedge the risk of China's regional dominance through Japan-U.S. alliance and also reduce the risk of U.S. abandonment through the maintenance of close economic ties with China (Hornung 2014; Wallace 2013). It is also argued that Israel and South Africa have utilized nuclear hedging as a strategy to reduce the risk of abandonment by their allies (Park and Peh 2020). In a similar context, North Korea's efforts on nuclear weapon programs can be understood as part of hedging strategy (Ring and Hwang 2020). The U.S. and China themselves have also used hedging strategy against each other to promote cooperation and minimize their chance of conflict by simultaneously employing engagement and balancing policies.

Similarly, South Korea has increasingly engaged in active hedging with both the U.S. and China (Chung 2009). Active hedging is a form of hedging engagement in which a state engages two great powers without cutting ties with one of them. While maintaining a strong tie with one great power in a dimension, a state can actively engage another great power in a different dimension for the purpose of hedging risks coming from both sides. In this regard, active hedging can be understood as simultaneous binding engagement with two great powers. This strategy could be effective for small or middle power states to strengthen their power and strategic importance in geopolitics and promote their national interests (Lake 1996).

The risks that South Korea tries to hedge are clear. High military and political dependence on the U.S. make South Korea vulnerable and susceptible to external influence, reduced commitment, or abandonment. As the recent case of defense cost-sharing negation between the Trump administration and the South Korean government for the year of 2020 shows, South Korea is vulnerable to exorbitant demands and associated threats of abandonment from the U.S. As a way to hedge such risk, South Korea has actively engaged China mainly in the economic dimension. In this way, South Korea intends to reduce its economic dependence on the U.S. and enhance its geopolitical importance. Since the establishment of diplomatic relationship in 1992, the bilateral trade volume between South Korea and China increased from $4.4 billion in 1991 to about $286 billion in 2018, which was about twice bigger than the trade volume with the U.S. Trade with China accounts for about a quarter of South Korea's total trade in 2019. Thanks to the South Korea-China Free Trade Agreements which went into effect in December 2015, their trade tie is expected to become stronger in the future. Their bilateral FDI also increased from about $43 million in 1991 to about $7.51 billion in 2018. In 2019, South Korea joined China-initiated Asian Infrastructure Investment Bank (AIIB). AIIB is often considered as a rival to the World Bank. Like the U.S. in the World Bank, China is the biggest shareholder in AIIB, enjoying the strongest voting power (about 26 percent of the total voting rights) in the bank. South Korea also joined Chiang Mai Initiative (CMI), a multilateral currency swap agreement, along with China and Japan in 2010. By participating in CMI, South Korea is expected to reduce its dependence on the International Monetary Fund (IMF), another U.S.-led international financial institution.

Even in the military dimension, South Korea shows its willingness to compromise China's interests. For example, as an effort to assuage China's security concerns after the deployment of Terminal High Altitude Area Defense (THAAD) system on the Korean Peninsula, the South Korean government made three No's policy announcement in 2017. They are no additional THAAD deployment, no agreement to the U.S. missile defense system, and no participation in trilateral military alliance with the U.S. and Japan. Overall, these indicators show that South Korea has strong interests in binding engagement with China.

South Korea has also significantly engaged the U.S. economically and militarily. As one of America's closest allies, South Korea has established close military, economic, and political relations with the U.S. In terms of bilateral trade, the U.S. has been always one of the three largest partners to South Korea. Under the 1953 Mutual Defense Treaty, U.S. military forces have maintained a continuous presence in South Korea. As of 2020, about 28,500 American troops are deployed in South Korea. By holding its alliance tie with the U.S. strong and actively engaging the U.S. particularly in the military dimension, South Korea has minimized the risk of China's regional dominance and security threats from North Korea. In fact, thanks to strong security commitments made by the U.S. to the Korean Peninsula, it has been possible for South Korea to actively engage China without serious security concerns (Chung 2009; Krieckhaus 2018).

The deployment of THAAD system in 2017 and the delay of wartime operational control (OPCON) transfer from the U.S. are just a few examples of many that show South Korea's continuous strategic interests in binding engagement with the U.S. The deployment of the defensive missile system was contentious among policymakers in South Korea particularly because of strong criticism from China.[1] However, the Seoul government eventually decided to deploy it after observing China's lukewarm responses to North Korea's nuclear test and satellite launch (Roehrig 2015), which highlights the strategic importance of the U.S. to South Korea and its national security. South Korea has also modernized its defense system through cooperation with the U.S. Currently, South Korea has more than $30 billion in active government to government sales cases with the U.S. under the Foreign Military Sales (FMS) system. Such sales include F-35 joint strike fighter, Aegis Combat Systems, and Global Hawk Unmanned Aerial Vehicle. The cooperative relations between South Korea and the U.S. have been continuously strengthened over the years.

1 Reportedly, China's sanctions over the deployment of THAAD system costs South Korea billions of dollars.

3. Conditions of successful hedging strategy

Largely, there are two key factors that ensure the success of hedging strategy: the maintenance of its strategic importance to both great powers as a regional power, and flexibility in its strategy of swiftly responding to changing environments. As the eleventh largest economy and the sixth most powerful military force in the world, South Korea's strategic importance to the U.S. or China cannot be exaggerated. Particularly in the time of great power competition, drawing cooperation from regional powers such as South Korea becomes an important foreign policy goal for both the U.S. and China to win the power competition.

As a way to increase its flexibility of responding to changing environments, South Korea has utilized a policy of strategic ambiguity or not taking a side with either great power when it comes to contentious issues. For example, Figure 1 shows South Korea's foreign policy positions in contested votes between the U.S. and China in the UN General Assembly from 1991 to 2018. It is well known that China and the U.S. reveal extremely divergent foreign policy preferences over UN resolutions, which generates enormous pressure on other states including South Korea to choose a position between the U.S. and China. Therefore, by examining South Korea's positions in contested votes between them, we can get an idea about how its strategic ambiguity policy has played out.

There are a few implications we can draw from the figure. First, the number of contested votes between the two great powers has increased over time. There were only about 20 contested resolutions in the early 1990s. But, the number increased to about 60 in the late 2010s. Surely, even in the UN, the two great powers are facing each other as big rivals. Relatedly, the figure shows that South Korea had a tendency of not taking a side between the U.S. and China in the 1990s. In about 60 percentage of cases, South Korea did not take a side with either power. However, since the 2000s, South Korea has tended to take a side with either the U.S. or China (more than 70 percent of cases), instead of staying neutral (less than 30 percent of cases). This implies that South Korea has tried to make its own voice on contentious issues more actively in recent years. From a different perspective, however, the result may imply the fact that it is getting hard for South Korea to not take a side with either, due to increasing pressure coming from both sides. Although the probability that South Korea takes sides with either power over contested resolutions has

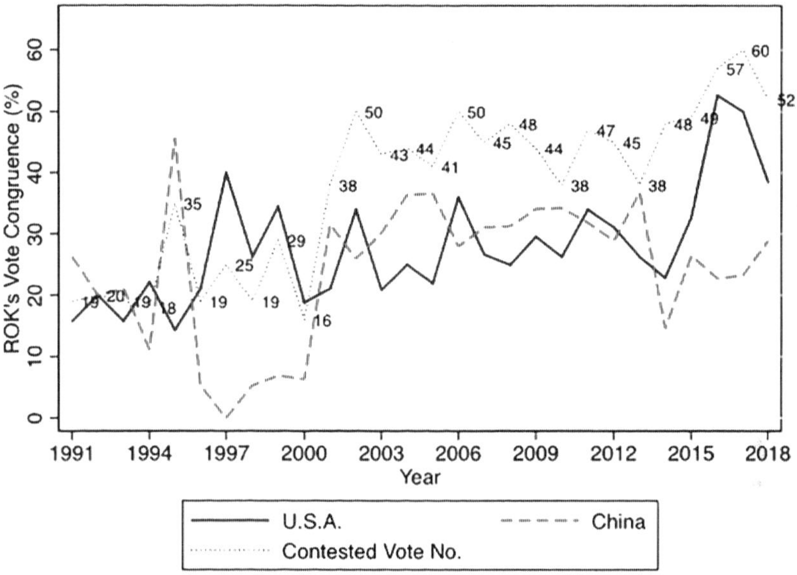

Figure 1. South Korea's positions in contested votes between the U.S. and China (1991-2018)

increased over time, however, there is still no clear evidence that South Korea's foreign policy preferences shift from the U.S. (China) to China (the U.S.) probably except the periods of two presidential leadership, Kim Dae-jung and Park Guen-hye. In these two periods, South Korea show high probabilities of supporting the U.S. rather than China. Overall, the figure presents empirical support that South Korea has maintained a policy of strategic ambiguity between the U.S. and China in international organizations like the UN.

However, analyzing a state's foreign policy preferences based on its votes on multilateral issues is quite limited in understanding its foreign policy positions and strategy on bilateral issues. Moreover, as the relations between the U.S. and China severely deteriorate, successfully implementing hedging strategy for South Korea becomes a difficult task. This is because the power struggle can fundamentally reshape geopolitics, and the great powers may relegate their relations with South Korea to a lower priority. Simply, the great power competition can generate big waves to easily knock out and sweep middle powers in any direction. Although the role of the U.S. as a security guarantor and sponsor for South Korea is important, the alliance can be used as a leverage of influence by the U.S. on South Korea as the power competition deepens. Likewise, since China is the most significant economic partner to South Korea, the economic tie may make South Korea vulnerable to external shocks and demand from China. Consequently, instead of reducing risks that come from both sides, the active hedging strategy can work as a trap that drags South Korea into the middle of struggle between the two great powers.

4. Improving Strategic Importance and Multilateralism

Then, how can South Korea effectively respond to challenges the great power competition poses and at the same time pursue its goals announced in the Korean Peace Process? South Korea is one of the countries significantly influenced by the power competition. This is mainly due to its economic structure, and its strong ties with both China and the United States, which is the key feature of the hedging strategy. When it comes to the economy structure, the South Korean economy is heavily dependent on international trade. South Korea, as the only OECD member state that maintains its trade volume greater than the size of its GDP, is highly vulnerable to external shocks. For example, currently about 79 percent of South Korea's total exports to China are intermediate goods and 29 percent of them are reprocessed for export purposes in China. This implies that U.S. tariffs on China and reduction of China's exports also cause collateral damage to South Korea. In another example, South Korea has been under pressure to join the U.S. in its economic sanctions on Huawei and its 5G technology. China also reciprocated with warning to South Korea's SK Hynix and Samsung of severe retaliation if they participated in the sanction. A decision on such contentious issue between the U.S. and China would be extremely costly for South Korea.

To reduce the risk of entrapment caused by the power competition and its security-trade dilemma, South Korea needs an alternative strategy. As discussed above, hedging or dual binding engagement strategy may not work for South Korea effectively in the time of fierce great power competition. Then, a viable alternative strategy that South Korea could take would be to promote its strategic importance in the regional politics and reduce its dependence on both great powers by aligning with other middles powers. By building and cultivating cooperative partnerships in economic, political, or military dimension with other middle powers, outside of the framework of the U.S.-China strategic competition, South Korea may be able to increase its strategic importance to great powers, which is one of the important conditions that enable the active hedging strategy to work. Using this strategy, South Korea can also minimize economic and security risks posed by the great power competition. Particularly with respect to the goal of creation of a new economic community on the Korean Peninsula, the power competition between the U.S. and China may present opportunities as well as challenges to South Korea. This is because the great power competition can create better environments for South Korea to build multilateral economic networks, thanks to shared concerns and interests with other middle powers.

To create a new economic community on the Korean Peninsula, the South Korean government has sought to promote greater inter-Korean exchanges and economic integration. Neighboring states' participation in the economic integration processes is essential for achievement of the goal. To this end, South Korea has promoted policies (i.e., the New Northern Policy and New Southern Policy) that aim to diversify and strengthen its economic and political ties with Russia, Mongolia, India and other Southeast Asian countries. For example, as the U.S.-China trade war deepens, South Korean firms have continued to move their supply chains from China to other destinations such as Vietnam. In fact, diversifying its trade partners across diverse regions and countries and thus reducing trade dependence on a specific region or partner has been South Korea's one of the key economic policies in recent decades (Hwang 2017).

Figure 2 shows the distribution of trade partners that South Korea has had in the last few decades. Similar to Gini index that is frequently used to measure the distribution of income in a society, the trade index is generated to measure the distribution of export and import partners to South Korea across countries. A high value in the index indicates that South Korea's export or import has been concentrated to only a few countries, while a low value indicates an enhanced diversity of trade partners. As the figure shows, South Korea has successfully diversified its export or import partners up until the late 2000s. However, in the 2010s, the direction of movements has changed. That is, the inequality of distribution of export or import partners increased, meaning that South Korea's trade

Figure 2. South Korea's distribution of export and import partners across countries

was concentrated to fewer numbers of countries.[2]

The main reason for the reverse trend in diversification in recent years is because of South Korea's growing trade dependence on China and the U.S. In terms of export share, China has been the top export partner for many years, accounting for about 27 percent of South Korea's total export. South Korea's export dependence on the U.S. has also increased from about 10 percent in the early 2010s to about 14 percent in the late 2010s. In terms of import share, the share of China increased from 16 percent to 23 percent in the 2010s, and the share of the U.S. increased from 7 percent to 13 percent in the 2010s. This growing dependence destabilizes the South Korean economy particularly in the time of the U.S.-China power competition, making the South Korean economy vulnerable to external shocks and political influence.

5. Shared interests with other middle powers

One notable thing is that, in the time of U.S.-China power competition, other middle powers have similar preferences/situations with South Korea. Shared concerns and interests may generate better environments for economic cooperation among middle

2 In the year of 2020, the data covers only up to September.

powers. For example, the growing great power competition may work positively for the improvement of South Korea-Japan relations. Japan is one of the key players that affect South Korean economy and politics. As well known, due to historical issues and associated trade disputes, South Korea-Japan relations have plummeted to its lowest levels in the last few years. Nevertheless, recently, we have observed some positive movements going on between the two rivals. In December 2019, Japan participated in a trilateral summit with South Korea and China to discuss North Korean nuclear issues and shared economic interests. That meeting was possible partly because of China's desire to play the role of regional anchor but mainly because of security and economic concerns shared by the three countries. Relatedly, in 2018, China and Japan expressed their common ground on the U.S.-China trade war (Landers 2018), which was an understandable move considering that trade with China took more than 20 percent of Japan's total trade. The three countries also agreed to work more closely to negotiate a trilateral free trade agreement.

South Korea and Japan are also joint partners of Regional Comprehensive Economic Partnership (RCEP), which includes 15 negotiation countries for free trade agreements in the Asia-Pacific region. RCEP is the biggest FTA in the world in terms of its economic size, accounting for about 30 percent of the world GDP and population. It was signed in November 2020 and will be effective once ratified by its member states. Economic difficulties that Japan suffers from the U.S.-China power competition ironically work to promote cooperation with South Korea, China, and other middle powers. Soon or later, we are likely to observe that South Korea and Japan sign free trade agreements together for the first time in their history, although they could be still multilateral agreements.

One of the multilateral policy tools that South Korea can utilize to promote multilateral economic cooperation could be Comprehensive and Progressive Agreement for Trans-Pacific Partnership (renamed from Trans-Pacific Partnership in January 2018 and became effective in December 2018). CPTPP is a multilateral trade agreement among eleven countries that include Australia, Brunei, Canada, Chile, Japan, Malaysia, Mexico, New Zealand, Peru, Singapore, and Vietnam. The participating economies represent about 13.4 percent of the world GDP. The U.S. and China may also join the agreement in the near future. Likewise, by participating in multilateral institutions, South Korea can reduce its dependence on the U.S. and China, promote economic cooperation with other middle powers, and thus enhance its chance to achieve the economic goal of the initiative.

6. Shared interests with North Korea

Meanwhile, to account for the success of the economic goal specified in the Korean Peace Process, we cannot underestimate the role of North Korea. An important question here is how North Korea perceives the power competition and how such perception affects its foreign policy. At a quick glance, the ongoing power competition does not necessarily work negatively for North Korea, particularly with respect to its relations with China. After North Korea's third nuclear test in 2013, China decided to participate in multilateral economic sanctions authorized by the UN Security Council. However, as the U.S.-China power competition and trade war causes fissures in the unity between the U.S. and China, recently, China along with Russia at the UN express their support for loosening or lifting economic sanctions on North Korea.

However, if we examine the situation more carefully, the ongoing power competition may signal two types of information to the North. First, North Korea may view the power competition as a signal of weakness of China unless they expect China to win the competition. China's defeat in the competition to the U.S. can strengthen North Korea's desire to diversify and develop its economic ties with others. Simply put, China cannot play as a big daddy for North Korea anymore. North Korea has significantly suffered from economic sanctions imposed on its economy. They have squeezed many North Korean industries, which damage North Korea's primary goal of economic development. Consequently, while maintaining a close tie with its strongest sponsor, the North Korean regime may seriously consider the need to improve its relations with neighboring states, particularly with the U.S. This may explain some backgrounds of North Korea's positive movements and gestures in its relations with the U.S. and South Korea in the last few years.

At the same time, however, the power competition may also signal high uncertainties and mistrust of the U.S. as a negotiation partner. The Trump administration aggressively pursued 'America First' foreign policy and its national interests even at the expense of its allies' costs. Its tendency to view its allies in economic and accounting perspectives rather than in holistic and strategic perspectives, and exorbitant demand for increases in defense cost-sharing to South Korea, Japan, and NATO members along with trade disputes with them may signal that the U.S. is not a reliable strategic partner in negotiation. The 2018 withdrawal from the Iran nuclear deal reached in 2015 only confirm this suspicion. Although the new Biden administration may return to a more multilateral approach in its foreign policy, it does not necessarily reduce uncertainties surrounding the U.S. as a negotiation partner.

Such perception may encourage North Korea to seek cooperation from other states. If Kim Jong-un believes that maintaining the status quo (i.e., North Korea with nuclear capabilities but with severe economic troubles) is the best strategy for the regime survival, the nuclear arsenal will remain as the best asset and there will be no serious improvements in the negotiation over denuclearization. However, if he wants to improve the economic situation, exchanging its nuclear weapon programs with enhanced security guarantees and the removal of economic sanctions would be a viable policy option for him in the long run (Ring and Hwang 2020). The ongoing power competition may signal to the North Korean leadership that the best chance to achieve economic development could be through multilateral cooperation beyond bilateral deals and negotiation with the U.S. and China. Without diversifying its economic, diplomatic, and political relations with other middle powers, North Korea's chance of survival or strategic maneuvering of the relations with the U.S. or China could be quite limited.

Due to its isolated position in world politics and economy resulting from its nuclear weapon programs and economic sanctions, North Korea's participation in multilateral economic institutions would be a remote contingency. Nevertheless, if both North and South Korea can increase their joint memberships in multilateral institutions in the future, they can reduce their economic or security dependence on China and/or the U.S. and thus minimize negative effects of the power competition on the Korean Peninsula. Overall, this evaluation indicates that the U.S.-China power competition presents both challenges and opportunities to South Korea with respect to the success of the Korean Peace Process.

III. Conclusion

According to the power transition theory, the U.S.-China conflict seems inevitable. Even if that is an accurate prediction of the ongoing power competition, however, the type of conflict could be non-violent. In other words, the fight can be done mainly in the economic or political dimension, not in the form of serious military confrontation. There are mainly three reasons for that. First, a high level of economic interdependence between the U.S. and China may incur great losses and costs to both sides if they engage in a military confrontation. Unlike previous cases of power transitional wars, the two superpowers heavily engage each other economically. Due to high opportunity or audience costs of war, neither side is strongly motivated to engage in a full-out war.

Second, domestic political situations in China may not be favorable for a military confrontation with the U.S. The political leadership in China has lost its popularity domestically in recent years mainly due to the way the government controls and governs the society. Public protests against the authoritarian government have increased over time in China (Zhong and Hwang 2016). Although nationalistic sentiments may encourage China's aggressive foreign policy in the short run when China confronts the U.S., economic troubles that militarized conflict eventually causes to the Chinese economy may backfire against the political leadership. Moreover, Chinese nationalism is not necessarily supportive of the regime. Those who are nationalistic in China are also people who strongly believe in democratic values and systems (Zhong and Hwang 2020). Although their understanding of democratic values and norms are different from the ones in the west to some extent, there are still high uncertainties about how militarized conflict with the U.S. can affect leaders' political survival in China.

Third, militarized conflict is very costly, and its outcome is uncertain. With high uncertainties of winning, even the U.S. cannot choose a military option easily. For example, according to the Pentagon report (Zakaria 2020), out of 18 simulation wars performed between the U.S. and China which might be triggered by the Taiwan issue, the U.S. won none. This projection may make American policymakers cautious about the use of aggressive foreign policy towards China. Therefore, despite turbulences and troubles the power competition generates, it may not escalate into a serious militarized confrontation.

Then, the main clashes between the U.S and China may break out in the economic dimension. While the U.S. tries to uphold the foundations of the liberal international order and its global leadership, China poses serious challenges to the order and the U.S. leadership. Consequently, the two economic powers may seek to decouple their economies or at least reduce their economic interdependence and integration particularly in the areas of vital national interests (Wright 2013). Amid high uncertainties, economic troubles and challenges generated by the power competition, South Korea has to find an answer to the new challenges. As discussed above, by building and consolidating relations with other middle powers, South Korea can mitigate negative effects that the U.S.-China power competition particularly in the economic dimension may cause to the Korean Peace Process.

Meanwhile, creation of a new economic community on the Korean Peninsula through bilateral and multilateral cooperation cannot be done easily without resolving other security related issues. Significant advancements in denuclearization in North Korea should be made along with/prior to economic cooperation and integration. A series of economic sanctions against North Korea that are concerned with North Korea's nuclear weapon programs needs to be reduced or removed. Before that, probably, the Korean War needs to officially end. In other words, three goals announced in the Korean Peace Process are not necessarily independent from each other. Since one strategy designed to achieve one goal is closely connected to another strategy that aims to accomplish another goal, we cannot evaluate them separately. However, at the same time, it would also be an accurate claim that to achieve each goal, continuous efforts in each strategy need to be made. Cooperation in low politics can also work as a stimulus for further cooperation in high politics. Creation of a new economic community on the peninsula cannot be done in the short run. To overcome challenges and grasp opportunities that the U.S.-China power competition may present, wisdom, patience, and tireless efforts would be necessary for South Korea and its leadership.

References

Allison, Graham. 2017. *Destined for War: Can America and China Escape Thucydides's Trap?*. New York: Houghton Mifflin Harcourt.

Bueno de Mesquita, Bruce. 2000. *Principles of International Politics*. Washington DC: CQ Press.

Chung, Jae Ho. 2009. "East Asia Responds to the Rise of China: Patterns and Variations." *Pacific Affairs* 82(4): 657-675.

Hornung, Jeffrey. 2014. "Japan's Growing Hard Hedge Against China." *Asian Security* 10(2): 97-122.

Hwang, Wonjae. 2017. *South Korea's Changing Foreign Policy: The Impact of Democratization and Globalization*. Lexington Books.

Krieckhaus, Jonathan. 2018. *Geopolitical Economy: The South Korean FTA Strategy*. Ann Arbor: University of Michigan Press.

Lake, David. 1996. "Anarchy, Hierarchy, and the Variety of International Relations." *International Organization* 50(1): 1-33.

Landers, Peter. 2018. "Japan and China Find Common Ground in Trump's Tariffs as Leaders Meet." *Wall Street Journal* (September 12).

Mearsheimer, John. 2001. *The Tragedy of Great Power Politics*. New York: W.W. Norton and Company.

Ministry of Culture, Sports and Tourism. 2020. *The Korean Peace Process*. Republic of Korea. March 3, 2020. https://www.korea.kr/special/policyCurationView.do?newsId=148865774

Park, Soul and Kimberly Peh. 2020. "Leveraging towards restraint: Nuclear hedging and North Korea's shifting reference points during the agreed framework and the Six-party Talks." European Journal of International Security 5: 94-11.

Ring, Jonathan and Wonjae Hwang. 2020. "Military and Economic Power Networks, Active Hedging, and Cooperation on the Korean Peninsula." *Asian Survey* 60(6): 1090-1115.

Roberts, Anthea, Henrique Choer Moraes, and Victor Ferguson. 2019. "The U.S.-China Trade War Is a Competition for Technological Leadership." *Lawfare Institutue*. May 21, 2019. https://www.lawfareblog.com/us-china-trade-war-competition-technological-leadership

Roehrig, Terence. 2015. "Caught in the Middle: South Korea and the South China Sea Arbitration Decision." In *Asian Yearbook of International Law*: Volume 21, edited by Lee Seokwoo, Lee Hee Eun, and Bautista Lowell, 96-120. Leiden: Boston: Brill

Wallace, Corey. 2013. "Japan's Strategic Pivot South: Diversifying the Dual Hedge." *International Relations of the Asia Pacific* 13(3): 479-517.

Waltz, Kenneth. 1979. *Theory of International Politics*. Reading, MA: Addison-Wesley.

Wright, Thomas. 2013. "Sifting through Interdependence." *The Washington Quarterly* 36(4): 7-23.

Zakaria, Fareed. 2020. "The New China Scare: Why America Shouldn't Panic About Its Latest Challenger." *Foreign Affairs* 99(1): 52-61.
Zhong, Yang, and Wonjae Hwang. 2016. "Pollution, Institutions, and Street Protests in Urban China." *Journal of Contemporary China* 25(98): 216-232.
Zhong, Yang, and Wonjae Hwang. 2020. "Why Do Chinese Democrats Tend To Be Nationalistic?" *Journal of Contemporary China* 29(121): 61-74.

Chapter 7

Sunrise, Sunset: The Rise and Fall of Inter-Korean Economic Relations

Inhan Kim
(Ewha Womans University)

Abstract

What explains the dramatic rise and fall of inter-Korean economic relations over the past two decades? The conventional explanation has been differences in the beliefs of political leaders. That is, liberal presidents such as Kim Dae-jung and Roh Moo-hyun pursued engagement policies with a firm belief that growing economic interdependence with North Korea would help it come out of isolation and moderate its foreign policy, while the conservative next two leaders were skeptical. Examining almost two decades of economic cooperation between the two Koreas, this paper asserts that the fate of inter-Korean economic relations has depended not just on the political leaders' beliefs but also on two external forces: Pyongyang's response to engagement efforts from Seoul and support from Washington. Throughout the sunshine period, the two Koreas were able to expand economic ties both in scope and quantity as both Pyongyang and Washington responded favorably to Seoul's sunshine policies. In contrast, economic cooperation shrank in scope and the overall volume of exchange fluctuated during—but not because of—the conservatives' rule in Seoul as Pyongyang rejected Seoul's proposals and instead accelerated its nuclear armament. This study projects poor prospects for Seoul's recent efforts to revive economic cooperation with Pyongyang.

Keywords: North Korea, South Korea, the United States, Sunshine policy, Economic cooperation, Engagement

I. Introduction

What explains the dramatic ups and downs of inter-Korean economic relations over the past two decades? Those relations kicked off at the turn of the twenty-first century under then South Korean President Kim Dae-jung's "sunshine policy" and expanded under the next president, Roh Moo-hyun. For the decade-long sunshine period, South Korean cruise ships set sail to Mount Kumgang in North Korea, carrying tourists, and the two Koreas opened a joint industrial complex in Kaesung (hereafter the KIC). However, economic cooperation between the two Koreas soon lost steam. The next president, conservative Lee Myung-bak, halted all economic projects with North Korea except the industrial complex in response to growing belligerence from Pyongyang. In February 2016, another conservative president, Park Geun-hye, shut down the joint industrial complex, severing the only remaining straw of economic ties between the two Koreas.

The conventional explanation for these ups and downs has been differences in the beliefs of political leaders.[1] That is, liberal presidents such as Kim and Roh pursued engagement policies with a firm belief that growing economic interdependence with North Korea would help it come out of isolation and moderate its foreign policy, while the conservative next two leaders were skeptical. This study puts the conventional wisdom under scrutiny, for two reasons. First, the fact that Kim and Roh pursued economic engagement does not explain why they achieved it. The conventional wisdom begs the question of how the leaders' beliefs, a variable on the individual level, became causally salient instead of other systemic and domestic political variables. The inference that there was economic cooperation just because the two liberal leaders embraced a noble vision is facile, risking confusing a necessary with a sufficient cause. Second, the intuitive conventional account has serious empirical flaws. The overall volume of

---

1 Jong-seok Lee, *Peace on a Knife's Edge: The Inside Story of Roh Moo-hyun's North Korea Policy*, trans. Se-woong Koo (Stanford, Calif.: The Walter H. Shorenstein Asia-Pacific Research Center, 2017); Chung-in Moon and David I. Steinberg, *Kim Dae-jung Government and Sunshine Policy*: Promises and Challenges (Seoul: Yonsei University Press, 1999); Chung-in Moon, *The Sunshine Policy: In Defense of Engagement as a Path to Peace in Korea* (Seoul: Yonsei University Press, 2012); Key-young Son, *South Korean Engagement Policies and North Korea: Identities, Norms and the Sunshine Policy* (New York: Routledge, 2009).

economic exchanges between the two states was growing even during conservative rule in Seoul, despite some fluctuations. In fact, it peaked during the Park presidency, a few months before the KIC closure. Another empirical problem of the conventional wisdom is related to the ongoing development of the Korean Peninsula. The incumbent president, Moon Jae-in, is known as an heir of the sunshine policy. However, as of September 2020, the two Koreas have shown no sign of resuming economic interactions. What, then, has decided the fate of economic relations between Seoul and Pyongyang?

This paper puts forward two arguments. First, political beliefs certainly made a difference in the rise and fall of inter-Korean economic relations, but not the way the conventional account has suggested. All four presidents pursued engagement. What divided them was their expectations about what North Korea should do. Liberal leaders were definitely more patient, sympathetic, and tolerant with Pyongyang. They believed that economic relations between the two Koreas must go on even with the north's provocations because they would help the North Korean leadership in Pyongyang realize that its external environment is benign and thus that it can eventually lower its guard. In contrast, the conservative leaders believed that Seoul should be ready to cut off economic ties with the north if Pyongyang behaved unacceptably and should expand the cooperation if Pyongyang behaved positively. Second, in addition to political leaders' beliefs, two external factors must be incorporated into the account: North Korea's response to engagement efforts from Seoul and support from the United States. To set off a virtuous cycle of economic engagement, a target's positive response to an initiator's call is crucial. If one side adopts a 'nice' strategy and both sides follow the rule of reciprocity, cooperation can evolve. The role of a third-party actor matters as well. The literature on conflict management has found that third-party actors have been important in either restraining or intensifying bilateral rivalries. For Korean Peninsula affairs, no state can be as decisive as the United States.

Throughout the Kim Dae-jung and Roh Moo-hyun periods, the two Koreas were able to expand economic ties both in scope and in quantity, as Pyongyang responded favorably to Seoul's sunshine policies and Washington threw its support behind Seoul's initiatives. In contrast, economic cooperation shrank in scope and the overall volume of exchange went up and down during the conservatives' rule in Seoul. Seoul's proposals for the expansion of economic cooperation were contingent on the progress of denuclearization; instead, Pyongyang accelerated its nuclear armament. The outcome was the severance of economic ties between the two Koreas in February 2016 by Ms. Park. It is also noteworthy that Washington has been increasingly critical of business projects pumping cash into Pyongyang since North Korea's fourth nuclear test in 2016. The U.N.-sponsored sanctions against North Korea have become stronger and tighter. They have targeted Kim Jong-un's financial resources enabling his nuclear weapon programs. This external condition forecasts poor prospects for Mr. Moon Jae-in's wish to restore economic ties between Seoul and Pyongyang.

This paper starts from theoretical debates about the pacifying effects of economic interdependence on states' foreign relations and notable scholarly works identifying hurdles impeding the growth of inter-Korean economic relations. It then discusses how, in theory, individual political leader's beliefs, positive or negative response from Pyongyang to Seoul's economic engagement and the absence or presence of support for it from Washington should work in tandem to decide the destiny of inter-Korean economic relations. A case study of South Korea–North Korea economic relations from 1998 to 2016 follows. The rich historical narrative presented here reveals the causal significance of the two external variables in determining the fate of the economic relations between the two Koreas, and helps check whether the conventional account stressing individual leaders' beliefs convincingly explains the ups and downs of the economic ties between Seoul and Pyongyang for the past two decades. This historical account is based on in-depth face-to-face and telephone interviews with former high-ranking government officials from the Kim Dae-jung to Park Geun-hye administrations, as well as extensive secondary sources. It also incorporates South Korean presidents' writings before their arrival in office, to examine how their preexisting vision and strategic goals for economic cooperation with the north have played out in their policy toward Pyongyang during their tenure in office. The case study also discusses Mr. Moon Jae-in's efforts to revive engagement with the north and headwinds confronting him.

II. Existing Literature

Whether economic interdependence induces peace has been a bone of contention among scholars of international relations. Liberal scholars have long believed that economic cooperation sets off for states a virtuous cycle leading to greater prosperity and more peaceful relations as economic exchanges enable common interests to emerge.[2] In contrast, realists are pessimistic about the pacifying effects of economic interdependence because of concerns about dependence and relative gains.[3] The debate between liberals and realists has inspired extensive research investigating the conditions under which economic interdependence fosters better political relations among states. Some scholars assert that it works only among democracies.[4] Another group argues that economic interdependence fosters peace only among advanced capitalist economies that share a common interest in maintaining stable financial and trade flows and contract-intensive economies backed by effective legal systems.[5] Still others call for attention to systemic variables such as the existence of regional trade institutions.[6]

The liberal hope that economic interactions would moderate foreign policies proved naïve in inter-Korean relations. Even during the heyday of economic engagement by Seoul, Pyongyang's belligerence persisted. It continued to wage military provocations against Seoul and, ultimately, develop nuclear weapons. The Korean Peninsula also lacks regional trade institutions; and while South Korea is an advanced capitalist democracy, North Korea is far from either status. The peninsula appears to be a barren ground for the seed of economic cooperation.

However, the breakdown of inter-Korean economic cooperation in just two

---

2 See Bruce Russett and John Oneal, *Triangulating Peace: Democracy, Interdependence, and International Organizations* (New York: W. W. Norton, 2001)

3 John J. Mearsheimer, *The Tragedy of Great Power Politics* (New York: W. W. Norton, 2001); Kenneth N. Waltz, *Theory of International Politics* (Reading, Mass.: Addison-Wesley, 1979).

4 Christopher F. Gelpi and Joseph M. Grieco, "Democracy, Interdependence, and the Sources of the Liberal Peace," *Journal of Peace Research*, Vol. 45, No. 1 (January 2008), pp. 17-34.

5 Erik Gartzke, "The Capitalist Peace," *American Journal of Political Science*, Vol. 51, No. 1 (January 2007), pp. 166-191; Michael Mousseau, "Market Prosperity, Democratic Consolidation and Democratic Peace," *Journal of Conflict Resolution*, Vol. 44, No. 4 (August 2000), pp. 472-507.

6 Edward D. Mansfield and Jon C. Pevehouse, "Trade Blocs, Trade Flows, and International Conflict," *International Organization*, Vol. 54, No. 4 (Autumn 2000), pp. 775-808.

decades does not necessarily validate realists' pessimistic view of the pacifying effects of economic interdependence. The Korean Peninsula is certainly the last place on this planet where the Cold War legacy is still lingering. Security concerns are acute between the two Koreas. However, the realist insight does not explain why Mr. Moon Jae-in endeavors to restore inter-Korean economic relations despite the advancement of North Korean nuclear capabilities. This incomplete explanation and the absence in the Korean Peninsula of many conditions necessary for economic interdependence to set off a virtuous cycle direct our attention to other political factors pertinent to inter-Korean relations.

Two fairly recent scholarly works contrast thriving economic relations across the Taiwan Strait with withering ones on the Korean Peninsula. They agree that economic cooperation across the Taiwan Strait is likely to continue to grow while inter-Korean relations are vulnerable to backpedaling. But they disagree about the sources of this variance. Scott Kastner has focused on the causal significance of the economic groups backing political leaders. According to him, leaders must surely consider the extent to which their policy decisions deviate from the interest of the coalitions that back them, else they risk defections.[7] Specifically, leaders backed by internationalist economic interests should expect to pay high political costs for pursuing policies detrimental to foreign economic exchange.[8] By this logic, the future for inter-Korean economic relations is not bright. In North Korea's political structure, hard-line nationalists are unlikely to be tolerant of bilateral economic exchanges with the south, and internationalists' economic interests are marginalized. It should be no surprise that North Korea recurrently stages provocations disrupting commercial interests and walks away from existing foreign economic arrangements.

Chan, Hu, and Sohn, employing two-level theory, show that Seoul's hope for inter-Korean economic cooperation has been constrained by domestic and international settings. According to them, Washington's confrontational approach to Pyongyang during the George W. Bush administration, including the axis of evil speech and the U.S. invasion of Iraq, accelerated Pyongyang's nuclear armament as a deterrent to a similar

7 Scott Kastner, *Political Conflict and Economic Interdependence across the Taiwan Strait and Beyond* (Stanford, Calif.: Stanford University Press, 2009), p. 22.

8 Ibid., p. 22.

attack.[9] North Korea's nuclear program and its first test in 2006 then strengthened its threatening image among South Koreans, while weakening the advocates of conciliatory policies in Seoul.[10]

These two studies share poignantly insightful pessimism about the future of economic cooperation between the two Koreas. Still, their explanations of the rise and fall of economic ties between Seoul and Pyongyang remain incomplete. For example, Chan and his colleagues cannot explain why economic cooperation between the two Koreas grew despite George W. Bush's open antagonism against North Korea's leadership. And Kastner cannot explain why inter-Korean economic relations had good times as well as bad ones? Still, both studies shed light on two important variables potentially determining the fate of inter-Korean economic relations: Pyongyang's response to Seoul's proposals and Washington's influence on the course of engagement. There is good reason to investigate how the two variables interact with South Korean political leaders' beliefs in economic engagement to decide the destiny of Seoul's proposals for economic cooperation with Pyongyang.

III. Argument

The role individual political leaders' beliefs play in international relations should not be overlooked. Personal beliefs held by individual leaders matter, as they provide road maps for decision makers who formulate and implement policy.[11] Elizabeth Saunders provides a similar claim. Noting that three U.S. presidents, Dwight D. Eisenhower, John F. Kennedy, and Lyndon B. Johnson, adopted different intervention strategies in the U.S. war in Vietnam, she attributes these different intervention strategies to different beliefs about the origins of threat—beliefs formed long before leaders faced actual crises and

9 Steve Chan, Richard Hu, and Injoo Sohn, "Politics of Détente: Comparing Korea and Taiwan," *The Pacific Review*, Vol. 26, No. 2 (2013), p. 213.

10 Ibid., p. 206.

11 Daniel L. Byman and Kenneth M. Pollack, "Let Us Now Praise Great Men: Bringing the Stateman Back In," *International Security*, Vol. 25, No. 4 (Spring 2001), pp. 107–146; Judith Goldstein and Robert O. Keohane, *Ideas and Foreign Policy: Beliefs, Institutions, and Political Change* (Ithaca, N.Y.: Cornell University Press, 1993).

even before they took office.[12]

The analyses provide a very useful insight for this study. South Korean political leaders' differing beliefs about the nature of the North Korean regime and what inter-Korean economic cooperation can do to Pyongyang might have shaped different approaches to dealing with North Korea. Liberal presidents were more sympathetic to North Korea than the conservative ones. Therefore, they were more tolerant than the conservative leaders. For liberal leaders, inter-Korean economic cooperation had to go on despite the north's military provocations, as it would help Pyongyang come out of its paranoid worldview and lower its guard in the long run. In contrast, the conservative leaders believed that inter-Korean economic cooperation should not fall into unilateral giving without return. Seoul should be ready to sever economic ties with the north in case of Pyongyang's unacceptable behaviors as well as expand the cooperation in case of Pyongyang's positive behavioral changes.

The importance of reciprocity in promoting cooperation and easing tension among states cannot be overstated.[13] International politics has no central authority to enforce promises made by states. However, Axelrod and Keohane have proposed that cooperation among states is still possible. Cooperation can get started by even a small cluster of actors who are prepared to reciprocate.[14] To set off a virtuous cycle of economic cooperation, a target's positive response to an initiator's call is crucial. A state can adopt a unilateral rapprochement toward a former enemy in the hope of making its strategic environment less dangerous. If one side takes the initiative and adopts a 'nice' strategy and both sides follow the rule of reciprocity, cooperation can evolve through a tit-for-tat mechanism.[15]

The implication drawn from the discussion above is straightforward: it takes two to tango. A state seeking to befriend its adversary sends a signal of benign intent through an offer on a matter of mutual interest. If the target state accurately interprets the act of

---

12 Elizabeth N. Saunders, *Leaders at War: How Presidents Shape Military Interventions* (Ithaca, N.Y.: Cornell University Press, 2011), p. 3.

13 See Robert Axelrod, *The Evolution of Cooperation* (New York: Basic Books, 1984); pp. 502-528; Robert O. Keohane, "Reciprocity in International Relations," *International Organization*, Vol. 40, No. 1 (Winter 1986), pp. 1–27.

14 Axelrod, *The Evolution of Cooperation*, p. 173.

15 Matthew Evangelista, "Cooperation Theory and Disarmament Negotiations in the 1950s," *World Politics*, Vol. 42, No. 4 (July 1990), p. 504.

accommodation as a potential peace offering and reciprocates, then the stage has been set for moving towards better relations, while rivalry will continue if the target exploits the sender's intent and fails to respond in kind.[16] On the Korean Peninsula, Seoul's initiative for economic engagement with Pyongyang is heavily dependent on how the north responds to it. Economic ties between the two will expand if Pyongyang unclenches its fist and holds the hand Seoul has extended, while they will shrink if Pyongyang turns away from Seoul's engagement proposal.

Another important variable to be considered is the role of a third party.[17] Mistrust arises when two disputants are uncertain about whether the other side prefers to reciprocate cooperation or exploit it. Then a third party may step in to resolve this problem. Great powers have served as mediators in many international conflicts and crises. For example, the United States has attempted to help mend relations between former enemies such as Egypt versus Israel and India versus Pakistan. Of course, not all international interventions have been successful. However, there is no dispute that third party players have been important in either restraining or intensifying bilateral rivalry.

For Korean Peninsula affairs, China and the United States have been the two most important outside actors. Beijing has constantly supported international efforts to build economic ties with Pyongyang. China has engaged with North Korea economically in the hope of encouraging its partner to follow in the steps of its own economic reforms and modernization.[18] It has welcomed any economic help toward its impoverished neighbor. In contrast, Washington has oscillated between support for and opposition to Seoul's economic engagement plans. What the United States does with South Korea's North Korean policy is certainly a key variable deciding the fate of inter-Korean economic relations.

The discussion above suggests that the destiny of economic cooperation between

---

16 Charles A. Kupchan, *How Enemies Become Friends: The Sources of Stable Peace* (Princeton, N.J.: Princeton University Press, 2010), p. 38.

17 Andrew H. Kydd, "When Can Mediators Build Trust?" *American Political Science Review*, Vol. 100, No. 3 (August 2006), pp. 449-462; Stephen John Stedman, "Spoiler Problem in Peace Processes," *International Security*, Vol. 22, No. 2 (Fall 1997), pp. 5-53; Barbara F. Walter, *Committing to Peace: The Successful Settlement of Civil Wars* (Princeton, N.J.: Princeton University Press, 2002).

18 Tat Yan Kong, "China's Engagement-oriented Strategy towards North Korea: Achievements and Limitations," *The Pacific Review*, Vol. 31, No. 1 (2018), pp. 76-95.

the two Koreas depends on what political leaders in Seoul expect from economic relations with Pyongyang and whether both Pyongyang and Washington respond favorably to Seoul's proposal for inter-Korean economic cooperation. Kim Dae-jung and Roh Moo-hyun saw economic cooperation with North Korea as necessary to ease tension on the peninsula by moderating its belligerence and ushering it into the world economy. Economic engagement had to go on even without concrete reciprocal measures from North Korea to ease tension. It was imperative to assure North Korean leaders that their external environment was benign. The two liberal presidents' common beliefs drove them to stay with economic engagement despite sporadic military provocations from North Korea. In contrast, both Lee Myung-bak and Park Geun-hye saw inter-Korean economic relations as an instrument to induce North Korea's behavioral changes in military affairs. They believed that the engagement should proceed in a reciprocal manner. Inter-Korean economic cooperation could be expanded if Pyongyang made meaningful progress toward denuclearization or waged no military provocations. It could decline otherwise, as the two leaders would lose hope for the strategic utility of economic inducement.

It is noteworthy that the difference in the beliefs of political leaders was a variable, not the variable, making inter-Korean economic relations materialize, expand, shrink, or even end. How Pyongyang responded to South Korea's engagement policy mattered as well. Inter-Korean economic cooperation would get momentum when Pyongyang accepted the hand Seoul extended. Moderate behaviors from Pyongyang perceived as reciprocal to Seoul's goodwill would provide a tailwind for engagement supporters, while its belligerence would narrow Seoul's latitude of action. Finally, whether Washington supported Seoul's engagement was also crucial. Given dense economic interdependence and asymmetric security relations, Seoul's North Korean policy had to be under constant consultation with Washington. Seoul's room for action would broaden with Washington's support while it would narrow with Washington's opposition.

IV. Case Studies

1. Sunrise: The Start and Expansion of Inter-Korean Economic Cooperation

As President Kim Dae-jung assumed the presidency of South Korea in February 1998, he carried out his own vision of peaceful coexistence and phased unification between the two Koreas. His peace initiative has been better known as the sunshine policy, deriving its name from Aesop's fable in which sun and wind competed to strip off a gentleman's coat (he took off the coat in response to warm sunshine rather than strong wind). President Kim firmly believed that in order to reduce tension on the peninsula and induce behavioral changes in the north, the first task should be to convince the regime that its external environment was benign.

The beginning of the sunshine policy was humble. In April 1998, Pyongyang rejected Seoul's proposal to send 200,000 tons of fertilizers in return for Pyongyang's agreement to discuss the issue of reuniting separated families. At the beginning, it interpreted the sunshine policy as an insidious scheme to "undress the north in all aspects of politics, economy, and military affairs." Furthermore, North Korea tested Mr. Kim's pacifist ideals in multiple cases. It infiltrated a submarine into the East Sea in June 1998; it tested a long-range missile in August 1998; and its navy clashed with a South Korean vessel in the Yellow Sea in June 1999. Despite such military provocations, President Kim remained steadfast in pursuing a warm relationship with Pyongyang.

His tenacious pursuit of the sunshine policy began to bear fruit by late 1998. Hyundai Asan, an affiliate of the South Korean conglomerate Hyundai, obtained from Pyongyang permission to develop a tourist resort at Mount Kumgang. The tour project was touted as the first tangible outcome of Mr. Kim's new North Korean policy. Later, he held a summit in June 2000 with North Korean leader Kim Jong-il, the first summit between the two Koreas in history; a few hundred families separated since the 1953 Korean War cease-fire united; North and South Korean governments agreed to create an industrial complex with South Korean capital and a North Korean workforce in Kaesong just a few miles north of the demarcation line. The next president of South Korea, Roh Moo-hyun, inherited the spirit of Kim's sunshine policy and expanded economic

Figure 1. Amount of inter-Korean trade, 1994-2018

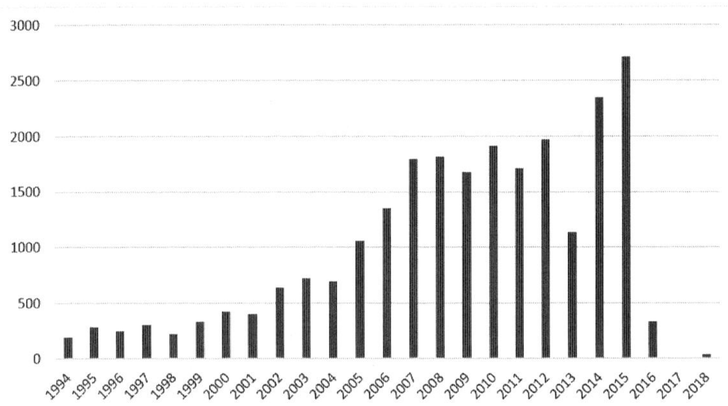

Amount Unit: Million USD
Source: Amount of Inter-Korean Trade, Ministry of Unification, Republic of Korea, https://unikorea.go.kr/unikorea/business/statistics/

Figure 4. Humanitarian Aid to North Korea from South Korea

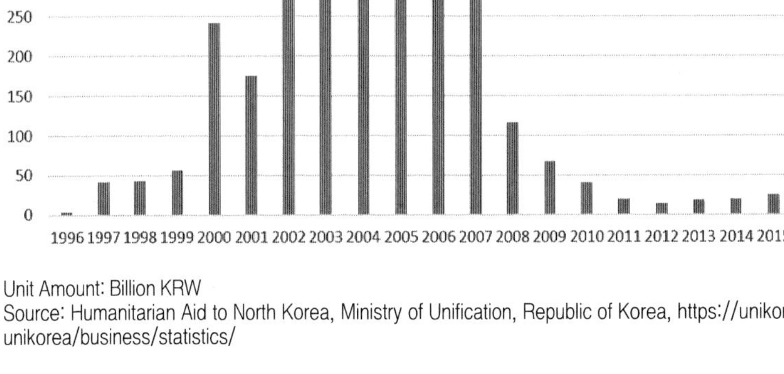

Unit Amount: Billion KRW
Source: Humanitarian Aid to North Korea, Ministry of Unification, Republic of Korea, https://unikorea.go.kr/unikorea/business/statistics/

ties with Pyongyang. The KIC opened in December 2004 and began to churn out a wide range of products. Roh also held an inter-Korean summit and signed the Peace Declaration of October 4, 2007.

During the sunshine period of 1998–2007, inter-Korean economic exchange displayed exponential growth in both quantity and quality. The volume of exchange grew by a factor of more than eight, as figure 1 below shows. After the KIC began to operate, its production output increased by a factor of more than twelve until 2007, from 1.4 million USD to 18.5 million USD, and the number of North Korean workers multiplied by four during the same time span. Humanitarian aid also expanded as figure 2 indicates below. Governmental and civilian aid from the south to the north increased more than tenfold over the Kim and Roh administrations.

What made all this possible? The conventional wisdom attributes the growth of inter-Korean economic relations to the longstanding personal faith of both Kim Dae-jung and Roh Moo-hyun in the need to offer North Korea economic incentives and induce the pacifying effects of economic cooperation. For example, Kim Dae-jung had proposed increased economic exchanges as an essential element of his three principles of peace on the Korean Peninsula long before his arrival in office. According to him, political, economic, social, cultural, and humanitarian interactions restore common national identity, and increased economic exchanges promote common interests.[19] The sunshine policy during his presidency can be seen as an embodiment of his longtime conviction. Mr. Roh Moo-hyun was on the same page. His writings after his retirement from the presidency consistently testify that the primary goal of Roh's North Korean policy was building peace and pursuing common prosperity between the two Koreas.[20]

But there were other factors contributing to the expansion of economic interactions during the Kim and Roh period: Pyongyang's receptiveness and Washington's support. Granted, at first Pyongyang balked. Then it discovered the benefits of economic cooperation with South Korea. The joint economic projects seemed to be a risk-free way to open up to the outside world to earn hard currency.[21]

---

19 Kim Dae-jung, *Building Peace and Democracy: Kim Dae-jung's Philosophy and Dialogue* (New York, N.Y.: Korean Independent Monitor, 1987), p. 232.
20 See Roh Moo-hyun, *Sŏnggong-gwa Chwajŏl* (Seoul: Hakkoje, 2009), pp. 210–220.
21 Congressional Research Service, *South Korea: Sunshine Policy and Its Political Context*, CRS Report for Congress, February 12, 2001, p. 19.

They allowed Pyongyang to extract benefits from Seoul essentially on its own terms. For example, the wages that South Korean companies paid for the workforce in the Kaesong industrial complex went to the North Korean government, which in turn paid individual laborers. Under this arrangement, the North Korean government had more than 100 million USD in foreign credits annually.[22] The same mechanism was applied to the tourist project at Mount Kumgang. In return for the exclusive rights to the tour project, Hyundai was obliged to pay 942 million USD to the north in monthly installments over a span of six years and three months.[23] Given the shortage of foreign credit due to limited access to foreign markets and the absence of revenue sources as a result of economic stagnation, getting involved in such profitable economic activities with few conditions attached was a no-brainer for North Korea.

But also, the sunshine policy enjoyed support from Washington. Bill Clinton wrote in his memoir, "I supported Kim Dae-jung's outreach to North Korea so long as it was clear that neither of us would allow the proliferation of missiles, nuclear weapons, or other weapons of mass destruction."[24] The next George W. Bush administration was originally reluctant to pick up North Korean policy where the former administration left off. [25] President Bush himself had little trust in North Korean leadership. He also believed that the previous administration had offered concessions to North Korea in return for a pledge to abandon its nuclear weapon programs, but to no avail. Nonetheless, throughout his tenure, Washington never vetoed Seoul's adherence to the sunshine policy. For example, after a review of the Clinton administration's North Korean policy, Colin Powell, secretary of state during the Bush administration's first term, made it clear that the United States would continue to engage North Korea.

2. Sunset: The Decline and End of Inter-Korean Economic Cooperation

Lee Myung-bak ended a decade-long rule by liberal presidents in South Korea. Lee and the people around him shared a belief that North Korean policy under the previous Kim and Roh administrations was flawed in many ways. His writing before

---

22 Yong-pyo Hong, "Interview with Sindonga: Taewha? Pukhaek Kodohwa Sigan Pŏrŏjul Ppun" [in Korean], Sindonga, April 2016, https://shindonga.donga.com/3/all/13/531992/2

23 Congressional Research Service, *South Korea*, p. 18.

24 Bill Clinton, *My Life* (New York: Alfred A. Knopf, 2004), p. 828.

25 George W. Bush, *Decision Points* (New York: Crown Publishers, 2010), p. 422.

his presidential campaign reveals his critiques against the sunshine policy: engagement spoiled North Korea by giving unilaterally without reciprocation and the former administrations had not paid enough attention to the problem of a nuclear North Korea.[26] Lee's administration set correcting these flaws as its top priority. However, it is noteworthy that Mr. Lee did not bid farewell to economic engagement with the north. On the contrary, he pledged that Seoul would continue the joint economic projects with Pyongyang.[27] What he wanted to discard was unprincipled unilateral giving from Seoul. He believed that North Korean policy should be designed and implemented to induce meaningful changes from North Korea. In other words, existing or future economic cooperation between the two should serve the goal of denuclearization and volitional reforms of North Korea. The outcome of his philosophy was the policy labeled "Vision 3000: Denuclearization and Openness." The initiative, also known as "De-nuke, Open 3000," pledged that South Korea would help North Korea achieve a per capita income of 3000 USD within 10 years in exchange for North Korea's denuclearization.[28] A comprehensive assistance package, covering the economy, education, finance, and infrastructure, would follow Pyongyang's voluntary denuclearization, and Seoul would help Pyongyang transform into an export-driven economy and get access to foreign investment.

North Korea responded to this initiative with a series of hostilities throughout Lee's five-year tenure. To name a few, North Korea conducted two nuclear tests, one in May 2009 and another in February 2013; launched a torpedo attack against the South Korean naval vessel *Cheonan* in March 2010; and bombarded Yeonpyong Island in November 2010. Proponents of engagement have claimed that military provocations in 2010 around the Yellow Sea and other belligerent acts should be understood as an expression of Pyongyang's sense of betrayal and disappointment that no hope existed for improvement in economic and political relationships between the two Koreas under conservative presidents.[29] The end of the sunshine rendered the status quo unbearable.

---

26 Lee Myung-bak, *Lee Myung-bak's Hŭndŭlliji Annŭn Yaksok* (Seoul: Random House Korea, 2007), p. 151.
27 Ibid., p. 167.
28 Lee Myung-bak, *Taetongryŏng-ŭi Shigan 2008–2013* (Seoul: RH Korea, 2015), p. 304.
29 See Keun-shik Kim. *Taepuk P'oyong Ch ŏngch'aek- ŭi Chinhwa-rŭl Wihayŏ* (Seoul, Korea: Hanwul Academy, 2011).

For Pyongyang, there was no remaining option but to go back to its former stance.

Nevertheless, the Lee administration was still committed to engagement. The volume of inter-Korean trade throughout the first two years of the Lee presidency was larger than that at any point during the sunshine decade. It was the scope of economic interactions that shrank throughout President Lee's tenure. For example, Lee suspended Mount Kumgang tours after a female tourist was shot dead by a North Korean soldier and in 2011, after the sinking of the *Cheonan*, imposed a ban on new investment in the KIC and inter-Korean trade, known as the May 24 measure. But these were all retaliatory measures against Pyongyang's provocations.

Another proof that the Lee administration stayed on the course of engagement is that it left the industrial complex in Kaesong still operating. According to a high-ranking official involved in North Korean affairs, President Lee was very close to shutting it down in response to the *Cheonan* attack, but he changed his mind at the last minute before the announcement of the May 24 measure. Why? The reason was that the administration recognized the importance of keeping in hand some leverage to both reward and punish North Korea's behavior in the future.[30] President Lee wrote in his memoir, "we should not put all eggs in one basket."[31] The outcome was the restoration of economic interaction in 2012 above the level of 2010.

Why, then, did his new approach to North Korea end up fluctuating, with ups and downs in economic relations? His new North Korea policy enjoyed full support from both the outgoing Bush administration and the incoming Obama administration. It was Pyongyang that rejected Seoul's new approach. Critics of Lee's North Korean policy contend that "De-nuke, Open 3000" was unrealistic from the beginning and that Pyongyang's rejection should not be a surprise. North Korea has never considered South Korea its counterpart in the nuclear weapons issue. Moreover, it did not consider 3000 USD close to an adequate incentive when weighed against its regime security and the cost it had paid to advance the program.[32] But a more fundamental reason for the rejection lay in North Korea's domestic politics—specifically, in the precarious power

30 Author's interview with a high-ranking official of the Lee Myung-bak government, June 18, 2018.

31 Lee, *Taetongryŏng-ŭi Shigan*, p. 323.

32 Moon, *The Sunshine Policy*, p. 120.

transition from Kim Jong-il to his son Kim Jong-un. Kim Jong-il suffered a stroke in 2008. From then on, the leadership succession became the most urgent issue inside Pyongyang. Kim Jong-il's third son, Kim Jong-un, rose to be the heir by fall 2010. But Kim Jong-un was too young and inexperienced. He did not have much apprenticeship time for running a country confronting many chronic economic problems, including energy shortage and starvation. The failure of currency reform in 2009 had aggravated economic hardship and people's complaints. Domestic political instability increases the incentive to promote domestic cohesion by inciting foreign crisis. This explains a series of militaristic provocations and the assertiveness of North Korea since 2009.[33] The ups and downs of inter-Korean economic cooperation during Lee's five-year rule had less to do with Lee than with Kim Jong-un.

Another conservative politician, Park Geun-hye, came to power in 2013. Her North Korean policy was labelled as a "Korean Peninsula Trust-Building Process" and known as *trustpolitik*. A guiding principle of her North Korean policy is well described in her 2011 article in *Foreign Affairs*. Her policy started from a realistic analysis that hostility was lingering and trust was missing in the relations between Seoul and Pyongyang. Therefore, the starting point should be building trust between the two. North Korea must keep its agreements made with South Korea and the international community to establish trust, and there must be assured consequences for actions taken.[34] North Korea's military provocation must not be forgiven, but its steps toward genuine reconciliation would be matched.[35] In short, her road map was that the south and the north should build up trust first by starting cooperation in small things; create an atmosphere for denuclearization; and then advance economic cooperation further with the resolution of nuclear issues.

However, North Korea greeted her proposal with a series of military provocations. Indeed, her first three years in office were full of escalation of tension by Pyongyang. First, on February 12, 2013, two weeks before her inauguration, North Korea conducted its third nuclear test. Second, in spring 2013 North Korea closed the Kaesong Industrial

---

33 Dong Sun Lee, "Causes of North Korean Belligerence," *Australian Journal of International Affairs*, Vol. 66, No 2 (April 2012), pp. 107–108.

34 Park Geun-hye, "A New Kind of Korea: Building Trust between Seoul and Pyongyang," *Foreign Affairs*, Vol. 90, No. 5 (September/October 2011), p. 14.

35 Ibid., p. 16.

Complex for three months, refusing to send workers to the complex. Third, it launched multiple missile tests—not just short- and intermediate-range but long-range missiles.

Until 2015, President Park pursued engagement. Inter-Korean trade increased, and South Korea provided humanitarian aid through international organizations. What ended President Park's engagement was North Korea's fourth nuclear test in early 2016, followed by the ICBM test. In response, President Park cut off all economic exchanges with North Korea. She declared a shutdown of the KIC and a halt to all types of humanitarian aid going to North Korea. What explains her decision?

Ms. Park's messages to South Koreans and my own interviews with both high- and mid-ranking officials in the Blue House and the government involved in the decision-making point to two reasons for her bold decision to close the KIC. First, President Park abandoned her hope for North Korea's voluntary denuclearization. Actually, the leadership in Seoul was optimistic about Pyongyang's exercising restraints in nuclear and missile tests through the second half of 2015. For the period, positive signs were looming: a series of high-level talks between the two were held, and there was a reunion of separated families. A high-level official recalled, "the leadership in the Blue House believed that the moment for easing tension had finally arrived."[36] However, it turned out to be a false conjecture. It became obvious that Pyongyang's determination to be a nuclear power was irreversible. The two tests were clear signs that North Korea had no intention of giving up nuclear weapons. The patience of the Park administration ran out.

Second, the security implications of the nuclear and missile tests in early 2016 were staggering. A nuclear North Korea with short-, mid-, and long-range missiles is a grave threat to the security of South Korea. Short-range missiles have already targeted the entire south. And North Korea's capability to strike American bases in the western Pacific or the American mainland with ICBMs carrying nuclear warheads may undermine the U.S. resolve and capability to take part in armed conflict between the two Koreas, a dreadful scenario that puts South Korea's survival in jeopardy.[37] Aware of these security implications, President Park described the nuclear test of January 2016 as "a grave threat

---

36 Author's interview with a high-ranking official of the Park Geun-hye government, September 19, 2019.

37 Il Park, Ji-young Park, and Kang Choi, *Pukhaekchindan-kwa Taeŭng* (Seoul, Korea: Asan Institute for Policy Studies, 2016), pp. 73–77.

not only to South Korea's security but also to its existence and future."[38]

Once North Korea's nuclear aspiration and its grave security implications were confirmed, President Park could not stay with the course of engagement. She needed to step up to call on a new kind of international response to North Korea's provocations. Within the Park government a consensus formed that Seoul should respond to Pyongyang's provocation with unwavering firmness, since the nuclear test fundamentally changed the security environment across Northeast Asia and the nature of North Korean nuclear capabilities. Earlier, China and Russia, skeptical about forming international sanctions that would tighten cash inflow to North Korea, had pointed to the KIC's continued operation.[39] To silence the skepticism, Park had to close the KIC.

In President Park's State Affairs Address to the National Assembly on February 16 (equivalent to the State of the Union Address in the United States), she asserted that cutting off economic relations with the north was a desperate measure to block the flow of foreign currencies into the north in order to "prevent it from upgrading its nuclear and missile capabilities."[40] Revenue generated from economic exchanges with the south, she said, had flowed to the leadership of the North Korean Workers' Party, which oversees nuclear and missile development, without any trickle-down effect improving the general well-being of the public. International actors were designing stronger sanctions to cut off North Korea's access to foreign credits in order to frustrate its weapons programs. South Korea would be the primary victim of North Korea's nuclear weapons and missiles. "As the party with the most at stake," Park argued, "it is only right for the south to use every means to make the north give up its nuclear ambitions."

Seoul paid a price for shutting down the KIC. The Park administration had to raise funds and help businesses embroiled in unexpected losses as a result of the closure. That is, Ms. Park's decision to close down the KIC in early spring was a delivery of costly signals to both Pyongyang and the world. To Pyongyang, President Park conveyed her anger and disappointment. To the world, she called for stronger action, showing Seoul's determination to incur any cost to stop nuclear threats from North Korea.

---

38 Park Geun-hye, "President's Press Conference at Chŏngwadae," January 13, 2016.

39 Author's interview with a senior diplomat of the Park Geun-hye government, December 18, 2019.

40 Park Geun-hye, "President's Address to the National Assembly," February 16, 2016.

3. Sunrise Again? Moon Jae-in's Dream to Restore Economic Ties with the North

President Moon Jae-in, who came to office in May 2017, has portrayed himself as an heir of the sunshine policy. Multiple writings he published before he held power testify that the basic philosophy of his North Korean policy is squarely aligned with that of Kim Dae-jung and Roh Moo-hyun.[41] Throughout his campaign, he pledged to revive the sunshine policy. Since being elected, he has vowed to restore economic cooperation with the north.

Since early 2018, Kim Jong-un has answered Moon's call for détente and showed refreshed interest in resuming inter-Korean economic relations. Kim and Moon have met four times so far, including three summits in 2018 alone. The ease of tension culminated in Mr. Moon's visit to Pyongyang in September 2018 and the joint declaration by Kim and Moon. In the declaration, they agreed to normalize the KIC and the Mt. Kumgang tourism project. [42] But, as of summer 2020, there was little sign of the reactivation—because now, the United States is reluctant to support it. The Trump administration has opposed economic interaction between Seoul and Pyongyang without meaningful steps forward toward denuclearization by North Korea. Trump has been adamant in keeping tight and strictly enforcing international sanctions designed to cut the flow of cash into North Korea. Secretary of State Mike Pompeo and Harry Harris, the U.S. Ambassador to South Korea, have repeatedly stressed in unison that sanctions against North Korea will be in place until Pyongyang makes significant progress in denuclearization and that the improvement in inter-Korean relations should keep pace with the denuclearization of North Korea.[43] Given this context, the restoration of inter-Korean economic ties appears to be remote.

---

41 See Moon Jae-in, *Moon Jae-inŭi Him, Sarami Mŏnjŏda* (Seoul, Korea: Purple Cow, 2012), p. 85.

42 "Pyongyang Joint Declaration of September 2018," https://www.ncnk.org/node/1633

43 Gardiner Harris, "Pompeo Hails Talks with North Korea but Says Sanctions Must Continue," New York Times, September 27, 2018, https://www.nytimes.com/2018/09/27/world/asia/mike-pompeo-north-korea.html; Harry Harris, "Keynote Address: Lasting Peace?- Prospects for Peace on the Korean Peninsula and the State of the ROK-U.S. Alliance 65 Years after the Armistice Agreement" (The Asan Institute-Wilson Center Conference, Seoul, October 17, 2018) http://en.asaninst.org/contents/lasting-peace-prospects-for-peace-on-the-korean-peninsula-and-the-state-of-the-rok-u-s-alliance-65-years-after-the-armistice-agreement-2/

V. Conclusion

This study challenges the conventional account that the fate of inter-Korean economic relations has depended solely on individual political leaders' ideology. Two liberal and two conservative presidents in Seoul all agreed that engagement with the north was necessary. The difference was not whether Seoul should pursue engagement but what Seoul should receive in return. Furthermore, the conventional account neglects two external factors: Pyongyang's receptiveness to Seoul's economic engagement overture and Washington's support for it.

For Kim Dae-jung and Roh Moo-hyun, inter-Korean economic cooperation was possible not simply because they believed in the importance of economic ties with the north. Pyongyang responded favorably to Seoul's engagement policy and Washington also supported it. In contrast, during the conservatives' rule, economic relations with the north fluctuated and eventually came to an end as Pyongyang rejected their proposals.

This study presents quite a somber prospect for the North Korean policy of the incumbent president, Mr. Moon Jae-in. Certainly, he is pursuing economic engagement with Pyongyang. After a series of summits with Kim Jong-un, he has portrayed himself as a mediator between North Korea and the world. He has called for easing sanctions on Pyongyang and emphasized the benefits of resuming economic relations between the two Koreas, starting from the reopening of the KIC and the Mount Kumgang tour. However, a formidable challenge lies ahead: the lack of U.S. support for easing international sanctions against North Korean weapon programs. Despite three historic summits with Kim Jong-un, President Trump consistently has asserted that the United States will continue to implement sanctions against North Korea maximally and will encourage all countries around the world to do the same. Furthermore, in the name of a secondary boycott, Washington has been willing to apply punishments against individuals and business entities that have evaded sanctions against North Korea. Any attempt of Seoul to restart economic projects with Pyongyang without Washington's support may invite the secondary boycott and jeopardize South Korea's economy. This is a risk Mr. Moon is unlikely to take.

References

Axelrod, Robert. *The Evolution of Cooperation* (New York: Basic Books, 1984).

Bush, George W. *Decision Points* (New York: Crown Publishers, 2010).

Byman, Daniel L., and Kenneth M. Pollack. "Let Us Now Praise Great Men: Bringing the Stateman Back In." *International Security*, Vol. 25, No. 4 (Spring 2001).

Chan, Steve., Hu, Richard., and Injoo Sohn. "Politics of Détente: Comparing Korea and Taiwan." *The Pacific Review*, Vol. 26, No. 2 (2013).

Clinton, Bill. *My Life* (New York: Alfred A. Knopf, 2004).

Congressional Research Service. *South Korea: Sunshine Policy and Its Political Context*, CRS Report for Congress, February 12, 2001.

Evangelista, Matthew. "Cooperation Theory and Disarmament Negotiations in the 1950s." *World Politics*, Vol. 42, No. 4 (July 1990).

Gartzke, Erik. "The Capitalist Peace." *American Journal of Political Science*, Vol. 51, No. 1 (January 2007).

Gelpi, Christopher F., and Joseph M. Grieco. "Democracy, Interdependence, and the Sources of the Liberal Peace." *Journal of Peace Research*, Vol. 45, No. 1 (January 2008).

Goldstein, Judith., and Robert O. Keohane. *Ideas and Foreign Policy: Beliefs, Institutions, and Political Change* (Ithaca, N.Y.: Cornell University Press, 1993).

Harris, Gardiner. "Pompeo Hails Talks with North Korea but Says Sanctions Must Continue." *New York Times*, September 27, 2018, https://www.nytimes.com/2018/09/27/world/asia/mike-pompeo-north-korea.html

Harris, Harry. "Keynote Address: Lasting Peace?- Prospects for Peace on the Korean Peninsula and the State of the ROK-U.S. Alliance 65 Years after the Armistice Agreement" (The Asan Institute-Wilson Center Conference, Seoul, October 17, 2018) http://en.asaninst.org/contents/lasting-peace-prospects-for-peace-on-the-korean-peninsula-and-the-state-of-the-rok-u-s-alliance-65-years-after-the-armistice-agreement-2/

Hong, Yong-pyo. "Interview with Sindonga: Taewha? Pukhaek Kodohwa Sigan Pŏrŏjul Ppun." [in Korean], *Sindonga*, April 2016, https://shindonga.donga.com/3/all/13/531992/2

Kastner, Scott. *Political Conflict and Economic Interdependence across the Taiwan Strait and Beyond* (Stanford, Calif.: Stanford University Press, 2009).

Keohane, Robert O. "Reciprocity in International Relations." *International Organization*, Vol. 40, No. 1 (Winter 1986).

Kim, Dae-jung. *Building Peace and Democracy: Kim Dae-jung's Philosophy and Dialogue* (New York, N.Y.: Korean Independent Monitor, 1987).

Kim, Keun-shik. T*aepuk P'oyong Ch ŏngch'aek- ŭi Chinhwa-rŭl Wihayŏ* (Seoul, Korea: Hanwul Academy, 2011).

Kong, Tat Yan. "China's Engagement-oriented Strategy towards North Korea: Achievements and Limitations." *The Pacific Review*, Vol. 31, No. 1 (2018).

Kupchan, Charles A. *How Enemies Become Friends: The Sources of Stable Peace* (Princeton, N.J.: Princeton University Press, 2010).

Kydd, Andrew H. "When Can Mediators Build Trust?" *American Political Science Review*, Vol. 100, No. 3 (August 2006).

Lee, Dong Sun. "Causes of North Korean Belligerence." *Australian Journal of International Affairs*, Vol. 66, No 2 (April 2012).

Lee, Jong-seok. *Peace on a Knife's Edge: The Inside Story of Roh Moo-hyun's North Korea Policy*, trans. Se-woong Koo (Stanford, Calif.: The Walter H. Shorenstein Asia-Pacific Research Center, 2017).

Lee, Myung-bak. *Taetongryŏng-ŭi Shigan* 2008–2013 (Seoul: RH Korea, 2015).

Lee, Myung-bak. *Lee Myung-bak's Hŭndŭlliji Annŭn Yaksok* (Seoul: Random House Korea, 2007).

Mansfield, Edward D., and Jon C. Pevehouse. "Trade Blocs, Trade Flows, and International Conflict." *International Organization*, Vol. 54, No. 4 (Autumn 2000).

Mearsheimer, John J. *The Tragedy of Great Power Politics* (New York: W. W. Norton, 2001).

Moon, Chung-in., and David I. Steinberg. *Kim Dae-jung Government and Sunshine Policy: Promises and Challenges* (Seoul: Yonsei University Press, 1999).

Moon, Chung-in. *The Sunshine Policy: In Defense of Engagement as a Path to Peace in Korea* (Seoul: Yonsei University Press, 2012).

Moon, Jae-in. *Moon Jae-inŭi Him, Sarami Mŏnjŏda* (Seoul, Korea: Purple Cow, 2012).

Mousseau, Michael. "Market Prosperity, Democratic Consolidation and Democratic Peace." *Journal of Conflict Resolution*, Vol. 44, No. 4 (August 2000).

Park, Geun-hye. "President's Address to the National Assembly," February 16, 2016.

Park, Geun-hye. "President's Press Conference at Chŏngwadae," January 13, 2016.

Park, Geun-hye. "A New Kind of Korea: Building Trust between Seoul and Pyongyang." *Foreign Affairs*, Vol. 90, No. 5 (September/October 2011).

Park, Il., Park, Ji-young., and Kang Choi. *Pukhaekchindan-kwa Taeŭng* (Seoul, Korea: Asan Institute for Policy Studies, 2016).

"Pyongyang Joint Declaration of September 2018," https://www.ncnk.org/node/1633

Roh, Moo-hyun, *Sŏnggong-gwa Chwajŏl* (Seoul: Hakkoje, 2009).

Saunders, Elizabeth N. *Leaders at War: How Presidents Shape Military Interventions* (Ithaca, N.Y.: Cornell University Press, 2011).

Son, Key-young. *South Korean Engagement Policies and North Korea: Identities, Norms and the Sunshine Policy* (New York: Routledge, 2009).

Stedman, Stephen John. "Spoiler Problem in Peace Processes." *International Security*, Vol. 22, No. 2 (Fall 1997).

Walter, Barbara F. *Committing to Peace: The Successful Settlement of Civil Wars* (Princeton, N.J.: Princeton University Press, 2002).

Waltz, Kenneth N. *Theory of International Politics* (Reading, Mass.: Addison-Wesley, 1979).

Implementation and Execution of the Korean Peace Process

Chapter 8.
Political Oppression, Human Rights, and UN Targeted Sanctions:
A Case of North Korea
Jiyoun Park (Jeonbuk National University)
Hyun Jin Choi (Kyung Hee University)

Chapter 9.
Bridge between South and North Korea:
Analysis of South Korean Aid to North Korea for Peace in the Korean Peninsula
Youngwan Kim (Hankuk University of Foreign Studies)
Jaeyoung Hur (Yonsei University)
Jiyoun Park (Jeonbuk National University)

Chapter 10.
What Do We Know and Do Not Know?:
Attitudes toward North Korea and Unification
Jaeyoung Hur (Yonsei University)
Sanghoon Park (University of South Carolina)

Chapter 11.
Japan and South Korea:
Can they get along by overcoming the challenges?
Atsushi Tago
(Waseda University and Peace Research Institute Oslo, PRIO)

Chapter 8

Political Oppression, Human Rights, and UN Targeted Sanctions: A Case of North Korea[1]

Jiyoun Park (Jeonbuk National University)
Hyun Jin Choi (Kyung Hee University)

Abstract

Why do some UN targeted sanctions (or 'smart' sanctions) cause collateral damage to the general population, while others minimize it? We suggest the scope and the effectiveness of smart sanctions, and the political institutions of target countries are critical determinants of sanctions' adverse effects on human rights. Leaders targeted by sanctions with a broad scope will have a greater incentive to oppress people to ward off potential support for challengers. The degree to which they can carry out successful oppression, however, hinges upon the effectiveness of sanctions implementation. Furthermore, we expect that authoritarian systems are more likely to encourage oppression than other ones. We conduct a quantitative analysis of 56 UN-imposed smart sanction episodes. Our study reveals sanctions with a broad scope that are less effective result in deteriorated human rights conditions especially in authoritarian countries. However, we find when sanctions with a narrow scope work effectively, they do not hurt innocent citizens. We illustrate the workings of our theory with an example of North Korea under smart sanctions (2006-2019).

Keywords: Smart sanctions, human rights, political oppression, UN targeted sanctions, sanction effectiveness, North Korea

---

1 This is a revised version of an article previously published by SAGE Publications, as: Park, Jiyoun and Hyun Jin Choi, "Are smart sanctions smart enough? An inquiry into when leaders oppress civilians under UN targeted sanctions," International Political Science Review (First published online June 26, 2020). Copyright © 2020 by SAGE Publications. Reprinted by permission.

I. Introduction

United Nations (UN) 'smart sanctions' are coercive economic measures against a target state — such as arms embargoes, asset freezes, and travel bans — that are designed to minimize harm to the general population who have no connections to those in power (Brzoska and Lopez, 2016: 60–78). The UN made a shift from 'comprehensive sanctions' to 'smart sanctions' after the UN sanctions on Iraq were found to have functioned as a lethal weapon against the civilian population (Lopez and Cortright, 1997: 14–18). Since then, the UN has made efforts to design economic sanctions so that they minimize the damage incurred by the general mass public but, at the same time, increase sanction effectiveness by causing direct damage to specifically identified individuals, entities, and/or regions (Biersteker Eckert, and Tourinho, 2016: 1–2). For the UN, the modified sanctions framework seemed like a much smarter policy tool than previous sanctions. Also, for human rights activists, smart sanctions appeared to be the best way to enforce norms in the global system without imposing unnecessary costs on the powerless in target countries (Drezner, 2011: 100).

However, even cleverly-designed smart sanctions aiming at political elites can sometimes hurt those with less power. Consider the example of smart sanctions against the Ivory Coast during 2005 through 2016. In 2005, the UN imposed a series of sanctions on the Ivory Coast through Security Council Resolutions (UNSCR) 1572, 1584, 1632 and 1633. The primary goals of the sanctions were to enforce the implementation of the peace agreement signed in 2003 and to constrain all stakeholders in the conflict – the Ivorian government and rebel leaders – with an arms embargo. These sanctions, which included an arms imports embargo, asset freeze, and travel ban, were clearly aimed at the political elites who posed a threat to the ongoing peace process and engaged in serious human rights abuse. However, they were largely ineffective in constraining the elites (Biersteker, Eckert, and Tourinho, 2016: 282). Instead, they led to the consolidation of authoritarian rule and greater corruption in the state-controlled economy (Biersteker, Eckert, and Tourinho, 2016). The arms embargo did not improve the political situation. Alongside growing tension over the presidential and legislative elections, the amount of violence against civilians increased sharply between 2010 and 2012. The Armed Conflict Location and Event Data Project (ACLED) recorded 164 violent events targeting civilians during this period, resulting in 748 reported deaths. More than half of these violent acts were perpetrated by the Ivorian military force and pro-government militias (Raleigh et al., 2010).

Why do some smart sanctions cause collateral damage to the general population, while others minimize it? There has been surprisingly little research on this question, despite its practical and theoretical importance. In this article, we argue that the scope and the effectiveness of smart sanctions, and the political institutions of target countries are critical determinants of adverse effects on human rights. Leaders who are targeted by sanctions with a broad scope will have a greater incentive to oppress people to cut off potential support for challengers. The degree to which they can carry out successful oppression, however, hinges upon the effectiveness of sanctions implementation. Furthermore, we expect that authoritarian systems with a small winning coalition, when targeted by sanctions, are more likely to encourage oppression than large-coalition systems.[2]

In the following section, we briefly examine the relevant literature on economic sanctions and develop a theoretical argument about the effects of smart sanctions on human rights in greater detail. Then, we discuss our data, methods, and the operational definitions of explanatory variables used for analysis. In the result section, we present and discuss statistical results, followed by an illustrative example of North Korea during the period 2006-2019. Smart sanctions on North Korea have been broadly targeted but largely unsuccessful in curbing Pyongyang's nuclear activities. These sanctions put North Korean people in greater danger of human rights violations. To prevent further harm to civilians, sanctions should be more narrowly targeted at Kim Jong-un's family and be much more effectively enforced through close coordination among relevant stakeholders.

---

2 Bueno de Mesquita et al. (2003: 51) defines the winning coalition as the number of supporters that a leader needs in order to remain in power. In general, liberal democracies require larger winning coalitions than do authoritarian regimes.

II. Smart sanctions, human rights, and political oppression

1. Human rights issues in the economic sanctions literature

Economic sanctions refer to the actions taken against a target country to accomplish a diplomatic goal through the withdrawal of trade or financial relations, or the threat to do so (Baldwin, 1985: 29-50). Less expensive than wars that entail military actions, economic sanctions have been valued as a useful tool of foreign policy (Davis and Engerman, 2003; Wallensteen and Staibano, 2005). It is clear that economic sanctions have fewer costs than war for sender countries (Garfield, 2002: 95). Meanwhile, economic sanctions must be designed to inflict a target country with economic losses that are borne by the civilian population. Certainly, the fundamental flaw of conventional sanctions theory is its assumption that damages inflicted on the ordinary people of the target country will lead to grassroots political pressure on their leader to change his/her policies or behavior (Tostensen and Bull, 2002: 375).

Even if the target suffers economic loss, which can lead to grassroots political pressure, there is no guarantee that this will result in policy change (Tostensen and Bull, 2002: 376). The target country may also have the capacity to 'adapt' in the face of economic hardship 'with a certain self-maintaining potential' (Galtung 1967: 409). In both cases, the problem is that most of the costs entailed in a sanction are directed against innocent people, many of whom find it difficult to survive without international aid. The sanctions imposed on Iraq are an exemplary case. The import ban on chlorine used to purify drinking water caused the spread of typhoid, dysentery, and cholera, and 6,000 children were reported starving to death every month (Mueller and Mueller, 1999). The number of Iraqi civilians who died during the implementation period of the sanctions is documented as higher than the number of people killed by atomic bombs in Hiroshima and Nagasaki (Mueller and Mueller, 1999: 51).

Since the mid-1990s, the UN has devised smart sanctions to avoid sanction-associated collateral damage. As the idea of smart sanctions comes to the fore, scholars have begun to pay close attention to the impact of economic sanctions on civilians' rights. Based on empirical analysis of 92 sanction episodes, for example, Shagabutdinova and Berejikian (2007) argue that smart sanctions that target elites rather than the general population are not only more humane, but also more effective than traditional sanctions. Others have focused on the domestic politics of target states, although none of them explicitly deals with the subject of smart sanctions. When economic sanctions produce greater pain to the leaders, they can diminish the coercive capacity of repressive leaders and subsequently lessen the leaders' repression against ordinary people (Blanton, 1999). The weakening of the regime's capacity by economic sanctions likely leads to the empowerment of opposition movements and dissidents, possibly leading to a shift of power in favor of anti-government groups. Increased leverage for these groups can, in turn, be used to minimize human rights violations (Peksen, 2009: 61). Moreover, the loss of support for leaders among influential groups, due to diminished resources resulting from economic sanctions, can further weaken the regime's coercive capacity (Wintrobe, 1990; Bueno de Mesquita et al., 2003).

On the other hand, Peksen (2009) argues that leaders could divert the cost of sanctions to civilians, to supply their supporters with more resources, resulting in a worsening of human rights conditions. Similarly, Escriba-Folch (2012) suggests that personalist regimes targeted by sanctions reduce public spending and increase repression more than other types of autocracy. This mechanism is especially true in authoritarian regimes where leaders can 'manipulate information flows for propaganda purposes' (Tostensen and Bull, 2002: 377). Further, after investigating the consequences of smart sanctions against African countries between 1992 and 2008, Carneiro and Apolinario (2016) find that the level of human rights protection is likely to worsen during the lifetime of the sanction's episode. Opposition groups, they argue, perceive a targeted leader as weakened by the sanctions, which may lead to more protest and oppression (Carneiro and Apolinario, 2016).

Overall, these studies suggested that a regime's willingness and ability to oppress civilians is influenced by the type and the intensity of economic sanctions. However, the above literature, except for Carneiro and Apolinario (2016), does not explicitly deal with the problem of collateral damage created by the new sanctions protocol, or the so-called smart sanctions. In addition, some of them yield contradictory results regarding the impact of economic sanctions on human rights, thus doing little to identify the specific conditions under which smart sanctions are improving or deteriorating human rights conditions.

This study departs from previous scholarship in two notable respects. First, we show how 'design and implementation' of sanctions influence the magnitude of political oppression. In so doing, we consider elite politics as the centerpiece for understanding the unintended effects of the smart sanctions policy. The level of human rights violations in the target country is not merely an unfortunate by-product of sanctions but rather the result of decisions made by elites. As political elites are agents of political oppression, it is crucial to explain the motives and strategies of elite groups targeted by smart sanctions. In this article, we develop a theoretical argument based on three conditions – the scope and effectiveness of smart sanctions and the political institutions of target countries – to explain when we should expect targeted elites to engage in oppression against ordinary citizens under smart sanctions. This argument builds upon the selectorate theory of Bueno de Mesquita et al. (2003), who demonstrated that authoritarian systems with a small winning coalition encouraged ruthless campaigns of political oppression. They stated: 'Such systems present a greater incentive to challenge the leader, a greater incentive for the leader to hang onto power by all possible means, a greater ability to recruit those who will carry out [oppression]' (Bueno de Mesquita et al., 2003: 346). We extend this theory by looking at the specific incentives and constraints that smart sanctions create for elites.

Second, we test our hypotheses using a sample of 56 smart sanction episodes against an incumbent regime between 1991 and 2016. Smart sanctions are designed to 'target responsible parties while minimizing collateral damage' (Drezner, 2003: 107), inferring a situation in which human rights violations are less likely to occur. Thus, this sample of smart sanctions may be the 'least likely' to support our argument. However, on the other hand, if the empirical evidence fits the prediction of our theory, we have strong evidence in favor of our theoretical claims. Next, we articulate an argument about the relationship between smart sanctions and political oppression when leaders face an economic challenge to their rule.

2. Hypotheses

Smart sanctions do not target civilian populations, but they can influence the actors, such as leaders and ruling elites, that oppress them. This article proposes the mechanism by which smart sanctions can inadvertently deteriorate human rights conditions in the target country. It can help us understand why the humanitarian costs of targeted sanctions have varied so much across episodes. As we discuss in detail later, three conditions – the scope and the effectiveness of smart sanctions, and the political institutions of target countries – can explain how this mechanism leads to the oppression of citizens who are not the subject of sanctions.

Leaders do not rule alone. To stay in power, they must maintain the support of their winning coalition by ensuring a sufficient flow of resources to the ruling elites (Bueno de Mesquita et al., 2003; Heger and Salehyan, 2007). Such resources could include side-payments in the form of private goods, access to a formal political position (e.g., a seat in the cabinet), and indirect transfers of state resources through differential tax privileges or provision of jobs in the public sector. If members of the leader's coalition do not receive sufficient resources, they may choose to defect and join opposition movements (Bueno de Mesquita et al., 2003: 113). That is why leaders, especially those of authoritarian regimes, try to buy-off potential challengers and convince elites that they are better off sticking with the incumbent rather than defecting to the opposition.

We argue that a UN-imposed sanction provides a signal about the future of resource transfers to the ruling elites. Elites feel the effects of smart sanctions directly when they receive fewer services or private goods from the government. Given that elites care about their future flow of resources, a signal of decreased future resources can create problems for leaders about their political survival by tipping the balance in favor of challengers (Kirshner, 1997: 42). This temporary government weakness may trigger defection from the leader's coalition, thereby increasing the chance of leadership turnover in the upcoming election. When such threats emerge, leaders may use oppression to deter elites from joining the challenger's nascent coalition (Bueno de Mesquita et al., 2003: 341). Moreover, ordinary citizens outside the incumbent's coalition are likely to support the challenger because it gives them some chance of entering the new governing coalition (Bueno de Mesquita et al., 2003: 341). As a result, leaders under smart sanctions have an incentive to oppress citizens to discourage their support for the opposition.

Even when this mechanism operates, however, there is no guarantee that the imposition of smart sanctions will influence the human rights conditions in target countries. In some cases, for example, the scope of targeted sanctions may be too narrow to motivate potential challengers to move against the incumbent leader. We believe that the three conditions mentioned above make it more likely for this mechanism to contribute causally to the political oppression of ordinary people. We use these conditions to develop more precise hypotheses about the effects of smart sanctions on human rights.

First, the adverse humanitarian effects of smart sanctions are more likely when the sanctions aim to target larger numbers of individuals and/or goods. We assume that the elites of the regime have strong incentives to obtain an accurate assessment of future resource transfers. To the extent that smart sanctions provide a broader platform for targeting regime elites, the elites are likely to feel the effects of the sanctions directly. The motivation to mount or join a challenge to the leader increases as the scope of targeted sanctions expands, and the prospects for future resource transfers become less certain. The leader's motivation for political oppression as a deterrent increases as the risk of successful challenge increases. This leads to our first hypothesis:

> H1: Smart sanctions with a broader scope are more likely to have adverse impacts on human rights in target countries.

Second, the adverse effects of smart sanctions may depend on how effective the sanctions are in coercing or constraining a target's behavior. Leaders need loyal supporters and resources to carry out successful oppression. Members of the ruling coalition are more willing to participate in an act of oppression to protect the leader when they benefit significantly from the leader's rule (Bueno de Mesquita et al., 2003: 344). Thus, leaders must co-opt the principal organs of oppression (e.g., the military and secret police) by committing a sufficient flow of resources or side-payments to make them unwilling to shirk. However, an effective sanction may reduce the leader's ability to recruit machines of oppression by limiting the leader's access to economic and military resources (Peksen, 2009). An effective sanction also reduces the number of rewards provided to members of the ruling coalition and, hence, reduces their loyalty to the incumbent. Therefore, the government's oppression of citizens is unlikely to succeed when a sanction is highly effective. Based on this argument, we derive the following hypothesis:

> H2: The more effective smart sanctions are, the lesser the risk of human rights violations in target countries.

The third condition for the adverse effects of smart sanctions concerns the institutional traits of target countries. According to Bueno de Mesquita et al. (2003), the provision of private goods is central to political survival in non-democratic systems with small minimum winning coalitions. Leaders in such systems attract political support by promising benefits to their coalition members. Furthermore, this makes members of the incumbent's coalition 'loyal' to their present leader for fear of losing access to future benefits (Bueno de Mesquita et al., 2003). However, substantial decreases in private benefits – through economic sanctions, financial crisis, or foreign aid shocks, for example – reduce both the welfare and loyalty of regime elites, emboldening some in the leader's coalition to challenge the incumbent (Nielsen et al., 2011; Choi and Kim, 2018). When non-democratic leaders begin to lose power, they are more likely to do so through a coup, a revolt, or an assassination (Geddes et al., 2018: 178-180). Thus, leaders have strong incentives to hold onto power by punishing prospective challengers and their potential supporters.

To sum up, systems with a small winning coalition encourage political oppression when targeted by smart sanctions. When imposed with a sanction, such systems provide the elites with a powerful incentive to challenge the incumbent, and the leader with a greater incentive to employ every possible means to maintain power and a greater ability to recruit people who are willing to carry out oppressive actions against fellow citizens (Bueno de Mesquita et al., 2003: 346). This reasoning leads to our third hypothesis:

> H3: Smart sanctions are more likely to have adverse impacts on human rights conditions when the target country has a non–democratic system with a small winning coalition.

III. Research design

The unit of analysis for this study is the sanction episode (years). Data on UN-imposed targeted sanctions come from the Targeted Sanctions Consortium (TSC) database and the official website of the UN Security Council. They provide information on the type, purpose, target, impact, and outcome of 70 targeted sanctions imposed between 1991 and 2016. Unlike the prior comprehensive sanctions, the UN targeted sanctions are designed to minimize the unintended adverse effects on 'the most vulnerable segments of targeted countries' (UN Security Council, 2013: 3). This study investigates the conditions under which smart sanctions can deteriorate the human rights conditions in target countries, making this sample of sanctions a robust test of the hypotheses. Following the coding rule of the TSC, we assume that a new episode has begun when the UN Security Council adopts a new resolution that changes the nature of the targeted sanction. For the theory to work, sanctions should be directed against ruling elites (e.g. President, senior military commanders, and ruling party leaders). Hence, we exclude 14 episodes where non-state armed groups were the principal targets of sanctions. Also, as the purpose of this study is to assess the effects of 'ongoing' sanctions on human rights, we exclude the last year of the final episode from the sample when the UN Security Council resolution explicitly terminates the sanction. As a result, there are a total of 19 target countries, 56 sanction episodes, and 237 episode years.

1. Dependent variable: Political terror scale

The development of indicators for human rights has posed problems for researchers because of the complex and multidimensional nature of human rights (Apodaca, 2014: 168). Nevertheless, in line with Peksen (2009) and Carneiro and Apolinario (2016), this study focuses on the respect for 'physical integrity rights,' such as freedom from disappearances, extrajudicial executions, torture, and political imprisonment.[3] We use the Political Terror Scale (PTS), frequently used in previous research, to measure the protection of physical integrity rights in countries targeted by smart sanctions (Mukherjee, 2017; Art, 2016).

The PTS measures 'the levels of political violence and terror that a country experiences in a particular year' (Gibney et al., 2018), using data from different sources, including the Yearly Country Reports of Amnesty International (PTS-Amnesty), and the US State Department Country Reports on Human Rights Practices (PTS-US). Amnesty

3 We acknowledge that these rights cover a narrower spectrum of human rights than those covered by International Covenant on Economic, Social and Cultural Rights where, for example, the denial of the rights to food, adequate healthcare and education is considered as a violation of human rights. Although economic sanctions have important implications for socio-cultural rights, such a broader approach to human rights is beyond the scope of this article.

International deals with issues related to armed conflict, arms control, corporate accountability, the death penalty, detention, disappearances, discrimination, freedom of expression, indigenous people, international justice, living in dignity, refugees and migrants, sexual and reproductive rights, and torture in its annual reports. The US State Department's annual reports on human rights practices cover internationally recognized individual, civil, political, and worker rights, as outlined in the Universal Declaration of Human Rights and other international agreements. As a whole, these include the rights not to be subjected to torture or other cruel, inhuman, or degrading treatment or punishment, to prolonged detention without charges to disappearance or clandestine detention, and to other violations of the right to life, liberty, and the security of the person (US Department of State, 2016: Appendix A). The PTS is a five-level scale with each level meaning the following (Gibney et al., 2018):

> Level 1: Countries under a secure rule of law, people are not imprisoned for their view, and torture is rare or exceptional. Political murders are extremely rare.
>
> Level 2: There is a limited amount of imprisonment for nonviolent political activity. However, few persons are affected, torture and beatings are exceptional. Political murder is rare.
>
> Level 3: There is extensive political imprisonment or a recent history of such imprisonment. Execution or other political murders and brutality may be common. Unlimited detention, with or without a trial, for political views is accepted.
>
> Level 4: Civil and political rights violations have expanded to large numbers of the population. Murders, disappearances, and torture are a common part of life. In spite of its generality, on this level terror affects primarily those who interest themselves in politics or ideas.
>
> Level 5: Terror has expanded to the whole population. The leaders of these societies place no limits on the means or thoroughness with which they pursue personal or ideological goals.

We use the US State Department's PTS measure (PTS-US) as the dependent variable in our study. In the online supplementary material, we additionally present robustness checks using an alternative measure of human rights conditions based on the annual reports by Amnesty International (PTS-Amnesty).

2. Independent variables

The first independent variable is the scope of targeted sanctions. The TSC database classifies UN targeted sanctions under five different types: individual (e.g., asset freeze and travel ban), diplomatic (e.g., limiting diplomatic representation), sectoral (e.g., arms import embargo), commodity (e.g., diamond and petroleum imports ban), and financial sector (e.g., central bank asset freeze) sanctions. Based on the TSC's classification, this study measures the scope of each targeted sanction based on a three-point index, where the scope is 0 for episodes with a single type of sanction, 1 for those with two types of sanctions, and 2 for more than three types of sanctions.

The next independent variable is the effectiveness of targeted sanctions. This research uses the sanction effects established by the TSC. The TSC assesses sanction effectiveness in terms of the three different purposes of a sanction: coercion to change a target's behavior, the constraint of a target's engagement in a proscribed activity, or signaling the violation of an international norm by the target. According to Biersteker, Eckert, and Tourinho (2016),

> Sanctions with a coercive purpose seek to change the behavior of targets, often requesting them to fulfill a set of demands explicitly stated in the UN Security Council resolutions or asserted by a relevant actor … Constraining sanctions attempt to deny a target access to essential resources needed to engage in a proscribed activity, raising its costs or forcing a change in strategy … Signaling sanctions publicly assert the target's deviation from an international norm, producing at the same time an articulation or reframing of the norm and a statement of its practical applicability in that case (Biersteker, Eckert, and Tourinho, 2016: 21).

Effectiveness for each purpose is evaluated in accordance with two criteria: policy outcome and sanction contribution to that outcome. Policy outcome is measured on a five-point scale, with 1 representing the least effective and 5 representing the most effective. Sanction contribution is measured on a six-point scale, with 0 representing no contribution to policy outcome and 5 representing maximum contribution. As an indicator of effectiveness for each purpose, we use the multiplication of policy outcome and sanction contribution. Thus, we create three variables: coercion, constraint, and signaling.[4] Each variable has a 26-point scale, where 0 represents the lowest level of effectiveness, and 25 represents the highest level of effectiveness. Also, the TSC considers a sanction episode as 'effective' when policy outcome scores 4 or 5, and sanction contribution is 3 or higher. Hence, we create a dummy variable effective, which is coded 1 if at least two of these three variables are higher than or equal to 12; otherwise, it is coded 0.

Lastly, we test to see how institutional characteristics of target countries influence human rights conditions during the period of smart sanctions. We expect that small-coalition leaders of a non-democratic target country are more likely to respond to smart sanctions with heightened repression of political opposition and control of the civilian population than bow to international pressure. To measure the size of the minimum winning coalition, we utilize the index of electoral democracy (Polyarchy index) of the Varieties of Democracy (V-Dem) project (Coppedge et al., 2015). This index is constructed using five indicators of electoral democracy: (1) suffrage, (2) clean and fair elections (3) elected executive, (4) freedom of association, and (5) freedom of expression and alternative sources of information. The V-Dem Polyarchy index does not include measures of civil violence and/or political terror in its construction. This allows us to test how a target country's political institutions and smart sanctions interact to influence the human rights conditions in the target country.[5] A dichotomous variable autocracy is coded 1 if the Polyarchy index, which varies from 0 to 1, is less than or equal to 0.2, and is coded 0 otherwise.

---

4 The 'effectiveness' in some of smart sanctions could mean improved human rights conditions. To eliminate the possibility of tautological relations between sanctions' effectiveness and human rights conditions, we excluded an episode (DR-Congo 2010) where sanctions were used to coerce a change in rebel groups' human rights practices.

5 The Polity IV democracy index of Marshall and Jaggers (2011) includes civil violence components in its construction.

3. Control variables

We include the following control variables to capture factors that are known to influence a country's human rights through other channels. We include GDP per capita and civil war as indicators of socioeconomic development and political instability. Previous studies have shown that factors such as the individual country's economic development and the presence of violent conflict can have a significant impact on human right conditions (Mitchell and McCormick, 1988; McCormick and Mitchell, 1997; Neumayer, 2005: 942). Information on GDP per capita (in current 1,000 USD) is obtained from the World Bank. A dichotomous variable civil war equals 1 if the country is engaged in a civil war that reaches at least 25 battle-related deaths within a given year based on the Uppsala Conflict Data Program/Peace Research Institute Oslo (UCDP/PRIO) Armed Conflict Dataset (Gleditsch et al., 2002).

We also control for the presence of unilateral sanctions imposed by the United States. A dummy variable US Sanction is coded 1 if Washington imposed unilateral sanction(s) against a target in addition to those authorized by the UN Security Council. Lastly, the duration of sanctions has been found to influence the effectiveness of economic sanctions (Hufbauer et al., 2007: 171-172; Drezner, 1999: 124-127). It was also used to investigate the side effects of economic sanctions such as human rights violations (Hakimdavar, 2015: 92-93; Peksen, 2009). Hence, we include the variable duration, which is the number of years since the adoption of the UN resolution on economic sanctions. Table 1 provides a summary of statistics for all variables used in the analysis.

Table 1. Definitions and Summary Statistics for Variables

Variable	Mean	Std. Dev.	Min	Max
PTS-US	3.898	0.947	1.000	5.000
PTS-Amnesty	3.954	0.969	2.000	5.000
Duration	3.021	3.077	0.000	12.000
Scope	1.199	0.918	0.000	2.000
Autocracy	0.257	0.438	0.000	1.000
Coercion	5.343	4.017	1.000	16.000
Constraint	5.609	4.827	0.000	20.000
Signaling	7.332	4.581	1.000	20.000
Effective	0.195	0.397	0.000	1.000
GDP per capita	2.193	2.736	0.093	15.247
Civil war	0.427	0.496	0.000	1.000
US Sanction	0.830	0.377	0.000	1.000

IV. Results

A linear mixed-effects model is used to test our hypotheses. All models include random intercepts for each episode, which account for unobserved and/or time-invariant determinants of human rights conditions that are not considered in the estimation, along with robust standard errors clustered by episode. Table 2 reports the results of testing the effects of smart sanctions on human rights conditions of target countries, using PTS-US as a dependent variable. Model 1 is a baseline specification that includes control variables only. The coefficient for duration has a negative sign but is not statistically significant. It indicates that the human rights conditions of target countries have not significantly improved during the period of sanctions. At the same time, this result suggests that the overall human rights situation in target countries has, at least, not worsened since the introduction of the smart sanctions concept.

In Model 2, we add a set of explanatory variables – scope, coercion, and autocracy – and examine their interaction with duration. The purpose of this research is to investigate change in human rights conditions while the target country is under a sanction. Therefore, our main interest is to test the interactions between the explanatory variables and duration. The positive and significant coefficient for duration x scope indicates that human rights conditions are expected to deteriorate during the sanctions episodes that include multiple types of sanctions. For example, the political terror scale is predicted to increase by about 0.078 every year during episodes with more than two types of sanctions, when holding all other variables constant. This result shows that, even though the UN-imposed smart sanctions target specific individuals and items, human rights conditions in the target country become worse when various combinations of sanctions are employed; thereby providing support for H1.

Next, the interaction between duration and coercion is negative and statistically significant at the 5 percent level. It means that we have less risk of human rights violations when a sanction successfully coerces the target to change its behavior. Therefore, the finding is in line with H2. Also, the coefficient for duration x autocracy has the expected positive sign and is highly significant at the 1 percent level. It implies that when faced with smart sanctions, non-democratic countries with small winning coalitions are more likely to oppress civilian populations than democratic countries. The political terror

Table 2. Determinants of Change in Political Terror Scale (PTS-US) during Smart Sanctions

VARIABLES	Model 1	Model 2	Model 3	Model 4	Model 5
Duration	-0.023 (0.027)	-0.038 (0.033)	-0.070 (0.026)***	-0.027 (0.030)	-0.084 (0.023)***
Duration × Scope		0.058 (0.021)***	0.066 (0.012)***	0.081 (0.021)***	0.051 (0.016)***
Duration × Coercion		-0.017 (0.008)**			
Duration × Constraint			-0.013 (0.003)***		
Duration × Signaling				-0.020 (0.005)***	
Duration × Effective					-0.137 (0.027)***
Duration × Autocracy		0.226 (0.039)***	0.181 (0.075)**	0.150 (0.058)**	0.156 (0.064)**
GDP per capita	-0.036 (0.024)	-0.077 (0.029)***	-0.042 (0.024)*	-0.043 (0.024)*	-0.051 (0.024)**
Civil war	0.500 (0.097)***	0.469 (0.103)***	0.414 (0.098)***	0.434 (0.088)***	0.436 (0.086)***
US Sanction	0.579 (0.323)*	0.251 (0.516)	0.531 (0.354)	0.506 (0.336)	0.585 (0.344)*
Scope		0.326 (0.151)**	0.076 (0.144)	-0.001 (0.130)	0.079 (0.137)
Coercion		-0.033 (0.027)			
Constraint			-0.008 (0.015)		
Signaling				0.022 (0.025)	
Effective					-0.211 (0.188)
Autocracy		-0.572 (0.310)*	-0.367 (0.283)	-0.401 (0.236)*	-0.365 (0.252)
Constant	3.427 (0.332)***	3.729 (0.457)***	3.547 (0.364)***	3.439 (0.424)***	3.496 (0.361)***
Number of observations	237	177	211	237	237
Number of sanctions	56	44	51	56	56
R-squared (within)	0.095	0.305	0.297	0.288	0.263

Notes: Robust standard errors in parentheses, *** p〈0.01, ** p〈0.05, * p〈0.1

scale in the non-democratic countries is expected to increase by 0.188 each year during sanction when other variables are held constant. Thus, we find strong support for H3.[6]

In Model 3, the effect of constraint on human rights oppression is negative and statistically significant. That is, when smart sanctions are highly effective in constraining target countries, human rights conditions tend to improve in times of sanctions implementation. Similarly, Model 4 shows that the stronger the signaling effects of sanctions, the lower the political terror index appears over time. In other words, the less effective the sanctions are in their intended purposes, the worse the human rights situations of target countries become. Overall, these results provide support for the second hypothesis. The control variables offer additional insights. Coefficients for GDP per capita are negative and statistically significant in Models 2–4, indicating that wealthier target countries tend to have better human rights records than poorer ones. Civil war is positive and highly significant in all models. It implies that human rights conditions tend to deteriorate when target countries are involved in a civil war. However, US Sanction, which is positive and marginally significant in Models 1 and 5, fails to exhibit any significant effect in Models 2–4.

Model 5 includes a dummy variable effective, which identifies whether sanctions are considered effective for at least two purposes. As expected, the interaction between duration and effective is positive and highly significant at the 1 percent level. It suggests that human rights conditions are expected to improve over time when sanctions achieve their policy goals. Figure 1, which is based on Model 5, plots trajectories of the political terror scale for two hypothetical countries under smart sanctions, holding other variables at their means. The plot shows that political terror can quickly escalate in times of smart sanctions when an autocratic country is under multiple sanctions, and when these sanctions are not effective in coercing, constraining, and/or signaling a target. The predicted value of PTS-US is about 27% higher after six years of targeted sanctions. The opposite pattern is observed when a target country has no autocratic regime and is under a single sanction where at least two of three purposes are considered effective. This

6 We also tested how different forms of autocratic regime - military, single party, and personalist - influence human rights of target countries (Geddes, Wright and Frantz, 2018). However, none of the interactions between duration and autocratic regime type were statistically significant at the 0.1 level.

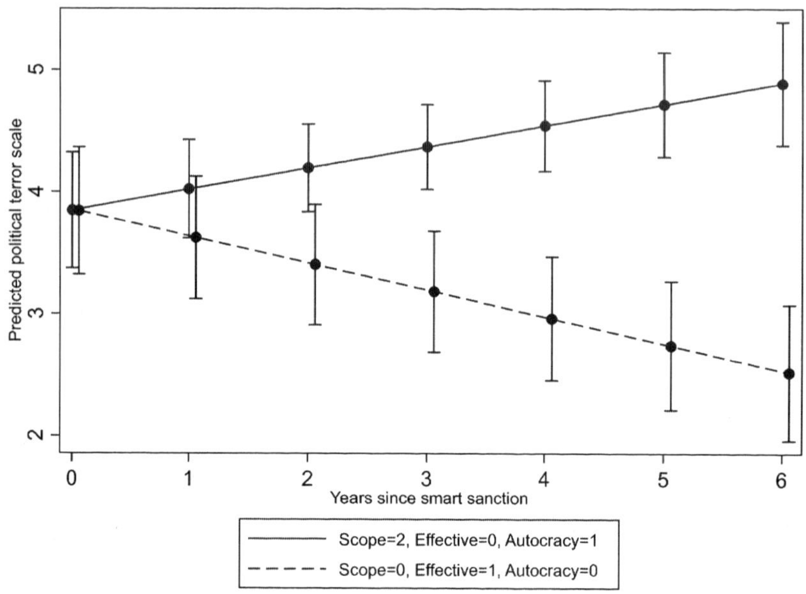

Figure 1. Predicted levels of political terror scale in times of smart sanction, with 95% confidence intervals.

result shows promise in that if sanctions with a narrow scope work effectively, they do not hurt innocent citizens. On the other hand, they can even improve the human rights conditions in target countries.

Illustrative example: North Korea under smart sanctions (2006 - present)

The North Korean case illustrates how political systems with a small winning coalition promote political oppression during UN-imposed smart sanctions. It also shows how this mechanism is influenced by the scope and effectiveness of the sanctions. In other words, the North Korean case lends support to our statistical results.

North Korea is widely regarded as an autocratic country. Three generations of the Kim family have ruled over the North Korean people since the end of World War II. Kim Jong-un became the country's supreme leader after his father's death in 2011. His first parliamentary election took place in March 2014 where Kim Jong-un was elected unanimously for five years in his constituency with 99.97% turnout. Regarding the election, Freedom House (2018) reported, '[North Korea] denies voters any choice and rules out any opposition to the incumbent leadership. The government uses the mandatory elections as an unofficial census, keeping track of whether and how people voted, and interprets any rejection of the preselected candidates as treason' (Freedom House, 2018: 2). In Kim's North Korea, a small group of supporters – especially those in the ruling Workers' Party and the military – wields sufficient instruments of power to ensure victory; hence, the size of the minimum winning coalition is very small.

Since 2006, North Korea has been under various forms of economic sanction, which have posed a challenge to the North Korean leadership. Within the notion of smart sanctions, the UN has targeted a wide range of individuals and items related to North Korea's nuclear weapons program. The first version of smart sanctions in 2006 prohibited the export of high-end military equipment to North Korea (UN Security Council, 2006). Since then, the UN has added more targets and items to coerce and constrain Pyongyang. For example, Resolution 2321 imposed a binding cap on North Korea's coal exports, its largest source of external revenue (UN Security Council, 2016), while Resolution 2371 banned the export of other critical commodities (e.g. lead, iron ore, and seafood) and restricted the number of North Koreans working abroad (UN Security Council, 2017). This resolution also added new financial sanctions to DPRK's overseas banks, and allowed member states to interdict North Korean vessels suspected of carrying prohibited items (UN Security Council, 2017).

However, these sanctions have not been successful in significantly modifying the regime's behavior. For the last 20 years, North Korea has continued to engage in proscribed activities, including ballistic missile launches and nuclear tests, suggesting that the UN has failed to pressure Pyongyang to abandon its nuclear and ballistic missile programs. Recently, the UN panel of experts found that North Korea has developed new and more sophisticated ways to evade international sanctions (UN Security Council, 2019). It details sanctions evasion activities by North Korea, including illicit ship-to-ship transfers of coal, oil, and other materials. The panel said, 'Financial sanctions remain some of the most poorly implemented and actively evaded measures of the sanctions regime' (UN Security Council, 2019).

While smart sanctions have failed to deny North Korea access to key resources, Kim Jong-un has reinforced oppression to deter potential threats to his leadership. According to the National Intelligence Service of South Korea, Kim Jong-un executed about 70 senior officials between 2011 and 2015 (Chosun Ilbo, 2015). This figure is much higher than the number killed by his father Kim Jong-il during his early years of rule. Among the executed elite members was Jang Sung-taek, Kim Jong-un's uncle, who was arrested and killed for treachery in 2013. Political terror has expanded to civilians in the midst of economic sanctions. North Korean authority maintains fear and control over the population using arbitrary arrest and punishment, torture in custody, and executions (Human Rights Watch, 2019). Human rights abuses have become more brutal under Kim Jong-un. For instance, he has presided over a major crack-down against civilians seeking to flee the country. The government announced that anyone trying to cross the border illegally would be shot on sight, and several episodes of killing have been reported (Han et al., 2018: 393). In addition, people in the so-called hostile class are often expelled from Pyongyang to remote farming or mining areas in the most impoverished conditions (Han et al., 2018: 103). Kim Jung-un needs tighter control over society, according to Park Hyeong-jung (a North Korea expert at the Korea Institute for National Unification), because public officials are becoming more corrupt and predatory, and citizens are starting to gripe under the pressure of targeted sanctions (NPR News, 2019).

V. Conclusion

This article has examined why some smart sanctions cause collateral damage to the general population in target states. We have argued that smart sanctions do not target civilian populations, but they can influence leaders who oppress the general public for their political survival. In this regard, first, we find that smart sanctions with a broader scope are more likely to have adverse impacts on the human rights conditions of target countries. The leader expects his/her political survival to be threatened by supporters who now expect a significant reduction in future resources as a result of sanctions. Thus, the leader is likely to intensify oppression to prevent this situation from arising. Second, the more effective smart sanctions are, the lesser the risk of human rights violations in target countries. This is because effective sanctions may reduce the leader's ability to recruit machines of oppression by limiting the leader's access to economic and military resources. Third, smart sanctions are more likely to have adverse impacts on human rights conditions when the target country has a non-democratic system with a small winning coalition. When non-democratic leaders lose power, supporters are more likely to replace the leader through a coup, a revolt, or an assassination. Therefore, the leaders have stronger incentives to hold onto power by punishing prospective challengers and their potential supporters.

Statistical analysis in this paper has substantiated the three hypotheses. We can conclude that when narrowly targeted sanctions work effectively, they do not contribute to human rights violations. Instead, they can even improve human rights conditions in target states. On the other hand, when broad-scope sanctions are not implemented effectively, there can be severe human rights violations in target countries. The case of North Korea can highlight the policy implications of these findings. Under the current UN-imposed sanctions, it is difficult to ignore the negative effects sanctions have on the human rights of North Korean people. When Pyongyang evades sanctions, imposing broadly targeted sanctions may put civilians in greater danger. For smart sanctions to be smarter and improve the human rights conditions in North Korea, they must be more narrowly targeted at the Kim family's leadership and be much more enthusiastically enforced through close coordination among relevant stakeholders.

References

Apodaca, Clair (2014) Human Rights Measurement. In Anja Mihr and Mark Gibney (eds) Human Rights. SAGE, 164–180.

Art, David (2016) Archivists and Adventurers: Research Strategies for Authoritarian Regimes of the Past and Present. Social Science Quarterly 97(4): 974–90.

Baldwin, A. David (1985) Economic Statecraft. Princeton, New Jersey: Princeton University Press.

Biersteker, Thomas, Sue E. Eckert, and Marcos Tourinho (2016) Targeted Sanctions. Cambridge: Cambridge University Press.

Blanton, Shannon L (1999). Instruments of Security or Tools of Repression? Arms Imports and Human Rights Conditions in Developing Countries. Journal of Peace Research 36: 233–244.

Brzoska, Michael and George Lopez (2016) Security Council dynamics and sanctions design. In Biersteker, Eckert, and Tourinho (eds) Targeted Sanctions. Cambridge: Cambridge University Press.

Bueno de Mesquita, Bruce et al. (2003) The Logic of Political Survival. Cambridge: The MIT Press.

Carneiro, Cristiane and Laerte Apolinario (2016) Targeted Versus Conventional Economic Sanctions International Interactions 42(4): 565-589.

Choi, Hyun Jin and Dongsuk Kim (2018) Coup, Riot, War: How Political Institutions and Ethnic Politics Shape Alternative Forms of Political Violence. Terrorism and Political Violence 30(4): 718-739.

Chosun Ilbo (2015) Kim Jong-un Continues Reign of Terror, 15 July 2019. http://english.chosun.com/site/data/html_dir/2015/05/14/2015051401073.html.

Davis, Lance and Stanley Engerman (2003) History Lessons: Sanctions: Neither War nor Peace. The Journal of Economic Perspectives 17(2): 187-197.

Drezner, Daniel (1999) The Sanctions Paradox. Cambridge: Cambridge University Press.

Drezner, Daniel (2003) How Smart Are Smart Sanctions? International Studies Review 5(1): 107-110.

Drezner, Daniel (2011) Sanctions Sometimes Smart: Targeted Sanctions in Theory and Practice. International Studies Review 13(1): 96-108.

Drezner, Daniel (2015) Targeted Sanctions in a world of Global Finance. International Interactions 41(4): 755-764.

Escriba –Folch, Abel (2012) Authoritarian responses to foreign pressure: Spending, repression, and sanctions. Comparative Political Studies 45(6): 683-713.

Freedom House (2018) Freedom in the World 2018: North Korea Country Reports. Washington DC: Freedom House.

Galtung, Johan (1967) On the Effects of International Economic Sanctions, with Examples from

the Case of Rhodesia. World Politics 19(3): 378-416.
Garfield, Richard (2002) Economic Sanctions, Humanitarianism, and Conflict after the Cold War. Social Justice 29(3): 94-107.
Geddes, Barbara, Joseph Wright and Erica Frantz (2018) How Dictatorships Work, Power, Personalization, and Collapse. Cambridge: Cambridge University Press.
Gibney, Mark, Linda Cornett, Reed Wood, Peter Haschke, Daniel Arnon, and Attilio Pisanò (2018) The Political Terror Scale 1976-2017, 12 December 2018. http://www.politicalterrorscale.org.
Gleditsch, Nils Petter, Peter Wallensteen, Mikael Eriksson, Margareta Sollenberg, and Havard Strand (2002) Armed Conflict 1946-2001: A New Dataset. Journal of Peace Research 39(5): 615-637.
Han, Dongho, Kumsoon Lee, Kyungok Do, Jehwan Hong and Sukyung Kim (2018) White Paper on North Korean Human Rights. Seoul: Korea Institute for National Unification. (In Korean)
Heger, Lindsay and Idean Salehyan (2007) Ruthless Rulers: Coalition Size and the Severity of Civil Conflict. International Studies Quarterly 51(2): 385-403.
Hufbauer, Gary Clyde, Jeffrey J. Schott, Kimberly Ann Elliott, and Barbara Oegg (2007) Economic Sanctions Reconsidered (3rd edition). Washington DC: Institute for International Economics.
Human Right Watch (2019) Report Country, 21 March 2019. https://www.hrw.org/world-report/2019/country-chapters/north-korea.
Kirshner, Jonathan (1997) The microfoundations of economic sanctions. Security Studies 6(3): 32-64.
Lopez, George and David Cortright (1997) Economic sanctions and human rights: Part of the problem or part of the solution? The International Journal of Human Rights 1(2): 1-25.
McCormick, James and Neil Mitchell (1997) Human Rights Violations, Umbrella Concepts, and Empirical Analysis. World Politics 49(4): 510-525.
Mitchell, Neil and James McCormick (1988) Economic and Political Explanations of Human Rights Violations. World Politics 40(4): 476-498.
Mueller, John and Karl Mueller (1999) Sanctions of Mass Destruction. Foreign Affairs 78(3): 43-53.
Mukherjee, Nisha (2017) Voting and Human Rights in Democratic Societies. Human Rights Review 18(3): 263-282.
Nielsen, Richard, Michael G. Findley, Zachary S. Davis, Tara Candland, Daniel L. Nielson (2011) Foreign Aid Shocks as a Cause of Violent Armed Conflict. American Journal of Political Science 55(2): 219–232.
National Public Radio (NPR) News (2019) Kim Tightens Leadership Over North Korea In Major Government Reshuffle, 12 April 2019. https://www.npr.org/2019/04/12/712628100/kim-tightens-leadership-over-north-korea-in-major-government-reshuffle.
Neumayer, Eric (2005) Do International Human Rights Treaties Improve Respect for Human Rights? Journal of Conflict Resolution 49(6): 925-953.

Peksen, Dursun (2009) Better or Worse? The Effect of Economic Sanctions on Human Rights. Journal of Peace Research 46(1): 59-77.
Raleigh, Clionadh, Andrew Linke, Håvard Hegre, and Joakim Karlsen (2010) Introducing ACLED: An Armed Conflict Location and Event Dataset Special Data Feature. Journal of Peace Research 47(5): 651-660.
ROK Ministry of Unification (2019) White Paper. Seoul: ROK Ministry of Unification (In Korean).
Shagabutdinova, Ella and Jeffrey Berejikian (2007) Deploying Sanctions while Protecting Human Rights Journal of Human Rights 6(1): 59-74.
Tostensen, Arne and Beate Bull (2002) Are smart sanctions Feasible. World Politics 54 (3): 373-403.
UN. UN Data, 21 March 2019. https://unstats.un.org/unsd/snaama/resQuery.asp
US Department of State (2016) Country Report on Human Rights Practices for 2016, 21 March 2019. https://www.state.gov/j/drl/rls/hrrpt/humanrightsreport/index.htm#wrapper
Wallensteen, Peter and Carina Staibano (2005) International Sanctions Between Words and Wars in the Global System. Routledge.
Wintrobe, Ronald (1990) The Tinpot and the Totalitarian: An Economic Theory of Dictatorship. The American Political Science Review 84(3): 849-872.
World Bank. World Bank Data, 21 March 2019. http://databank.worldbank.org/data/home.aspx

Chapter 9

Bridge between South and North Korea: Analysis of South Korean Aid to North Korea for Peace in the Korean Peninsula[1]

Youngwan Kim (Hankuk University of Foreign Studies)
Jaeyoung Hur (Yonsei University)
Jiyoun Park (Jeonbuk National University)

Abstract

This study suggests new approaches to conceptualize South Korean aid to North Korea as equivalent to Official Development Assistance (ODA) by looking at its historical background and present situation, as well as related laws. We review the characteristics and development of South Korean aid to North Korea, compare it to ODA, and suggest an innovative way of conceptualizing it as ODA. In particular, we assert that if South Korean aid to North Korea is considered ODA, South Korea would be able to effectively assist North Korea and become a more influential and responsible donor in international society. In addition, it will motivate two Koreas to work together for peace in the Korean peninsula.

Keywords: Korean peninsula, South Korean aid, North Korea, Peace.

---

1 This is a revised version of an article previously published by Johns Hopkins University Press, as: Hur, Jaeyoung, Jiyoun Park, and Youngwan Kim. "Same Money, Different Names: Analysis of South Korean Aid to North Korea." Asian Perspective 41:4 (2017), 645-671. © 2017 Institute for Far Eastern Studies, Kyungnam University. Reprinted with permission of Johns Hopkins University Press.

I. Introduction

While the two Koreas share the same ethnicity, history, culture, and language, they remain the only formerly united country left divided from the initiation of the Cold War. The tension between these two countries has significantly increased due to the development of nuclear weapons of the Democratic People's Republic of Korea (henceforth North Korea). The tour to Geumgang Mountain has ceased over the last several years and, more importantly, the Gaeseong industrial complex was shut down after North Korea's fourth nuclear test. After the Moon Jae-in administration began, there has been the expectation for the better relationship between South and North Korea, but the tension in the Korean peninsula has been increased after the failed negotiation between the United States and North Korea. In spite of this situation, the Republic of Korea (henceforth South Korea) has provided a significant amount of aid to North Korea for cooperative, humanitarian, and economic reasons since the 1990s.[2]

South Korea, as a member of the OECD DAC (Organization for Economic Cooperation and Development, Development Assistance Committee), and new donor in the international community, has provided USD 4.41 billion of aid to North Korea from 1995 to 2018. Nonetheless, South Korean aid to North Korea is not currently considered as Official Development Assistance (ODA). There are two different perspectives on South Korean aid to North Korea. One perspective is that it should not be considered to be ODA as South Korea still considers North Korea a part of its own territory (just as North Korea likewise views South Korea as its territory). Following this logic, South Korea is just transferring money to its own territory for its own people, not providing aid to people in another country. The other perspective argues that it is time to accept the fact that the two Koreas are de facto independent and separate countries; thus South Korean aid to North Korea should be considered ODA. This enables the actual amount of South Korean foreign aid to be calculated, enabling the efforts of South Korea as a donor to be more recognized in the international community.

2 Even though South Korea has provided the significant amount of aid to North Korea after 1995, the amount of South Korean aid to North Korea has decreased during the Lee Myung-bak administration (2008–2012) and more significantly decreased during the Park Geun-hye administration (2013–2017).

In this chapter, we attempt to understand why South Korean aid to North Korea has not been considered as ODA so far and why it is currently understood it the way it is. After addressing these issues, we propose a new approach to South Korean aid to North Korea following the new international standard for ODA. We argue that it is possible to treat South Korean aid to North Korea as ODA within the legal framework of South Korea if we relax the application of legal articles of South Korean laws related to international development cooperation. With South Korean aid to North Korea recast as ODA, moreover, North Korea will be willing and able to receive aid from South Korea with the help of the international community. In addition, South Korea can be a more influential donor by fulfilling its duty as a donor. More importantly, the new concept of Total Official Support for Sustainable Development (TOSSD) can be applied to South Korean aid to North Korea. With this new approach, we believe that South Korea can be more actively engaged in the peace process in the Korean peninsula.

Following this introductory section, the second section of the chapter explains the historical aspects and current issues regarding South Korean aid to North Korea. The third section deals with how South Korean aid to North Korea differs from ODA in terms of principles, goals, and implementation actors. The fourth section proposes a new way to understand South Korean aid to North Korea by analyzing its difficulties and merits. The final section concludes and explains the implications and limitations of ODA.

II. Historical Aspects and Current Issues

In 1995, following a large flood, North Korea requested emergency aid from the international community (Haggard and Noland 2013). In response, the international community initiated emergency aid for flood damage and food requirements in North Korea because the country's severe food shortages were revealed. South Korea also aided North Korea in 1995; however, the size of its aid was insignificant compared to what other countries offered. The government of South Korea at that time advocated a hardline policy toward North Korea; thus Seoul was not actively involved in the provision of aid to North Korea—indeed, a number of high-level policymakers in South

Korea regarded the government of Kim Jong-il unstable after the death of Kim Il-sung and expected food shortages would cause Kim's regime to topple.

However, after 1998, when President Kim Dae-jung took office, the size of South Korean aid to North Korea started to increase as the relationship between the two countries began to improve with the inter-Korean summit of June 2000 (Son 2006). In addition to food, fertilizer, and medical supplies, South Korea actively aided North Korea by reconstructing the railroad and roads, which are foundations of the Mt. Geumgang tour, and the Gaeseong industrial business complex. President Roh Moo-hyun, who succeeded Kim Dae-jung in 2003, continued to follow the preceding government's policy toward North Korea. However, the policy of openness toward North Korea could not be continued, because public opinion moved in a negative direction as North Korea carried out nuclear tests and South Korea's position in the Six-Party Talks weakened (Snyder 2010). Moreover, the size of aid to North Korea shrank considerably once the Roh Moo-hyun government was succeeded by the Lee Myung-bak administration. The communication between the two Koreas was cut off during the Park Geun-hye administration.

From the start of Moon Jae-in administration, it is expected that there would be better relations between two Koreas. When two Koreas had the summit meeting, they even agreed to support each other in various aspects. However, several failed results from the summit meeting between North Korea and the United States made South Korea unable to support North Korea. The UN sanction has been still effective. Currently, there is no way for South Korea to support North Korea except humanitarian assistance, in which North Korea is not willing to comply with.

South Korean aid to North Korea is implemented through the Inter-Korean Cooperation Fund (IKCF). IKCF was established in August 1990 by the Inter-Korean Cooperation Fund Act, as President Roh Tae-woo's July 7, 1988 declaration (the Special Declaration for National Self-Esteem, Unification, and Prosperity) permitted closer relations between the two Koreas through economic, social and humanitarian projects. The government's funding was initiated in March 1991 (Kim 2012). The purpose of this fund was to promote exchange and cooperation by building trust and contributing to the recovery of the national community by activating exchanges of human resources.

As shown in Figure 1, the total volume of South Korean aid to North Korea from

Figure 1 South Korean Aid Flow to North Korea

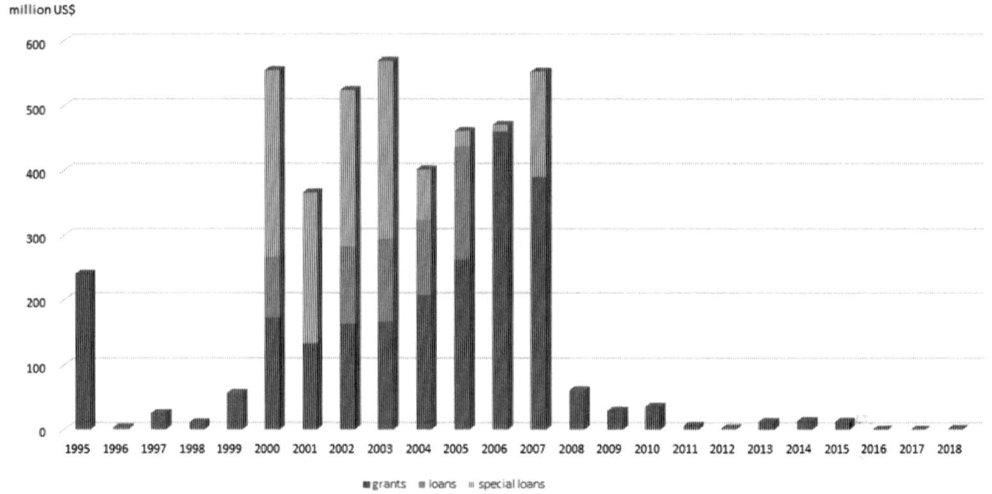

* Calculated by reflecting the average exchange rate for each year based on the statistical data of the Ministry of Unification and rounded off.
** Special loan: loan for the light water reactor project
Source: Ministry of Unification, "Aid Information" https://hairo.unikorea.go.kr/stat/StatInternalYearTotal.do (December 12, 2020); Economic Statistics System of the Bank of Korea, http://ecos.bok.or.kr/ (December 12, 2020).

1995 to 2018 was USD 4.41 billion, and all funds were provided through the IKCF (Park 2015). The total volume of South Korean aid to North Korea (USD 4.41 billion) equates to around 21 percent of South Korean ODA to all recipients (USD 20.84 billion) from 1995 to 2018.[3] The conditions of assistance were USD 2,468 million in grants, and USD 1,941 million in concessional loans. The concessional loans were for food and energy that were completely and directly funded by the South Korean government. As shown in Figure 2, government grants can be subcategorized into three channels: direct government support and support via nongovernmental or international organizations. Direct government support covers mainly food, fertilizer aid, and emergency aid, while support via nongovernmental channels includes aid for the sectors of agriculture,

3 A review of the volumes of assistance by year shows that aid to North Korea is more than that of ODA from 2000 to 2003. South Korea provided USD 468, 308, 452, and 494 million to North Korea in 2000, 2001, 2002, and 2003, respectively. In comparison, South Korean ODA was USD 212, 265, 279, and 366 million in 2000, 2001, 2002, and 2003, respectively.

Figure 2 South Korean Grant Flows to North Korea by Channel

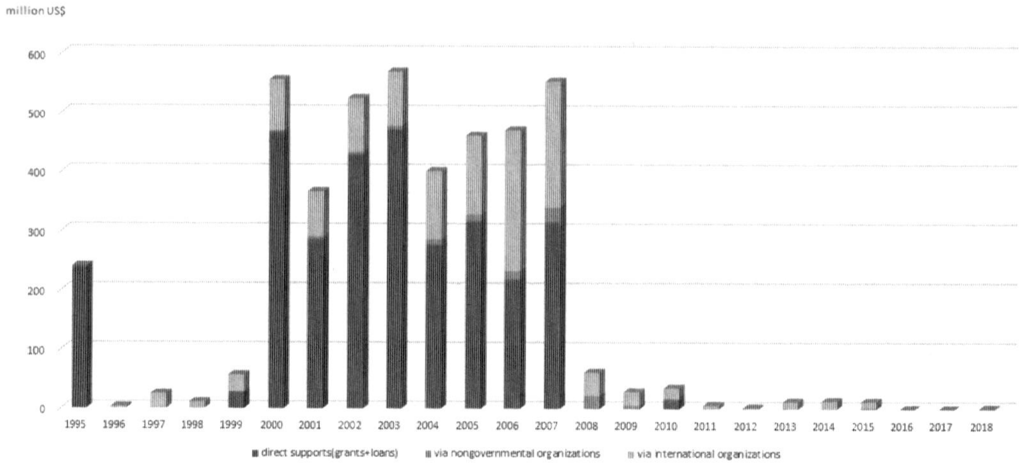

* Calculated by reflecting the average exchange rate for each year based on the statistical data of the Ministry of Unification and rounded off.
Source: Ministry of Unification, "Aid Information" https://hairo.unikorea.go.kr/stat/StatInternalYearTotal.do (December 12, 2020); Economic Statistics System of the Bank of Korea, http://ecos.bok.or.kr/ (December 12, 2020).

public health, and social welfare. International organizations' support focuses on food and medical aid for marginalized groups in North Korea. The amount of aid provided through each channel was USD 3,062 million, USD 110 million, and USD 1,236 million, respectively.

At present, internal and external challenges complicated distinguishing South Korean aid to North Korea from ODA. With regard to internal factors, the transparency of aid provided to North Korea is an issue (Haggard and Nolan 2013; Park 2016). Since 1995 when the aid was started through IKCF, the two Koreas have accomplished positive outcomes, such as increased exchanges and cooperation, active economic cooperation among businesses, and summits between South and North Korea. However, the nonstop military provocations by North Korea raised questions about whether South Korea should continue its aid to North Korea. Moreover, whether food aid was actually distributed to the public was a question. Furthermore, aid to North Korea programs lacked a strict monitoring process from planning to distribution; in contrast, ODA rules require a strict monitoring system, including policy planning, implementing, and evaluating projects (Moon 2013).

Due to the lack of transparency in the process of aid distribution, there is no way to determine how humanitarian assistance, such as food and fertilizer, has contributed to improving the food situation or crop production, or how this aid was distributed to the North Korean people. Thus, to obtain and secure transparency, the general rules of ODA need to be applied to South Korean aid to North Korea. Contemporary South Korean aid to North Korea that does not follow the general rules of ODA has a critical weakness in the current situations (Park and Moon 2015).

There are also problems related to the domestic politics of South Korean aid to North Korea. The size of aid was expanded during the tenure of Presidents Kim Dae-jung and Roh Moo-hyun, when reconciliation and cooperation, peace, and prosperity were the main policies of South Korea toward North Korea. However, these policies created a rift among South Korean citizens. Hence, the Lee Myung-bak and Park Geun-hye governments decreased the amount of aid given to North Korea. However, controversy persists around South Korean aid to North Korea about whether it represents a "dissipation of money" due to the lack of broad domestic political support for providing it (Jo 2008, 187).

Despite the lack of consensus among South Koreans, South Korean aid to North Korea can be practically beneficial. If South Korean aid to North Korea aims to develop every aspect of North Korean society, potential unification costs can be decreased (Jonsson, 2006). Therefore, aid to North Korea can be delivered with greater consent from South Korean people (Lee, 2005). In doing so, it is important to give North Korea the correct idea about the international community's development support; this development support has to enhance the welfare of people, not the government of North Korea, such as supplying drinking water, family planning, anti-poverty measures, and self-assistance capacity. In this respect, it is said that aid to North Korea should be changed from one-off supports, such as providing fertilizer, to development and cooperation methods, such as provision of greenhouse supplies and support for afforestation (*Yonhap News* 2015). If South Korean aid to North Korea is provided by respecting general rules and revealing transparent data on quantity and allocation, this would change public consensus and raise sympathy among South Korean people.

Among the external problems South Korea faces in the international arena is its prestige within the international community. Even though South Korea has been transformed from a recipient to a donor, South Korea is not being considered as a significant donor by international community (Watson, 2013). In other words, the exclusion of South Korean aid to North Korea into international ODA makes the total amount of South Korea aid appear less than it actually provides. The size of South Korea's ODA appear small given the fact that it has the 10th highest GDP in the world in 2019. The average size of ODA of twenty-nine OECD DAC member countries is 0.31 percent, while South Korean ODA is just 0.14 percent per GNI in 2018. Specifically, South Korean ODA is only one-third the size of other countries when it is compared to Canada, Spain, Italy, and Australia, all of whom have GDPs similar to South Korea.

In particular, South Korea failed to reach the goal of increasing the size of its ODA per GNI to 0.25 percent by 2015, which was promised by the Lee Myung-bak administration. However, if aid to North Korea is calculated as ODA, the goal would be on the horizon. For example, the size of South Korean ODA per GNI was 0.02 percent excluding but 0.06 percent including grant to North Korea in 1995, and also it was 0.07 percent excluding but 0.09 percent including grant to North Korea in 2007.[4] In this way, the contribution of South Korea to the international community could be shown to be far more than is currently perceived (Chun, Munyi and Lee, 2010; Shin and Jung, 2015).[5]

The second external problem in differentiating South Korean aid to North Korea from its ODA is that it is difficult for North Korean development issues to be discussed between South Korea and other donors. One barrier is that the South Korean government has a different statistical system for aid to North Korea from the one for ODA. The absence of common information and a statistical system poses a challenge for South Korea for cooperating with other donors on North Korean development needs as a global issue.

---

4 See the OECD website at https://stats.oecd.org/Index.aspx?DataSetCode=CRS1# and UN website at https://unstats.un.org/unsd/snaama/resQuery.asp.

5 Shin and Jung (2015) presents a rudimentary comparison of IKCF with ODA. Only a part of IKCF is compared with ODA. In contrast, our chapter discusses South Korean aid to North Korea itself as a main subject of an argument.

III. Comparative Analysis of South Korean Aid to North Korea and ODA

This section discusses comparisons between South Korean aid to North Korea and ODA. By analyzing official publications of the South Korean government, including the White Papers on Korean Unification and the International Development Cooperation Annual Comprehensive Implementation Plans, we show how South Korean aid to North Korea and ODA are similar and at the same time different from each other in terms of their goals and purposes.[6] Furthermore, we identify actors relevant to providing aid to North Korea and ODA to illustrate their similarities and differences, focused on the implementation process.

The basic goal of South Korean aid to North Korea is to protect the basic rights of North Koreans, and thus, in the longer term, contribute to the restoration of the Korean national community. The goals and principles of South Korean aid to North Korea by period can be examined through the White Papers on Korean Unification.[7] The Kim Young-sam administration, which lasted from 1993 to 1998, identified the goals of South Korea's assistance to North Korea as the alleviation of North Korea's food shortage and the improvement of intra-Korean relations. The Kim Young-sam administration states its position on the principle of assistance to the DPRK as follows. "Rice aid to the

---

6 There are three general theories of donor motivations: idealism, realism and constructivism. ODA exists for the purpose of economic development and the welfare improvement of the recipient countries based on idealism. Emphasizing humanitarianism in the international community prompts a clash between communism and humanitarianism in the ODA world (Lumsdaine 1993). On the other hands, realists argue that there is no aid that is not tied to national interest and argue that foreign aid policy is politically motivated, even if done for non-political purposes such as humanitarianism. (Morgenthau 1962,). Certainly, Constructivism defines relations between nations through identity and interest formed in the process of interaction. Their identity and interests are formed by shared norms, and the shared norms determine nations' behaviors (Wendt 1999). Since the various agreements and declarations in the international community, including the MDGs and the SDGs, have the status of common norms, powerful states such as the United States can even easily deny them. Motivations for aid may depend on the situation and the environment, and the priorities will change according to the policy goals of each country. The purpose of this study is to analyze South Korean aid to other countries and North Korea based on those theoretical viewpoints.

7 The ROK government issues a White Paper on Korean Unification and makes public its position on South-North relations and ROK policies toward North Korea. The White Paper on Korean Unification especially introduces the detailed status of and plans for assistance to North Korea since 1995.

DPRK is hoped to be preferentially dealt with internally because it is an internal issue for Koreans, and it is advisable that assistance to the DPRK at the international level is handled cautiously in acknowledgment of the importance of procedure, and by taking into consideration the special and unique nature of the South-North relations" (Ministry of Unification 1995). Simultaneously, the administration has expressed the principle that "at the international level, South Korea, as a member state of the UN, will participate in UN assistance to North Korea on a scale that is in accordance with its economic power" (Ministry of Unification 1997).

During the Kim Dae-jung and the Roh Moo-hyun administrations, the goals of South Korean aid to North Korea were to uphold the universal value of humanitarianism, and a spirit of brotherly love based on the premise that South and North Koreans are one. In particular, at the international level, the basic principle is that humanitarian assistance should not be linked to the political situation of the country receiving assistance and thus, in the same context, the necessity to assist North Korea from a humanitarian point of view is emphasized (Ministry of Unification 2000).

Initially, the goal of aid to North Korea of the Lee Myung-bak and Park Geun-hye administrations was to provide assistance in full consideration of North Korea's humanitarian situation, South Korea's financial capacity, national consensus, and so on. However, after the sinking of the *Cheonan* corvette and the attack on Yeonpyeong Island, all assistance projects to North Korea were postponed with the exception of humanitarian assistance to the most vulnerable people of North Korea such as infants and the elderly. The basic position of the South Korean government has been consistently that humanitarian assistance to North Korea will be rendered regardless of the political situation, at least in limited sense (Snyder and Byun 2011; Ministry of Unification 2016). For the Moon Jae-in administration, there has been no substantial aid provided to North Korea due to the UN sanctions.

Meanwhile, the basic goal of the South Korean government's international development cooperation includes principles such as reducing poverty and improving the quality of life of people in developing countries, reinforcing friendly and cooperative relations and mutual exchanges with developing countries, respecting the principles of the UN Charter, promoting the international community's mutual harmony and cooperation, and others (Kim and Oh 2012; The Committee for International Development

Cooperation 2014). The basic principles of South Korean international development cooperation can be examined in detail in the International Development Cooperation Annual Comprehensive Implementation Plans (Annual Implementation Plans).[8] South Korea first launched the Comprehensive Plan for Improving Korean ODA in 2005, and has announced the Annual Implementation Plan every year since then. From 2006 to 2008, the implementation goals of international development cooperation were to 1) contribute to the achievement of the Millennium Development Goals, 2) provide the foundation of economic cooperation with developing countries in order to promote the overseas expansion of South Korean companies, and 3) advance a Korean model of international development cooperation (Prime Minister's Office 2005; 2006; 2007). Since the Lee Myung-bak administration, global goals, such as contributing to the maintenance of international peace through humanitarian assistance, have also been emphasized.

At the same time, ODA has also been deployed for South Korean national interests. For example, the Lee Myung-bak administration established the New Asia Diplomacy assistance and expansion of peace-building projects for reconstruction in post-conflict areas as specific and important directions for international development cooperation (Prime Minister's Office 2009). Similar to the Lee Myung-bak administration, the Park Geun-hye administration also sought to expand and enhance external relations through ODA. Moreover, the Park administration mentioned the effort to secure a domestic support base and the effort to enhance the efficiency of development cooperation as additional directions for implementation (Prime Minister's Office 2013; 2014; 2015).

The goals and implementation principles of South Korean aid to North Korea and ODA can be distinguished as follows. First, in terms of goals, South Korean aid to North Korea and ODA are similar in that both aim to protect basic human rights, enhance the quality of life of people in the receiving country, and improve relations with the recipient country. The only difference is that the former targets North Korea while

8 The ROK government makes the Annual Implementation Plan through the Korea Official Development Assistance website of the Committee for International Development Cooperation (http://www.odakorea.go.kr), the Office for Government Policy Coordination. The Annual Implementation Plan, which has been reported every year from 2006 to 2016, includes in its content the ROK government's international development cooperation implementation plans and assessments. This study reviews the Annual Implementation Plans from 2006 to 2016 to trace the evolution of the ROK government's official position on international development cooperation.

the latter targets developing countries. Second, the principles of implementation differ. In the case of assistance to North Korea, the unique relationship between South and North Koreas as divided nations is being emphasized, while in the case of international development cooperation the common principles of the international community are stressed. However, the current implementation principles of the two forms of assistance simultaneously entail both global principles and the principle of achieving special national interests.

The actors and implementation processes of South Korean aid to North Korea and ODA need to be examined through the relevant laws. The Inter-Korean Exchanges and Cooperation Act prescribes the necessary matters to facilitate reciprocal exchange and cooperation between South and North Korea.[9] This Act especially entrusts the MOU to coordinate the policies regarding inter-Korean exchange and cooperation, and establish the inter-Korean Exchange and Cooperation Promotion Council (the Council) to decide important matters.

The Council deliberates upon and resolves matters related to the overall control, coordination, and support of cooperative projects, including assistance to North Korea, and the promotion of cooperation among relevant ministries and agencies. As the main supervising organ, the MOU supervises the execution of the Council resolution matters. The funding source for aid to North Korea is the Inter-Korean Cooperation Fund (IKCF), which is executed based on the Inter-Korean Cooperation Fund Act (IKCF Act). Article 7 of the IKCF Act stipulates the basic policies on the operation and management of the IKCF, the operation plans of the fund, and reports on the settlement of accounts and other matters deemed necessary by the Minister of Unification, which should be decided through Council resolution. The IKCF Act was legislated to establish the IKCF in accordance with the Inter-Korean Exchanges and Cooperation Act in order to provide assistance for the mutual exchange and cooperation between South Korea and North Korea, and to provide for matters related to the operation and management of the fund.[10] As the main body for operating and managing the fund, the MOU is in charge of

9 The Act was legislated in 1990 and amended 13 times. It includes regulations on the establishment and functions of the Inter-Korean Exchange and Cooperation Promotion Council, visits, and trade between South Korea and North Korea, cooperative projects, and others.

10 The IKCF Act was legislated in 1990 and amended 10 times. It stipulates the establishment,

establishing basic policies on the operation and management of the fund. It also designs the annual operation plans of the fund and the report on the settlement of accounts, determining the assistance policies of the IKCF projects, and consulting with relevant ministries on these projects.

The Export-Import Bank of Korea (Korea Exim bank) is in charge of the fund at the working level. Specifically, it is responsible for the management of the fund (management of the fund accounts, handling the accounting, and management of surplus money), consultation on and appraisal of the requested assistance projects, execution of the fund, and post-management of the assistance project and fund. According to Article 7.2 of the IKCF Act and Article 5 of the Presidential Decree, the Korea Exim bank is the financial institution entrusted with administrative affairs concerning the operation and management of the IKCF.

In accordance with the Framework Act on International Development Cooperation (Framework Act), institutionally South Korean ODA has three dimensions: overall policy-making and coordinating institutions, supervising ministries, and implementing agencies (Prime Minister's Office 2014). First, the Committee for International Development Cooperation (CIDC) is the overall supervisory and coordination committee of ODA, which is chaired by the Prime Minister and composed of the heads of central administrative organs and relevant public organizations, and civilian experts. The CIDC is the highest-level government body that deliberates and decides on key issues related to ODA and it coordinates strategies and policies of ODA in order to implement the international development cooperation policies more comprehensively and systematically.[11]

---

financial resources, operation and management, reporting, and redemption of the fund. The Act also regulates diverse uses of the fund. Among these, assistance to North Korea falls within the scope of Article 7.6: "Financing and subsidization of the funds necessary for inter-Korean exchange and cooperation, which contributes to the restoration of the reliability among the Korean people and the national community, and support of any project of the fund." For this reason, all assistance to North Korea is executed through the IKCF. See Haggard, Ryu, and Boydston (2015).

11 The CIDC was first established under the Prime Minister in 2006 through a Presidential Decree and was upgraded to a de jure committee through the promulgation of the Framework Act in 2010. The CIDC has a Working Committee and a Sub-Committee for Evaluation affiliated to it. Meanwhile, the Office for Government Policy Coordination serves as the secretariat of the CIDC in accordance to the Framework Act and supports the operations of the CIDC and its committees through the working-level support of ODA policy formulation, ODA evaluation, ODA project coordination, and others.

Next, as the supervising ministries of bilateral concessional loans and bilateral grants, the Ministry of Strategy and Finance (MOSF) and the Ministry of Foreign Affairs (MOFA) establish a five-year Mid-Term ODA Policy Plan and an Annual Implementation Plan for each channel as described above, and monitor the implementation progress, respectively. The MOSF manages the Economic Development Cooperation Fund (EDCF) by the mandate of the Fund Management Council and entrusts the Korea Exim bank with the operation of the fund; it also supervises identification and selection, implementation, and evaluation of concessional loan projects.

To implement ODA, the MOFA oversees the establishment, implementation, and coordination of grant policies by formulating the basic mid-term policies and annual implementation plans, and regional and country-specific ODA plans in the grant sector, and implements ODA projects through the Korea International Cooperation Agency (KOICA), which is the implementing agency. In accordance with the Economic Development Cooperation Fund Act and the related Enforcement Decree, the Korea Exim bank is entrusted by the Minister of MOSF with the operation and administration of the EDCF and implements concessional loans, while KOICA (Korea International Cooperation Agency), established on the basis of the Korea International Cooperation Agency Act, is responsible for grant projects.

The implementation processes of South Korean aid to North Korea and South Korean ODA have similarities and differences. They are similar in that both are implemented according to what is a three-level process, involving an overall coordinating institution, supervising ministries, and implementing agencies. However, there are differences in implementation process in that South Korean aid to North Korea reflects the independent initiative of the MOU in that the overall coordinating institution and supervising institution are the same. The ODA implementation is more complex. It falls under the supervision of the Office for Government Policy Coordination. The MOSF and the MOFA supervise concessional loans and grants based on the nature of the assistance. Moreover, in the case of the assistance to North Korea, the Korea Exim bank is the exclusive implementing organization, while in the case of international development cooperation projects are implemented by either the Korea Exim bank or the Korea International Cooperation Agency (KOICA) depending on the nature of the project.

IV. Innovative Ways of Understanding South Korean Aid to North Korea

As explained previously, the main difference between South Korean aid to North Korea and ODA is that the former targets North Korea and the latter focuses on developing countries, among which North Korea is included. The current problems regarding South Korean aid to North Korea and ODA could be alleviated to a certain extent were South Korean aid to North Korea considered a type of ODA. The practical contents of South Korean aid to North Korea and ODA are similar: both aim to protect basic human rights and improve the quality of life of people in the receiving countries. Therefore, from the perspective of assistance goals, there is no great problem in regarding South Korean aid to North Korea as a type of international development cooperation. Moreover, the implementation process of assistance to North Korea is similar to that of ODA and divided into the same three levels: overall coordination, supervision, and implementation. In other words, there appears to be no special reason why South Korean aid to North Korea should be considered differently from ODA based on the implementation process.

However, there are also several problems associated with considering South Korean aid to North Korea as ODA. We address these issues along with new ways of conceptualizing South Korean aid to North Korea. First, the main issue is whether North Korea can be seen as a recipient country—that is, whether it can be seen as a different country from a South Korean perspective. When considering the fact that South Korea and North Korea are both UN member states, North Korea can indeed be viewed as a separate country from South Korea.[12]

However, the Constitution of South Korea does not acknowledge North Korea as an independent and separate country. According to article 3 of the Constitution of the Republic of Korea, "the territory of the Republic of Korea shall consist of the Korean peninsula and its adjacent islands."[13] Hence, South Korea regards North Korea as special

12 South Korea and North Korea became member states to the UN, each having a separate seat, on September 18, 1991, at the 46th Session of the UN General Assembly.

13 For relevant laws, refer to National Law Information Center website at http://law.go.kr/engLsSc.do?menuId=0&subMenu=5&query=.

territories. "Special territories" can be understood as objectives of national reunification, as stated in article 4, where it says "the Republic of Korea shall seek unification and shall formulate and carry out a policy of peaceful unification based on the basic free and democratic order." Moreover, article 3 of the "Development of Inter-Korean Relations Act" states that "inter-Korean relations are not relations between nations, but special relations established temporarily in the course of pursuing unification," and regards inter-Korean trade as intra-national, not as international trade.

In article 2 of the "Korea International Cooperation Agency Act" and article 2 of the "Foreign Economic Cooperation Fund Act," it is stated that recipients are "determined by the Minister of Foreign Affairs and Trade" and "designated as such by Minister of Strategy and Finance." Because of South Korean laws, North Korea is neither considered as an object of ODA nor included in the statistics of ODA.

Table 1. ODA Definition, starting with 2018 Data

The DAC defines ODA as "those flows to countries and territories on the DAC List of ODA Recipients and to multilateral institutions which are:

i. provided by official agencies, including state and local governments, or by their executive agencies;
ii. and each transaction of which:
a. is administered with the promotion of the economic development and welfare of developing countries as its main objective; and
b. is concessional in character. In DAC statistics, this implies a grant element of at least
- 45 per cent in the case of bilateral loans to the official sector of LDCs and other LICs
- 15 per cent in the case of bilateral loans to the official sector of LMICs
- 10 per cent in the case of bilateral loans to the official sector of UMICs
- 10 per cent in the case of loans to multilateral institutions

Source: OECD, "Official development assistance – definition and coverage," at www.oecd.org/dac/stats/officialdevelopmentassistancedefinitionandcoverage.htm#Definition.

Nevertheless, there is still potential to interpret aid to North Korea as ODA. In Table 1, not only "countries" but "territories" are considered as recipients according to the definition of ODA by OECD DAC. Therefore, South Korean aid to North Korea could be interpreted as ODA, as South Korea regards North Korea as "special territories." To wit, this does not violate the highest law of South Korea, the "Constitution of the Republic of Korea," nor the "Development of Inter-Korean Relations Act." However, as stated above, articles of the "Korea International Cooperation Agency Act," and the "Foreign Economic Cooperation Fund Act" are the legal basis of development support. The stated countries "determined by the Minister of Foreign Affairs and Trade," and "designated as such by the Minister of Strategy and Finance" become obstacles to recognizing South Korean aid to North Korea as ODA.

In other words, the reason why South Korea does not regard its aid to North Korea as ODA is because it understands ODA as an act carried out by one country to "other countries." However, because the definition of ODA establishes ODA recipients as countries and territories on the global list, the argument that aid to North Korea cannot be regarded as ODA is not a position not shared by the international community, but a problem with domestic laws.

We can find ways to avoid a clash between domestic laws and international standards. If articles stating "countries determined by the Minister" of the "Korea International Cooperation Agency Act," and "Foreign Economic Cooperation Fund Act" are replaced with "countries and territories determined by the Minister," it would be possible to provide aid to North Korea through KOICA, and the resources of EDCF. Moreover, this would possibly also include aid to North Korea via the Inter-Korean Cooperation Fund (IKCF) as ODA—if other conditions (countries, concession rates, purpose, etc.) are valid—because North Korea is a territory on the OECD DAC recipient list.

Second, we should consider the issues related to the process of implementing South Korean aid to North Korea. When South Korea provides aid to North Korea, it suffers from the domestic criticism that aid to North Korea involves the mere transfer of money toward the North Korean government, rather than humanitarian or development assistance. Even though there is no clear proof that South Korean aid to North Korea has been actually used for nuclear tests, there is the suspicion that money from South Korea is not used for the sectors it is intended for in North Korea. South Korea cannot monitor how its aid to North Korea is used. Even food aid can be used to stabilize the control of North Korean government over the general public.

However, this issue could be overcome if South Korea were to provide aid to North Korea as ODA with the help of international organizations. For instance, South Korea could provide its food aid to North Korea in coordination with the World Food Programme (WFP). As WFP strictly monitors the distribution process through pre-inspection, implementation, and evaluation of aid, aid to North Korea can reach the general public and alleviate the harsh life conditions of the North Korean people.

The third issue is whether North Korea is willing or able to receive South Korean aid once South Korea starts to provide it as ODA. In September 2005, North Korea rejected international humanitarian assistance. Instead, it officially requested development assistance (*Dong-A Ilbo* 2005). Thus, it can be understood that North Korea wants to receive ODA from donors in order to develop infrastructure or technologies instead of receiving short-term humanitarian assistance (Easterly 2007). North Korea appears willing to receive ODA from South Korea. However, to activate a development assistance program in practice, the level of openness of North Korea has to be similar to that of other recipient countries. Owing to continuing North Korean nuclear tests, the international community has implemented economic sanctions against North Korea. As the level of the economic sanctions becomes higher and higher, North Korea is likely to be more isolated from international society. Securing a sufficient level of openness to provide development assistance therefore becomes a problem (Morrow 2006).

To address this issue, South Korea needs to take the initiative by reconceptualizing its aid to North Korea. South Korea emphasizes its own experience of development from being a recipient to being a donor and attempts to maintain a vigorous foreign aid policy toward low-income and marginalized countries as a donor.[14] Emphasizing its development experience, South Korea should persuade the international community to provide North Korea ODA. It can assert that aid to North Korea will ultimately contribute to the settlement of peace in the Korean peninsula (Jun, Jeong, Son and Kim 2010). In this way, South Korean aid to North Korea can be considered as ODA, and North Korea can receive it. If aid to North Korea is converted to development assistance, the "special nature" of this aspect of inter-Korean ties could fade. Paradoxically, however, the "special nature" can be used in support of the argument for South Korea undertaking this initiative.

The last issue is related to the changing concept of ODA. Since the end of 2012, the international community, led by the OECD, has prepared to develop a new measurement of total official support. In the DAC High Level Meeting in December

---

14 See Korea International Cooperation Agency at http://stat.koica.go.kr/.

2014, the OECD agreed to develop a new concept of Total Official Support for Sustainable Development (TOSSD). TOSSD is designed to "complement ODA by increasing transparency and monitoring important new trends that are shaping the international development finance landscape, including: the leveraging/catalytic effect of ODA; the use of blended finance packages; and the use of innovative risk mitigation instruments in development cooperation."[15] Under the rubric of TOSSD, different types of official supports to the recipient can be included and the total volume of ODA will be increased owing to change in the concept of ODA. Donors hope to include the various sources of support to recipients and expand the scope of ODA.

Following this trend toward new ways of measuring ODA, South Korean aid to North Korea can be included as ODA or TOSSD. It is a good time for South Korea to include aid to North Korea as one of its official forms of support. By doing so, South Korea can follow new trends, and the volume of Korean support to recipients will be significantly increased as explained previously. South Korea moreover does play by the rules because North Korea is a country that desperately needs to receive support from outside. Furthermore, TOSSD emphasizes the importance of peace and security when donors provide aid to recipients. As explained previously, South Korean aid to North Korea could comply fully with this concept because doing so contributes to the maintenance of peace in the Korean peninsula.

V. Conclusion

In this chapter, we attempt to understand the historical background and conceptualization of South Korean aid to North Korea. We find that South Korean aid to North Korea is not clearly understood because of the special relationship between the two sides of the demilitarized zone. Because South Korea does not include its aid to North Korea within its measure of ODA, South Korean ODA half of its actual support to foreign countries. We address the issues related to this problem. By changing how

15 See the OECD website at www.oecd.org/dac/financing-sustainable-development/tossd.htm.

South Korean laws related to international development cooperation are applied, South Korean aid to North Korea could be considered ODA. Moreover, the implementation and monitoring of its support to North Korea can be done through interactions with the international community. The new concept of TOSSD can also include South Korean aid to North Korea as one of type of support to foreign countries.

This chapter has some limitations. Above all, it is descriptive in nature. However, limited research has been published analyzing South Korean aid to North Korea from the perspective of international development cooperation. Our chapter can serve as a new framework to conceptualize the aid relationship between South and North Korea. Second, our study may lack generalizability toward a more theoretical understanding of international development cooperation in general. Because we address a very special case, i.e., the two Koreas, there is little room to develop a general theory applicable to other cases. Nonetheless, we can say that such an approach will possibly improve understanding of a special relationship between two Koreas. Third, we analyze the conceptualization of South Korean aid to North Korea rather than the operationalization of it. That is why we do not suggest how South Korean aid to North Korea should be provided and operated. In addition, we do not argue that South Korean aid to North Korea and ODA should be merged and implemented together. We do not even agree that the merger of these two is more promising or would improve implementation. The reason why we do not presentation recommendations for implementation policies is that we need to first focus on the conceptual dimensions of South Korean aid to North Korea and changes thereof. The issue of how to better implement of South Korean aid to North Korea should be dealt with as a future study. However, our analysis helps one understand South Korea more clearly as a donor, with an under-recognized amount of ODA due to the exclusion of South Korea aid to North Korea. With a newly expanded concept of its ODA, South Korea can be understood as a more important donor, which could galvanize it to put more effort into expanding its aid to other countries. As a new status, South Korea will have the better motivation to make its relationship with North Korea, which will contribute to peace in the Korean peninsula more positively.

References

Chun, Hong-Min, Elijah N. Munyi, and Heejin Lee. 2010. "South Korea as an Emerging Donor: Challenges and Changes on Its Entering OECD/DAC." *Journal of International Development*, vol. 22, no. 6 (August), pp. 788–802.

Dong-A Ilbo. 2005. "NK, Change the food aid system." September 10.

Easterly, William. 2007. *The White Man's Burden: Why the West's Efforts to Aid the Rest Have Done So Much Ill and So Little Good.* New York: Penguin Books.

Haggard, Stephan, and Marcus Noland. 2013. *Famine in North Korea: Market, Aid and Reform.* New York: Columbia University Press.

Stephan Haggard, Stephan, Jaesung Ryu, and Kent Boydston. 2015. "South Korean Aid to the North: An Accounting 1991–2015." Peterson Institute for International Economies – North Korea: Witness to Transformation (blog), July 20, at https://piie.com/blogs/north-korea-witness-transformation/south-korean-aid-north-i-accounting-1991-2015 (accessed August 20, 2016).

Jo, Dongho. 2008. "Balamjighan daebukjiwon-ui gaeseonbanghyang: Daebukjiwongwa ODAui bigyoleul batang-eulo" [Policy recommendations for improving assistance to North Korea: Based on comparison with official development assistance]." *Bigyogyungje Yeongu [The Comparative Economic Review]*, vol. 15, no. 1, pp. 153–205.

Jonsson, Gabriel. 2006. *Towards Korean Reconciliation.* Burlington: Ashgate.

Jun, Seung-Hoon, Yeon-Seung Jeong, Gwang-Ju Son, and So-Won Kim. 2010. *Gaebalhyeomnyeok Gyeongheomui Daebukjiwon Hwaryong Bangan* [The methods of aid to North Korea with development assistance experiences]. Sungnam: KOICA.

Kim, Ji-hyung. 2012. "The Development of the Discussions on Unification during the Early Post-Cold War Era." *International Journal of Korean History*, vol. 17, no. 1, pp. 171–205.

Kim, Eun Mee and Jinhwan Oh. 2012. "Determinants of Foreign Aid: The Case of South Korea." *Journal of East Asian Studies*, vol. 12, no. 2 (May), pp. 251–274.

Lee, Keum-Soon. 2005. "Daebuk indojeok jiwon-ui Silhyoseong Yeongu: pyeong-gajipyowa gwaje" [A study on the effectiveness of the humanitarian assistance to North Korea: Measurement and policy directions]. *Tongil jeungchak yeongu [Unification Policy Studies]*, vol. 14, no. 2, pp. 42–43.

Lumsdaine, D. H. 1993. *Moral Vision in International Politics: The Foreign Aid Regime, 1949–1989.* Princeton: Princeton University Press.

———. n.d.b. <Home page>, at www.unikorea.go.kr/main.do (accessed July 4, 2016).

———. 1995. *1995 Tong-ilbaegseo [White Paper on Korean Unification]*. Seoul: Ministry of Unification.

———. 1997. *1997 Tong-ilbaegseo [White Paper on Korean Unification]*. Seoul: Ministry of

Unification.
———. 2000. *2000 Tong-ilbaegseo [White Paper on Korean Unification]*. Seoul: Ministry of Unification.
———. 2012. *2012 Tong-ilbaegseo [White Paper on Korean Unification]*. Seoul: Ministry of Unification.
———. 2016. *2016 Tong-ilbaegseo [White Paper on Korean Unification]*. Seoul: Ministry of Unification.
Moon, Kyungyon. 2013. "Daebukjiwon Dillemawa Geukbokbang-an mosaek" [Dilemmas in aid to North Korea and searching for a solution]." *Geulrobel jeongchi yeongu [Journal of Global Politics]*, vol. 6, no. 1, pp. 5–37.
Morgenthau, Hans. 1962. "A Political Theory of Foreign Aid." *The American Political Science Review*, vol. 56, no. 2, pp. 301–309.
Morrow, Daniel. 2006. "Possible World Bank Assistance to North Korea: Issues and Challenges." *Asian Perspective*, vol. 30, no. 3 (Fall), pp. 37–67.
OECD. n.d. "What is total official support for sustainable development (TOSSD)?" at http://www.oecd.org/dac/financing-sustainable-development/tossd.htm.
OECD. 2016. "OECD DAC Member Profile: Korea." At www.oecd.org/dac/korea.htm (accessed July 20, 2016).
Park, Jiyoun. 2015. "Gugjesahoe Daebugjiwon Bunseog" [International aid to North Korea from 1945 to 2014]. *Sooeun Bookhan Gyungje [Korea Exim North Korea Economic Review]*, vol. 12, no. 1, pp. 76–80.
———. 2016. "Norms and Realities of Applying the Aid Discourse on Fragile States to North Korea," *Asian Politics and Policy*, vol. 8, no. 4 (October), pp. 559–574.
Park, Jiyoun, and Kyungyon Moon. 2015. "Hangugjeongbuui Daebugjiwon 'Tong-gye'e daehan Bipanjeog Gochal: OECD Gong-yeogugbogochegye(CRS)waui Bigyoleul Jungsim-eulo" [A Review of 'statistics' on ROK's aid to the DPRK: Comparing with OECD CRS]. *Dongseo Yeongu [East and West Studies]*, vol. 27, no. 1, pp. 5–27.
Prime Minister's Office. 2005. *2006 Annual Implementation Plan*. At www.odakorea.go.kr (accessed July 6, 2016).
———. 2006. *2007 Annual Implementation Plan*. At www.odakorea.go.kr (accessed July 6, 2016).
———. 2007. *2008 Annual Implementation Plan*. At www.odakorea.go.kr (accessed July 6, 2016).
———. 2009. *2010 Annual Implementation Plan*. At www.odakorea.go.kr (accessed July 6, 2016).
———. 2013. *2014 Annual Implementation Plan*. At www.odakorea.go.kr (accessed July 6, 2016).
———. 2014. *2015 Annual Implementation Plan*. At www.odakorea.go.kr (accessed July 6, 2016).
———. 2015. *2016 Annual Implementation Plan*. At www.odakorea.go.kr (accessed July 6, 2016).
Shin, Sang-hyup, and Somin Jung. 2015. "A Study on the Integration of the IKCF into Korea's ODA: Is it Possible?" *International Area Studies Review*, vol. 19, no. 3, pp. 3–31.
Snyder, Scott. 2010. "Changes in Seoul's North Korean Policy and Implications for Pyongyang's Inter Korean Diplomacy." In Kyung-Ae Park, ed., *New Challenges of North Korean Foreign Policy*. New York: Palgrave Macmillan, pp. 153–172.

Snyder, Scott, and See-won Byun. 2011. "Cheonan and Yeonpyeong: The Northeast Asian Response to North Korea's Provocations." *Rusi Journal*, vol. 156, no. 2 (April/May), pp. 74–81.

Son, Key-young. 2006. *South Korean Engagement Policies and North Korea: Identities, Norms and the Sunshine Policy*. New York: Routledge.

The Committee for International Development Cooperation. 2014. *Hankuk ODA Baekseo [Korea's Official Development Assistance White Paper]*. Seoul: The Committee for International Development Cooperation.

Watson, Iain. 2013. "Governments and NGOs in Asian Overseas Development Assistance: Assessing South Korea's Model of Foreign Aid." *Asian Studies Review*, vol. 36, no. 1 (March), pp. 79–103.

Wendt, Alexander. 1999. *Social Theory of International Politics*. Cambridge: Cambridge University Press.

Yonhap News. 2015. "Unification Minister Hong Yong-pyo said Support for North Korea should be changed from a single event to development and cooperation" November 6.

Chapter 10

What Do We Know and Do Not Know?: Attitudes Toward North Korea and Unification

Jaeyoung Hur (Yonsei University)
Sanghoon Park (University of South Carolina)

Abstract

This article examines whether existing explanations of South Korean attitudes regarding North Korea and Korean unification adequately explain changes after the declaration at Panmunjom on April 27, 2018. This study uses the National Consciousness Survey Data to estimate these shifts in attitude. Our results show that South Korean attitudes shifted following the Panmunjom Declaration for Peace, Prosperity, and Unification of the Korean Peninsula. We show that existing explanations for generational effects do not explain the national attitude shifts on unification; our study demonstrates that a wide divergence exists between younger and the older generations, and younger generations are more likely to display a negative attitude toward North Korea and unification even after the Declaration. We also show that the prospects of unification evoke different attitudes across generations. Our results imply that the Panmunjom Declaration is a prominent political event, but it is necessary to analyze it without overestimating it.

Keywords: The Panmunjom Declaration, Attitudes on Korean Unification, Attitudes toward North Korea, Generations, Prospects of unification

I. Introduction

The unification policy in South Korea has been up and down with various handovers of administration. Conservative administrations tended to take a strong stance against North Korea, while liberal administrations led the engagement policy as a basis for reconciliation and cooperation. President Jae-In Moon, elected in a shift of power from the conservative administration over the past decade, is leading the inter-Korean relationship to a new phase. The new administration is pushing for policies that require inter-Korean cooperation, which was not the case under the conservative administration. For instance, the inter-Korean relationship is rapidly changing in political, cultural, and military policies, such as the joint inter-Korean rail investigation, the withdrawal of the demilitarized zone guard post (DMZ GP), the linkage of the arrowhead roads in DMZ for the KIA (Killed in Action) Recovery and Identification project, and the promotion of forest cooperation.

Indeed, the inter-Korean relationship faced several historical events in 2018. North Korea sent athletes, cheering squads, and art troupes to the Pyeongchang Winter Olympics. After alleviating these tensions and creating an atmosphere of cooperation, South Korea and North Korea held three summit meetings together. The series of meetings led to the Panmunjom Declaration on April 27, and the Pyongyang Joint Declaration on September 19. Similarly, incumbent leaders of the United States and North Korea held their first summit in history. At the first meeting, between the US and North Korea, the leaders adopted the Singapore Joint Statement, promising a joint effort to build a lasting and substantial peace regime on the Korean peninsula. US–North Korea relations, as well as inter-Korean relations, are on a new path, and we are in a unique international situation concerning the Korean Peninsula.

The Panmunjom Declaration reminds us of the 10.4 Inter-Korean Joint Declaration in 2007, which made South Koreans expect that it is possible to solve the inter-Korean relations with reconciliation and cooperation. In particular, the Panmunjom Declaration is an effort to improve North Korea relations entirely after the 5.24 measures, which cut off relations with North Korea. The world has indeed paid attention to the Panmunjom Declaration, and the Korean government has shown optimistic expectations. However, there are also criticisms that the Panmunjom

Declaration's contents are not much different from the past 10.4 South-North Summit Declaration, which eventually failed to manage the inter-Korean relationship and North Korea's nuclear development. It implies that the Panmunjom Declaration has only a symbolic meaning, rather than a political event that can bring about substantial change.

Do the recent changes fundamentally address North Korea's ongoing threat to the security of South Korea and inter-Korean relations? In other words, the question is whether the Panmunjom Declaration is meaningful enough to change the inter-Korean relationships fundamentally like the previous declarations, such as the South-North Joint Declaration in June 2000, and the North–South Summit Declaration in October 2007. If so, at least, it is not too much to say that the Panmunjom improves the attitudes toward North Korea and the unification of South Koreans. Existing studies have explained the differences of opinions of Korean people toward the unification issues in terms of political ideology and generational preferences. However, members of Korean society have experienced various policy changes and the development of national guidance from North Korea. One can question whether the changes caused by the Panmunjom Declaration will lead to the same results as previous declarations.

For the Pyeongchang Winter Olympics of 2018, 80% of Koreans in their 20s and 30s opposed the formation of the joint South Korean and North Korean women's ice hockey team (Seong and Hong, 2018). The "National Consciousness Survey on Inter-Korean Integration 2017," published by the Korea Institute for National Unification, found that negative attitudes toward the need for unification, unification tax, and expected benefits for unification were significantly higher for Koreans in their 20s and 30s than for other age groups. Besides this, respondents were divided as to whether they regarded the two Koreas as a single nation. This change paradoxically shows that we need to consider unification issues from different perspectives for a changing future, and suggests that existing theoretical analysis needs to reconsider whether they are producing meaningful results under such changing contexts.

This study examines whether the political event of the Panmunjom Declaration has changed the attitudes and perceptions of Korean people toward unification. If the Panmunjom Declaration is indeed a significant event, we can expect to observe immediate changes in attitudes and perceptions toward inter-Korean relationships, which might affect the success or failure of future policies. As a result, it is difficult to say that the event has changed the attitudes toward North Korea and unification after the Panmunjom Declaration. It means that the Panmunjom Declaration might not fundamentally change the long-term view of respondents on inter-Korean relations.

This chapter is organized as follows. In the next two sections, we review the theoretical and empirical studies on the issues of unification and North Korea relations. In Section 4, we develop the conceptual framework of our analysis. Following this, Section 5 describes the dataset and empirical models we have constructed to test our hypotheses about changes after the Panmunjom Declaration. Section 6 presents and discusses our empirical results, and we conclude by addressing issues for further inquiry.

II. The Effect of Political Events on Attitudes toward North Korea and Unification in South Korea

1. Attitudes toward North Korea and Unification in South Korea

Since the end of 1998, when the Dae-Jung Kim administration was attempting to improve inter-Korean relations, scholars have been actively producing research related to inter-Korean relationships. The research on inter-Korean relationships is diverse. Some studies discuss the government's countermeasures related to military provocations. Others diagnose the nature of a particular administration's policy toward North Korea, while still others examine the people's attitudes toward unification and North Korea policy.

Studies that derive implications through empirical research using surveys can provide leverage for policymakers. Since these studies contribute to looking at public attitudes on the issues of unification and North Korea issues, it helps policymakers establish policy that corresponds with the demand of the public. For sustainable unification and North Korea policies, it is necessary to understand the attitudes toward unification and North Korea of the people at the micro-level.

Many scholars have investigated the changes and trends of South Koreans using surveys. Some find that respondents' attitudes toward unification and North Korea differ depending on their political ideologies, political sophistication, and the level of partisanship. For example, the more someone has a liberal ideology, the more likely one is to support the Moo-hyun Rho administration's moderate policy toward North Korea. At the same time, the more conservative one is, the more likely one is to advocate the Myung-bak Lee administration's firm policy toward North Korea (Song and Kwon, 2013).

However, it is an unrealistic assumption that every voter correctly understands his political ideology. Sophisticated voters will choose to vote based on their political ideology or policy evaluation, but if voters are not sophisticated, they are less likely to vote based on political motivation (Campbell et al., 1960; Luskin, 1987). In Korean politics, political sophistication plays a role as a variable that mediates the political ideology of voters. Only those groups with a high degree of sophistication show the empirical results of discriminatory policy preferences in the attitude toward the the United States-Republic of Korea relationship, the North Korean policy direction, and the North Korean nuclear issues (Ryu, 2012).

Partisanships can be a shortcut for political information or cues, which can have significant impacts on individual voters' policy preferences. It is costly for voters to gain proper and precise political information. When voters obtain specific information to understand any policy, even a slight increase in costs can be felt. On the other hand, partisan cues, represented by political parties, help voters to predict and understand the position of candidates or specific policies, albeit at a high cost (Rahn, 1993; Bartels, 2000; Klar, 2014). An empirical analysis of voters' attitudes toward North Korea policy after the 20th general election in 2016 shows that supporters of the Democratic Party felt more efficacy in social and cultural exchange, inter-Korean economic cooperation, and regular talks than those of the Saenuri Party (Jung, 2016).

There are many studies on the effects of individual tendencies such as political ideology, political sophistication, and partisanship on an individual's behavior or personal attitude. However, it is not possible to clearly explain where these political tendencies come from or what changes them. In terms of partisanship, Campbell et al. (1960) propose the concept of party identification, defined as affective orientation. According to their study, party identification is a psychological attachment to preferred partisan groups. It is assumed to have an ongoing tendency, as it is a sort of emotional bond. Thus, Campbell et al. (1960, 146–147) argue that party identification is formed in the individual's early socialization process. It implies that individuals have specific party identification before they reach voting age. Also, an individual's nearest social environment, especially the family, has the most significant influence on forming a partisan preference. Campbell et al. (1960, 161–165) show that the longer the party identification has been formed, the higher the intensity of party identification increases. In other words, they argue that older individuals are more likely to enhance their party identifications. Bartels (2000) also shows that a more substantial influence of party identification on voting behavior was attributed to the fact that party identification preceded other political attitudes.

However, while partisanship matters, its influence can vary depending on its social setting. Here, the social context implies the social circumstances to which individuals belong. Klar (2014) disaggregates the partisan differences within groups, because groups are homogeneous and heterogeneous and between-group variations are distinctive. Klar (2014) found that within each group, the partisan gap still holds. In the context of American politics, we can understand that homogeneous partisan groups which have only Democrats or only Republicans, have very different partisan effects than heterogeneous groups, which have a mix of individuals from both parties.

Also, it is possible to consider the possibility that individual voter' economic considerations will affect unification and North Korea issues. A simple proposition that voters judge ruling parties when the economy goes down (or up) theorizes economic voting (Fiorina, 1981; Abramowitz, 2008). In South Korea, several studies have revealed that economic voting usually works in presidential elections (Lee, 2008; Jang, 2013; Moon, 2018). Reward–punishment voting, which allows governments and ruling parties to have democratic accountability to voters, explains how voters' evaluations lead to voting choice. It suggests that not only can direct economic and economic downturns at the national and household levels affect how the people perceive the issues in the future, but they can also affect the success or failure of specific policies beforehand. For example, the effects of political events, such as the North–South Summit talks, are characterized by position issues that are influenced by ideology and partisanship. In addition, it is closely related to the voter's retrospective or prospective evaluation (Kim, 2007). In the past, nationalism-based legitimacy mainly explained the issue of unification.

Still, over time, the consideration of the real benefits that can be achieved by nations and individuals through unification began to emerge (Choi, 2016). The issues related to unification and North Korea are shifting from a past-oriented approach to a pragmatic approach (Cho and Han, 2014). As the division of the two Koreas is prolonged, the homogeneous national identity is weakened. Therefore, the attitudes toward unification and North Korea vary, depending on people's assessment of the realistic political turmoil and economic burden that unification will bring.

Changes in social composition in the context of the generation– age cohort may have changed attitudes toward unification and North Korea. For example, Koreans who were in their 20s during the administrations of Presidents Dae-Jung Kim and Moo-hyun Roh had a strong tendency to approve aid to North Korea and oppose preemptive strikes on North Korea. Other generations that share different social experiences, such as post-war industrialization or the Korean War, show a distinct tendency to disagree with aid to North Korea (Chang, 2018). Also, the younger generation in South Korea considers national identity and material interests at the same time in terms of unification, and they find the latter more important. It means that attitudes toward inter-Korean relationship may be affected by a costs-and-benefits consideration. The negative attitude toward North Korea may be due to the long-term infraction of inter-Korean relations (Cho and Han, 2014). Conversely, if there is a prospect that the benefits of a relationship between the two Koreas will outweigh the costs, people will likely show a positive attitude change toward North Korea and unification.

2. The Influences of Political Events

Political events may occur under highly controlled conditions and can become predictable. At the same time, political events may occur under uncontrolled and unpredictable conditions. For example, we can predict the outcome of a political event such as an election that develops under a given system and rules. On the other hand, events that occur outside of the political actors can have unexpected results. Therefore, political events vary, and the effects of such events also vary (Smith, 2005).

Existing studies have explored what the effects of a political event are and how it affects different outcomes in various ways. A line of inquiry examines the direct influence of political events. For instance, Smith (2005) argues that a politically significant event may influence the image of political parties. A political event has internal and external factors. Internal factors make consumers learn from events and change the motivations of individual consumers. External factors are about image power, which is the perception of how influential the events are.

Healy et al. (2010) attempt to figure out the relationship between political events and voters' evaluation of the government's performance. They suggest that political events that people may think are irrelevant can actually affect the decisions people make on Election Day. Healy et al. (2010) draw their hypotheses from the psychological literature that makes an association between voter well-being and decision-making. They find that a voter with negative information from a political event may perceive a separate news story about the government policy in a less positive light (Healy et al., 2010, 12807). These studies show that political events can be essential information that changes the motivation of actors and directly affects their political behavior.

Another line of studies focuses on frame building and frame effects. Lim and Seo (2009) present how the US government and the US news media framed the speech of President George W. Bush in 2002 and how it affected the public perception of US citizens toward North Korea. The results show how the frame built by the two counterparts, the government and the news media, can affect the public's attitudes toward the country in question. In sum, a political event can affect the motivation of engaged actors, or a political event is mounted in the hope that it will be influential. In terms of the latter case, a political event may not bring fundamental changes.

Theorizing about factors affecting inter-Korean relations is inevitably influenced by major real-world events surrounding inter-Korean relationships. In other words, events occurring in North Korea or events such as a consensus between the two Koreas can drive actual and theoretical changes by affecting attitudes toward (and images of) North Korea and unification in South Korean society rather than any other internal or external changes (Kim, 2017, 158; Kim et al., 2008; Kim et al., 2003).

Besides the discussions of existing studies on the attitudes toward North Korea and unification, we focus on the effect of the Panmunjom Declaration as a politically critical event. The Panmunjom Declaration can be understood as a kind of turning point that hints at the transition in hard policy positions toward unification and North Korea. Considering the results and outcomes of several official talks with North Korea in the past, the Panmunjom Declaration may also have affected people's perception toward North Korea. Before and after the Panmunjom Declaration, various media outlets suggested the prospect that the Korean Peninsula issue would develop favorably in the future (Kim, 2018; Smith and Kim, 2018). After the Declaration, President Jae-In Moon's first year of approval exceeded 80% (Oh, 2018; Cho, 2018).

When we classify the main events of the inter-Korean relationship into "conflictive" versus "cooperative," different types of events would have differing results in Koreans' attitude toward North Korea and unification. Conflictive events that cause tensions between the two Koreas, such as the North Korean nuclear test, may increase the likelihood that people will show a negative attitude toward North Korea and unification. On the contrary, events that ease tensions, such as summit talks, are more likely to reduce the perception of the possible threat posed by North Korea and to encourage positive attitudes toward unification. In other words, the main event of the inter-Korean relationship can influence the attitudes of South Korean society members (Kim, 2017, 160-161, 171). If so, the Panmunjom Declaration can be an event with the effect of alleviating hostile perceptions of North Korea, as the summit between South and North Korea, which took place over ten years after President Myung-Bak Lee's administration imposed full sanctions against North Korea on May 24, 2010. It implies that we need to consider whether there has been any significant change in people's perception of North Korea. In other words, when an incident creates an atmosphere of reconciliation between the two Koreas, it is necessary to analyze whether the event fundamentally changed the understanding of the people who experienced the event.

Members of South Korean society are involved in conflictive or cooperative events with North Korea. They have experienced policy cycles in the past two decades in which North and South Korea repeat both cooperation and conflict. How to judge the success or failure of policies for managing North Korea can affect South Korean attitudes toward North Korea and unification. For example, those who believe that the appeasement policies of previous South Korean administrations toward North Korea have failed may not expect North Korea to change substantially despite the Panmunjom Declaration.

The recent tendency that the younger generation in South Korea shows more conservative attitudes suggests that the same type of events may have various influences. The characteristics of the young generation, which have been seen in previous studies such as "Cooperation with North Korea, Pro-unification, and Self-Defense," have been affected by conservative characteristics as shown in studies such as "Strong against North Korea, Passive or Anti-unification, and Korea-US Alliance" (Bae, 2018). Since the early 2000s, younger generations who have experienced tensions between the two Koreas are likely to have formed a negative perception of and attitudes toward North Korea and unification (Hur, 2014).

III. Research Design

1. Research Hypotheses

This study seeks to investigate whether the Panmunjom Declaration changed the attitude toward North Korea and unification. First, we explore the determinants of the attitude toward the North Korean leadership and the attitude toward North Korea in general. On the one hand, the ministry of defense of South Korea primarily designated as "enemies" those which support the hereditary regimes of Il-Sung Kim, Jong-Il Kim, and Jong Un Kim of North Korea such as the Communist regime of the Democratic People's Republic of Korea, paramilitary organizations, and domestic support in South Korea until 2018. On the other hand, the Ministry of Unification defines North Korea as a dual entity. North Korea is not only a political and military confrontation, but also a partner to cooperate with to build a national community. In this reality, the two Koreas have maintained hostile relations since the Cold War yet have sought cooperation to achieve peaceful unification. Kim et al. (2003) describe the paradoxical attitudes of South Koreans toward North Korea as ambivalent.

One of the studies on attitude toward North Korea argues that the level of trust in North Korea is discriminatory, according to different leaders and administrations (Lee, 2013, 130-131). It means that if the Panmunjom Declaration had a significant effect as an event showing inter-Korean cooperation, we can expect that the perception of the North Korean leadership would have changed in a positive direction compared to before Panmunjom. Differences in the perceptions of North Korea and unification may appear, according to cohorts that have experienced different events. For instance, the generation that experienced the events of the conflictive period may have a different attitude toward North Korea compared to those who underwent the easing period. The latter can also be more likely to support unification.

Koreans currently in their 20s and 30s who experienced changes in ethnic identity while experiencing tensions with North Korea may not have seen the Panmunjom

Declaration as being more meaningful than other generations did. Therefore, although the Panmunjom Declaration may have had a positive effect on South Korea's perception of North Korea, generations who have experienced conflict between the two Koreas are likely to show a conservative tendency toward North Korea's policy and unification consciousness. Thus, we expect that younger generations (people in their 20s and 30s) show a more conservative attitude toward North Korea and unification than other generations, even after the Panmunjom Declaration (Hypothesis 1).

Secondly, we examine the changes in attitude toward unification among South Koreans. Because the cost and benefits of unification vary depending on the conditions, the results of individual utility calculations based upon them may also differ. If the younger generation in Korea considers national interests and realistic interests simultaneously in terms of unification, but considers realistic interests more critical, it cannot overlook the effect of the "crunched" relationship with North Korea that influenced the consideration of costs and benefits at the time. Choi (2016) shows that people who think unification will be beneficial respond positively to the need for unification, while most of those who think negatively about unification are less likely to support unification. It implies that the negative responses to the interests of unification may be due to the negative prospects of the long-term conflictive inter-Korean relationship.

After the Panmunjom Declaration, a positive outlook on the inter-Korean relationship can lead to a positive attitude toward unification based on reasonable considerations. In terms of the attitudes toward unification, we expect that the prospects for unification affect the need for unification differently across generations (Hypothesis 2). The more positive the prospects for unification, the more likely the older generations will favor unification (Hypothesis 2-1). Otherwise, even with a positive outlook on unification, the younger generations will not change their attitude toward unification as they experience the failure of appeasement policies and repeated North Korean provocations (Hypothesis 2-2).

This study argues that the Panmunjom Declaration is different from previous political events, which can have two competing implications. On the one hand, it can be a sign that the Jae-In Moon administration will convert the hardline policy toward North Korea that has persisted for about ten years into an appeasement policy. On the other hand, it can be a repeat of the failed political events of the past. If so, it is difficult to assert that the Panmunjom Declaration will improve the inter-Korean relationship fundamentally.

2. South Korea before and after the Panmunjom Declaration

It is difficult to assert that a political event is critical. We can only ex-post the influence of the event through the results it brings. When the government determines a political event, and it is influential, we can expect that the event can have a macro-level influence on political– economic indicators. The upper panel of Figure 1 shows the nominal Gross Domestic Product (GDP) and real GDP growth rates between the first quarter of 2016 and the second quarter of 2018 following the Panmunjom Declaration. The upper panel shows that it is difficult to observe significant changes in South Korea's economic size and growth rate before and after the declaration of Panmunjom.

Also, North Korea's provocation of South Korea is the kind of conflictive event that can affect the attitudes of South Koreans toward North Korea and unification; 2015 was a time of heightened military tension in the inter-Korean relationship. On July 11, 2015, about 10 North Korean soldiers broke into the military demarcation line, and on August 4, 2015, North Korea initiated a provocation that buried a mine in the DMZ's western front. As a result, the South Korean government warned North Korea and resumed the cross-border loudspeaker broadcasting campaign it had waged against North Korea for the previous 11 years as a punishment. In response, North Korea launched a shelling attack on August 20 in Yeoncheon, Gyeonggi-do. To resolve the military conflict triggered by North Korea's landmine provocations and artillery bombardment, senior officials from both sides met August 22–25, and drew up the "August 25 Agreement" to release the tensions between South and North Korea. The August 25 agreement states that South Korea would suspend loudspeaker broadcasting and cancel semi-exhibition status. The agreement also requires North Korea to be cooperative about family reunions and to encourage exchanges and collaboration at the civilian level.

Since 2016, North Korea's military provocation has shown a sharp increase. In particular, along with conventional military provocations, North Korea conducted military provocations, such as the experiment of strategic weapons; the fourth nuclear test; a missile launch experiment at Gwangmyeongseong Lake on February 7; a submarine-launched ballistic missile (SLBM) test launch on April 24 from the Sinpo-class submarine, at least five Hwaseong 10 (Musdan) medium-range ballistic missile launches; a test launch of the North Star ballistic missile (SLBM) from a new submarine on August 24; and a nuclear test on September 9.

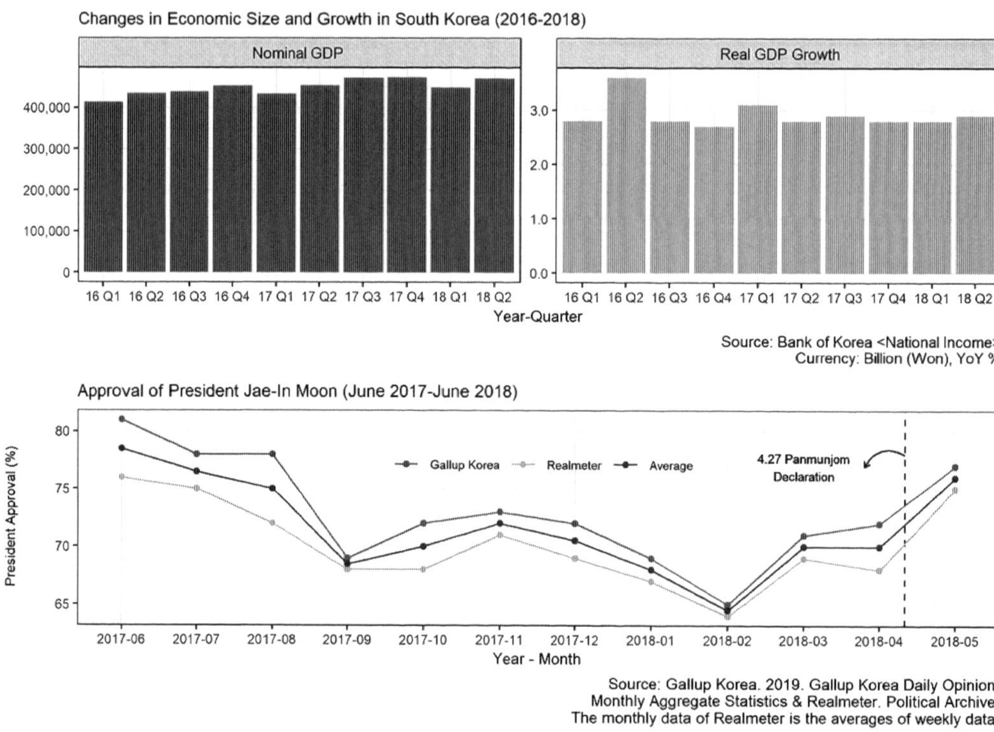

Figure 1. Political and Economic Situation in South Korea (2017-2018)

In 2017, North Korea continued the military provocation with a political slogan that promises the construction of great power. South Korea then announced a pledge to appease North Korea in the process of holding a presidential election on May 9, but North Korea neglected it. Jong-Un Kim's regime continued to provoke military tensions in South Korea, as well as in the United States and Japan. In 2018, starting from the

Pyeongchang Winter Olympics, the atmosphere of reconciliation between the two Koreas was created, and there was no North Korean missile launch. Thus, North Korea expanded its military provocations from 2015 to 2017, and by 2018 it showed signs of easing the tensions. In other words, the people of South Korea were exposed to the threat of North Korea's provocation until April 27, 2018, when the Panmunjom Declaration was announced. In sum, Figure 1 and North Korea's military provocation log show that it is difficult to observe the kind of macroscopic changes that can cause rapid changes in the attitudes toward North Korea and the unification of South Koreans, before and after the Panmunjom Declaration.

On the contrary, the lower panel of Figure 2 implies that the Panmunjom Declaration may have a critical influence on the South Koreans. It shows the monthly approval ratings of the presidential administration conducted by Gallup Korea and Realmeter. According to the lower panel, President Jae-In Moon's approval rates continued to decline, beginning in June 2016, and began sharply rebounding in February 2018. In February 2018, President Jae-In Moon and Yeo-Jung Kim, the vice director of the Central Committee of the Workers' Party of North Korea, had a meeting. Yeo-Jung Kim delivered a letter from Jong-Un Kim, chairman of the State Council, and verbally asked President Jae-In Moon to visit Pyongyang. This shows that the Panmunjom Declaration can be an influential event on the attitudes toward North Korea and unification compared to other events. Therefore, we will take a look at the discriminatory results from previous studies that appeared through public surveys after the Panmunjom Declaration in the context of the impact of political events.

3. Data

The data used in this paper is the Korean Broadcasting System (KBS) National Unification Consciousness Survey of 2018 conducted by KBS (hereafter, KBS survey). KBS surveyed for five days from August 3 to August 7, 2018. It weighted population proportions by gender, age, and region based on the registered population in July 2018. It is made up of 1,000 men and women over the age of 19 who live in cities and provinces. The KBS survey contains questions on the attitude toward North Korea in terms of leadership and general perception and attitudes toward unification after the Panmunjom Declaration. Also, it shows the least time difference from the Panmunjom Declaration.

Therefore, among the available survey data, it is the most suitable for use in the empirical analysis for this study.

It should be noted that this is not panel data that surveys the same respondents at different times. It is difficult to find significant events that could affect the attitude toward North Korea and unification at that time except for the Panmunjom Declaration. However, it does not mean that we can interpret that the change after the Panmunjom Declaration is due to the effect of the political event. It is necessary to consider that there are no available panel surveys to analyze the Panmunjom Declaration before-and-after. Hence, the KBS survey can be helpful for an empirical analysis of the individual level of attitudes toward North Korea and unification after the event, although the data have several limitations. If we are not overconfident of the results of the analysis, we can expect to find significant implications that will help us understand the changing attitudes of South Koreans toward North Korea and unification after the Panmunjom Declaration.

IV. Dependent Variables

1. Attitudes toward North Korea: Leadership, and General State

The dependent variables of interest are the attitudes toward North Korea, and unification. We use two questions to classify the attitude toward North Korea—North Korean leadership, or North Korea in general. We expect attitudes toward North Korea to be differentiated into North Korean leadership and North Korea as a general state. First, we look at the question about North Korean leadership: "What do you think of Jong-Un Kim's North Korean regime and its ruling leadership group?" The responses on North Korean leadership were given on a five-points scale, with 1 meaning "very dissatisfied" to 5, meaning "very satisfied." Also, we asked the question, "What do you think about North Korea?" to measure general attitudes toward North Korea. The responses are also measured on a five-point scale from 1, "I think North Korea is a hostile entity," to 5, "I think South Korea should support North Korea."

2. Attitudes toward Unification

We asked, "What do you think about unification?" Responses were measured on a four-point scale. The most frequent response is the opinion that respondents prefer unification if it creates no burdens (45.5%). Only 8.9% of respondents say that they do not prefer unification. A quarter of the respondents answer that they prefer the status quo (25.2%), and only 20.4% say they prefer unification unconditionally.

Figure 2. Distributions of Dependent Variables

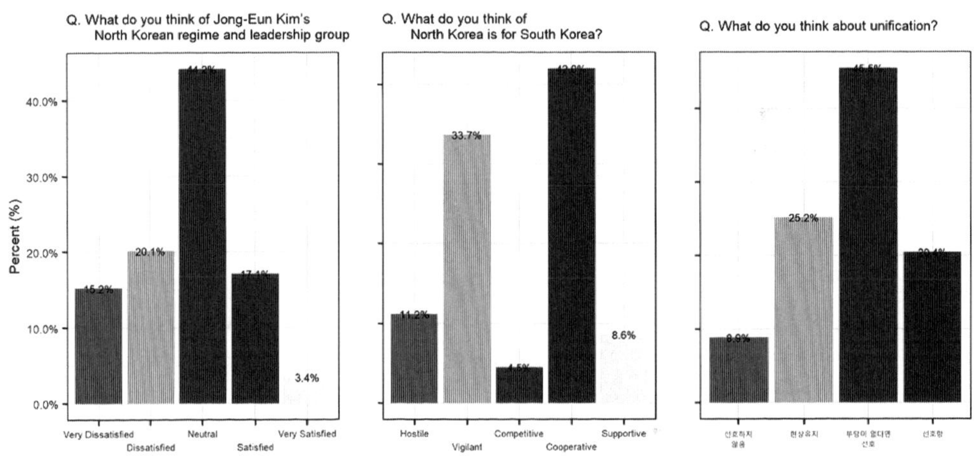

V. Explanatory Variables

One of the main explanatory variables in this study is generations. We investigate how the generations are associated with the attitudes toward North Korea and unification after the Panmunjom Declaration. Generations are categorical variables measured in 10-year units based on age. The younger generations, in their 20s and 30s, are those who experienced several provocations of North Korea and the failure of appeasement policies. It means that the Panmunjom Declaration may not be an event critical enough to change their political attitude fundamentally. Instead, the younger generation can accept the Panmunjom Declaration as part of the repetitive North Korean warfare tactics.

Thus, we expect that the younger generations would persist in conservative views on North Korea regardless of its leadership and general perception. However, the older generations, in their 40s and 50s, who experienced the period of successful appeasement policies, would expect that the Panmunjom Declaration will bring peace again. Lastly, the oldest generation surveyed, those in their 60s and over, is expected to show a negative attitude toward the leadership, but not as a general perception. Since the oldest generation are those who experienced the Korean War or its immediate aftermath, for them, North Korea is both an enemy of the Korean War and, at the same time, belongs to the same Korean nationality. Therefore, unlike the previous studies, we expect a nonlinear relationship between different generations and attitudes toward North Korean leadership. Conversely, the relationship between generations and attitudes toward North Korea in general would not be distinctive across the generations since South Koreans have learned through a series of events that the people who are ruled in North Korea do not influence the inter-Korean relationship. The reference category among the generations are those in their 20s, who are expected, in this survey, to show conservative or negative attitudes toward North Korea even after the Panmunjom Declaration.

The other explanatory variable of interest is the prospect of unification. This variable consists of responses to the question, "When do you think unification will happen?" The longer the period of unification, the more negative the prospect. It is because we can view the negative responses for the expected unification period as a kind of "time of hesitation" that expects a transitional period, such as the preparation period for unification, considering the burdens, costs, and social problems that will arise from unification. Moreover, responses that the time when unification is possible is "near" or "impossible for the long term" means that the motivation and expectations for unification are low (Jeong, 2013, 82).

Finally, we control for other variables that can potentially affect the attitudes toward North Korea and unification. The variables include the regions where respondents live, gender, education level, income level, evaluations of North Korea policies under the Jae-In Moon administration, all drawn from the KBS survey data. Conventional wisdom asserts that regionalism has driven the outcomes of elections in the post-democratization period in Korea (Kim et al., 2008). We have observed a regional divide in which the electorate of the Youngnam and the Honam regions were opposed.

Even the Youngnam region is divided into two parts: northern Youngnam, with the city of Daegu, and southern Youngnam, with the cities of Pusan and Ulsan (Kang, 2000; Kim, 2010; Yoon, 2012).

Evaluations toward North Korea's policies under the Jae-In Moon administration is a proxy variable of political ideology or party identification, considered in previous studies. Political ideology mostly measures the spectrum of liberal or conservative, and party identification measures a respondent's attachment to a particular party as a primary political variable. The political ideology or party identification in current studies is used to explore the determinants of attitudes toward North Korea and unification. However, the KBS survey data used in this study do not include questions that directly measure the political ideology or party identification of respondents. We expect that the evaluations will show the ideological tendency because voters in South Korea have shown significant differences in policy issues in terms of North Korea support and the ROK-US alliance (Park et al., 2012). Socio-demographic variables, such as gender, education level, and income level are also included.

VI. Empirical Findings

The dependent variables are the attitudes toward North Korea and unification, measured on a major five-point scale. Also, the variables have a discrete, not continuous, ranking. Therefore, we use ordered logistic regression to estimate the relationship between dependent variables and explanatory variables. The results of ordered logistic regression are natural logarithms of the odds ratio that show the probability of selecting each category of the dependent variable. Although coefficients of ordered logistic regression are in linear forms, it implies the nonlinear relationship between explanatory variables and the dependent variable. Hence, it is difficult to derive a direct implication through the coefficients. In this study, we show some of our results with predicted probabilities.

1. Attitudes toward North Korea after the Panmunjom Declaration

Table 1 is the result of examining the determinants of North Korea's perception through ordered logistic regression analysis for respondents after the Panmunjom

Declaration. In Model 1, respondents of all generations except those in their 30s were more likely to show more positive attitudes toward North Korean leadership compared to those in their 20s when we hold other explanatory variables constant. In other words, we can understand that the 20s and 30s are more likely to show negative attitudes and antipathy toward the North Korean leadership than other generations. Model 2 analyzes the determinants of North Korea in general. We cannot find any significant differences among generations compared to those in their 60s and older in terms of attitudes toward North Korea in general in Model 2. Although we changed the reference category from people in their 20s to those over 60, we cannot find statistically significant differences across the generations in terms of the attitudes toward North Korea in general.

Table 1. Ordered Logistic Regression: Attitudes toward North Korea after the Panmunjom Declaration

	Attitudes toward North Korea	
	Leadership	General
Generation: 30s	0.313 (0.203)	-0.041 (0.206)
Generation: 40s	0.521** (0.201)	0.133 (0.203)
Generation: 50s	0.574** (0.208)	-0.110 (0.206)
Generation: 60+	0.403 (0.209)	-0.182 (0.209)
NK policy Eval.	1.427*** (0.085)	1.219*** (0.082)
Region: Honam	-0.196 (0.206)	0.073 (0.201)
Region: PK	-0.049 (0.167)	0.095 (0.172)
Region: TK	-0.086 (0.204)	-0.285 (0.204)
Socio-demographic: Gender	0.595*** (0.122)	0.386** (0.121)
Socio-demographic: Education	-0.266* (0.122)	0.032 (0.123)
Socio-demographic: Income	0.174** (0.054)	0.170** (0.055)
cut1	2.594*** (0.451)	1.911*** (0.444)
cut2	4.071*** (0.462)	4.319*** (0.464)
cut3	6.557*** (0.489)	4.558*** (0.467)
cut4	8.785*** (0.524)	7.307*** (0.497)
Log-likelihood ratio	386.212	311.067
Observations	996	996

Note: *$p < 0.05$ **$p < 0.01$ ***$p<0.001$. Standard errors in parentheses. PK/TK are abbreviations of the regions: PK: Pusan/Ulsan/Kyeongnam TK:Taegu/Kyeongbuk.

2. Attitudes toward Unification after the Panmunjom Declaration

Table 2 examines the competing hypotheses about attitudes toward unification from previous studies, and the second hypothesis, that the prospects of unification affect the attitudes toward unification differently across generations. In particular, we break down the second hypothesis into two statements. First, the more positive the prospects for unification, the more likely it is that older generations will prefer unification. Secondly, the younger generations will not change their attitudes toward unification even they have a positive outlook on unification, since they have experienced the failure of appeasement policies and repeated North Korean provocation.

Model 3 is a basic model composed of variables that can influence attitudes toward unification derived from previous studies. Model 3 includes demographic variables, as well as variables that indicate the degree of interest in unification, and evaluation of the current government's policy toward North Korea policy. Respondents showed that the higher the interest in unification, the more they prefer unification. Likewise, the more supportive the current government's policy is toward North Korea, the more likely people will respond that they prefer unification. Model 4 shows the influence of generations on attitudes toward unification. Since the reference group is people in their 20s, we can interpret the results as effects of generations in comparison with those in their 20s on attitudes toward unification after the Panmunjom Declaration. Unlike previous studies, all generations did not show statistically significant differences from people in their 20s. Previous studies point out that the younger generations, such as those in their 20s and 30s, tend to prefer unification less, since the generations are more likely to approach unification issues with a view to utility maximization rather than historical nationalism, and will feel that unification is not practical (Cho and Han, 2014). However, after the Panmunjom Declaration, the generations do not show statistical differences between each other, which are contrary to previous studies.

Model 5 analyzes the relationship between the prospect for and the attitudes toward the unification. The longer the expected period of unification is, the more negative the prospect is, because we can consider it a transitional period. In other words, the expected period for unification is not only the preparation period for unification, but also the time of hesitation when we take into account the burdens, costs, and social issues that will arise from unification. Moreover, the response that the time when unification is

Table 2. Ordered Logistic Regressions: Attitudes toward North Korea after the Panmunjom Declaration

	Base	Generation	Prospects	Full
Generation: 30s		0.137 (0.209)		1.239* (0.619)
Generation: 40s		0.057 (0.206)		-0.118 (0.633)
Generation: 50s		0.304 (0.211)		1.971** (0.604)
Generation: 60+		0.307 (0.217)		1.787*** (0.535)
Prospects of unification			0.421*** (0.049)	0.693*** (0.117)
30s × Prospects				-0.284 (0.158)
40s × Prospects				0.033 (0.158)
50s × Prospects				-0.443** (0.149)
60+ × Prospects				-0.375** (0.134)
Interests of unification	1.247*** (0.092)	1.230*** (0.093)	1.085*** (0.094)	1.090*** (0.095)
NK policy Eval.	0.657*** (0.081)	0.672*** (0.083)	0.498*** (0.084)	0.515*** (0.086)
Region: Honam	-0.220 (0.212)	-0.232 (0.211)	-0.156 (0.215)	-0.188 (0.215)
Region: PK	-0.044 (0.172)	-0.046 (0.172)	-0.017 (0.173)	-0.023 (0.175)
Region: TK	0.049 (0.205)	0.039 (0.205)	0.140 (0.207)	0.103 (0.209)
Socio-demographic: Gender	-0.144 (0.123)	-0.151 (0.123)	-0.252* (0.125)	-0.291* (0.126)
Socio-demographic: Education	-0.013 (0.111)	0.064 (0.123)	-0.028 (0.113)	0.065 (0.125)
Socio-demographic: Income	-0.044 (0.054)	-0.041 (0.055)	-0.080 (0.055)	-0.071 (0.056)
cut1	2.404*** (0.405)	2.777*** (0.474)	2.636*** (0.412)	4.109*** (0.617)
cut2	4.543*** (0.422)	4.914*** (0.488)	4.916*** (0.433)	6.435*** (0.638)
cut3	7.123*** (0.455)	7.504*** (0.52)	7.625*** (0.47)	9.187*** (0.669)
Log-likelihood ratio	377.507	380.96	455.642	479.648
Observations	996	996	996	996

Note: * p〈0.05; **p〈0.01; *** p〈0.001. Standard errors in parentheses. PK/TK are abbreviations of the regions: PK: Pusan/Ulsan/Kyeongnam, TK:Taegu/Kyeongbuk.

possible is near or impossible for the long term means that motivation and expectations for unification are low (Jeong, 2013, 82). In Model 5, respondents display negative attitudes toward unification as they are more cynical about the prospect for unification, which was statistically significant.

Lastly, we constructed Model 6 to test the second research hypothesis. When the Panmunjom Declaration brings about fundamental changes in recognition of unification by respondents, we expect that the more positive the prospects for unification are, the more likely the generations who have experienced past cooperative events will show positive attitudes toward unification. Alternatively, respondents may accept the

gure 3. Changes in Predicted Probabilities by Generation on Attitudes toward Unification

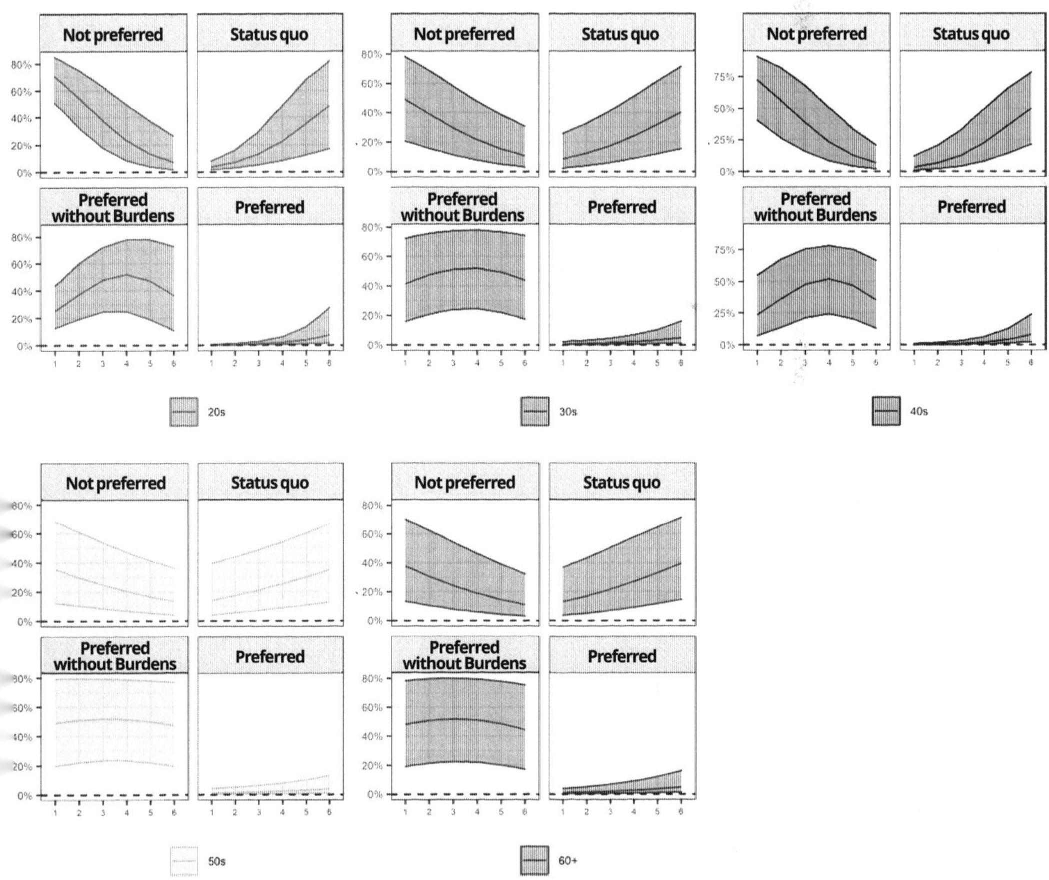

Panmunjom Declaration as a part of North Korea's stick-and-carrot strategy, not as a substantial change in the benefits and costs of unification. We examine the interactions between the two variables on the dependent variable by changing the prospects for unification by the predicted probability in Figure 3.

Although Model 6 presents that the 50s and 60s are statistically different from the 20s, Figure 3 show the details, which we need to think about their implications. When the prospects become positive, all generations show similar patterns that they are more likely to prefer unification, and less likely to oppose to it. However, the 50s and 60s are different in terms of the answers of "preferred without burdens" and "Status-quo." The 50s and 60s do not show much variations by varying prospects of unification, while the 20s, 30s and the 40s show greater variations as the prospects become positive when they answer "preferred without burdens." With the answer of "Status quo," all the generations are more likely to hold the status-quo as the prospects of unification become positive, but the younger generations (20s, 30s and 40s) show greater increasing rates. It implies that the younger generations are also sensitive to the prospects of unification when they judge the inter-Korean relationships.

VII. Conclusion and Implications

This study investigates the attitudes toward North Korea and unification based on data from the KBS National Unification Consciousness Survey of 2018. From the data, the generations who feel the most opposition to North Korean leadership appear to be people in their 20s and 30s. However, people in their 20s perceive North Korea in general to be relatively moderate. It tells us that people in their 20s have the most substantial attitudinal gap between the leadership and their perception of North Korea in general.

The generational change also appears in the analysis of attitudes toward unification after the Panmunjom Declaration. Variables such as the degree of interest in unification, and the evaluation of current governmental North Korea politics, are consistently related to the attitude toward unification, but generational variables have different impacts on unification preferences across the generations. For instance, people in their 30s, 50s, and 60s and above are more likely to prefer unification conditional on increasing positive prospects of unification compared to people in their 20s. In other words, people in their 20s became the generation that least prefers unification across the generations. However, when we compared people in their 20s to people in their 40s in Table 4, it shows that the tendencies of both are similar in changes of predicted probabilities. It implies that the 20s are the generation that shows the most negative attitudes toward North Korea leadership and unification; their attitudes are not static, but conditional to the external environment, such as the change in inter-Korean relationships.

We focus on the effect of the Panmunjom Declaration and attempt to verify whether it had a positive effect on the prospects for future unification like the previous inter-Korean cooperation cases. If respondents from all generations improved in their attitude toward unification as the unification prospects change after the Panmunjom Declaration, we could expect that the declaration is the event that has brought about a significant change in unification. However, it is difficult to say that the event improves the prospects of unification (Figure 10 and Figure 11), and people in their 20s show consistent negative attitudes toward North Korean leadership and unification. In terms of unification, in particular, even when the prospects of unification increase, people in their 20s are more likely to have the most negative attitudes toward unification on average. In particular, the younger generations and the 40s seem to estimate the costs and benefits by the extent to the expected unification timing.

The changes, which are difficult to find in previous studies, clearly show that the generations of our society are changing. Generational changes have been observed as fragmentary events since 2017. For example, the strong antipathy from people in their 20s and 30s over the 2018 Pyeongchang Winter Olympics over the formation of the single inter-Korean women's ice hockey team was challenging to find before that. Similarly, this paper also consistently showed a negative attitude toward North Korea and unification from the younger generation, which can be said to capture the facets of generational changes in our society.

The results of this study show that the significant events driving changes in inter-Korean relations can be made on the supply side, but we should also pay attention to the changes that appear in the ordinary people, who are the consumers, and other parties of the inter-Korean relationship. The changes after the Panmunjom Declaration suggest that the people who experience essential events in the inter-Korean relationship form significantly different attitudes or prospects for North Korea and unification. Thus, the government, as a supplier in the unification and North Korea issues, not only provides one-sided policy options but should also embrace the people's perceptions and attitudes, which are sensitive to changes in the real world. At the same time, to establish the justification logic of unification based on generational changes, it is necessary to ensure long-term consistency in at least unification and North Korea policy. Without policy consistency, citizens cannot set the expected costs and benefits of unification to their standards, which will make people anxious because of the uncertainty of inter-Korean relations.

Lastly, we should note that the Panmunjom Declaration is a prominent political event but we do not need to overestimate it. The agreement between the Panmunjom Declaration and the September 19 Pyongyang Joint Declaration made significant progresses in many areas. However, the two Koreas seem at a standstill, as the second North American summit in Hanoi in February 2019 concluded without much success. Although South Korea has long held political discussions related to North Korea and unification since the division, we could not solve the fundamental problem. Political leaders should consider public opinion to secure the driving force for solving unification and North Korea problems. In particular, in order to fundamentally change the perception toward North Korea and unification, a domestic effort to supplement it is urgently needed—not a one-off event.

References

Abramowitz A (2008). "Forecasting the 2008 Presidential Election with the Time-for-Change Model." *PS: Political Science & Politics*, 41(4), 691–695.

Bae JS (2018). "Generation and Ideology Factors of Evaluation on North Korea and Security Policy." *Korean and World Politics*, 34(2), 99–135.

Bartels LM (2000). "Partisanship and Voting Behavior, 1952-1996." *American Journal of Political Science*, 44(1), 35-50.

Campbell A, Converse PE, Miller WE, Stokes DE (1960). *The American Voter*. Riley, New York.

Chang KY (2018). "Aging and Generational Effects on South Korean Attitudes toward North Korea's Nuclear Threat." Journal of Future Politics, 8(2), 33–57.

Cho JH (2018). "North Korea leader Kim Jong Un scores surprising favorability among South Koreans after summit: Poll finds 78 percent of S. Koreans responded positively to his trustworthiness." URL https://abcnews.go.com/International/north-korea-leader-kim-jong-scores-surprising-favorability/story?id=54933996.

Cho JM, Han JT (2014). "A Comparative Analysis on the Perceptional Differences of the Younger Generations between South and North Korea regarding the Reunification Issues." *Journal of East and West Studies*, 26(1), 149–178.

Choi JY (2016). "Differentiated Perceptions of the Benefits and the Necessity of Korean Reunification." *National Strategy*, 22(3), 113–138.

Fiorina MP (1981). *Retrospective Voting in American National Elections*. Yale University Press, New Haven.

Healy AJ, Malhotra N, Mo CH (2010). "Irrelevant events affect voters' evaluations of government performance." Proceedings of the National Academy of Sciences of the United States of America, 107(29), 107 (29) 12804-12809; DOI: 10.1073/pnas.1007420107.

Hur SJ (2014). "Generation Replacement and Changing Perception on North Korea: Cohort Analysis." *Peace Studies*, 22(2), 73–112.

Jang Sj (2013). "Economic Democratization and the 18th Presidential Election: Issue Voting and Political Knowledge." *Korean Party Studies Review*, 12(1), 87–112.

Jeong EM (2013). "The Changes of Attitude toward Reunification between North and South Koreans: Focusing on Analysis of the Surveys, 2011˜2013." *Journal of Peace and Unification Studies*, 5(2), 74–104.

Jung DJ (2016). "South Korean Citizens' Attitudes toward Unification after the 2016 National Assembly Election: Ideological Polarization or Partisan Bias?" *Korean Political Science Review*, 50(5), 131–161.

Kang WT (2000). "Regionalist Voting and Rational Choice: A Critical Review." *Korean Political Science Review*, 34(2), 51–67.

Kim H, Choi JY, Cho J (2008). "Changing cleavage structure in new democracies: An empirical analysis of political cleavages in Korea." *Electoral Studies*, 27(1), 136–150.

Kim Jh (2010). "The Change of Korean Regionalism: A View on Voting Behaviors and Political Parties." *Journal of Contemporary Politics*, 3(2), 89–114.

Kim P (2017). "Effects of Inter-Korean Events on the Conception of Unification." *Journal of peace and unification*, 9(2), 157–184.

Kim S (2018). "Summit in 2000 made history with big hopes." URL: https: //koreajoongangdaily.joins.com/news/article/article.aspx?aid=3047405.

Kim TH, Namkung G, Yang YS (2003). "Korean People's Foreign Policy Beliefs and National Images of North Korea." *Korean Political Science Review*, 37(3), 151–174.

Kim YT (2007). "The 2007 Presidential Election and Effects of "North Korean Variables"." *The Journal of Political Science & Communication*, 10(2), 65–77.

Klar S (2014). "Partisanship in a social setting." *American Journal of Political Science*, 58(3), 687–704.

Lee JC (2008). "Economic Voting in the 17th Presidential Election: Economic Perception and Voting Behavior." *Journal of Contemporary Politics*, 1(1), 111–136.

Lee SS (2013). "Do We Trust North Korea?: An Analysis of Korea Trust Process with Survey Data." *Korean Political Science Review*, 47(4), 113–133.

Lim J, Seo H (2009). "Frame flow between government and the news media and its effects on the public: Framing of North Korea." *International Journal of Public Opinion Research*, 21(2), 204–223.

Luskin RC (1987). "Measuring Political Sophistication." *American Journal of Political Science*, 31(4), 856–99.

Moon WJ (2018). "Economic Voting, Electoral Punishment, and Democracy: The Effects of Objective and Subjective Economic Evaluations on the Support of Incumbent Party Candidates." *Peace Studies*, 26(2), 5–44.

Oh J (2018). "Moon's approval rating surges after inter-Korean summit." URL https://www.upi.com/Top{_}News/World-News/2018/05/07/Moons-approval-rating-surges-after-inter-Korean-summit/5181525665543/.

Park KM, Han JT, Lee JH (2012). "The Constructive Characteristics of Ideological Conflicts in South Korea." *Korean Party Studies Review*, 11(3), 127–154.

Rahn WM (1993). "The Role of Partisan Stereotypes in Information Processing About Political Candidates." *American Journal of Political Science*, 37(2), 472–96.

Ryu Js (2012). "The Roles of Political Knowledge through Political Ideology in Formation of Policy Preferences." *Journal of Korean Political Science Reviews*, 21(2), 53–86.

Seong Yc, Hong Sj (2018). "President Moon's approval rating drops below 60% for first time since inauguration." URL http://english.hani.co.kr/arti/english{_}edition/e{_}national/829656.html.

Smith G (2005). "Politically Significant Events and Their Effect on the Image of Political Parties." *Journal of Political Marketing*, 4(2-3), 91–114.

Smith J, Kim C (2018). "From nuclear weapons to peace: Inside the Korean summit declaration." URL https://www. reuters.com/article/us-northkorea-southkorea-declaration-exp/from-nuclear-weapons-to-peace-inside-the-korean-summit-declaration-idUSKBN1HY1ZY.

Song YH, Kwon SH (2013). "Determinants of Individuals' North Korea Policy Preferences: Survey Evidence for Roh Moo-hyun and Lee Myung-bak Administrations." *The Journal of Asiatic Studies*, 56(1), 153–182.

Yoon Ki (2012). "Regionalism and the 19th National Election." *Korean Journal of Political Science*, 20(2), 113–138.

Chapter 11

Japan and South Korea: Can they get along by overcoming the challenges?

Atsushi Tago
(Waseda University and Peace Research Institute Oslo, PRIO)

Abstract

Japan and South Korea have been facing varieties of bilateral issues. Those challenges between the two democracies in East Asia indeed prevent further regional cooperation like East Asian Community, and they could jeopardize the regional and potentially global peace and security. Nevertheless, an optimistic view over the two countries might not be dead (yet). Japan and South Korea co-hosted the FIFA World Cup in 2002. Also, there has been a new development of DCA (defense cooperation agreement) between the two countries, while it has been under serious pressure of withdrawal of the commitment on both sides. As a major alliance partner of the United States of America, Japan and South Korea could have been a strong ally with each other in theory. This study, based on those two competing views, will uncover why the two countries tend to overtly fight with each other. Also, this study will seek to answer how the two countries can stop engaging in such a negative interaction and make some practical cooperation to stabilize peace and security in East Asia.

Keywords: Japan, South Korea, Cooperation, Disputes, Survey Experiment

I. Introduction

Japan and South Korea have been facing varieties of bilateral issues including the territorial dispute over the Dokdo/Takeshima, formal apology over the colonial rule since 1911 to the end of World War II, disagreements over the Yasukuni visit by the Prime Minister, and what shall be (or shall not be) taught in history textbook. Those challenges between the two democracies in East Asia indeed prevent further regional cooperation like East Asian Community, and they could jeopardize the regional (and potentially global) peace and security in the future. This type of pessimistic view seems to be dominating in both countries, and it may be the course of diplomacy that Suga and Moon governments are following.

Nevertheless, an optimistic view over the two countries might not be dead (yet). Japan and South Korea co-hosted the FIFA World Cup in 2002. Also, there has been a new development of DCA (defense cooperation agreement) between the two countries, while it has been under serious pressure of withdrawal of the commitment on both sides. As a major alliance partner of the United States of America (i.e., two countries are sharing the key national security institutional partner country) and as a democracy with high economic interdependence, Japan and South Korea could have been a strong ally with each other in theory.

This study, based on those two competing views, will uncover why the two countries tend to overtly fight with each other as they did so in 2018 December over the radar targeting against a Japanese SDF maritime patrol aircraft (Kawasaki P-1) by South Korean Navy destroyer, ROKS Gwanggaeto the Great (DDH-971).[1] Also, this study will

1 On December 20, 2018, according to Japanese government, South Korean Navy destroyer, ROKS Gwanggaeto the Great (DDH-971) used its fire-control radar (FCR) against a Japanese SDF maritime patrol aircraft (Kawasaki P-1) that was in surveillance operation off the Noto Peninsula in the Sea of Japan/East Sea at around 3 p.m. in Japan Standard Time. The Ministry of Defense (MOD) of Japan claimed that the use of the FCR at a plane is violation of the Code for Unplanned Encounters at Sea (CUES) and the act of locking with the FCR is generally considered as a hostile act one step before actual firing. The Japanese MOD also claimed that the radar hit the plane multiple times, and no response was made to communication from the Japanese aircraft against the South Korean destroyer. By contrast, the South Korean government denied the Japanese claims a day after Japan made an accusation. According to the statements of the South Korean military, its destroyer did not employ the FCR but it used MW08 radar for an ongoing rescue operation. When the Japanese aircraft arrived at the site, it was participating in the

seek to answer how the two countries can stop engaging in such a negative interaction but make some practical cooperation to stabilize peace and security in East Asia.

The first section provides an illustrative survey experiment on an invisible crisis (such as a scramble of airplanes in airspaces where the two countries' Air Defense Identification Zones co-exist) to explain why two countries cannot hold silence over a situation where none can really objectively confirm what happens and they end up with creating a visible crisis. The second and third sections illustrate two kinds of survey experiments to understand how cooperation among the two countries can be achieved, especially by the third-party interventions.

II. Indivisible crisis in East Asia

As mentioned in the introduction, starting from December 2018 to March 2019, Japan and South Korea engaged in a series of diplomatic denouncements against each other on a situation, which could have been hidden to the public and may have been handled behind closed doors among the two governments' officials. Whatever happened between the Japanese SDF maritime patrol aircraft (Kawasaki P-1) and the South Korean Navy destroyer (ROKS Gwanggaeto the Great), two governments could have prevented overt denouncement-game and saved each others' face by solving the problem in a back door channel. The puzzle here is why two countries cannot be wise enough to select a discreet diplomatic interaction to talk about this type of incident.

This puzzle, based on some scientific research, could be explained by the motive of gathering the third-party's support for the country. That is, a state cares of international public opinion to side it, and the denouncement message is considered as an effective message to increase those foreign public support in this type of situation. To confirm that, there have been multiple survey experiments conducted in Japan, South Korea and the

rescue of a distressed North Korean fishing boat. While South Korean claim suggested that the location of the incident was approximately 100 km northeast of the Liancourt Rocks, Japanese claimed that it was off the coast of the Noto Peninsula. From the final two weeks of December 2018 to the end of January 2019, two governments were involved in repeated verbal fights over the incident.

United States of America (e.g. Kohama, Inamasu and Tago 2017).

Kohama and her coauthors conducted their first Internet-based, between-subjects survey experiment in November 2014, through Nikkei Research Inc. Over 2,000 people residing in Japan participated in the experiment. The sample involved a wide range of population in terms of age, gender, income level, educational background and ideology and the randomized experiment did not aim to acquire a representative sample.

The experiment was designed as follows. Upon answering several practice questions, all participants were presented with the following scenario, in which the scrambling of fighter jets occurs between two anonymous countries:

> Country A and Country B maintain conflicting territorial claims over land and sea. They also contest over airspace, leading to an increasing number of cases where fighter jets of the countries fly simultaneously in the disputed airspace. As a result, a "near–miss" incident recently occurred where their fighter jets approached very close to each other.
>
> Following the incident, the government of each country publicized the following announcements….
>
> *Country A*: [*one particular statements is randomly shown*]
> *Country B*: [*one particular statements is randomly shown*]

The scenario was based on actual incidents which occurred a few times between China and Japan in 2014. The first incident was reported on May 24 and was followed by verbal fights between the Chinese and the Japanese governments. Similar incidents occurred on June 11 and reportedly in early August 2014. Because scrambling is not a rare event, we believe that the scenario is sufficiently realistic yet generalizable. In fact, according to the Yonhap News Agency (https://jp.yna.co.kr/view/AJP20170112003800882), there were over 400 cases of "intrusion" of airplanes of Japanese Air Self-Defense Forces to South Korean Air Defense Identification Zones in 2016.

Participants are then randomly assigned a message from each side of the disputing countries, which adopts one of the following tones: denouncing the other side, self-promoting itself, or remaining silent. The denouncing message is such that the opposing party's action is "extremely dangerous and abnormal, which can lead to a serious incident." The self-promoting comment states that "our activity is a part of regular warning and surveillance, which is legitimate." The no-comment announcement simply states, "we have no comment." Considering that diplomacy is characterized by two-sided actions, we constructed six unique pairs of messages, such as "self-promotion versus denouncement," as treatments. All combinations are listed in Table 1.

Table 1: List of treatments

Country A/Country B	(a) Remains silent	(b) Self-promotes	(c) Denounces
(a) Remains silent	Group 1		
(b) Self-promotes	Group 2	Group 3	
(c) Denounces	Group 4	Group 5	Group 6

Source: Kohama, Inamasu and Tago 2017. Note. The exact sentence for each announcement is the following: (a) "We have no comment." (b) "Our activity is a part of regular warning and surveillance, which is legitimate." (c) "A(B)'s action is extremely dangerous and abnormal, which can lead to a serious incident."

After being randomly exposed to one of the stimuli, each participant reported their support level for each country, choosing from "support," "somewhat support," "somewhat oppose," "oppose," and "don't know." Each answer was indexed from 1 to 4, where higher values mean higher support. Finally, subjects answered some post-experimental questions regarding their personal background including age, gender, income, education, and ideology.

The most striking finding of this experiment was the strong positive effect of verbal attacks (denouncement) on the attacker's popularity (see Figure 1). The results indicated little evidence of a backlash effect by diplomatic negative campaigns. Rather, the denouncing message significantly increased the attacker's popularity unless the opponent also attacked (here, the notations of "the attacker" and "the attacked," instead of Country A and B, was used for convenience of explanation of the outcome --- the notations were just for labeling purposes and did not necessarily imply that "the attacker" adopted an assertive action or strategy in a substantive way).

The left panel of Figure 1 indicated the level of support for the statement by the attacker, holding the strategy of the attacked constant. The bars indicated the mean popularity level and the lines show the 95% confidence interval. The bars in the leftmost

Figure 1. Popular support for the attacker and the attacked.

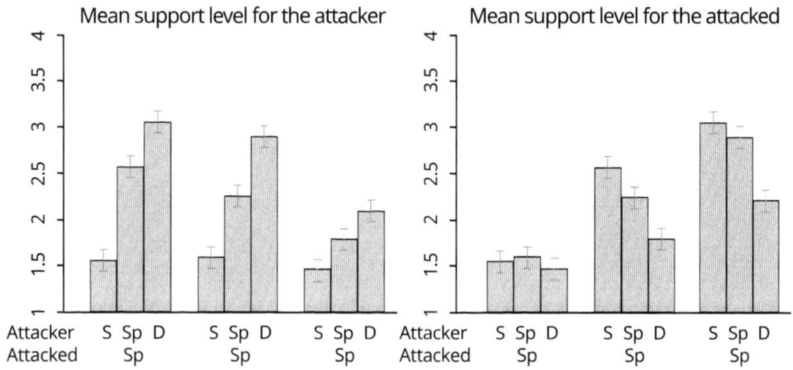

S: remain silent, Sp: self-promote, D: denounce

Source: Kohama, Inamasu and Tago 2017. Note: Whiskers indicate 95% CI.

part of the left panel indicated the foreign public support for the attacker when the other side (i.e. the attacked) remained silent. Each bar in the left part corresponded to the attacker's three strategies—silence, self-promotion, and denouncement, respectively. Hence, the comparison between silence and denouncement indicated the average treatment effect of a negative attack on the attacker's favorability, given that the attacked country remained silent.

When the opponent side remained silent, for example, the mean popularity of the attacker was 1.56, which indicated that people were somewhat opposing it. Mean popularity increased to 2.57 (i.e., by one level of support) with self-promotion. When the attacker verbally denounced the silent opponent, the mean popularity obtained an even higher score of 3.05, which was equal to "somewhat support." The difference among the three strategies was statistically significant at the 5% significance level ($p = 0.00$).

Given that the counterpart remained silent, only 12% of the respondents support (including somewhat support) the attacker who also remained silent. Yet the attacker attracted support from 62% of respondents when it selected self-promotion and 76% when it selected denouncement. Accusing the silent counterpart was an extremely effective way of raising the attacker's own popularity.

Similar dynamics emerged when the attacker faced an opponent who self-promotes. The attacker's mean popularity increased from 1.60 to 2.11 by switching from silence to self-promotion (p = 0.00). Likewise, when the attacker adopted the denouncement strategy, its mean popularity reached 2.89, which was significantly higher than that with the self-promotion strategy (p = 0.00). The gain was as large as a 27% increase in full or partial support.

However, the utility of denouncement substantially deteriorated if both sides relied on it. The mean popularity of the attacker gained with silence, self-promotion, and denouncement was 1.47, 1.80, and 2.10, respectively, in this case. The overall low favorability indicated the negative impact of accusation by the attacked. In addition to the overall modest favorability, the benefit of denouncement compared with the other strategies also diminished. Although the denouncement promised the highest support and the difference was significant (p = 0.00), the size of the effects was not as high as in other cases. The substantive advantage was also limited because respondents are on average still leaning toward opposition. Mutual verbal fights, therefore, did not help disputants promote their positive image. This implies that mutual denouncements harm both and could avoid it if the two governments are fully aware of a (long-term) negative effect of verbal fighting. The mechanism here implies that denouncement-game forces the states to reveal information that could have been hidden to the general public and end up with mutual denouncement of others.

III. Impossible bilateral cooperation by bilateral initiative

Given the fact that the denouncement would beat two other messages (silence and self-justification) and strong anti-Korea and anti-Japan sentiments among the general public, the author is pessimistic about a political initiative that both or either one of the leaders would call for bilateral cooperation in the near future. Statistical data by joint research of Japanese Genron-NPO and South Korean East Asia Institute (EAI) in Figure 2 somehow support this pessimistic view about the two countries' cooperation.

Both in Japan and in South Korea, the majority of people are answering that the impression of the other country is either "very bad" or "relatively bad". In a relative sense, South Koreans are harsher against Japanese than Japanese are against South Koreans;

Figure 2: Impression of South Korea and Japan in respective countries

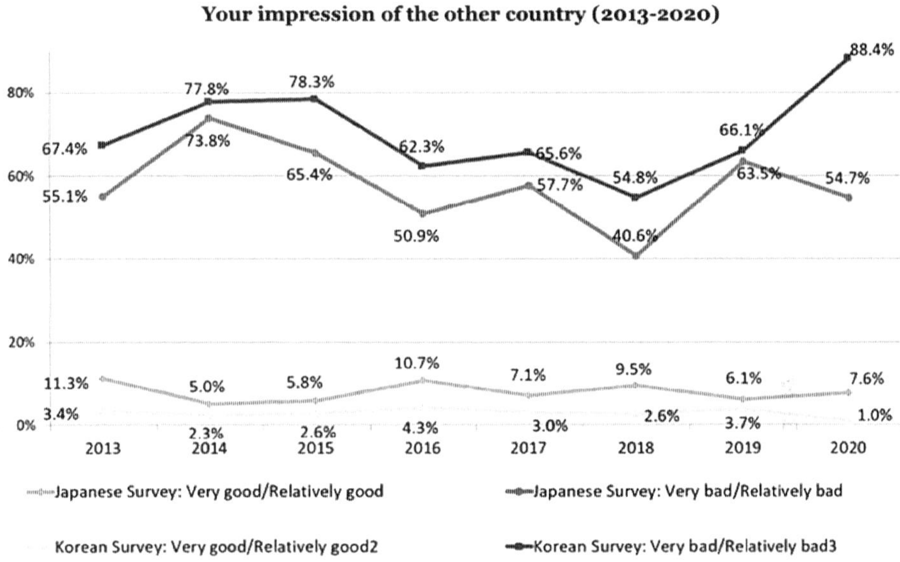

Source: Genron-NPO (https://www.genron-npo.net/en/opinion_polls/archives/5562.html)

60-80% of the respondents tell that the impression of Japan as very bad or relatively bad. Only 2-3% of South Korean people would answer the impression of Japan as "very good" or "relatively good". As for Japan, the negative impression of South Korea is about 40-74% and the positive impression of it is about 5-11%. In any case, the public opinion data of the two countries indicate the bilateral, mutual distrust among the two democracies in East Asia.

The mutual negative views toward the other country can be a product of the unfortunate history of the two countries. However, we can also see some fluctuations even in the last several years. For instance, in 2018 data, Japanese negative perception toward South Korea became as small as 40%. In the same year, South Korean negative perception toward Japan was only 54.8%. In early 2018, there was the winter Olympic game in South Korea, and at that occasion, President Moon and Prime Minister Abe met in person, which is at least a better situation than the winter of 2020 since Prime Minister Suga is putting some, probably unacceptable conditions for South Korea in order to meet President Moon.

IV. A Promise of the Third party intervention

With a very hostile bilateral public opinion toward each other, we really cannot expect bilateral rapprochement unless there would be a surprising event among the two countries to transform the view of the people. However, if we recall the bilateral history in the early 2000s, we could notice that the two countries had a much nicer relationship and even co-hosted the FIFA World Cup. Since the Genron-NPO and EAI had started their comparable public opinion survey from 2013, we cannot show the same data for years like 2002 and 2003.

Like FIFA, an international third party may help out the two countries to promote bilateral cooperation. In this particular study, I would like to seek two kinds of international intervention that could potentially affect Japanese and South Korean rapprochement and cooperation; the International Court of Justice and the United States of America.

One of the most serious issues among the two countries is the territorial dispute over Dokdo/Takeshima. Two countries are demanding each other that the islands (internationally also known as Liancourt Rocks) belong to it, respectively. One of the solutions of the problem is bringing the issue to the international institution either for mediation or legal settlement. While either one of the countries must give up its claim over the islands, international institutions could provide a leader of the losing country with some "political cover". In this study, I would show a tentative, experiment-based evidence of the power of international court settlement as a political cover.

With Daina Chiba and Kazunori Inamasu, I conducted an online survey experiment in Japan in November 2014. The experiment was designed as follows. Upon answering several practice questions, all participants were presented with the following scenario (for Group called "Pattern 1" and "Pattern 2"):

Pattern 1:

Japan and South Korea are under a territorial dispute over the Takeshima/ Dokdo island. Recently, two governments had a negotiation to judge which of the two states has the territorial rights over the island. The following are the outcome of the negotiation.

1. Territorial right (sovereignty) over the island is entitled to South Korea.

2. However, as to the natural resources around the island, two nations must peacefully talk and manage jointly.

Pattern 2:

Japan and South Korea are under a territorial dispute over the Takeshima/ Dokdo island. Recently, International Court of Justice (ICJ), a main organization of the United Nations, had a chance to judge which of the two states has the territorial rights over the island. The following are the outcome of the judgement.

1. Territorial right (sovereignty) over the island is entitled to South Korea.

2. However, as to the natural resources around the island, two nations must peacefully talk and manage jointly.

The key difference between the two groups appears in the main paragraph. While pattern 1 tells that the "two governments had a negotiation to judge ", pattern 2 tells that the "International Court of Justice (ICJ), a main organization of the United Nations, had a chance to judge." In case of pattern 2, Japanese government could use a political cover of the international court to persuade its population over the loss of the claimed territory (Allee and Huth 2006). There were three more groups in the whole experiment but the most

Table 2: List of treatments

Pattern 1	Pattern 2	Pattern 3	Pattern 4	Pattern 5
ROK wins & Bilateral Negotiation	ROK wins & ICJ Verdict	Unclear & Bilateral Negotiation	Unclear & ICJ Verdict	JPN wins & ICJ Verdict

Source: Author

Figure 3:

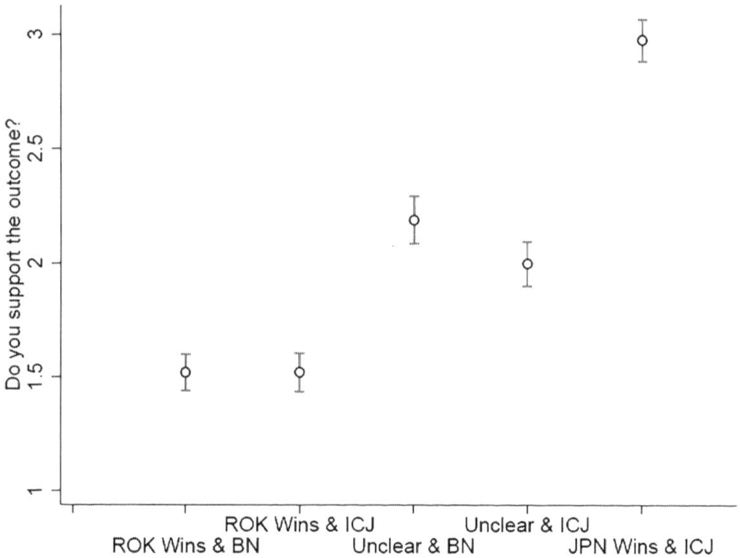

Source: Author

Figure 4:

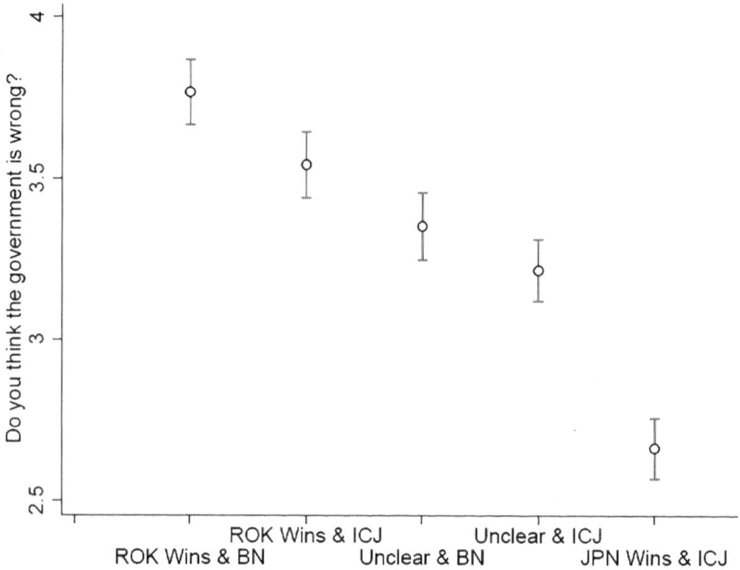

Source: Author

important part here is the difference of patterns 1 and 2 to observe the intervention effect of international institutions.[2]

Figure 3 shows that Japanese people overwhelmingly support the outcome that Japan secures the territorial claim over the islands and obtains sovereign control. The worst case for them is the South Korean win over the conflict; the score of 1.5 in the total scale of 1 to 4 suggests that the outcome is unacceptable to the majority of the people. In the middle, the people do not like it but somehow feel acceptable for "unclear" solution cases. The most important fact is that there was no difference between "Pattern 1" and "Pattern 2". By contrast, Figure 4 shows disapproval rate for the cabinet that brought the mentioned outcome either by bilateral negotiation or by ICJ verdict. Now we see the difference between "Pattern 1" and "Pattern 2". Japanese tend to support the lost cabinet more if it was judged by the ICJ.

This evidence could be a hope for the two countries. Even compared with the case where the outcome is unclear and the bilateral negotiation brought the result, the Japanese people tend to consider the government is less "wrong" if it is brought by the ICJ verdict. We can confirm that there is a political cover of the ICJ to make the people think their own government less responsible for the undesired outcome of the territorial dispute. Unfortunately, the same experimental evidence is not available for South Korea, but as long as South Korea is a democracy like Japan and its president needs to care for the general public, use of a political cover of the ICJ could be a wise option for it to move forward for solving the territorial dispute.

V. A Promise of the further Third party intervention

Other than the ICJ, we can think of another third party for South Korea and Japan; the United States of America. The US government has been under a long-term security commitment to the two countries via the Treaty of Mutual Cooperation and Security between the United States and Japan, and the Mutual Defense Treaty Between

2 Patterns 3, 4 and 5 are listed in Table 2. We replaced 1) who won the case - either South Korea or Japan, and 2) where the outcome was reached - via bilateral negotiation or a judgement by the ICJ.

the United States and the Republic of Korea. For the U.S. military, South Korean and Japanese mutual distrust and antagonism is one of the key challenges for East Asian peace and security since it could jeopardize the security cooperation against North Korea and China.

Therefore, the U.S. has been engaging in a PR campaign to Japan and South Korea to inform the necessity of the bilateral cooperation and they even made a short video clip, which can be seen in their government websites. For instance, in September 2016, USPACOM (then, now it is known as United States Indo-Pacific Command: USINDOPACOM) created a short PR video clip in the immediate aftermath of the North Korean Nuclear Weapon test. The 38 seconds-long video features US B-1 Strategic Bombers (B-1Bs) conducting "sequence flights" with ROK and Japanese air forces in response to the nuclear test (Figure 5).

Figure 5: Short video by US military calling ROK-Japan cooperation

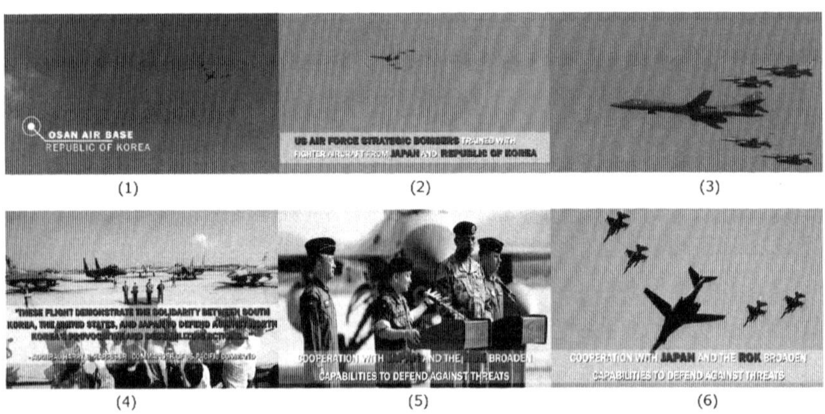

Source: Asaba et al. 2020. The movie can be seen from the US Indo-Pacific Com's Facebook website [https://www.facebook.com/indopacom/videos/10155688211942588/ (6 November 2020, date last accessed)].

As it can be seen in Figure 5, the movie emphasizes the importance of cooperation between the two countries by suggesting lines like "These flights demonstrate the solidarity between South Korea, the United States and Japan to defend against North Korea's provocative and destabilizing actions... " and "Cooperation with Japan and the ROK broaden capabilities to defend against threats". The video was uploaded on the official Facebook website of Hawaii based U.S. Pacific Command and watched by the people more than 100,000 times.

If this type of American "intervention" via web media may affect the people's perception toward South Korea in Japan and toward Japan in South Korea, we can again hope for another third party engagement to ease the tension between the two countries. That is, we need to test if the video message changes the hearts and minds of South Korean and Japanese in terms of the bilateral cooperation against potential threat, i.e. North Korea and others.

To test this, Yuki Asaba and his co-authors conducted two online survey experiments in South Korea and Japan. The first study (hereafter, study 1) was done only in Japan on 15 January 2017 via Yahoo Crowdsourcing service (http://crowdsourcing.yahoo.co.jp). The team collected 1,050 participants by paying a 10 yen incentive as an incentive. The second study (hereafter, study 2) was done simultaneously in South Korea (sample size = 800) and Japan (sample size = 741) as an online survey experiment during the period of 10-15 July 2017. Likewise the first study, the team paid incentives to the respondents. They employed the services provided by Yahoo Crowdsourcing in Japan and Macromill Embrain (http://www.embrain.com/eng/) in South Korea.

Both in the study 1 and 2, the team made the experiments a very simple design with only two groups. For the treatment group, they used the 38-second long video made by USPACOM in September 2016 (Figure 5). For the control group, they searched for a PACOM made video with the same length and created in a similar time of the year and not related to Japan nor South Korea. They found a 38-second video entitled "Exercise Koolendong 16: Movement-to-Contact Drill" featuring a US-Australian military exercise, uploaded to the PACOM Facebook account on 15 August 2016 (Figure 6 for key scenes). It was seen over 5,190 times and received 'likes' from 424 viewers, with 41 shares. In the experiment setting, half of the respondents saw the control video while the other half saw the treatment video. The control video was important as a placebo since they were measuring how the content and message of the video changes people's perceptions (Iyengar and Kinder 1987).

The team measured the attitudes toward Korea–Japan cooperation by using questions like 'Do you agree or disagree with the following statements? – Korea (Japan) should promote economic cooperation with Japan (South Korea) or Korea (Japan) should promote security cooperation with Japan (South Korea)' and five-point Likert scale choices. Other than the key attitude questions, they asked the respondents' age, gender, political party identity, education (in four-point scale), and political ideology (in ten-point scale).[3] See more on Appendix.

The results of the experiments can be seen in Figures 7 to 10. The coefficient plots to test the hypotheses are shown. Asaba et al. (2020) run simple OLS regressions to obtain a comparable unit-change effect of the video manipulation (i.e. seeing the trilateral military cooperation video) in relation to other key variables such as gender, education, political interest, and so on.

The upper left panel of Figure 7 shows the coefficient for security cooperation as the dependent variable. The upper right panel is for economic cooperation. The effects on case by case cooperation and environmental cooperation are shown in the lower left and right panels, respectively. The panels indicate statistically significant positive effects in generating Japanese attitudes to support more cooperation with South Korea. For instance, the video increases positive attitudes by 0.14 in coefficient size, which is roughly equivalent to the effect of a one unit move (out of 10 total) in political ideology. While the video is just about the military countermeasure against North Korea, it promoted a variety of cooperative attitudes in the field of economic policies and environmental protection.

Figures 8 and 9 show the coefficients for key independent variables for the study 2 in Japan and South Korea (July 2017). There, we can find statistically significant positive effects in generating an attitude to support more cooperation in security and case-by-case issues with South Korea in Japan. However, the reverse was not true. South Koreans were not affected by the video and thus do not support cooperation with Japan by USPACOM.

---

3 In the second study that aims to do a Korea–Japan comparison by using the exact same study design as the first study, to ensure if the manipulation was received correctly by the respondents, they additionally asked if the respondents remember accurately what they saw. For the control group, 90% of Japanese and 93% of Koreans answered that the U.S. military was in the video while 79% of Japanese and only 42% of Koreans answered that Australian military was there as well. For the treatment group, 96% of Japanese and 97% of Koreans answered that the U.S. military was in the video while 73% of Japanese and only 51% of Koreans answered that Japanese SDF was there as well. As for South Korean military presence in the same treatment video, 81% of Japanese and 83% of Koreans answered correctly.

Figure 6: Control video

Source: Asaba et al. 2020. The movie can be seen from the US Indo-Pacific Com's Facebook website [https://www.facebook.com/indopacom/videos/10155556857872588/ (6 November 2020, date last accessed)].

Figure 7: Survey in Japan (2017. Jan)

Source: Asaba et al. 2020.

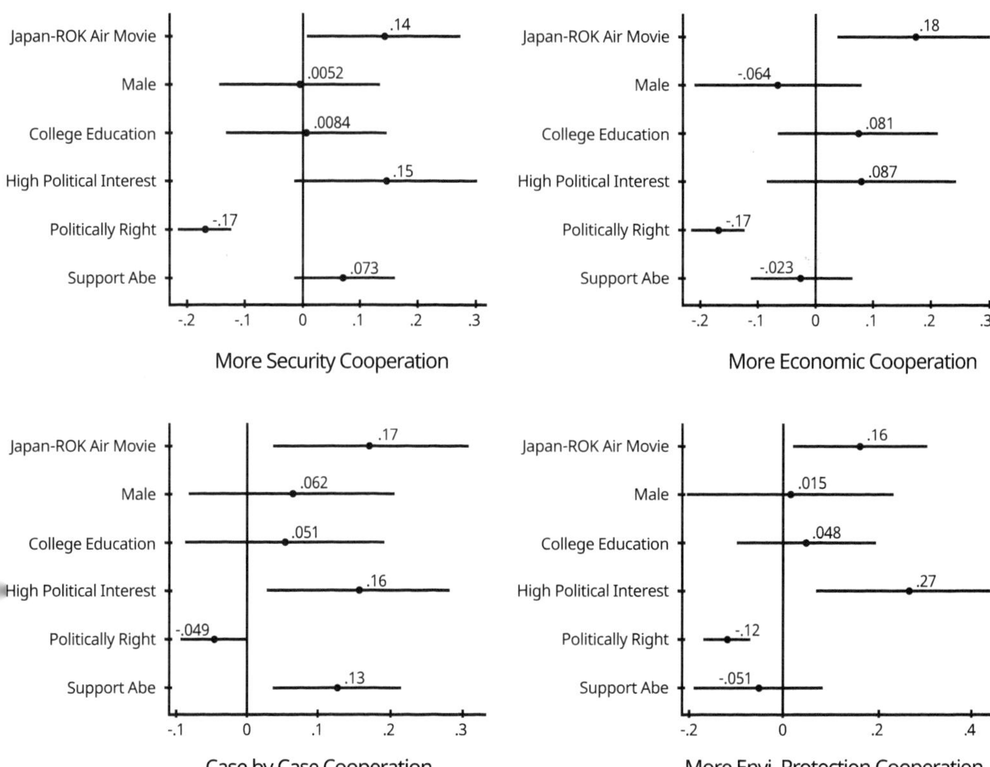

Figure 8: Survey in Japan (2017. July)

Source: Asaba et al. 2020.

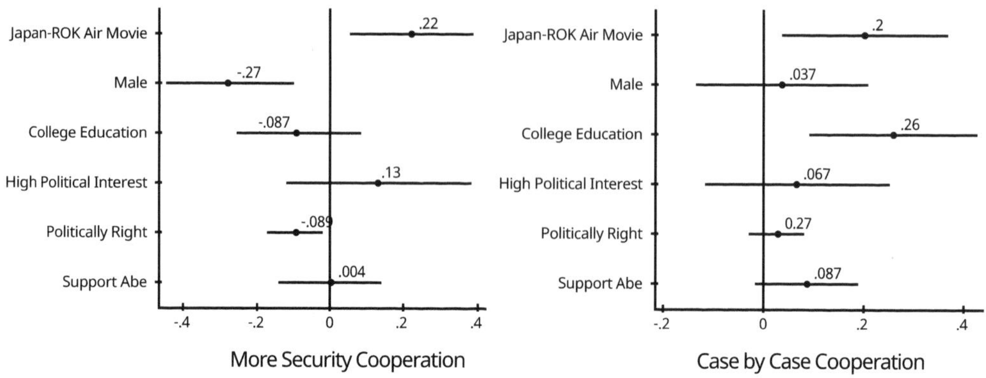

Figure 9: Survey in South Korea (2017. July)

Source: Asaba et al. 2020.

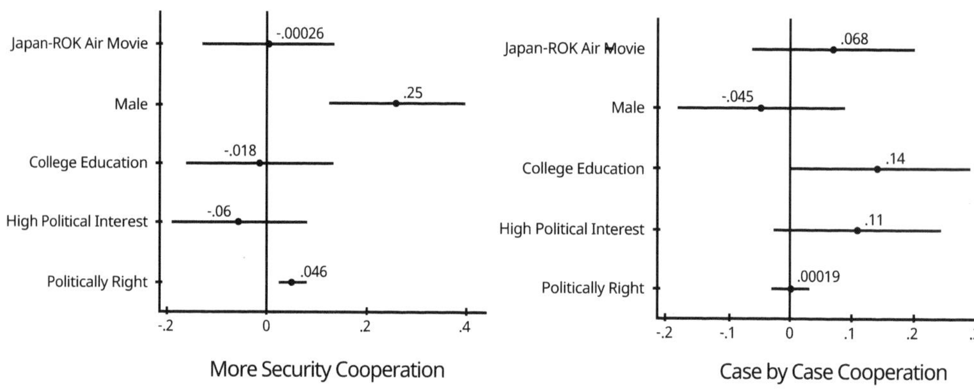

Figure 10 shows two plots of coefficients including interaction terms of right wing (in Japan) and left wing (in Korea). In both Japan and Korea, the video indeed had an effect on the specific group of people. For Japanese right wing people, the video impresses them that the Korean air force could work with the Japanese SDF and U.S. air force to counter North Korea, the shared enemy. They start thinking of the shared enemy more and thus consider South Korean as a reasonable partner to cooperate for the common goal in national security. Normally, without seeing the video, the Japanese right wing people tend to deny cooperation with South Korea (−0.8 is the coefficient for the right); however, this recovers to the baseline after seeing the US-made video (+0.66). Likewise, in South

Figure 10: Survey in Japan and South Korea (2017. July)

Source: Asaba et al. 2020.

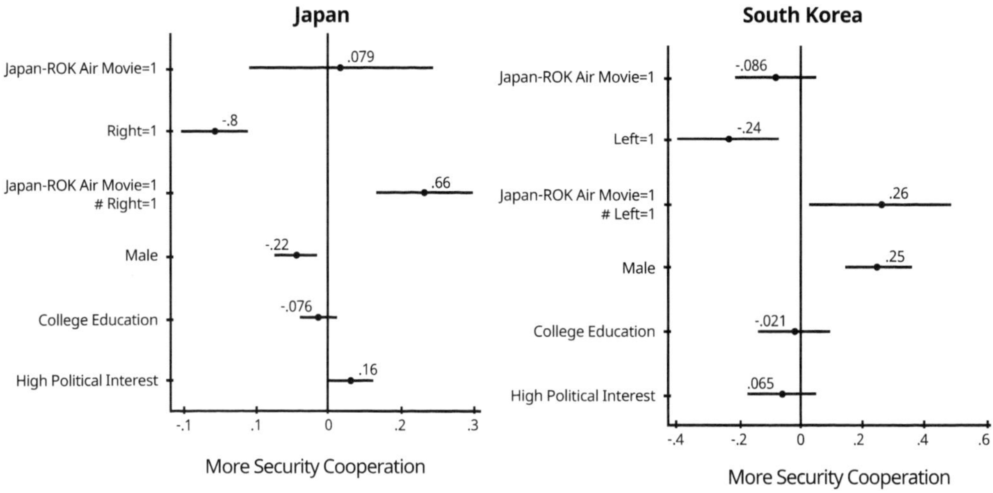

Korea, the Korean left wing people tend to think it less ideal to cooperate with Japan for their national security (-0.24) but they see cooperation as positive if they watch the video (+0.26). The left-wing Korean people, who are more dovish toward North Korea and believe more in diplomatic solutions with it, may not fully realize how Japan could be a crucial national security partner in a time of actualized crisis with North Korea until they watch a military-made video.

VI. Conclusion

The challenges lying ahead of South Korea and Japan are not easy to solve. Given the very hostile perception of the general public against each other, the author of this short article does not believe that the bilateral political leadership would not be able to commit a better relationship by themselves. The two countries would need a third party intervention to get along and this study shows some evidence of hope for both international institutional and American intervention to generate better perception on political cooperation among South Korea and Japan.

Mutual distrust among the leading democratic economy in East Asia is damaging to the regional and even global peace and security. Japan, in its declining stage of the national power mainly due to its mismanagement of national economic policies and population decrease with rapidly expanding aged generation, cannot afford making another enemy next door. South Korea, even much faster aging society and larger socio-economic divide in its society, would like to utilize its resources inward rather than fighting against next door democracy. There should be a way out in the two countries' antagonism. The wise politicians of the two countries could use political cover of third party intervention like the ICJ verdict and ask mutual alliance partners, i.e. the U.S., to mediate a difficult and salient conflict of the two countries.

For the two countries' leadership, what I am concerned with is a case like the 2018 December incident would happen again. Mutual denouncement was inevitable once it started to be visible to the general public. For both democratic Japan and South Korea, I would not claim that the secrecy and closure of information is always better; however, as long as its parliamentary control is assured in a closed door session and the national security secret can be handled in a manner to avoid further escalation, an invisible crisis like the 2018 December incident, may be discreetly handled and solved without mutual denouncement via a back door channel.

Acknowledgement

The experiment studies shown in this short article were financially supported by the JSPS (Japan Society for the Promotion of Science).

Appendix

The text used in Asaba et al. (2020) was as follows.

[Control condition]

[page1] In the next page, we will show you a short video on international security in Asia-Pacific region. Please click the arrow and start the video. Please watch the video carefully because we will ask you questions related to the video afterwards (you cannot move forward unless you finish watching the video). Note: there will be sound in the video.

[page2] This video is made by the United States Pacific Command, featuring joint exercise between Australian and US armed forces. The Australian and American forces are often conducting this type of drill and increase their capability for joint operation. Please answer the following questions after you finish watching the video.

[Treatment condition]

[page1] In the next page, we will show you a short video on international security in Asia-Pacific region. Please click the arrow and start the video. Please watch the video carefully because we will ask you questions related to the video afterwards (you cannot move forward unless you finish watching the video). Note: there will be sound in the video.

[page2] This video is made by the United States Pacific Command, featuring the coordinated protection of US B-1 strategic bombers by Japanese SDF and Korean armed forces. Cooperation among Japan and South Korea ---- both American allies --- is increasingly important to counter North Korean nuclear weapon testing and ballistic missile testing. Please answer the following questions after you finish watching the video.

Q. Do you agree or disagree with the following statements?

Korea/Japan should forcefully claim sovereignty over Dokdo/Takeshima, even if it increases tension between (South)Korea and Japan.

Disagree, Somewhat disagree, Neither agree nor disagree, Somewhat agree, Agree

Korea/Japan should promote economic cooperation with Japan/South Korea.

Disagree, Somewhat disagree, Neither agree nor disagree, Somewhat agree, Agree

Korea/Japan should promote security cooperation with Japan/South Korea.

Disagree, Somewhat disagree, Neither agree nor disagree, Somewhat agree, Agree

Korea/Japan should promote cooperation with Japan/South Korea, just on the issues that would

contribute to Korea/Japan's own national interest.
Disagree, Somewhat disagree, Neither agree nor disagree, Somewhat agree, Agree

Korea/Japan should promote cooperation with Japan/South Korea on anti-pollution measures.
Disagree, Somewhat disagree, Neither agree nor disagree, Somewhat agree, Agree

Korea/Japan should promote cooperation with Japan/South Korea on disaster countermeasures.
Disagree, Somewhat disagree, Neither agree nor disagree, Somewhat agree, Agree

Reference

Allee, Todd L., and Paul K. Huth (2006) "Legitimizing Dispute Settlement: International Legal Rulings as Domestic Political Cover." *American Political Science Review* 100(2): 219–234.

Asaba, Yuki, Kyu S. Hahn, Seulgi Jang, Tetsuro Kobayashi, and Atsushi Tago (2020) "38 Seconds above the 38th Parallel: How short video-clips produced by the US military can promote alignment despite antagonism between Japan and Korea," *International Relations of the Asia-Pacific*. 20(2): 253–273.

Iyengar, Shanto, and Donald R. Kinder (1987) *News That Matters: Television and American Opinion*. Chicago: University of Chicago Press.

Shoko Kohama, Kazunori Inamasu and Atsushi Tago (2017) "To Denounce, or Not To Denounce: Survey Experiments on Diplomatic Quarrels," *Political Communication*, 34(2): 243-260.

Future of the Korean Peace Process

Chapter 12.

Be Careful What You Wish For:

Security Challenges Facing the Korean Peninsula During a Potential Unification Process

Mason Richey (Hankuk University of Foreign Studies)
Daewon Ohn (Hankuk University of Foreign Studies)
Jangho Kim (Hankuk University of Foreign Studies)
Jae Jeok Park (Hankuk University of Foreign Studies)

Chapter 13.

Challenges and Opportunities of the 'Korean Peace Process' in the Moon Jae-in Government:

Lessons from 'NAPCI' in the Park Geun-hye Government

Eunmi Choi
(The Asan Institute for Policy Studies)

Chapter 12

Be Careful What You Wish For: Security Challenges Facing the Korean Peninsula During a Potential Unification Process[1]

Mason Richey (Hankuk University of Foreign Studies)
Daewon Ohn (Hankuk University of Foreign Studies)
Jangho Kim (Hankuk University of Foreign Studies)
Jae Jeok Park (Hankuk University of Foreign Studies)

Abstract

There is a lacuna in the literature analyzing the mid-term (6-24 months) period after a DPRK contingency that results in the Pyongyang regime's relatively sudden and unmanaged fall. This chapter helps fill that gap, particularly with respect to security issues that would challenge Korean unification efforts during such a period. Following an Introduction, Section I first makes the case for a DPRK contingency being the most plausible end to the Pyongyang regime. Assuming the scenarios from Section I, Section II addresses the question of what critical issues a unifying Korea will face over the mid-term, and how dealing with these challenges will condition the type of end-state that a unified Korea will embody. In particular, we examine three challenges: (a) mid-term security provision related to potential weapons proliferation, cyber-security, organized criminality, and human security; (b) the foundations of institution-building through measures dealing with issues of transitional justice, disputed land title claims, and generating broad domestic stakeholder buy-in in a unifying Korea; (c) the disposition of Korea's strategic alignment in Northeast Asia that will have undergone a major alteration of the regional system. Section III concludes with policy recommendations concerning what efforts should be made now to prepare for the situations described in Sections I and II.

Keywords: North Korea, contingency, regional security, Korean peninsula, Northeast Asia

---

1 With the permission of Taylor and Francis, this chapter is a slightly revised reproduction of Richey, Mason, et al. "Be careful what you wish for: Security challenges facing the Korean Peninsula during a potential unification process." Asian Security 14.3 (2018): 263-281.

I. Introduction

As Niels Bohr famously quipped, "Prediction is difficult, especially about the future." Politics is no exception to this observation, of course, and the hazards of divining the future are evident when looking at the record of forecasts for the end of North Korea (DPRK). Experts have proclaimed the downfall of the Kim-led regime as a result of numerous upheavals and crises: the loss of communist patrons following the end of the Cold War, the first dynastic transition from Kim Il-sung to Kim Jong-il, crippling famine during the 1990s, economic sanctions from many corners of the international community, a disastrous currency reform in 2009, the hasty power transition to Kim Jong-un, and the DPRK-China border shutdown during the 2020 COVID-19 pandemic.[1] Obviously the Pyongyang regime led by the Kim dynasty remains in power—with the current Kim seemingly firmly in the saddle—and DPRK analysts are left to wonder why their projections were not realized.

Nonetheless, the most likely outcome for the DPRK is some form of governance dissolution—e.g., party/government collapse, military coup, mass revolt—and just because Pyongyangologists have been wrong about this in the past does not mean they will be in the future. Indeed one of these governance dissolution scenarios may occur sooner than expected. Thae Yong-ho, former DPRK Deputy Ambassador to the United Kingdom, and among the highest ranking DPRK defectors in history, fled to the ROK in 2016 and has since given numerous interviews claiming the Pyongyang regime's brittle support and predicting its downfall by the 2020-2025 period.[2] For his part, recently retired US Forces Korea (USFK) Commander Walter Sharp said in a May 2016 address that "due to internal instability, the regime might collapse on a faster timeline than we previously imagined."[3] Consequently he argued for the imperative of military, security, and geopolitical preparation for the aftermath of sudden DPRK regime collapse.

This point has also been emphasized in more detail by Wendy Sherman, US Undersecretary of State in the Obama administration (and an expert deeply connected with the US State Department's up-to-date perceptions of the DPRK). She argued at a 2016 Washington, D.C. forum that the US and South Korea (ROK) should be prepared for a sudden DPRK regime collapse or coup, and make plans accordingly, including working with Northeast Asian regional powers to sketch out plans for military-military deconfliction, discuss the handling of DPRK nuclear weapons, and identify ways of managing large immigration flows, etc.[4] For his part, Zhu Feng, influential Director of the Institute of International Studies at Nanjing University, made the same claim, from a Chinese point of view, at the 2017 World Knowledge Forum in Seoul.[5]

Indeed, there is a lacuna in the literature analyzing the mid-term (6-24 months) period after a DPRK contingency that results in the Pyongyang regime's relatively sudden and unmanaged fall. There is no shortage of operational plans for the immediate aftermath of various DPRK collapse scenarios, the most (in)famous of which is the US Department of Defense's OPLAN 5029; the Chinese of course have their own less well-known plan.[6] These plans are dominated by military considerations necessary for providing security (including human security) and stability in a failed state. There is also a plethora of works on the long-term fate of a unified Korea. Analyses for this situation tend toward theoretical and normative arguments about unified Korea's type of state (unitary state, federation, confederation), government (parliamentary, presidential, semi-presidential), domestic institutions (economic system, social programs, etc.), and external relations (e.g., how to manage relations with the US, Japan, and China).[7] Scholars have spent less effort trying to figure out the interstitial scenarios between an abrupt end to the Pyongyang regime and the end-state of a nascent unified Korea.[8] Our task in this article is to remedy this gap in the literature by tackling what a unifying Korea would face in the mid-term.

That said, there is perhaps a good reason for the comparative neglect of this topic in favor of examinations of the short-term and long-term issues pertaining to Korean unification: mid-term analyses must make assumptions about the likely nature of the immediate situation following a DPRK contingency, while *also* connecting and justifying how responses in this environment would evolve into (hopefully) preferred long-term outcomes institutionalized in a unified Korea. Short-term planning only has to consider the contingency situation in its immediacy, while long-term analyses are free to be normatively ambitious about the unified country without attending much to how to achieve desired results. In contrast, this article must account for several plausible conceptions of the short-term aftermath of a DPRK contingency, while also remaining flexible with respect to how various responses to such an aftermath could establish uncertain path dependencies.

As a methodological note, we are agnostic about exactly what kind of state and government a unified Korea will (or should) be. However, we do point out that our argument assumes a more or less successful transition from a collapse or coup contingency scenario to the mid-term unification project. Practically speaking, this means (at least) successful peace-making/peace-keeping and thus a lack of widespread open conflict on the Korean peninsula; basic service provision and a functioning humanitarian operation for those in the northern half of the Korean peninsula; a working provisional central government of a unified Korea; a managed situation with regard to the presence of soldiers from the ROK, US, China, and other polities having participated in a presumptive stabilization operation; a set of more or less enforceable measures regarding human mobility between the southern and northern halves of the Korean peninsula; and successful disarmament, demobilization, and re-integration (DDR) of the vast bulk of the DPRK military.

The article proceeds in the following way. Following this Introduction, Section II first makes the case for a DPRK contingency being the most plausible end to the Pyongyang regime, and then explicates which two contingency scenarios are most probable—namely, an abrupt collapse of party (Korean Worker's Party) and government, or a slower-motion, yet still surprising change of leadership that is uncontrolled, but possibly led and managed by China. Assuming the scenarios from Section II, Section III addresses the question of what critical issues a unifying Korea will face over the mid-term, and how dealing with these challenges will condition the type of end-state that a unified Korea will embody. In particular, we examine three challenges: (a) mid-term security provision related to potential weapons proliferation, cyber-security, organized criminality, and human security; (b) the foundations of institution-building through measures dealing with issues of transitional justice, disputed land title claims, and generating broad domestic stakeholder buy-in in a unifying Korea; (c) the disposition of Korea's strategic alignment in a Northeast Asia that will have undergone a major alteration of the regional system. Section IV concludes with policy recommendations concerning what efforts should be made now to prepare for the situations described in Sections II and III.

II. The Likely Fate of North Korea's Ruling Regime

It is important to recall why some form of DPRK contingency is the most likely terminus of the Pyongyang regime led by the Kim dynasty and managed by a relatively small group of elites.[9] Quite simply, it is difficult to imagine a more plausible alternative to a collapse or coup situation on the Korean peninsula.

Alternative (a) is DPRK reform—both economic and, potentially, political—following the "developmental dictatorship" models of countries such as China, Vietnam, or Myanmar. This path is attractive, as it implies a reasonable level of continuity on the Korean peninsula and in the Northeast Asian regional system, which would in turn buttress peace among the region's stakeholders. Indeed, especially China's leaders—who are fearful of both major conflict and ROK-led unification—have admonished Pyongyang to adopt reform since the early 1990s. The DPRK has roundly rejected this advice, for instance declaring at the 7th Worker's Party Congress in May 2016 that "[d]espite the filthy mind of bourgeois liberty and 'reform' and 'openness' blowing in our neighborhood, we let the spirit of *songun* [military-first] rifles fly and advanced according to the path of socialism that we had chosen."[10] The DPRK has grudgingly bowed to the necessity of gray markets, but the regime remains committed to refusing comprehensive reform because its institutions and leadership would lose power.

Alternative (b) is unification by military invasion. To begin with, it is worth recalling that imposed unification following conflict is the stated policy of neither the current DPRK nor the ROK. Moreover, this possibility is improbable because both the ROK and the DPRK are deterred from launching an attack by the enormous escalation risk (especially nuclear risk) attendant to inter-Korean war. Although a threat to the ROK, the US, and Japan, the DPRK's nuclear weapons arsenal actually reduces the likelihood of an intentional[11] invasion of the DPRK by the US-ROK alliance, and this is in addition to the fact that the DPRK's conventional deterrent (artillery and rocket forces within easy range of Seoul and environs) and chemical/biological weapons hold the ROK hostage.[12] On the DPRK side, the Kim regime is a rational actor, not suicidal, and an attempt at forced Korean unification by invasion would result in the US extended deterrent (possibly nuclear) being activated to destroy the Kim regime.[13]

Alternative (c) is a gradual, peaceful transition of one country's politico-economic system to that of the other.[14] This is in fact the official position of both protagonist polities, although they each envision very different mechanisms and institutions for accomplishing this metamorphosis. Of course, these "officially" endorsed outcomes are also non-starters, as each government would demand that the other adopt its system as the unification end-state.[15] This would relegate one side's elites to oblivion, and thus they would have no incentive to enter this unification path.

And so there remains alternative (d), a contingency (e.g., collapse, coup, perhaps brought about by succession difficulties if Kim Jong Un, who is an obese smoker reportedly suffering from a number of chronic maladies, died suddenly.) on one side and the other side's attempt to absorb it. The Pyongyang regime's brittle[16] political legitimacy and the country's overall precarity (especially its horrendously maldeveloped economic fundamentals) militate that most scenarios envision an abrupt[17] collapse of the DPRK and its rapid absorption and unification on the South's terms. This remains the case despite the lifeline extended to the DPRK by China, although there is a plausible alternative collapse scenario that envisions a slower process of DPRK regime disintegration, and in which Beijing plays a role in guiding the DPRK to a pro-Chinese, post-Kim dynasty political arrangement.[18] Under this scenario, Korean unification would be unlikely, and even if it were to take place, it would be on looser terms favorable to Beijing's geopolitical vision for Northeast Asia.

There are other collapse possibilities of course—notably DPRK collapse and gradual absorption, as well as a one people/two states solution (something like Austria and Germany)—but they are generally considered implausible.

But does this schema not forget at least one possibility: that inertia prevails and the DPRK continues on its path of economic maldevelopment and political repression? In fact, we have not seen mass elite defections[19] or popular uprisings that reliably signal regime change in authoritarian states. Nonetheless, there are new reasons to think that the current regime has entered a particularly fragile period. In the first place, domestic challenges are mounting. These include the long-term trend of decreasing regime control over economic forces (e.g., tolerated marketization[20]) due to loosened agricultural collectivization and the futility of the public distribution system, and weakening of the government's monopolistic control of information (due to ICT and foreign media penetration into the formerly hermetic country).[21] In the short-term, this has saved the Kim regime, but in the medium-/long-term this development is a major risk.[22] That is, paradoxically, toleration of markets, which have increased living standards in the DPRK, even allowing the formation of a sort of middle class that one usually associates with successful governance, entails a growing group of people who do not rely on the state or party, and are therefore a threat to the DPRK regime precisely at the moment when its repressive/control systems are being undermined.[23]

These structural collapse risks—which undermine the regime's fundamental legitimacy and control—are reinforced by more unpredictable risks emanating from the DPRK's economic maldevelopment. As Victor Cha put it already in 2016, "North Korea is one pandemic away from collapse," a proposition being tested at the time of this writing, as the DPRK is suffering major economic fallout due to its border closure with China as a response to COVID-19.[24] Another such unpredictable threat is natural and/or man-made environmental disasters. Indeed, the country is prone to severe drought, flooding, and famine, while Pyongyang's now-shuttered underground nuclear test site (Punggye-ri, near the Chinese border) is a threat to leak major amounts of radiation, which a high-ranking defector argues would perhaps precipitate an uncontrolled mass emigration to China and/or Beijing's intervention in the DPRK.[25]

Second, the international environment is similarly unfavorable. Indeed, the DPRK's acceleration of its nuclear weapons program is widely viewed as a desperate sprint to achieve de facto nuclear state status before international sanctions hit with full force, which Kim fears could threaten his regime.[26] International sanctions (UNSCR 2270, 2321, 2356, 2371, 2375, and 2397) in place after the DPRK's 2016-2017 round of nuclear bomb and missile tests have become much stronger than previous sanctions rounds, targeting industries (inter alia, shipping, coal and iron ore exports, hydrocarbon imports, international financial system access, textile exports, seafood exports, aviation fuel imports), entities and institutions (the National Aerospace Development Agency), and individuals in the regime. Reports indicate that these sanctions are beginning to bite: the DPRK's trade deficit with China (upon which the DPRK is dependent) is ballooning, prices are rising (inter alia, for oil and rice), and the DPRK won is volatile.[27] The DPRK itself has acknowledged that sanctions are hurting its economy enormously, even establishing a Sanctions Damage Investigation Committee (presumably for tallying the damage in case future negotiations lead to a reparation possibility).[28] Going forward, sanctions will limit DPRK access to international finance, foreign exchange, private (especially luxury) goods instrumental in ensuring regime loyalty, and materiel and know-how for nuclear weapons and missile programs.[29] In addition, numerous polities—especially the US (via self-enforcing executive orders that constrain China's ability to evade the sanctions) and the EU—have passed enhanced sanctions going beyond UNSCR sanctions.[30] In addition to the US's base secondary sanctions codified in Executive Order 13466 and 13722 (and subsequent modifications), the Treasury Department has promulgated financial sanctions—under section 311 of the USA Patriot Act—and sanctions that much more seriously restrict DPRK access to international banking. Under rules passed in May 2016 and September 2017, banks worldwide with connections to the US financial system are prohibited from processing DPRK/DPRK-related financial transactions. For its part, the EU has taken steps to close down DPRK-backed businesses that engage in various forms of fraud to earn hard currency that is remitted back to the Pyongyang regime.[31]

The US and its allies are weary of the status quo, and over time it is more likely that they will begin to pressure the Pyongyang regime in ways that will threaten its survival. This course of action was most vividly demonstrated by US president Donald Trump's twin "maximum pressure" and "summit diplomacy" approach to Pyongyang, but other, more orthodox voices (with a vision more consonant of what one would expect from a Joe Biden administration) have also called for more assertive policies. To wit, the following comments from Evans Revere, a former top diplomat in the US State Department and current advisor in the Albright Stonebridge Group (a consultancy led by former US Secretary of State Madeleine Albright and considered very well connected to the US government thinking about US foreign policy, including that related to the DPRK):

> "I have come to the conclusion—after seeing everything else we have tried fail to achieve the objective of freezing and then eliminating North Korea's nuclear weapons program—that we need to try something different. And that 'something different' is to begin to put at risk the one thing that the North Koreans treasure more dearly than their nuclear weapons, which is the stability and the future prospects for survivability of the regime··· [W]e have tried engagement, we have tried removal of sanctions, we have tried commitments to normalize relations, we have tried the establishment of liaison offices. On the dark side we've tried threats and sanctions and pressure, etc., and none of this has worked··· So if they

> define these weapons as key to their survival, what we need to do is to say to the North Koreans, 'You will not be able to survive if you go down this path.' And the way to do that… is to ratchet up sanctions to an unprecedented degree; and that's the course the U.S. is on right now. The steps that have been taken by the administration so far are helpful, but they are also rather preliminary. I think there is a lot more coming…"[32]

Indeed, during both the late Obama and early Trump administrations, the US and ROK posture toward the DPRK grew more hawkish, notably including military measures complementing much toughened sanctions. In 2015, USFK Commander Curtis Scaparrotti led a secret strategy session—at the Special Operations Command Wargame Center—that included planning for regime change and collapse scenarios.[33] Also in 2015, the ROK re-started retaliatory propaganda loudspeaker broadcasts into the DPRK (these measures are currently out-of-favor under the progressive Moon Jae-in government in Seoul, but could return if a conservative wins the next ROK presidential election). These broadcasts, which undermine the party's legitimacy and sap military support crucial to regime survival, alarmed Pyongyang sufficiently that it started cross-border firing (which the ROK returned), setting up a near escalation to full-blown conflict.[34] In July, 2016 US Pacific Command concluded a deal to install a THAAD (Terminal High Altitude Area Defense) battery on ROK territory, a part of a larger US increase in DPRK-focused militarization around the Korean peninsula.[35] In early February 2017 then-US Defense Secretary James Mattis traveled to Seoul for official meetings with ROK leaders in which he outlined a more aggressive US posture vis-à-vis the DPRK, including the possibility of pre-emptive strikes against DPRK nuclear and missile facilities.[36] Also in February, then-USFK Commander Vincent Brooks indicated the same line of thought about pre-emptive strikes, as did Bob Corker, the chairperson of the US Senate Foreign Relations Committee.[37] Throughout the summer and fall of 2017, the Trump administration adopted a highly hawkish posture vis-à-vis Pyongyang.[38]

Among other objectives, a *sotto voce* diplomatic and strategic goal of these measures—from intensifying sanctions throughout the Obama administration to increased military presence in Northeast Asia under Trump—was to pressure Pyongyang in such a way as to dovetail with other domestic and international factors capable of inducing governmental collapse or regime change.[39] The typical argument against the DPRK collapse thesis is that China—given its regional and global geopolitical/ geostrategic interests, and in light of its professed policy preferences—would obviate such collapse-inducing factors from reaching criticality, thus preventing it from occurring.[40] That is, China would take extraordinary measures to prevent collapse from becoming even a concrete possibility as a result of either international pressure or domestic DPRK factors; and if imminent danger of collapse were to emerge, Beijing would rescue the regime, or, barring that, ensure that a China-friendly, status quo-friendly replacement regime would gain power when a DPRK contingency was still in its earliest stages, and thus controllable.

This argument is imminently sensible, but its logic rests on at least two factors: (a) the interest and ability of the DPRK regime to play the role of tributary state, which requires deference to, and respect for, China; and (b) Beijing's continued perception that its geopolitical/geostrategic and security interests are better served by propping up the DPRK than by its collapse.[41] There are signs that these conditions may not hold in the long term.[42]

(a) As for the former, at points in recent years the DPRK leadership's relationship with China was significantly degraded. Numerous factors contributed to this: the execution of Jang Song-thaek (China's closest contact to the Pyongyang regime) and the purge of many elements of his faction; Kim Jong-un's refusal to attend Beijing's September 2015 celebration of the 70th anniversary of victory in WWII; and missile/rocket and nuclear bomb tests in 2012, 2013, 2016, and 2017. This set of incidents led to China's assent to and enforcement of the aforementioned enhanced UNSC resolutions, the toughest international sanctions ever. Considering that China has served as the DPRK's lifeline, this degeneration in their relationship (even if currently seemingly patched-up) makes Pyongyang vulnerable to endogenous and exogenous shocks.

(b) As for the latter, in recent years Chinese leaders have seemingly begun to re-think the value of the relationship with the DPRK.[43] This is most obvious in the country's increasing support for UN sanctions against the DPRK, including for UNSCR 2094 in 2013 (which Beijing co-sponsored). Moreover, China's paramount leader, Xi Jinping, failed to meet with Kim Jong-un before having met multiple times with ROK president Park Geun-hye. The state visit hosted for Xi in the ROK in 2014 marked the first time that a new Chinese leader visited the ROK prior to the DPRK since Ziang Zemin in 1995 (a momentous capstone to the establishment of official diplomatic relations between the ROK and China, which Deng Xiaoping achieved in 1992).

Analysts are likely still correct that, overall, China's interest preference order for the Korean peninsula is stability/status-quo first, China-friendly unification second, and denuclearization third.[44] Nonetheless, the gap between those interests is closing, as increasingly China's greater strategic ambitions—which are widening beyond Northeast Asia to the rest of the Asia-Pacific, to Central Asia, and even beyond—become more difficult with a DPRK-sized millstone around Beijing's neck. Indeed, Beijing's leaders may eventually decide that the risk-cost of the status quo in the DPRK outweighs the current benefits, and opt for trying to manage a slower-motion, yet still surprising change of leadership. This might also entail a unification scenario, and although the geopolitical consequences would be different than an unmanaged scenario, many of the same domestic issues would remain.

In any event, there is a real likelihood that at some point Chinese leaders will choose to drop the DPRK millstone through one mechanism or another (e.g., relative neglect in favor of other priorities, trading it away in a grand bargain, etc.).[45] After all, the DPRK is only one marginal (albeit important) state in a sub-region of a greater East Asian theater in which China is rising to challenge US primacy.[46] As the US counters China's attempts to re-order East Asia—via maritime claims in the South China Sea, the establishment of the Belt and Road Initiative, etc.—both the possibility and necessity of protecting Pyongyang will decline in the face of the claims on Beijing's resources needed for mitigating the US's regional strategic interest advancement. This is all more likely as Pyongyang's bellicosity incentivizes (and provides diplomatic cover for) the adoption and deployment of US strategic assets (and those of its regional allies) that aim at deterring[47] the DPRK yet inevitably form part of a potential US containment line vis-à-vis China.[48]

III. Middle-term Issues Facing a Unifying Korea

Assuming a DPRK contingency situation—collapse, coup, mass revolt, etc.—as the proximate cause of the end of the current Pyongyang regime, the reactive and doubtlessly chaotic crisis management during the initial aftermath will transform over time into a mixture of immediate challenges and forward-looking struggles to lay institutional foundations for unified Korea.

1. Selected security risks entailed in DPRK collapse.

(a) Perhaps the most worrisome problem is proliferation of weapons of mass destruction, especially nuclear weapons. A chaotic end to the Pyongyang regime would likely result in degraded control of NBCR weapons (nuclear, biological, chemical, radiological). In anticipation of this, there would be an immediate scramble by regional actors—primarily the US and China—to secure the DPRK's nuclear bombs, delivery systems, fissile material, nuclear weapons processing and production technology, (e.g., uranium enrichment centrifuges), and related equipment.[49] This would be difficult even in the best of circumstances, but the confusion of a contingency situation coupled with an unprepared and under-resourced Chinese PLA (People's Liberation Army), as well as an undermanned[50] ROK and US military force, means that there is a significant probability that some materiel is at risk of going missing, perhaps in the hands of those with an incentive to proliferate it: e.g., disaffected or opportunistic members of the former DPRK military, state security, or worker's party.[51] Mutatis mutandis, the same logic applies to conventional weapons, from small arms and light weapons (SALW) to larger systems.

An additional NBCR proliferation risk is the DPRK's military scientists, who, in a post-contingency environment, will see their skills rendered unmarketable domestically and thus perhaps seek to sell their know-how internationally.

The above possibilities are not only a general threat to global nonproliferation efforts, but also a specific threat to regions of the world already facing security difficulties due to various forms of political instability. For example, likely buyers of such goods and services would be violent extremist groups in Southeast Asia, the Middle East, or North Africa (from which extremist groups have access to Europe). The DPRK already has inroads to these regions: various authoritarian Southeast Asian governments, such as Myanmar, have historically had connections to the DPRK military; Iran and North Korea cooperate on missile technology; and Pyongyang covertly helped Syria build a nuclear reactor that Israel bombed in 2008. As recently as 2017, Pyongyang attempted on multiple occasions to ship chemical weapons to the Assad government in Damascus.[52] Other weapons clients have included Libya, Yemen, and Hezbollah, each of which has connections with DPRK military officers.

(b) Increased cyber-terrorism and cyber-crime represent another set of security risks that would likely emanate from the former DPRK during the mid-term transition period toward a unified Korea. The DPRK's cyber-warfare units employ an estimated 6,000 trained military hackers, with approximately 1,800 working for the elite Bureau 121.[53] These elite cyber-warriors are considered responsible for several high-profile hacking attacks including the 2013 DarkSeoul attack (which caused 700mnUSD damage to the ROK economy in general and banks and media companies in particular), the crippling 2014 Sony Pictures attack, and the 2017 Wannacry ransomware attack. A group of DPRK hackers—known to cyber-security experts as the Lazarus group—appear to be responsible for using the SWIFT system to steal 101mnUSD from Bangladesh Bank.[54] In addition, Pyongyang's cyber-warriors have apparently carried out lower-profile, yet still serious hacking attacks against ROK targets: e.g., the ROK satellite GPS-signal jamming in 2016 and 2015 hacking attacks (including extortion to stop the attacks) against a nuclear power plant operated by Korea Hydro (the ROK's main nuclear power company).[55] Even more worryingly, from a terrorism perspective, a recent DPRK defector formerly connected to the military's hacking units has stated that Pyongyang's cyber-warriors are increasingly learning to carry out infrastructure sabotage (along similar lines as the US-Israeli Stuxnet attack).[56]

Like the country's nuclear scientists, the DPRK's cyber-warriors will face unemployment/underemployment following a regime collapse or unmanaged coup. Considering their skill set, over the mid-term of the unification process they will have the ability and incentive to sell their black-hat abilities to unscrupulous entities interested in attacking businesses and governments worldwide. An added layer of complexity to this issue is that most experts say a significant number of the DPRK's elite cyber-warriors are frequently stationed internationally (in order to have easy, invisible access to servers), which means it will be difficult to identify and track them in the case of DPRK contingency situation.

(c) The DPRK has an estimated 300,000-400,000 people working for the country's various security services (State Security Department, Ministry of Public Security, Military Security Command, etc.).[57] In the mid-term aftermath of a DPRK contingency, the remnants of these organizations represent a multipronged security threat, including insurgency and organized crime. It is true that the DPRK does not have obvious fault lines—religious sectarianism, multi-ethnic and/or multi-racial societies, a history of warlordism—that have played an important role in fanning insurgency and organized criminality in toppled or failed states such as Iraq, Afghanistan, Somalia, and Libya. Nonetheless, there is a significant probability that the DPRK security services would produce organized crime and insurgent groups following collapse or coup. In the first place this is due to the current nature of these organizations, which are likely widely reviled by much of the rest of the DPRK citizenry (meaning that they face retribution for current repressive actions, and are thus incentivized to band together), and as insular as they are diffuse (meaning that they share bonds of solidarity, are spread throughout many parts of society, and have a flatter structure than the military (and therefore are less susceptible to top-down de-mobilization)). As importantly, many of the security services would likely have members facing drastic cuts to economic well-being and social status, which would incentivize organized criminal activities and perhaps even outright resistance to the newly unified Korea. In addition, the security services are already inextricably linked to an ingrained culture of corruption in the DPRK, have significant experience in black markets and illicit activities, and will have undergone decades of indoctrination of hatred against the US, the ROK, Japan, (even) China, and other countries whose crisis managers will not be greeted as "liberators." Finally, the northern part of the Korean peninsula has mountainous geography, difficult terrain, and extremely poor infrastructure, all of which would make very difficult any efforts by the new central government of a unified Korea to control and eradicate organized crime and insurgency.

(d) There will be numerous human security challenges facing a Korean peninsula in the process of unification. These range from public health and safety issues, to a continuing need for humanitarian aid and food assistance for those living in the northern half of the peninsula, to policies related to the movement of people across the current DMZ. For instance, health security would need to be improved, not only in terms of provision of basic health care (which will be a major challenge, as the already poor DPRK health system will be in dire straits following a contingency), but especially in terms of prevention of breakout of infectious diseases with human reservoirs in the DPRK. A prominent example is extreme-/multi-drug resistant tuberculosis. About 3,500 annual cases are currently quarantined in the DPRK, but in a chaotic situation they could cross the current DMZ, become disease vectors, and propagate to other regions of the peninsula (or even to other countries). A major public safety threat will be anti-personnel land mines. Quite obviously the current DMZ (which is densely mined) will be a particular focus for removal efforts, but it is likely the case that Pyongyang has placed mines in and around many sensitive security and military locations throughout the DPRK. Another question with human security implications is that of when/where/how to allow movement of people across the current DMZ, an issue that may be compounded both by large numbers of internally displaced people and a significant number of former DPRK citizens who try to cross into northeastern China (which would likely close the border, exacerbating a migration crisis). This issue will likely begin during the earliest phases of a collapse or coup scenario, but resolving it would likely extend well into the mid-term phase of unification.

2. Generating buy-in for a unified Korea's civil institutions

In the mid-term period following the initial, reactive aftermath of a DPRK collapse or coup, the primary political task will be cultivating loyalty to the unified Korea across the spectrum and throughout much of the social and government hierarchy of the current DPRK (and, probably less problematically, in the current ROK). It is a mistake to assume that national sentiment will do enough work in this regard: there will be winners and losers (on both sides), and their material outcomes will affect their loyalty to the unified Korea. That loyalty will come as much on the back of well-designed institutions (including political institutions) as it will through "pre-political" national identity. These institutions—from economic to political—will need to create stakeholders in the unified country. Many of those institutions are readily identifiable: some form of market liberalization and fair contract enforcement, massive structural funding for economic development (perhaps through PPPs), democratic politics (multi-party elections, rule of law), and the construction of civil society. Today's DPRK citizens will need to experience these institutions as sufficiently beneficial, from an early stage in the unification process, in order for the stakeholder effect to do the work of cultivating loyalty to the new state. Without economic prosperity, the rest of the unification tasks will become radically endangered. Citizens from the south will also need to feel that, at least in the long run, they will benefit (hence the "daebak" ("bonanza") rhetoric that some ROK administrations have used to describe unification); it is also imperative that they do not look down at their northern consanguines, much less engage in widespread discrimination, as this will undermine the northerners' loyalty to the newly unified country. All of this is relatively simple to understand and easily supportable. But there are trickier issues. Transitional justice will be just such a thorny issue. One of the principal difficulties will be dealing with the DPRK elite. On the one hand, those in the military, the party (WPK), the government, the various secret and security services, etc. sufficiently responsible for the disastrous human rights, political rights, and economic record of the DPRK will need to be at a minimum excluded from renewed leadership roles, and many will face criminal prosecution for crimes against humanity (especially those sufficiently responsible for the gulag system). On the other hand, it is not obvious what "sufficiently" means. Where does one draw the line on who is prosecuted and who is amnestied and even rehabilitated? This is an essential question, as in a unified Korea—just as in many other states, from Germany, to Japan, to South Africa, to Iraq—making some members of a terrible old regime stakeholders in the new one plays an important role in preventing political destabilization due to insurrection, guerilla warfare, and organized criminality (and not doing so incentivizes these behaviors). Unfortunately, one cannot be a stakeholder if one is facing prison or the gallows.

Where to draw the line is also a very difficult question because the nature of the current regime makes unmanageably large numbers of people substantially complicit in grave crimes (sometimes as both perpetrator and victim), and there will be difficulty in piecing together forensic evidence of gulag abuses for reparations. A reasonable position may be that leaders on the secretary level and above should be prosecuted; junior officials, officers, and party cadres should be amnestied but barred from government/military service; and those otherwise implicated in lower-level violations should participate in Truth and Reconciliation commissions, but otherwise face no sanction. Of course, reasonable people can disagree on whether or not that is a just assignation of censure. The overriding lesson, however, is that although the DPRK system may not remain, some of its operators will. In any event, this division of consequences is also driven by a practical consideration. Under many current models, Korean courts will be responsible for handling such trials, as is currently foreseen by the ROK constitution, but their resources, and thus case capacity, are limited.

Another major "stakeholder" and justice issue combining political considerations and security concerns (as well as economic one) is the issue of disputed land claims. Many ROK citizens hold (illegally expropriated) land titles in the DPRK, whose citizens also occupy and (for example) farm said land (but do not own it because property belongs to the state). These conflicting land claims will have to be adjudicated and compensation paid. This will also stress the Korean court system. Simply giving the land to the southern title holders will effectively destroy the possibility of self-sufficient livelihoods for many current DPRK citizens (encouraging insurrection and other criminal behavior), while ignoring current ROK citizens' claims would violate the very sense of the rule of law that a unified Korea should represent. Meanwhile, systematically awarding land to the ROK title holders while paying compensation to the northern occupiers will lead to windfall-induced inflation. Awarding title to northern occupiers while compensating southern title holders would open up the possibility of quick-turnaround land sales (to businesspeople) by northerners with limited/non-existent experience in real estate markets. This would result in windfall profits that would quickly evaporate due to either the exigencies of daily consumption or windfall-induced inflation.

3. Unified Korea's strategic alignment in Northeast Asia

Peninsular unification following a DPRK collapse or coup would have a transformative effect on the Northeast Asian regional order. These geopolitical transformations would change the context in which polities approach relations to China, Japan, and Russia (inter alia). Obviously, there are risks involved. Notably, China would be largely disadvantaged by the transformation, as it would suddenly have borders contiguous to territory that would be part of the US-Korea-Japan constellation. Given a realigned region in which it were deprived of its buffer state, it would likely upgrade and modernize its military, as well as adopt a different posture—possibilities that could lead to a security dilemma. Thus, it is even a distinct possibility that China—defying both Korean and US desires—would work hard to undermine unification.

If a putative Chinese strategy of undermining Korean unification were to fail, one scenario might be that China would use leverage in other places to maintain its interests. For example, it might compensate by exerting more pressure on Taiwan, the

South China Sea, and disputed maritime territories such as the Senkaku/Diayou islands. These potential actions would affect global commons—e.g., sea lines of communication (SLOCs), or overflight rights—whose secure access is vital for the international economy.

Yet another scenario is that the current US-ROK security cooperation would be weakened without the presence of the DPRK. After all, the US-ROK alliance is primarily for DPRK deterrence, which would be unnecessary after unification. Notably a unified Korea could theoretically gravitate more to China on security cooperation (reflecting the weight of their economic relationship). This specific scenario is unlikely, but certainly possible. Perhaps more plausibly, one can also imagine a scenario in which the US-Korea alliance withers away in the face of a more independent, "balancer-role" Korea that might emerge after unification.

Whatever the modalities, the value of the US-Korea alliance will come into question, and, even if the alliance remains in force, its raison d'être will clearly change from countering Pyongyang to other objectives. The main reason for the continuation of the alliance would be that it could take on a role of contributing to regional stability in East Asia. This fits the concept of a so-called "alliance for order insurance," which is defined as an alliance that "serves as an essential arrangement for retaining or cultivating security arrangements to respond to an undesirable long-term security trend that may occur in the process of order-maintenance."[58] This understanding of alliances views them as existing to insure against "defaulting relative to whatever balancing or hedging strategy may be appropriate to implement at some point in the future, even though the question of who needs to be guarded against or why currently remains unclear."[59] Put differently, an order insurance alliance is intended to obviate the necessity of choosing between specific strategies (such as hedging or balancing) by building a security architecture that prevents the emergence of unwanted security-related situations in general.[60]

For a unified Korea, such a concept would have several important advantages. First, a newly unified Korea will be weak, as it struggles to overcome the challenges of combining two systems, and a strong security alliance with a trusted partner is the most efficient and least risky way to maintain a regional order that is conducive to the new country's consolidation. Moreover, from a purely practical standpoint, the transition from a ROK-US alliance to a unified Korea-US alliance would be comparatively seamless, relative to a switch to a (for example) security arrangement with China, as the sunk costs and interoperability with the US are significant. It is also clear that the US would likely be a willing partner for such an order insurance alliance, as this approach would serve the US's status quo geopolitical preeminence in the region. Meanwhile, there is no guarantee that China, for example, would be interested in the same kind of alliance, as Chinese leadership has a different understanding of the relationship between major and minor powers (one that is perhaps more "traditional" and "tributary based," as is in many ways China's current relationship with the DPRK).[61]

The logic behind the continuation of the ROK-US anti-Pyongyang alliance qua unified Korea-US alliance for order insurance is not without flaws. To begin with, millions of former DPRK citizens—including, especially, military, security, and intelligence personnel who have been trained to distrust the US—would be suddenly asked to enter an alliance with a former enemy. Assuming that this problem could be managed, the primary difficulty, however, is that a meaningful alliance involves more than regular leadership summits and invocations of the facticity of the alliance—that is, operational activities and joint training, intelligence sharing, interoperable hardware development, established relations between military commands, and other means of maintaining the capability to work as an alliance (if necessary) are crucial to its existence. In the current situation, the ROK-US alliance does all of these things; most famously these essential elements of the alliance come together in annual ROK-US military exercises. Something similar would be necessary for a Korea-US alliance to be credible, and the downside is that it would (rightly or wrongly) almost certainly feed China's fear of encirclement and containment by US-led alliances, and therefore likely provoke a potential security dilemma situation that would possibly destabilize the region. Ironically, this consequence would be precisely the outcome that the alliance for order insurance would be designed to prevent.

A related difficulty with the continuation of the ROK-US alliance as a unified Korea-US alliance during the mid-term unification process would be the stationing of US troops on the Korean peninsula. Ceteris paribus one imagines that the US and a unified Korea would be loathe to antagonize China by positioning US troops north of their current locations, but even if all US troops were to be based below the Han River, it is likely that China would still be displeased with the presence of US troops in a country directly on its border. It would, in turn, take measures to respond to the perceived security threat: this could include accelerated upgrading of the PLA/PLAN, repositioning and re-posturing troops responsible for the Korean peninsula, and/or causing problems in unrelated areas (South China Sea, Taiwan Strait, East China Sea). Certainly, the US has alliances with countries in which it does not have significant troop presence, so there is no ironclad rule that an alliance requires such. However, not keeping a troop presence as part of the Korea-US alliance would make the operationalization of the alliance more difficult (see above), and be interpreted as a downgrade vis-à-vis the alliance status quo. The latter could be especially problematic, as it would call into question the credibility of the alliance, which, in turn, might provoke its testing. Like authority in general, alliances work best precisely when they are not questioned, and to do so in the context of a fraught post-unification Northeast Asia would be to invite escalation.

In addition to a strategy of alliance for order insurance, a unified Korea might find the Korea-US alliance valuable against hypothetical specific perceived threats. As historically dominant power on the Korean peninsula, China would be one candidate for threat perception by a unified Korea. This sentiment would be buttressed by contemporary China's growing power and revisionist geopolitical aspirations in Northeast Asia and beyond. On the other hand, for many Koreans, Japan is considered a greater potential threat than China. The residual animosity of the Japanese colonization of Korea remains a potent component of Korean national identity (in both the north and the south), and an altered regional security environment following Korean unification might be interpreted by Koreans as an opportunity for Japan to reassert its designs on regional dominance. As that has historically led Japan to attack the Korean peninsula, Korean leaders (and the population at large) may desire a Korea-US alliance as a way to deter that eventuality.

The prospect of nuclear weapons in Northeast Asia would also be a critical aspect of considerations about the continued value of a unified Korea-US alliance. On the one hand, the US's extended nuclear deterrence is a model of protection against general risk of nuclear attack (ipso facto this tends to support the status quo). In the context of a Korea-US alliance the US nuclear umbrella would presumably cover Korea in the case of any country that launched a nuclear attack against it (or threatened to do so imminently). On the other hand, insofar as a handful of East Asian states either have nuclear weapons or are threshold nuclear powers (China, Russia, and Japan), US extended deterrence would disincentive a hypothetical nuclear attack (or imminent threat of nuclear attack) from the countries that a unified Korea's population and government might feel are its greatest potential threats (China and Japan).

From the perspective of the US, there is a major advantage to the US's extended deterrence for unified Korea: namely, it would clearly reduce the incentive for the fledgling country to acquire its own nuclear deterrent. The ROK is already a latent nuclear power (having knowledge and technological capability to quickly develop, test, and operationalize nuclear weapons), and if it (or a successor unified Korea) felt compelled to become a nuclear weapon state, it would lead a series of regional (and perhaps) global dominos to fall: Japan (a threshold nuclear state), Taiwan (a latent nuclear power), Iran, Saudi Arabia, Turkey, and others. This would obviously be a dramatic blow to global nonproliferation efforts.

It is worth noting that the US extended deterrence within the context of an alliance with a unified Korea is not without problems. In the first place, there are many questions about the capabilities—e.g., weapons, radar/sensors, ancillary equipment, personnel, command-and-control—and ongoing training/operational activities that would need to be installed on the Korean peninsula in order to make the nuclear umbrella functional. These elements of extended deterrence would likely be considered hostile by some or all of Korea's neighbors, thereby heightening regional security tensions and exacerbating potential security dilemmas. Second, there are important issues of doctrine and geographical coverage that would need to be dealt with. For example, would the nuclear umbrella cover today's DPRK territory (i.e., would a nuclear strike on that territory of a unified Korea trigger retaliation by the US)? If so, China and Russia would suddenly find themselves with a US extended deterrence policy that reaches their borders (which is not the case now in East Asia, insofar as currently the US nuclear umbrella is only in force for the ROK); if not, perhaps precisely out of deference to Chinese and/or Russian sensibilities, then the unified Korea would find itself only partially covered by extended deterrence. The latter would probably be untenable, if for no other reason than that it would strain the overall credibility of US extended deterrence on the Korean peninsula. Finally, insofar as a unified Korea—in a changed Northeast Asian system—would consider US extended deterrence to apply to Japan also, the US would have a very delicate, complicated, perhaps impossible balancing act with its Northeast Asian allies. If improperly handled, the US's alliance network in the region could fall apart.

Finally, it is worth pointing out briefly why the US would be interested in continuing the ROK-US alliance in its new form with a unified Korea, given the various complications and entanglements. There are at least three reasons. There is always the possibility that by the time of Korean unification the US could fall into one of its periodic infatuations with isolationism, but, barring that (and the attendant domestic political pressures that might compel US political leaders to back away from Northeast Asian security issues), geopolitical reasons are the first answer to the question of why the US would continue the alliance. Specifically, abandoning a unified Korea as an alliance partner would reduce the US's ability to project military and diplomatic power in the region, signal weakness to Beijing, jeopardize the alliance with Japan, and otherwise drastically reduce US political influence in East Asia. Such a series of events would also have a knock-on effect on the ability of the US to project power and wield influence in other regions.

Second—and related—the US would lose a substantial portion of its ability to influence the regional security order in a way that would protect US economic interests. Everything from protecting SLOCS to negotiating advantageous trade deals would become more fraught with the loss of US power in the region, a necessary effect of the abandonment of the unified Korea-US alliance. Third, as mentioned above, the prospect of regional nuclear proliferation would increase dramatically if the US pulled out of its East Asian alliances, an effect that would radiate to other parts of the world, and eventually force the collapse of the global nonproliferation regime. This is a risk that no state should take unless absolutely necessary, and one that few serious US politicians would make under all but the most exigent circumstances.

IV. Conclusion

Korean unification has many upsides—not least the fact that it would put an end to ghastly human rights violations the predatory DPRK regime visits upon its own people. But the creation of a unified Korea will be highly disruptive, massively expensive, and fraught with security and geopolitical challenges. In short, unification, which may not occur for a significant period of time, carries great risks and uncertainty. Strategic thinking is tasked precisely with considering the mid-/long-term future's known and unknown scenarios and possible states of affairs, deciding where opportunities and difficulties are to be found among the uncertainties, and then describing measures for seizing the positives and mitigating risks. In what remains, we provide a selected set of considerations to this end. The general thrust of our approach is that some elements of the mid-term process of Korean unification should be internationalized, for reasons both practical (the tasks to be accomplished are legion, and will outstrip the capacities of Korea and the US) and conceptual (Korean unification will affect the international and regional Northeast Asian systems, which necessitates a role for other affected states).

The best way to respond to future risks is to be vigilant in preparing for them in advance. One obvious place to start in terms of future Korean unification is augmenting available manpower necessary for meeting some of the challenges described above. The ROK's total strength of current armed forces stands at 599,000 active personnel (and 3,100,000 reserves), out of which most are arranged into 24 ground force divisions. As for the US, its presence on the Korean peninsula is currently at 28,500 troops, while that in Japan (which could be mobilized in the case of a DPRK contingency and its aftermath) is roughly 50,000. Even at these numbers, a newly unified Korea's ability to provide state security (an ongoing requirement even during the mid-term of the unification process), fight weapons proliferation, counter organized crime and insurgency, and provide human security (public health, etc.) will be compromised.[62] The DPRK has a larger active military (1,300,000 troops), a reserve force of 600,000 soldiers, and a reserve paramilitary of nearly 6,000,000 personnel. Although they are mostly poorly trained, badly equipped, and perhaps weakly motivated, these forces' size alone means the security challenges listed above would be difficult to accomplish in the face of even minimal resistance to co-optation by the unified Korean government. The situation is aggravated by the fact that the ROK is facing a country-defining demographic change. As its population stagnates and ages, by 2022 the ground force divisions will shrink to 14-16 (down from 24), with accompanying loss of manpower (Bennett 2013). The US would theoretically be able to mobilize additional troops to assist, but it would be unlikely that the US would commit to making up the gap alone.

Recommendation 1: Mitigate future shortages of manpower for peace-keeping through: (a) identifying and working with international partners—including allies such as those in Europe, Australia, or India, as well as fraught powers such as China and

Russia—who could supply personnel[63] for security tasks (i.e., filling so-called "security gaps"); (b) messages (psychological operations) targeting active and reserve DPRK soldiers, in which they are informed that under unification conditions they can expect opportunities to be co-opted (as opposed to abandoned), such that they are incentivized to avoid insurgency and organized criminality; (c) establishing weapons buy-back programs to remove excess small-arms and light-weapons from potential problem elements of the former DPRK military and security services.

Creating stakeholder buy-in will be crucial to the success of Korean unification, along with establishing economic fundamental and humanitarian assistance (where and when necessary), setting up new political institutions and possibly bringing selected influential DPRK elites into some positions of authority, and managing the issue of mobility flows and internally displaced people. As we show above, ensuring processes of transitional justice and land title dispute settlement will be an important part of that effort. There will be major challenges to these two efforts.

In the first place, transitional justice would certainly involve the employment of the Korean (and perhaps international) court system, in order to try those suspected of sufficiently grave crimes against humanity. Given the elevated number of potential suspects subject to due process, it is nearly certain that a responsible execution of this overall judicial effort would place an almost impossible burden on Korea's judges and pre-trial detention capacities. Second, transitional justice in a unified Korea would likely require the establishment of Truth and Reconciliation commissions to deal (especially) with human and civil rights violations/violators under the DPRK system. The manpower and expertise to run such commissions will be in short supply in a unified Korea. Third, the adjudication of disputed land title claims will present both practical difficulties (including lack of manpower and expertise to handle the cases), as well as legal and economic challenges (i.e., questions of what the correct legal decision should be for who owns property, and how that should be dealt with in order to ensure that the formal titling and compensation (for those who lose their land title) plans accomplish the objective of stakeholder buy-in).

Recommendation 2: Prudent preparation for Korean unification should include planning: (a) to learn in general how historically divided nations (e.g., Germany, Ireland) have gone through peace processes and/or processes of (re)unification; (b) to establish hybrid Korean-International courts (including international judges) for trying sufficiently grave cases of human rights violations/violators under the DPRK system; (c) to identify states that potentially could offer manpower to manage pre-trial detention of those suspected of grave human rights violations under the DPRK regime; (d) to incorporate the experience and expertise of other countries' (e.g., South Africa, Cambodia) and the international community in establishing and running transitional justice programs in general and Truth and Reconciliation commissions in particular; (e) to learn from reunified Germany how it handled (practically, juridically, and normatively) the resolution of land title disputes between East and West Germans; (f) to organize a "roadmap" for paying southern Koreans claiming compensation for land titles awarded to northern Koreans (conditional on their holding the land title for a vesting period that would create a northern stakeholder class and prevent hasty windfall sales).

Concerning the continuation of the ROK-US alliance qua unified Korea-US alliance, the main objective in preparing for its possibility should be to take steps now that would mitigate possible future risks inherent in continuing the alliance. In practice, this means lessening the fears of China, Russia, and (to a lesser extent) Japan. In this regard, both the general idea of the Korea-US alliance and its specific execution (inter-operable technological development, military exercises, US troop presence, etc.) are what would generate potential security dilemmas.

Recommendation 3: (a) Strategic diplomacy (if necessary, sotto voce) now and in the future to persuade Beijing, Tokyo, and Moscow that a potential unified Korea-US alliance would be primarily about maintaining regional stability to the non-detriment of vital Chinese, Japanese, and Russian interests[64]; (b) Increasing transparency and information sharing vis-à-vis (especially) China with respect to selected weapons systems and/or doctrines, in order to include China in US-led alliance dynamics and reduce potential miscalculation of capabilities and intentions; (c) Re-thinking the concept of extended deterrence in East Asia after the fall of the DPRK.

Although from a security standpoint the world—and especially the US and the ROK—has a lot of exigent requirements to deal with currently, and thus it may seem that DPRK collapse and peninsular unification are sufficiently distant scenarios that they do not deserve much attention, policy-makers should remember the following: strategy is about long-term thinking, thinking beyond the horizon and around the corner, establishing a solid context for reacting to unforeseen and unforeseeable events, if not shaping them yourself. Not doing so invites punishment by the inevitable changes of history itself.

1 Armin Rosin, "The Long History of (Wrongly) Predicting North Korea's Collapse," *The Atlantic*, August 6, 2012, https://www.theatlantic.com/international/archive/2012/08/the-long-history-of-wrongly-predicting-north-koreas-collapse/260769/

2 Arirang TV, "Arirang Special," Arirang TV Special, Episode 374, January 25, 2017, https://www.youtube.com/watch?v=oGQ_S4h4uk0; Jenny Lee, "Analysis: Is North Korea's Collapse Imminent?," VOA, January 30, 2017, http://www.voanews.com/a/north-korea-analysis-is-collapse-imminent/3699107.html. Naturally skepticism is warranted regarding Thae's comments, as selection effects predispose him to exaggerate Pyongyang's weakness.

3 Ahn Jong-Sik, "Both U.S. and North Korea brace for sudden change," DailyNK, June 1, 2016, http://www.dailynk.com/english/read.php?num=13922&cataId=nk03600

4 Yong In-yi. "Wendy Sherman: must prepare for possible North Korean 'coup or collapse'," *Hankyoreh*, May 5, 2016, http://www.hani.co.kr/arti/english_edition/e_northkorea/742632.html

5 Zhu Feng, "Remarks at the Forum 'Endgame: A Hard Debate on North Korean Nuclear Threat'," World Knowledge Forum—Seoul, South Korea, October 18, 2017.

6 Bruce Bennett and Jennifer Lind, "The Collapse of North Korea: Military Missions and Requirements," *International Security* 36(2) 2011: 84-119; Shannon Tiezzi, "Does China Have a Contingency Plan for North Korea," *The Diplomat*, May 7, 2014, http://thediplomat.com/2014/05/does-china-have-a-contingency-plan-for-north-korea/; Global Security, "OPLAN 5029—Collapse of North Korea," http://www.globalsecurity.org/military/ops/oplan-5029.htm.

7 Marcus Noland, *Avoiding the Apocalypse: The Future of the Two Koreas* (New York: Institute for International Economics, 2000); Ministry of Unification (Republic of Korea), White Paper on Korean Unification (2014), http://eng.unikorea.go.kr/content.do?cmsid=1819; Sue Mi Terry, "Unified Korea and the Future of the U.S.-South Korea Alliance," CFR Discussion Paper (December 2015); Tara O, T*he Collapse of North Korea: Challenges, Planning, and the Geopolitics of Unification* (Basingstoke, UK: Palgrave Macmillan, 2016).

8 An exception to this is Bruce Bennett's *Preparing for the Possibility of a North Korean Collapse*, which contains sections on the mid-term issues that most stakeholders of a unify*ing* Korean peninsula would face. See: Bruce Bennett, *Preparing for the Possibility of a North Korean Collapse* (Santa Monica, CA: RAND Corporation, 2013), http://www.rand.org/content/dam/rand/pubs/research_reports/RR300/RR331/RAND_RR331.pdf. See also: Kyuryoon Kim et al, *The Attraction of Korean Unification: Inter-Korean and International Costs and Benefits* (Seoul, South Korea: Korea Institute for National Unification, 2013), http://repo.kinu.or.kr/handle/2015.oak/2297.

9 This article is, of course, an exercise in academic counter-factual thinking, as the authors' aim is to identify some major medium-term issues`` that a unifying Korea *would* face, *assuming* a DPRK collapse or coup. Indeed the DPRK has not yet collapsed, and many Chinese analysts argue that it is inconceivable that Beijing would let the regime in Pyongyang fall (notwithstanding a recent editorial in the *South China Morning Post*, which is known to hew to Beijing's viewpoint, arguing that the regime's days are numbered (See: Deng Yuwen and Huang Ting, "Collapse of the North Korean Regime Appears Inevitable, and the World Needs to Prepare for It," *South China Morning Post*, May 18, 2016, http://www.scmp.com/comment/insight-opinion/article/1946189/collapse-north-korean-regime-appears-inevitable-and-world). However, the scholarly counter-factual thinking

in this article is not without a connection to *actual, practical, present* concerns of strategic preparedness. Just to give one example, the US's *Military Review* argues for why strategic planning for DPRK collapse and follow-up Korean unification is a necessary endeavor (See: Bryan Port, "North Korean Collapse or Korean Unification: The Importance of Preparation Over Prediction," *Military Review* (September-October 2016): 8-19. http://usacac.army.mil/CAC2/MilitaryReview/Archives/English/MilitaryReview_20161031_art006.pdf).

10 Ruediger Frank, "The Seventh Party Congress in North Korea: A Return to a New Normal," 38North.org., May 20, 2016, http://38north.org/2016/05/rfrank052016/#_ftn3

11 That said, there is of course the possibility of miscalculation by the DPRK or the US-ROK alliance, for example disproportional US-ROK retaliation following a DPRK provocation (ballistic missile launch, nuclear test detonation, small-scale artillery salvo against ROK territory). This scenario could lead to unintentional escalation to total war (including military invasion), which the DPRK would almost certainly lose in such a way that the Kim regime would fall and a potential unification scenario could emerge that would be different from that of a collapse or coup scenario.

12 Robert Kelly, "America Must Manage North Korea, Not Destroy It," *The National Interest*, September 5, 2017, http://nationalinterest.org/blog/america-must-manage-north-korea-not-destroy-it-22175;
Joshua Rovner, "Nobody Loves Deterrence, But We'll Keep Doing It Anyway," War on the Rocks, October 9, 2017, https://warontherocks.com/2017/10/nobody-loves-deterrence-but-well-keep-doing-it-anyway/.

13 Mason Richey, "Turning It Up to Eleven: Belligerent Rhetoric in North Korea's Propaganda," *Parameters: The US Army War College Quarterly* 46(4) 2017: 93-104, https://ssi.armywarcollege.edu/pubs/parameters/issues/winter_2016-17/11_Richey.pdf

14 One variant of this is a "negotiated confederation" leading to a "one country, two systems" model in which the North would retain significant autonomy and many of its leaders would remain in power in some way. Arguably this was the intended outcome of the "Sunshine Policy," and is now arguably considered dead-letter. See: Chung In Moon, "The Sunshine Policy and the Korean Summit: Assessments and Prospects," *East Asian Review* 12(4) 2000: 3-36; Patrick Cronin et al, *Solving Long Division: The Geopolitical Implications of Korean Unification* (Washington, DC: CNAS, 2015), https://s3.amazonaws.com/files.cnas.org/documents/Korean-Unification-151204-final.pdf; Andrei Lankov, *Tigers and Bears: Saying the Unthinkable about Korean Unification* (Washington, DC: NK News Publishing, 2016).

15 Cronin et al, 2015, *Solving Long Division*; Lankov, 2016, *Tigers and Bears.*

16 From late 2016 extending into 2017 the ROK faced political turmoil stemming from the impeachment of President Park Geun Hye. Rather than provoking an existential political crisis in the ROK, however, Park's impeachment was peacefully handled through established constitutional and statutory mechanisms, underlining the robustness of the ROK's democratic institutions. That said, the more the ROK is focused on domestic politics, the less attention it can devote to preparation and planning for a DPRK contingency. As the authors outline in Parts II and III, this preparation and planning is crucial.

17 Just because the collapse scenario is abrupt does not mean that it will take place in the very near-term, however. It is entirely possible that Kim Jong-un remains in power for the next decade or longer. If that were the case, the unification challenges (and policy recommendations) described in this article would still be valid, albeit with some alterations. For example, on the one hand, the longer Kim Jong-un remains in power while refusing reform, the greater the DPRK will come to rely on gray markets. This entails that the DPRK populace would be more thoroughly socialized into market thinking, thereby making some unification challenges easier. On the other hand, the longer Kim remains in power, the greater Pyongyang's military capabilities (especially nuclear and missile) will be. This will present greater challenges to non-proliferation during the unification period.

18 Andrei Lankov, "A developmental dictatorship (with North Korean characteristics)," NKNews, July 4, 2016, https://www.nknews.org/2016/07/a-developmental-dictatorship-with-north-korean-characteristics/

19 This is not to say that high-level defections have not been occurring, as illustrated by Thae Yong-ho.

20 The establishment of private markets (*jangmadang*) has led to the rise of middle class *à la coréenne*. The regime is deeply ambivalent about this class of *donju* (literally: "moneymasters"), as they are responsible for the fact that the DPRK economy has not utterly failed (and with it, the state), while at the same time they represent a threat to state political control. Historically the regime's approach to this dilemma is a cycle of market crackdowns and toleration (accompanied by unofficial taxes on market stalls and extortionate bribes paid to police and security forces).

21 Michael Holtz, "As North Korea's economy grows, Kim tries to wield a double-edged sword," *CSMonitor*, May 1, 2017, https://www.csmonitor.com/World/Asia-Pacific/2017/0501/As-North-Korea-s-economy-grows-Kim-tries-to-wield-a-double-edged-sword

22 Jonathan Corrado, "Will Marketization Bring Down the North Korean Regime?," *The Diplomat*, April 18, 2017, https://thediplomat.com/2017/04/will-marketization-bring-down-the-north-korean-regime/; Bryan Harris, "North Korea begins journey from feudalism to crony capitalism," *FT.com*, June 21, 2017, https://www.ft.com/content/db738fb8-3ed2-11e7-82b6-896b95f30f58; Holtz, 2017, "Double-edged sword"; Andrei Lankov, "North Korea's economy is improving—but this may not save Kim Jong Un," NKNews, August 14, 2017, https://www.nknews.org/2017/08/north-koreas-economy-is-improving-but-this-may-not-save-kim-jong-un/

23 Corrado, 2017, "Will Marketization Bring Down"; Lankov, 2017, "North Korea's economy"; Melanie Hart and Renee Ding, "Getting Real on Sanctions Is Key to Pressuring North Korea," Center for American Progress, September 5, 2017, https://www.americanprogress.org/issues/security/reports/2017/09/05/438371/getting-real-sanctions-key-pressuring-north-korea/

24 Keegan Hamilton, "North Korea Is 'One Pandemic Away From Collapse' Says Former US Nuclear Negotiator," Vice News, March 11, 2016, https://news.vice.com/article/a-former-us-nuclear-negotiator-says-north-korea-is-one-pandemic-away-from-collapse

25 Elizabeth Shim, "Defector: North Korea's next nuclear test could lead to collapse," UPI, March 14, 2017, https://www.upi.com/Top_News/World-News/2017/03/14/Defector-North-Koreas-next-nuclear-test-could-lead-to-collapse/6641489489192/; Martin Seitz, "North Korea's Impending Perfect Storm," *The Diplomat*, August 25, 2017, https://thediplomat.com/2017/08/north-koreas-impending-perfect-storm/

26 Jake Maxwell Watts and Ben Otto, "New North Korea Sanctions Are in a Race With Pyongyang's Missile Development," *Wall Street Journal*, August 6, 2017, https://www.wsj.com/articles/enforcing-new-north-korea-sanctions-poses-challenge-1502050649; Leif-Eric Easley, "North Korea's Nuclear and Missile Tests Are Aimed at Splitting its Rivals," *Foreign Policy*, September 3, 2017, http://foreignpolicy.com/2017/09/03/north-koreas-tests-are-aimed-at-splitting-its-rivals/

27 VOA News, "Oil to Keep Flowing, but UN Sanctions Hit North Korea Hard," VOA News, September 12, 2017, https://www.voanews.com/a/north-korea-sanctions-crude-oil/4025246.html; Stephen Haggard, "Monday Morning Roundup: More on the Sanctions." North Korea: Witness to Transformation, October 2, 2017, https://piie.com/blogs/north-korea-witness-transformation/monday-morning-roundup-more-sanctions; William Brown, "Volatility in North Korea's Currency Trading: Does a Rising Won Mean Trouble Ahead, or Progress?," 38North, November 20, 2020, https://www.38north.org/2020/11/wbrown112020/

28 Phil Helsel and Stella Kim, "North Korea Says Sanctions Cause 'Colossal' Damage But Won't Work," NBC News, September 29, 2017, https://www.nbcnews.com/news/north-

korea/north-korea-says-sanctions-cause-colossal-damage-won-t-work-n806146

29 Laura Smith-Park and Richard Roth, "Toughest UN sanctions yet to cost North Korea $800 million," CNN, December 1, 2016, http://edition.cnn.com/2016/11/30/asia/un-north-korea-nuclear-sanctions/; Reuters, "China puts temporary ban on North Korean coal imports," Reuters, December 22, 2016, http://www.reuters.com/article/us-northkorea-nuclear-un-china-idUSKBN14007R; Stephen Haggard, "Sanctions: Things Are About To Get Interesting. Very Interesting," North Korea: Witness to Transformation, September 21, 2017, https://piie.com/blogs/north-korea-witness-transformation/sanctions-things-are-about-get-interesting-really; Stephen Haggard, 2017, "Monday Morning Roundup."

30 White House, Presidential Executive Order on Imposing Additional Sanctions with Respect to North Korea. The White House, September 21, 2017, https://www.whitehouse.gov/presidential-actions/presidential-executive-order-imposing-additional-sanctions-respect-north-korea/; Stephen Haggard, 2017, "Monday Morning Roundup"; Consilium, Press Release: North Korea: EU adopts new sanctions. Consilium of the European Union, October 16, 2017, http://www.consilium.europa.eu/en/press/press-releases/2017/10/16/north-korea-sanctions/

31 NKNews, "European Commission designates N. Korean insurance companies, individuals," NKNews, July 3, 2015, https://webcache.googleusercontent.com/search?q=cache:oHLkVDw1jxsJ:https://www.nknews.org/2015/07/european-commission-sanctions-hit-n-korean-insurance-company-individuals/+&cd=4&hl=ko&ct=clnk&gl=kr

32 Chad O'Carroll, "Make North Korea 'stare into the abyss'," NKNews, May 30, 2016, https://www.nknews.org/2016/05/make-north-korea-stare-into-the-abyss/

33 Bill Gertz, "U.S. Commander in Korea Leads Secret Strategy Session," *Washington Free Beacon*, January 26, 2015, http://freebeacon.com/national-security/u-s-commander-in-korea-leads-secret-strategy-session/

34 Ian Williams, "North Korea Puts Army on 'Quasi State of War,' Sets Loudspeaker Deadline," NBC News, August 21, 2015, http://www.nbcnews.com/news/north-korea/north-korea-puts-army-quasi-state-war-sets-loudspeaker-deadline-n413636

35 US Department of Defense, "US to deploy THAAD missile battery to South Korea," DOD News, July 11, 2016, https://www.army.mil/article/171316

36 Jeong Ho Nam, "The real reason for Mattis' visit," *Korea Joongang Daily*, February 6, 2017, http://mengnews.joins.com/view.aspx?aId=3029481

37 Seung Eun Lee, "Pre-emptive strikes on North Korea worth weighing: Corker," *Korea Joongang Daily*, February 2, 2017, http://koreajoongangdaily.joins.com/news/article/article.aspx?aid=3029308; Yong Weon Yu, "USFK Chief Hints at Preemptive Strikes Against N. Korean Missiles," *Choson Ilbo*, February 10, 2017, http://english.chosun.com/site/data/html_dir/2017/02/10/2017021001270.html

38 Evan Osnos, "The Risk Of Nuclear War With North Korea," The New Yorker, September 18, 2017, https://www.newyorker.com/magazine/2017/09/18/the-risk-of-nuclear-war-with-north-korea

39 Jisi Wang, "Understanding Strategic Distrust: The Chinese Side," in *Addressing U.S.-China Strategic Distrust* (eds. Jisi Wang and Kenneth Lieberthal) (New York: Brookings Institute, 2016), https://www.brookings.edu/wp-content/uploads/2016/06/0330_china_lieberthal.pdf

40 Paul Stares, "Assessing the Risk of Regime Change in North Korea," 38North.org, December 16, 2016, http://38north.org/2016/12/nkinstability121616/

41 Daewon Ohn and Mason Richey, "China's Evolving Policy towards the Democratic People's Republic of Korea under Xi Jinping," *Asian Studies Review* 39(3) 2015: 483-502; Leif-Eric Easley and In-Young Park, "China's norms and its near abroad: understanding Beijing's North Korea policy," *Journal of Contemporary China* 25(101) 2016: 651-668. http://www.tandfonline.com/doi/full/10.1080/10670564.2016.1160497

42 Stares, 2016, "Assessing the Risk of Regime Change."

43 Ohn and Richey, 2015, "China's Evolving Policy"; Stares, 2016, "Assessing the Risk of

Regime Change."

44 Ohn and Richey, 2015, "China's Evolving Policy"; Wang, 2016, *Understanding Strategic Distrust*; Andrei Lankov, "China's position on North Korea hasn't changed," NKNews, June 8, 2016, https://www.nknews.org/

45 For an explanation of the logic of a Chinese grand bargain with the US, and how that might affect the Korean peninsula, see: Charles Glaser, "A U.S.-China Grand Bargain: The Hard Choice Between Military Competition and Accommodation," *International Security* 39(4) 2015: 49-90.

46 Bruce Jentleson, "The Post-Trump World in Context: The US and the Northeast Asian Strategic Order," *Global Asia* 11(4) 2016: 50-57.

47 Richard Bush (ed.), *Alliances and partnerships: U.S. commitments in the Asia-Pacific* (New York: Brookings Institute, 2016); Brendan Taylor, "Sino-US Competition and Nuclear Non-Proliferation on the Korean Peninsula," *Global Asia* 11(4) 2016: 28-33.

48 THAAD deployment is one salient example of this, as is the so-called "minilateral" linkage of US-led alliances (See: Bush, 2016, *Alliances and partnerships*). For detailed analyses of how the Korean peninsula fits into the US-China dyad, see: Scott Snyder, *China's Rise and the Two Koreas* (Boulder, Co: Lynne Rienner, 2009); Andrew Scobell, "The View from China," In *Asia at a Tipping Point: Korea, the Rise of China, and the Impact of Leadership Transitions* (ed. Gilbert Rozman) (Seoul: Korea Economic Institute, 2012); SINA, "张琏瑰, '年以来的朝美、朝中关系与朝核问题'" [Zhang Liangui: "North Korea-US relations, North Korea-China relations and the North Korean nuclear issue"], July 31, 2013, http://blog.sina.com.cn/s/blog_5b016db90101asa9.html; Scott Snyder and S.W. Byun, "China-Korea Relations: China's Red Line on the Korean Peninsula," *Comparative Connections*, May 2014, file:///C:/Users/SONY/Downloads/1401qchina_korea.pdf; Yun Sun, "Uncertain Futures: China, Trump and the Two Koreas," 38North.org, February 9, 2017, http://38north.org/2017/02/yuns020917/

49 Bennett, 2013, *Preparing for the Possibility.*

50 Both parties, especially the US, will have to handle NBCR weapons locating, securing, and dismantling, despite the fact that the US will not have sufficient disposal teams available, while unified Korea will be prohibited by international law from handling (i.e., possessing, even for neutralization and disposal purposes) nuclear weapons (See: Bennett, 2013, *Preparing for the Possibility*). This presents a host of complications (See: Mason Richey and Daewon Ohn, "Options for Increasing Europe's Security Role on the Korean Peninsula," IES Policy Brief, 2014/06 (July 2014), http://www.ies.be/files/2014_6_PB.pdf

51 Richey and Ohn, 2014, "Options for Increasing Europe's Security Role."

52 Samuel Ramani, "A Closer Look at Iran and North Korea's Missile Cooperation," *The Diplomat*, May 13, 2017, https://thediplomat.com/2017/05/a-closer-look-at-iran-and-north-koreas-missile-cooperation/; Martin Chulov, "Two North Korean shipments to Syria intercepted in six months, UN told," *The Guardian*, August 22, 2017, https://www.theguardian.com/world/2017/aug/22/two-north-korean-shipments-to-syria-intercepted-in-six-months-un-told

53 Reuters, "In North Korea, hackers are a handpicked, pampered elite," Reuters, December 5, 2014, http://www.reuters.com/article/us-sony-cybersecurity-northkorea-idUSKCN0JJ08B20141205; BBC, "North Korean hackers 'could kill,' warns key defector," BBC, May 29, 2015, http://www.bbc.com/news/technology-32925495

54 CNN Money, "North Korea suspected in fed probe of 'Lazarus' bank hacks," CNN Money, May 28, 2016, http://money.cnn.com/2016/05/27/technology/bank-hacks-north-korea-lazarus/

55 WSJ, "North Korea Blamed for Nuclear-Power Plant Hack," *Wall Street Journal*, March 17, 2015, http://www.wsj.com/articles/north-korea-blamed-for-nuclear-power-plant-hack-1426589324

56 BBC, 2015, "North Korean hackers."

57 Bennett, 2013, *Preparing for the Possibility.*

58 Jae Jeok Park, "The persistence of the US-led alliances in the Asia-Pacific: an order insurance explanation," *International Relations of Asia-Pacific* 13(3) 2013: 337-368.

59 Ibid.

60 Cronin et al, 2015, *Solving Long Division.*

61 Easley and Park, 2016, "China's norms."

62 Byung Gun Chae and Esther Chung, "US reviews posture for conflict in Korea," *Korea Joongang Daily*, February 11, 2017, http://koreajoongangdaily.joins.com/news/article/article.aspx?aid=3029737&cloc=etc%7Cjad%7Cgooglenews

63 The additional personnel required to cover the "security gaps" would depend on factors on the ground, which are difficult to predict, but a reasonable starting-point assumption would be planning for mustering additional international forces totaling at least one-third of the future demographically-induced ROK military reduction. Given current mid-term predictions for ROK troop reductions (170,000), the number would be roughly 55,000, and this is likely a low-end estimate. See: Bennett, 2013, *Preparing for the Possibility.*

64 Wang, 2016, *Understanding Strategic Distrust*; Taylor, 2016, "Sino-US Competition."

Chapter 13

Challenges and Opportunities of the '*Korean Peace Process*' in the Moon Jae-in Government: Lessons from '*NAPCI*' in the Park Geun-hye Government[1]

Eunmi Choi
(The Asan Institute for Policy Studies)

Abstract

The '*Korean Peace Process*' is the Moon Jae-in government's policy toward North Korea for resolving conflicts and confrontation which has been prevalent on the Korean Peninsula for a long period time and to realize denuclearization. The North Korean nuclear issue was still difficult to solve. In spite of several historic meetings, North Korea and the U.S. eventually failed to reach an agreement on denuclearization. In this study, first, I examine the progress and current situations of the *Korean Peace Process*. Second, I analyze the advantages and limitations of the (neo-)functional approach by comparing them with the examples of previous governments, especially focusing on the Northeast Asia Peace and Cooperation Initiative in the Park Geun-hye government, which is the very model of the application of the neo-functional approach to solve the North Korean issue, and explore its effectiveness and limitations. Third, I research the challenges and opportunities of the *Korean Peace Process*, and then give my insight on the *Korean Peace Process* and the way forward. As a result of this study, it has proved functionalist approach would be difficult to reach an eventual solution to the North Korean nuclear issue, even though it could help to ease tensions on the Korean Peninsula and in Northeast Asia.

Keywords: the Korean Peace Process, Northeast Asia Peace and Cooperation Initiative (NAPCI), multilateral cooperation, regional policy, functionalist approach

---

1 This study includes excerpts from Eunmi Choi (2020), "Where is NAPCI? The Challenges and Limitations of the (Neo-)Functionalist Approach for Multilateral Cooperation in Northeast Asia," *National Strategy* Vol.26, no.3: 181-208(in Korean).

I. Introduction

How to achieve peace on the Korean Peninsula? How will we resolve the North Korea and North Korean nuclear problems? How to build peace and prosperity in Northeast Asia? This is a challenge faced by all previous and current governments, and a problem for all of us who are living in the contemporary era.

After the Cold War, building a peace system in the Korean Peninsula beyond ideological confrontation with North Korea was a top priority for all South Korean governments, and each government dealt with this issue in different ways. These ways have sometimes appeared in the form of pressure and sanctions on North Korea, and sometimes in the form of dialogue and cooperation. Even though the ways taken by each government were different, all governments were focused on pursuing the same direction to resolve the North Korean nuclear issue and build peace on the Korean Peninsula.

There are two main ways to solve this problem. The first is to try to resolve the North Korean nuclear issue through direct talks with the North, and the second is to create an environment for dialogue. If the former is a direct way of dialogue on North Korean nuclear issue, the latter involves talking indirectly when it is difficult to communicate directly with North Korea due to internal and external factors. The indirect way takes more time and effort than the direct way to achieving the ultimate problem-solving solution. However, it can be considered as a contingency option. Also, it has the advantage of being able to continue the bond of exchange and cooperation in spite of it being low-level communication.

The Moon Jae-in government proposed the "*Korean Peace Process*" to resolve conflicts and confrontation which has been prevalent on the Korean Peninsula for a long period time and to realize denuclearization. It is a long-term and comprehensive policy led by the South Korean government to realize peace and prosperity on the Korean Peninsula as well as Northeast Asia together with North Korea, regional neighbors, and the international society. In order to implement this policy, it places importance on three values; 'Peace', 'Mutual Respect', and 'Openness'. Firstly, 'Peace' is the highest priority which we should uphold as well as being the foundation for prosperity. Secondly, the spirit of 'Mutual Respect' means to pursue co-prosperity in the Korean Peninsula by defining South Korea's stance as the "3-Nos", which means no desire for the North's collapse, no pursuit of unification by absorption, and no pursuit of unification through artificial means. Thirdly, 'Openness' means open to the public, so that the South Korean government pursues the *Korean Peace Process* through public participation and interaction with its people.[2]

By carrying out the *Korean Peace Process*, we have seen remarkable progress over the last few years, especially from 2017-2019. There have been two historic meetings between North Korea and the U.S. and 3 meetings between South Korea and North Korea. After a long period of conflict and antagonism, it led to people having high expectations that peaceful unification on the Korean Peninsula is approaching. However, the North Korean nuclear issue was still difficult to solve. In spite of several historic meetings, North Korea and the U.S. eventually failed to reach an agreement on denuclearization, only confirming their differences on the issue. Despite the consideration of the difficulties of the nuclear issue itself and the worldwide crisis of Coronavirus disease (hereafter, COVID-19) in 2020 there were no real achievements or pragmatic progress in the boisterous meetings. So, now it is still in place.

In that sense, alternative ways to change the stagnant situation have been considered to restart and bolster the *Korean Peace Process* in order to solve the North Korean nuclear issue. One of these ways is to utilize the COVID-19 situation. Amid the change in international order caused by COVID-19, the government aims to shift from the existing military security discussions to the human security[3] dialogues, and to provide opportunities for improvement in inter-Korean relations through health and medical cooperation.[4] The idea is that we can convince the United Nations to remove or reduce sanctions on North Korea, especially sanctions related to the prevention of epidemics and humanitarian aid, facing the COVID-19 crisis. It is expected that if the two Koreas build

---

2 Ministry of Unification. "Moon Jae-In's Policy on the Korean Peninsula" https://www.unikorea.go.kr/eng_unikorea/policylssues/koreanpeninsula/goals/ accessed on December 1, 2020.

3 The 1994 United Nations Development Program (UNDP) annual report presented the threat from infection to human society as a kind of human security that destroys human daily life. In the report, health security was presented as one of the emerging concerns of human security. For more details see http://hdr.undp.org/sites/default/files/reports/255/hdr_1994_en_complete_nostats.pdf.

4 edaily. (2020.5.14.) https://www.edaily.co.kr/news/read?newsId=04090166625768920&mediaCodeNo=257 ;The National Unification Advisory Council. http://webzine.nuac.go.kr/tongil/sub.php?number=2545 accessed on November 19, 2020.

trust through health and medical cooperation projects and humanitarian aid, and if talks take place between the authorities, they will be able to secure momentum to resume the denuclearization and peace negotiations.[5]

The other is to utilize the Olympics which are supposed to be held in Tokyo in 2021 and Beijing in 2022. President Moon Jae-in suggested this idea at the 15th East Asia Summit (EAS) in 2020.[6] He said, if the Northeast Asian relay Olympics are successfully held as a 'healthy and safe Olympics', mankind will be able to further raise hopes for overcoming the COVID-19 and achieving peace, with the trust and cooperation of the member countries. Then, as the first step, in November 2020, some high-level officials and major figures of the South Korean government presented their opinion officially to hold the Summit Meeting between South Korea-North Korea-U.S.-Japan at the Tokyo Olympic in 2021.

These ideas are based on the "functionalist and neo-functionalist approaches" to lead high-level cooperation from low-level cooperation through common interests in non-political and non-military areas. Will these ideas and approaches bear fruit? Though I support the ideas to revive the embers of cooperation and turn them into new opportunities, which have been caused by external shocks by COVID-19, it needs more objective, sober, and in-depth analysis and judgments.

In this study, first, I examine the progress and current situations of the *Korean Peace Process*. Second, I analyze the advantages and limitations of the (neo-)functional approach[7] by comparing them with the examples of previous governments, especially focusing on the Northeast Asia Peace and Cooperation Initiative (hereafter, NAPCI) in the Park Geun-hye government, which is the very model of the application of the neo-functional approach to solve the North Korean issue, and explore its effectiveness and limitations. Third, I research the challenges and opportunities of the *Korean Peace Process*, and then give my insight on the *Korean Peace Process* and the way forward.

---

5 Policy Briefing of the Republic of Korea. https://www.korea.kr/news/contributePolicyView.do?newsId=148871893 accessed on November 19, 2020.

6 Cheong Wa Dae of the Republic of Korea. "15th East Asia Summit" (2020.11.14) https://www1.president.go.kr/articles/9508 accessed on November 19, 2020.

7 In this study, I use the term '(neo-)functionalist approach' which can be applied to functionalist and neo-functionalist approach. However, I will use the terms separately, if it needs to be distinguished.

II. The 'Korean Peace Process' in the Moon Jae-in Government

1. What is the 'Korean Peace Process'?

The '*Korean Peace Process*' is the Moon Jae-in government's policy toward North Korea for completing denuclearization on the Korean Peninsula, eliminating threats of war and hostile tensions between the two Koreas, and establishing lasting peace settlement. It emphasizes the efforts and processes to create the future of a '*New Korean Peninsula Regime*' in which the two Koreas develop a new economic community.

The idea started from President Moon's 'Belin Declaration' on July 6, 2017. In the speech, he emphasized 'only peace on the Korean Peninsula', 'denuclearization of the Korean Peninsula', 'establishing a permanent peace regime', 'drawing a new economic map on the Korean Peninsula', and 'nonpolitical exchange and cooperation projects by separating it from the political and military situation'.[8]

The '*Korean Peace Process*' has three goals. The first is to resolve the North Korean nuclear issue and establish permanent peace in the Korean Peninsula. The second is to develop sustainable inter-Korean relations, and the third is to realize a new economic community on the Korean Peninsula.[9]

In order to achieve these aims, it has four strategies. The first one is taking a step-by-step and comprehensive approach. It means to take a two-track approach of pressure and dialogue. Also, it pursues the fundamental elimination of security threats by establishing a peace regime on the Korean Peninsula and facilitating improvement in relations between North Korea and the international community. The second one is to tackle the issues of inter-Korean relations and the North Korean nuclear threat simultaneously. For this, the South Korean government hopes to reestablish channels for inter-Korean dialogue and cooperation, and facilitate multilateral talks for the resolution of the nuclear issue. The third is to ensure sustainability through institutionalization. Specifically, the South Korean government aims to push ahead with a 'National Unification Contract' based

8 Inter-Korean Summit. http://koreasummit.kr/Policy/Berlin accessed on December 1, 2020.

9 Inter-Korean Summit. http://koreasummit.kr/Policy/Policy_North accessed on December 1, 2020.

on a national consensus to ensure policy consistency toward North Korea. Also, it plans to enact a 'New Inter-Korean Basic Agreement' in order to establish sustainable inter-Korean relations. The last one is to lay the foundation for peaceful unification through mutually beneficial cooperation. It aims to restore national homogeneity and build an inter-Korean community by expanding various inter-Korean exchanges. Then, it pursues 'natural unification' that occurs as part of the process of promoting the coexistence and co-prosperity of the two Koreas and recovering the Korean national community.[10]

For this, it has five principles; first, the 'ROK-led initiative' in promoting inter-Korean reconciliation and cooperation, and in establishing peace and co-prosperity on the Korean Peninsula. Second, 'strong defense' based on the solid ROK-US alliance for deterring North Korea's provocation and maintain peace on the Korean Peninsula. Third, 'mutual respect' with North Korea, fourth, 'interaction with the people' to draw a national consensus and agreement on unification issues, and fifth, 'international cooperation' through 'openness'.

2. Progress and Current Situation

During the past three years the '*Korean Peace Progress*' seems to have made some progress such as North Korean athletes participating in the 2018 Pyeong-chang Winter Olympics, three inter-Korean summit meetings (1st 4.27; 2nd 5.26; 3rd 9.18-20) in 2018 and two U.S.-North Korea summit meetings in 2018-19 (1st 2018.6.12; 2nd 2019.2.27). Then, North Korea's dismantlement of its nuclear test site in Punggyeri (2017.5.24), implementation of military agreements, settlement of separated families, inter-Korean exchanges in sports and culture, and economic cooperation projects such as railways.[11]

At the historic U.S.-DPRK summit held in Singapore on June 12, 2018, the two countries agreed to establish a new U.S.-DPRK relationship, establish a peace regime on the Korean Peninsula, make efforts to completely denuclearize, and excavate and repatriate the remains of prisoners of war and missing persons. In particular, by reaffirming the 'Panmunjom Declaration' regarding the resolution of North Korea's

10 Ministry of Unification. https://www.unikorea.go.kr/eng_unikorea/policylssues/koreanpeninsula/strategies/ accessed on December 1, 2020.

11 Policy Briefing of the South Korea. https://www.korea.kr/special/policyCurationView.do?newsId=148865774# accessed on December 1, 2020.

nuclear weapons program, the leaders of South Korea, North Korea, and the U.S. shared the common goal of complete denuclearization. Also, the two Koreas have laid an institutional foundation for continuing discussions on easing military tensions and building trust on the Korean Peninsula. Furthermore, the South Korean government has tried to secure international support through close communication with neighboring countries.

However, the second summit between the U.S. and DPRK, failed to reach a complete agreement, because of the two leaders' different thoughts about denuclearization and their strategic misjudgment. After that, it seems that the *Korean Peace Process* had stalled. In June 2020, DPRK blew up the 'inter-Korean liaison office' which had been set up to foster better ties with South Korea in Kaesong. The reason given was that they took offense at a South Korean civic groups' sending leaflets into North Korea and the failure of the inter-Korean agreements. Despite President Moon's talk of peace on the Korean Peninsula, the DPRK still engaged in aggressive displays, for example, the poor timing of the DPRK's recent military parade which displayed their ICBMs in October 2020. Additionally, the roles and practices of the other countries, such as Japan, China, and Russia who are directly and indirectly engaged in the DPRK nuclear issue, were hard to determine. It seems that they were left out of the issue. Thus, with the *Korean Peace Process* still ongoing, it is hard to evaluate whether the situation on the Korean Peninsula is getting better. Even though there were many meetings and historic events, we couldn't see any tangible achievement compared to the elevated expectations about the North Korean nuclear issue. Rather, we can say that it didn't pan out.

In sum, in terms of positive evaluation, the *Korean Peace Process* presented a blueprint for permanent peace on the Korean Peninsula. Also, it emphasized the South Korean government's role in leading efforts for reconciliation and cooperation for peace and prosperity on the Korean Peninsula. Furthermore, it takes a problem-solving approach by a playing mediating role between the United States and North Korea who are parties to the Armistice Agreement. However, we also need to think about the practical limitations, approaches to reach peace and South Korea's role in order to reach the next step and gradual development. For example, Is it a feasible approach? Can we respond to policy changes in North Korea and the United States? Is South Korea capable of being a mediator and a driver? How to establish relations with neighboring countries who are likely to be affected by anything that happens with North Korea? And how to get support from the neighboring countries? These questions are raised continuously when we proceed to develop policies toward North Korea.

In that sense, it is necessary to review the former governments' policies toward North Korea and Northeast Asia. In addition, researching and analyzing the regional polices of the former governments is important. Knowing the pros and cons of previous policies helps us to develop the current policy. The following chapter will cover this in more detail.

III. Lessons from the Former Governments' DPRK and NEA Regional Policies: Focusing on NAPCI in the Park Geun-hye Government

1. The Former Governments' Policies for NEA Regional Cooperation

Previous governments have made various efforts for peace, prosperity and cooperation in this region, seeking cooperation with neighboring countries even in the volatile situation on the Korean Peninsula caused by geopolitical specialties surrounded by superpowers and the North Korean nuclear threat.

The South Korean government's efforts to raise and clarify the need for regional multilateral cooperation in East Asia which began in July 1986 after the proposal of the '*Helsinki-type Conference of all nations of Asia-Pacific*' by M. Gorbachev, General Secretary of the Central Committee of the Communist Party of the Soviet Union. In October 1988, South Korea proposed the formation of a '*Consultative Conference for Peace in Northeast Asia*' involving six Northeast Asian countries for the first time under the Roh Tae-woo government, and in May 1993, the Kim Young-sam government proposed a '*Northeast Asia Security Dialogue*'. After that, the Kim Dae-jung government in April and November 1999 proposed '*Northeast Asia Multilateral Security Dialogue*' in which 6 countries participated. During the Rho Moo-Hyun government, the "*Era of Peace and Prosperity in Northeast Asia*" initiative was proposed at the inauguration in February 2003. Then the 'Presidential Committee on Northeast Asian Cooperation

Initiative' was organized in order to realize the initiative. After that, the Lee Myung-bak government pursued global diplomacy based on pragmatism, and thus proposed the "*New Asia cooperation diplomacy*", and the "*New Asia initiative*". During the Park Geun-hye government, "*Northeast Asia Peace and Cooperation Initiative (hereafter, NAPCI)*" was proposed to overcome deepened 'Asian Paradox' by having dialogues about soft security issues and accumulating cooperation customs. Then, the Moon Jae-in government proposed the "*Northeast Asia Plus Community of Responsibility*", which is very similar concept of NAPCI which was proposed in the Park Geun-hye government.

Even though the names are all different, these ideas and initiatives aim to build peace and prosperity in the Korean Peninsula, and to establish stable relations with Northeast Asia countries. Also, these ideas and initiatives are focusing on creating a foundation for North Korea to live with Northeast Asian countries and encouraging them to accept North Korea. Among these initiatives, NAPCI is the very model of the application of the neo-functional approach to solve the North Korean issue. It was an attempt by the Korean government to revive the embers of cooperation and turn them into new opportunities.

2. What is NAPCI?

1) Background and Purpose

'*Northeast Asia Peace and Cooperation Initiative (NAPCI)*' is the Park Geun-hye govenment's regional initiative and cooperation policy in Northeast Asia. In Northeast Asia, there is a phenomenon known as the *Asia Paradox*, which is the growth of political and security conflict in spite of deep economic interdependency. NAPCI was proposed in order to convert the regional structure of confrontation, from conflict and tension to dialogue and cooperation based on the idea of 'trustpolitik'. NAPCI explains that Asian leaders should pay attention to resolving various problems which hinder Asia's cooperation, build more lasting peace on the Korean Peninsula, and pursue reconciliation in Northeast Asia.[12]

Specifically, NAPCI emphasized that Northeast Asia should successfully

12 Park Geun-hye. "A Plan for Peace in North Asia" *The Wallstreet Journal* (2012.11.12.) https://www.wsj.com/articles/SB10001424127887323894704578114310294100492 accessed on November 11, 2020.

implement measures for building political and military trust, strengthening economic cooperation, and for human security, which is the notion that genuine world peace is possible only when basic values that are beneficial to all the people are guaranteed, such as military reduction, arms control and disarmament, human rights, environmental protection, social stability and democracy.

From this perspective, NAPCI sought to build trust by inducing gradual changes in the perceptions of countries in the region, forming a consensus on multilateral security cooperation, and creating small but meaningful practices of cooperation. The goal was to create a foundation for sustainable peace and prosperity in the Korean Peninsula and Northeast Asia by creating conditions for expanding the width and depth of multilateral cooperation.

2) Main Concepts and Approaches

NAPCI was a multilateral dialogue process aimed at creating a regional peace and cooperation order among Northeast Asian countries, and its plan was to build trust by accumulating practices of dialogue and cooperation from non-traditional security areas and expanding the scope of cooperation to traditional security areas in consideration of the situation in Northeast Asia where competition and conflict persist. This is a process-oriented approach that values the process of cooperation, not aimed at institutionalization, such as the establishment of a specific organization within a short period of time. Thus, flexibility in the field of agenda and format was the main characteristic of NAPCI (The Sejong Institute 2017, 40-41).

The main participants of NAPCI were stakeholders in the region, including South Korea, the U.S., Japan, China, Russia, Mongolia, and North Korea. Also, it is open to the EU, ASEAN, OSCE, and NATO, as well as offshore countries such as Southeast Asia and Europe under the principle of open participation. Thus, it created opportunities for wide-ranging dialogue with many dialogue partners. In other words, through the process and habits of dialogue, it aims to induce gradual changes in the perception of countries in the region and create a multilateral cooperation order in Northeast Asia through the formation of a consensus on multilateral security cooperation.

Under these goals, it set the seven soft security cooperation agendas that are urgent but less politically sensitive and therefore, more likely to lead to participation. It includes *'nuclear safety'*, *'energy security'*, *'environment'*, *'disaster'*, *'cyberspace'*, *'health'* and *'drugs'*. Also, it proposed a top-down approach that promotes functional and agenda-specific cooperation by combining political will by regularizing high-level inter-governmental dialogue while pursuing a bottom-up approach. This approach promotes political will through dialogue and cooperation in the field of soft security, and expected two-way spillover effects from which cooperation can continue.

Based on this idea, the government aims to create sustainable peace and prosperity in Northeast Asia by establishing conditions for expanding the width and depth of multilateral cooperation, stably managing the elements of division in the region in a multilateral framework, and opening a new path of cooperation by creating a foundation for sustainable peace and prosperity in Northeast Asia. In addition, it hoped to encourage North Korea to join the regional common interest in soft security cooperation, which would create momentum for dialogue to resolve current issues such as nuclear issues, and ultimately contributing positively to sustainable peace and stability on the Korean Peninsula and in Northeast Asia.

In order to achieve these purposes, specific methods of implementation were devised. These methods consisted of two tracks; one involved inter-governmental cooperation (Track 1 cooperation) and the other, public-private cooperation (Track 1.5 cooperation). Also, various efforts were made, such as conducting discussions to achieve cooperation by participating countries and agenda items. Lastly, cooperative implementation projects were assigned to various agencies and officials from participating countries were appointed. The details are as follows.

3) Development Process and Achievements

- Inter-governmental Cooperation (Track 1 cooperation)

According to the *Sejong Institute* (2017), for about three years from 2013 to 2016, the beginning of the implementation of NAPCI, efforts were made to obtain consent, cooperation, support from relevant countries and inform the international community. Specifically, in order to achieve inter-governmental cooperation, which is also the starting point of NAPCI, the South Korean government dealt with NAPCI at the various summit and major bilateral talks, focusing on directly and indirectly related European and Asian countries, and made efforts to induce neighboring countries to participate through understanding and cooperation with each other. As a result, less than a year after its implementation, it secured support from major countries such as the United States, China and Russia, and got support and consent from 10 multilateral consultative bodies and 30 countries.

In addition, a cooperative mechanism was created in Northeast Asian countries for the seven major cooperation agendas mentioned above. In this process, a high-level intergovernmental meeting was held to promote and strengthen the power of NAPCI. Then, from 2014, the '*Northeast Asia Peace and Cooperation Forum (hereafter, NAPC Forum)*' and '*Inter-governmental Consultative Meeting*' which involved major countries have been held.

At the '*NAPC Forum*' and '*Inter-governmental Consultative Meeting*', major regional powers discussed the possibility and status of multilateral cooperation in Northeast Asia and future development directions. In particular, the '*Inter-governmental Consultative Meeting*' held in 2015 and 2016 secured support and consent from the relevant countries on major cooperation issues and adopted the Chair's Summary. Furthermore, to promote NAPCI in earnest, a high-level official from each country was designated as a contact point. Specifically, South Korea designated a 'Director-General for Policy Planning' from the Ministry of Foreign Affairs (MOFA), in the U.S., an 'Assistant Secretary for East Asian and Pacific Affairs' from the U.S. Department of State was designated. China provided a 'Deputy Director General of Department of Asian Affairs' from MOFA, whereas Japan appointed a 'Deputy Director-General of the Asian and Oceanian Affairs Bureau' from the MOFA. In Russia, an 'Ambassador-at-Large in charge of the North Korean nuclear issue', from Ministry of Foreign Affairs, and in Mongolia, a 'Director-General of the Multilateral Cooperation Bureau' of MOFA was assigned. The designation of the person-in-charge could facilitate smoother communication and cooperation, and above all, it provided a framework for maintaining cooperation even if the regime changed.

- Public-Private Cooperation (Track 1.5 Cooperation)

Public-private cooperation of NAPCI was initiated for the efficient promotion of functional cooperation focusing on the seven agendas, 'nuclear safety', 'energy security', 'environment', 'disaster', 'cyberspace', 'health' and 'drugs', mentioned above. At the initial stage of NAPCI, the South Korean government was pushing for government-level cooperation on the seven major cooperative agendas (see Table 1).

Specifically, in the field of '*Nuclear Safety*', the cooperation efforts were launched in earnest through the proposal to establish the regional mechanisms to guarantee nuclear security among Northeast Asian countries in President Park Geun-hye's congratulatory speech on August 15, 2014. Then, the "Top Regulator's Meeting (TRM) on Nuclear Safety among China, Japan and Korea" and "Forum on Northeast Asia Nuclear Safety Cooperation (TRM+)" were held in 2014, and the "Forum for Enhancing Public Confidence on Nuclear Safety in Northeast Asia" the "Korea-Japan-China Expert Workshop on Nuclear Safety Research Cooperation" in 2016.

In the field of '*Energy Security*', the South Korean government held the "Northeast Asia Energy Security Forum" in 2013, "International Gas Trading Hub Symposium", the "International Oil Hub Symposium" and the "Pacific Energy Summit" in 2014, and the "Symposium on Transition to a Low-Carbon Economy and Future of the Energy Industry" in 2015, continuing discussions on energy security.

In addition, in the field of '*Disaster Management*', while holding the "Table-Top Exercise (TTX)", the South Korean government took the opportunity to have the "Northeast Asia Disaster Management Cooperation Conference", and confirmed the possibility of further cooperation in 2015.

In the field of '*Environment*', the cooperative foundation was strengthened and solidified in areas such as air pollution, nature conservation, marine protection, low-carbon cities and the prevention of desertification, through regular meetings of the "North-East Asian Sub-regional Programme for Environmental Cooperation" participated in by high-level officials from each country in 2015.

Furthermore, in the field of '*health*', the "Korea-Japan-China Forum for Communicable Disease Control and Prevention" is held regularly, and in the field of '*Drugs*', a separate session was arranged among the countries involved in NAPCI on the occasion of the "Anti-Drug Liaison officials' Meeting for International Cooperation (ADLOMICO)" in 2014. Lastly, in the field of '*cyberspace*', a foundation for regional cooperation was attempted through the hosting of the "Northeast Asia Peace and Cooperation Initiative (NAPCI) and EU-ROK Cooperation" and the "Inter-Regional Conference on Cyber/ICT" in 2015.

Based on the progress in the area mentioned above, NAPCI held the "NAPC Forum" in 2014 by integrating such efforts in various fields, and the Forum has been continued to date. The "NAPC Forum" was created at the time of its launch as a Track 1.5 conference for experts and government officials to explore specific cooperative measures in the field of non-traditional security, which provided an opportunity to enhance understanding and support among the parties involved. Also, it aims to build trust and foster a culture of cooperation through the establishment of networks with participating agencies and people and the accumulation of multilateral dialogue practices (The Sejong Institute 2017, 90).

Despite such diverse efforts and achievements, the government-led top-down approach has revealed limitations in advancing cooperation and expanding external relations between the parties beyond government-level support and consent.

The primary reason is that it was not known to domestic and foreign partners who are engaged in the seven functional areas and who are supposed to lead the cooperation. The South Korean government made a lot of effort to promote NAPCI to the international community, but it didn't pay that much concern to its functional partners compared to the efforts on sharing the idea to international society. In addition, the contents or methods of cooperation were not discussed in the process of securing the support of each country for NAPCI, and therefore, there were many short-term, irregular meetings without the parties who were supposed to be involved in the cooperation.

Furthermore, the agendas of meetings were mainly focused on the need for multilateral and regional cooperation in a comprehensive way, so the partner parties who were supposed to cooperate under the name of NAPCI were often excluded from the meeting. Conversely, some scholars who deal with international politics and multilateral cooperation were over-represented at various cooperation conference. In other words, there was a consensus among countries on cooperation, but the areas of cooperation and the parties involved were excluded from the discussion, it caused practical problems when NAPCI moved on to the next steps for cooperation.

Moreover, international cooperation on the seven agendas presented in NAPCI is already being pursued by other related ministries other than the Ministry of Foreign Affairs, which revealed problems of overlapping and coordinating work among ministries. This raised the need for the establishment of a "public-private cooperation network private-led (bottom-up approach)" between the government and the private sector to develop the NAPCI to the next level and have practical "sustainability" beyond

Table 1. Public-Private Cooperation led by government-level (top-down approach)

Area	Progress and Achievements
Nuclear safety	Top Regulator's Meeting (TRM) on Nuclear Safety among China, Japan and Korea (2014) Forum on Northeast Asia Nuclear Safety Cooperation (TRM+) (2014) Forum for Enhancing Public Confidence on Nuclear Safety in Northeast Asia (2016) Korea-Japan-China Expert Workshop on Nuclear Safety Research Cooperation (2016)
Energy security	Northeast Asia Energy Security Forum (2013) International Gas Trading Hub Symposium (2014) International Oil Hub Symposium (2014) Pacific Energy Summit (2014) Symposium on Transition to a Low-Carbon Economy and Future of the Energy Industry (2015)
Disaster management	Northeast Asia Disaster Management Cooperation Conference (2015)
Environment	North-East Asian Sub-regional Programme for Environmental Cooperation (2014)
Health	Korea-Japan-China Forum for Communicable Disease Control and Prevention (annual)
Drugs	Anti-Drug Liaison officials' Meeting for International Cooperation (2014)
Cyberspace	Northeast Asia Peace and Cooperation Initiative (NAPCI) and EU-ROK Cooperation (2015) Inter-Regional Conference on Cyber/ICT (2015)

it just being a conceptual "idea" (The Sejong Institute 2015; 2016). In other words, the establishment of a public-private network led by private sector was promoted to discuss specific cooperative measures beyond the need for cooperation, advance those measures, and maximize the efficiency of cooperation through systematic management and sustainable discussions.

It means that in the early stages of NAPCI there had been a discussion of the idea and direction of the government-centric, but in the subsequent stages, there was an attempt to move towards practical cooperation through the linkage of the people and the government in order to achieve substantial cooperation and results.

The public-private network-building project[13] implemented under this

13 It was implemented over multiple occasions for about seven months from May 20, 2016, about nine months from March 10, 2017, and about five months from July 12, 2018, and as research projects of the Ministry of Foreign Affairs (Choi 2018).

background has achieved many tangible and substantial results (see Table 2). The government's first action to achieve this was to designate 'The Sejong Institute' as a public-private network-building institution. It had a person-in-charge to manage and oversee cooperation in each of the seven agenda areas, and it established cooperative relations with stake-holding institutions in each of those areas.

Specifically, major cooperative agencies and officials were selected in four areas: 'nuclear safety', 'environment', 'disaster management', and 'cyberspace' to create a foundation for cooperation and to make significant progress.

In terms of domestic efforts, MOU documents were signed between the 'Sejong Institute' and the 'Korea Institute of Nuclear Safety (KINS)' in the field of '*Nuclear Safety*', and the 'Korea Environment Institute (KEI)' in the field of '*Environment*' for NAPCI. Also, the 'National Disaster Management Research Institute (NDMI)' offered its support as an advisory institution in the field of '*Disaster Management*'. These three agendas were selected as primary concerns for the establishment of public-private networks. It led the cooperative organization in the following manner: "Ministry of Foreign Affairs - Sejong Institute - each major cooperative organization." Furthermore, utilizing the system, each institution prepared separate sessions at big conferences, such as the 'Jeju Forum' and the 'Annual Conference of The Korean Association of International Studies' for discussions on NAPCI. It was an effort to broaden the scope of discussion and increase interest among experts and academia which had previously been limited.

In terms of international efforts, during the carrying out process of NAPCI, there was a strengthening of networks with experts and institutions from each country that could support and consent to the purpose of NAPCI and share their opinions. Also, it intensified the international solidarity with cooperative institutions in each functional cooperative area. As a result, an MOU document on NAPCI was signed between the 'Sejong Institute' and the 'Hiroshima Peace Institute (HPI)' in Japan. Also, one was signed by the 'Sejong Institute' and the 'Institute of Strategic Studies (ISS)' in Mongolia. Additionally, the 'Institute of Strategic Studies, Far East Federal University (FEFU)' in Russia, and the 'China Institutes of Contemporary International Relations (CICIR)' in China declared their support for and cooperation NAPCI.

In addition, there were various achievements by securing major foreign partner institutions, focusing on the cooperative agencies for functional cooperation. In the field of '*Nuclear Safety*', A 'ROK-U.S.-Japan' workshop and a 'ROK-China-Japan' workshop were held sequentially to advance discussions. In the field of '*Environment*', international joint projects centered on South Korea, China, Mongolia, and Russia were carried out to advance multilateral cooperation in the region. In addition, in the field of '*Cyber space*', cooperation tasks and measures were discussed in detail through the establishment of networks centered on South Korea, Russia, and Mongolia.

These discussions on cooperation in each agenda were not only presented at the "*Northeast Asia Peace and Cooperation Initiative Network Symposium 2016*" held voluntarily at the private level for the first time, but also separate sessions for functional cooperation were held at the "*NAPC Forum*" in 2016 and 2017 to check cooperation and discuss future plans. As such, the cooperative system was strengthened through the public-private network building project, and each cooperative field was able to expand its external relations with self-sustaining power, and achieved practical results such as implementing joint cooperation projects.

IV. Critical Review on NAPCI and its Lessons

As noted above, NAPCI achieved great progress with the participation and support of neighboring countries. In the initial stage of the implementation of NAPCI, the involved countries achieved a consensus that they can cooperate with minimal political burden on the issues and engage in a dialogue without any burden on the institutions' resources and budgets, in spite of doubts about the South Korean government's ability to sustain these policies.

However, it was not easy to continue active dialogues amid lingering security threats in Northeast Asia, including the North Korean nuclear issue. Additional issues were caused by the questions of the feasibility of regional peace through non-traditional security cooperation discussions. Other factors that hindered the process were questions about sustainability amid instability in domestic politics caused by the presidential impeachment in South Korea. Additionally, other factors that were a hindrance were a lack of interest and support in the country, which was weaker than international

Table 2. Public-Private Cooperation led by private-level (bottom-up approach)

Area	Progress and Achievements
Building institutional network	■ Domestic (Nuclear Safety) MOU with KINS (Environment) MOU with KEI (Disaster Management) get support from NDMI as an advisory institution
	■ International (Japan) MOU with HPI (Mongolia) MOU with ISS (China) get support from CICIR (Russia) get support from FEFU
Building cooperation network on each agenda	(Nuclear Safety) a 'ROK-U.S.-Japan' workshop and a 'ROK-China-Japan' workshop (Environment) international joint projects centered on ROK, China, Mongolia, and Russia (Cyber space) cooperation tasks and measures were discussed between ROK, Russia, and Mongolia.

support[14], and reduced government support in terms of supplying sufficient budget to the project. Moreover, it was difficult to give precedence to discussions on non-traditional security issues amid changes in the international environment, such as the security crisis in Northeast Asia caused by North Korea, the international community's pressure on North Korea as a result of their nuclear threats, the deployment of Terminal High Altitude Area Defense (THAAD) on the Korean Peninsula and the intensifying conflict between the U.S. and China. In this situation, the impeachment of and subsequent power vacuum left by President Park Geun-hye directly influenced the policy implementation. The continued decline in related budgets[15] has also made it difficult to

14 Despite the changes in the international situation and complex dynamics in the region, there were voices from the political, government and academic circles cheering on the vision and goals of NAPCI, including Vershbow (2014), Kim (2015), Snyder (2015), and Riterer (2015).

15 The budget for the 'Northeast Asia Peace and Cooperation Initiative' and 'Northeast Asia Peace and Cooperation Platform' decreased by 43% from 17.6 billion KRW in 2015 to 10.04 billion KRW in 2020 (Choi 2020). Meanwhile, the budget for the establishment of the 'Northeast Asia Peace and Cooperation Platform', an axis of peace for the 'Northeast Asia Plus Community of Responsibility', has decreased, but the budget for the 'New Northern Policy', an axis of prosperity, is 38.2% from 387 million KRW in 2019 to 535 million KRW in 2020, and the budget for the 'New Southern Policy (strengthening exchanges and cooperation with ASEAN and Southeast Asian countries)' is 1.55 billion KRW to 1.8 billion KRW in 2020. - MOFA. http://www.mofa.go.kr/www/brd/m_20537/view.do?seq=364166

implement the policies related to NAPCI.

Nevertheless, a more fundamental reason for disappointing progress on NAPCI lies in the limits of NAPCI itself. As explained previously, NAPCI aims to expand cooperative regional order and change regional structure from conflict to cooperation by beginning with the soft security issues which are common threats to this region. Then it ultimately aims to expand its cooperation field further to the hard security sector. From the point of view of international politics, it is based on functionalist and neo-functionalist approaches to promote cooperation by providing a political framework for functional cooperation and accumulating practices of dialogue in the field of non-traditional security. And this approach is expected to encourage collaboration in non-political and functional areas, which are relatively less sensitive than political areas where interests and conflicts exist between countries. Then it is anticipated to spread the benefits of future cooperation to other areas and ultimately reach cooperation in the political and traditional security areas.

In order for this approach to work properly, however, the ideological orientation and values of the participating countries and similarities in local culture must be established as preconditions. But Northeast Asia is a region where ideological confrontation and differences in values still remain, so there is a limit to taking this approach without solving this problem. This has already been pointed out by Hemmer and Katzenstein (2002), in a classic study of Northeast Asian regional cooperation.

As for NAPCI, it is undeniable that there were environmental restrictions for policy implementation, such the lack of motivation that resulted from the presidential impeachment and changes in the atmosphere of the international environment caused by the North Korean nuclear threat. Also, there were various problems at the working level such as overlapping inter-ministerial work, insufficient establishment of secretariat, budget, manpower and organization.

However, even if all of these problems were resolved, the process nor methods were not clearly presented for cooperation in non-traditional (or, non-political) security to cooperation in traditional (political) security, so that it made it difficult to achieve the

---

accessed on July 1, 2020.

goal.[16] That is, the lack of concrete action plans for the transition from soft security cooperation to hard security cooperation and plans for an implementation process made it difficult to promote cooperation. According to the study of Northeast Asia Peace and Cooperation Initiative Team (2014), which specifically explained the main contents, characteristics, and future roadmaps of NAPCI, it is important from a justifiable point of view, but no specific method has been suggested.[17]

As it is well known, the functionalist approach is suitable to explain the international institutions such as the United Nations to which almost all countries in the world are members due to its more generalized focus which makes membership easier to attain. However, the neo-functionalist approach has been applied in European and Latin American countries that are seeking regional economic integration which requires a great deal more political will to accomplish which contrasts with the more generalized nature of the functionalist approach. Thus, functionalism focuses on the principle of unity, and presupposes the separability of the political and non-political sectors so as to minimize political conflict. From this point of view, an explanation of cooperation in non-political fields that can facilitate international cooperation can be applied. On the other hand, neo-functionalism emphasizes the importance of political issues and shows that political motivation combines with economic purposes to accelerate the movement of unity (Delgado 1978; Kim 2004).

The main idea of NAPCI was that the effects from cooperation will spillover from non-traditional security to cooperation in traditional security area, while distinguishing cooperation between political and non-political sectors. However, it needs political will

16 Fundamental criticism of multilateralism also supports this perspective. According to a realistic approach, based on the structure of power in world politics, powerful countries that are less interfered with by other countries are likely to take bilateral relations to maximize their own interests even within multilateral organizations. Also, they are unwilling to join the majority of cooperation mechanisms even while undermining their own control (Kahler 1993, 295-296). Meanwhile, the neoliberal approach highlights the difficulty of reaching consensus in multilateral cooperation. It is not easy to narrow the gap if there are differences in the establishment of the organization or system (Park 2007).

17 NAPCI needs to show a certain linkage between soft and hard issues in regards to peace on the Korean Peninsula as a result of spillover effect when it enters a settlement period. It is believed that the participation of North Korea in any form should be visible. Also, it needs a minimal progress in the nuclear issue at the least, even if not a complete denuclearization. Then NAPCI can get a logical justification and then it can be further solidified. - The Northeast Asia Peace and Cooperation Initiative team (2014, 84-85).

from each country in order to achieve the goal. In this process, the other countries had no choice but to take political considerations into account when they faced with the dilemma of politically supporting and participating in cooperation mechanisms within the NAPCI. Furthermore, it was difficult to find a link that could transit to cooperation in the traditional security area by fostering a culture of cooperation in the non-traditional security area. In other words, while taking a (neo-)functionalist approach, it began without coming up with a way to overcome the empirical limitations of the approach.

By the way, among the seven cooperation agendas mentioned above, the four agendas, 'nuclear safety', 'environment', 'disaster management', and 'cyberspace', have reached the stage of establishing a public-private network and implementing multilateral cooperation projects. However, each meeting on the agenda was centered on professional discussions in the focused fields, far from the hard security areas such as the North Korean nuclear issues. During the process, various cooperation projects at the private-level supported by the Korean government had been carried out. Nevertheless, it was difficult to anticipate the spillover effect, which resulted from functional cooperation through public-private cooperation and organic links spreading to cooperation in the political area. This is the same as not providing much momentum for cooperation in one area to spread to cooperation in another, as pointed out in the limitations of (neo-)functionalism, and not finding a link between cooperation in non-political issues leading to political cooperation. Rather, political conflicts often affected cooperation in non-political areas, and clearly revealed the limitations of having a (neo-)functionalist approach.

For example, it was not mentioned anything about NAPCI at the '*East Asia Summit*' and the Chairman's Statement at the '*ASEAN+3 Summit Meeting*' in 2015 unlike the other previous meetings. It was related to the North Korean nuclear issue and it means that the soft security issue was overwhelmed by hard security issues such as North Korean missile test (Kim 2016, 15-16). In addition, Japan was not reluctant to participate in NAPCI because of the conflict between South Korea and Japan during the Park Geun-hye government. Also, the high-level officials of China and Russian government did not participate in '*Inter-governmental Meeting*' of NAPCI in 2016 because of the THADD issue (The Sejong Institute 2017). In the end, there were many cases of political conflicts affecting non-political cooperation which were pointed out as limitations of the neo-functionalist approach. These limitations were involved in the process of promoting the

NAPCI and there were no ways to overcome them.

Haas (1975) who advocated neo-functionalism also acknowledged the limitations of neo-functionalism theory on his own when the European Community's collective responses to the economic crisis in the 1970s were not in place, and European integration plunged into recession, leading to criticism of the optimistic and objective elements inherent in the neo-functionalist approach (Hong 2005, 9). In other words, as neo-functionalists argued, it was expected that a chain of integrations should occur in which the integration across functional areas spreads into the surrounding areas in order to overcome the imbalance caused by integration in a particular field. However, it retreated in the 1960s and 1970s due to the lack of related debates. Eventually, Haas himself declared the abolition of the unified theory in less than 20 years. Even though the (neo-) functionalist approach has already displayed its limits in history, the idea of NAPCI repeated the empirical limitations of the (neo-)functionalist approach without preparing countermeasures against the limitations.

The principle of NAPCI included an optimistic viewpoint about the spillover effects of non-traditional security cooperation to traditional security cooperation. Moreover, it was emphasized in the concept of NAPCI to take lessons from the Organization for Security and Co-operation in Europe (OSCE)'s experience in applying the comprehensive security concept to the Korean Peninsula and Northeast Asia, and then establishing Confidence Building Measures (CBMs). However, it was difficult to apply the idea in this region, because of the lack of historical, cultural and political homogeneity, the lack of multilateralism experience, different thoughts about the Cold War and its heritage, and differences in military and security strategies based on each nation's different national interests (Hwang and Yoo 2010). These factors have weakened the possibility of cooperation through a neo-functionalist approach in Northeast Asia. Some scholars argue that OSCE's experience should be selectively accommodated according to the situation in Northeast Asia (Song 2002; Seo 2009, etc.), because the situations in Northeast Asia are different from those in Europe. However, there are several prerequisites that the neo-functionalist approach requires, such as the ideological orientation and values of the participating countries, the cultural similarities, and the development of high levels of economy and industry, and it is difficult to achieve these prerequisites in a short period.[18] That is, the OSCE's experiences cannot be applied to Northeast Asia, because even the prerequisites cannot be fulfilled.

Thus, with the existence of political friction resulting from these factors, it is difficult to expect cooperation spillover effect in the face of the North Korean issue, without finding a way to spread the scope of cooperation in the political sector through cooperation in the non-political sector.

In sum, the core idea of NAPCI aimed to encourage North Korean participation in the Northeast Asian community and it also aimed to foster acceptance of North Korea among Northeast Asia countries through cooperation on soft security issues that the countries are facing with. This is based on the (neo-)functionalist approach to expect a spillover effect from the cooperation on soft security issues to hard security issues. As analyzed above, it is very hard to realize, especially in Northeast Asia. Rather, there were many examples of political conflict impairing cooperation in non-political areas. In that sense, it is unlikely that the North Korean nuclear issue will be resolved through the functionalist approach, such as cooperation on health area during COVID-19 crisis and utilizing the Olympics in coming years. It helps to ease tensions on the Korean Peninsula and in Northeast Asia, but it would be difficult to reach an eventual solution to the North Korean nuclear issue. So, it is necessary to think about ways to make substantial progress in resolving this issue for the success of the *Korean Peace Process.*

V. Conclusion: The Korean Peace Process and the way forward

The *Korean Peace Process* is an opportunity and a challenge for South Korea and stake-holding countries in Northeast Asia. At the initial stage of the 'Process', we could see the historic meetings between the U.S and North Korea. In addition, amid the mood of reconciliation between the DPRK, South Korea and the U.S., expectations

18 Prof. Endo Ken, who is an expert on European Studies and regional integration in Europe, strongly argued that the preconditions are definitely necessary for progressive dialogue in military area. - 2020 NAPC Forum (2020.12.3) hosted by the ROK's MOFA and Korea National Diplomatic Academy.

for reunification have also risen. However, as evaluated above, it is difficult to give high marks based on the current situation, progress and results. Therefore, we should review the ongoing progress for the resumption of the *Korean Peace Process*.

First, in order to resolve the North Korean nuclear issue, we must face the issue, not by working around it, but by focusing on tangentially related issues such as health issues. Even though it is difficult to deal with, it means that the South Korean government continues to make efforts for resolving the North Korean issue which would be evidence to North Korea of South Korea's sincerity.

Second, it is necessary for the South Korean government to consider its practical role in resolving the North Korean issue. We should balance between 'ideal' and 'reality'. In the history of the South Korean government's regional policies, the South Korean government referred to itself as a 'balancer' in Roh Moo-hyun government, a 'facilitator' in Park Geun-hye government, and a 'driver' in Moon Jae-in government. Even though it shows the character of each government, and how they planned to implement their policies, sometimes there have been cases where it exceeded the actual capacity of the government or was not appropriate for South Korea's position. Therefore, a sober judgment on the South Korea's role between reality and ideals is required.

Third, we have to foster and strengthen close cooperation and linkage with neighboring countries. The South Korean government should not just explain the idea of the *Korean Peace Process* to other countries, but persuade the establishment of a peace regime on the Korean Peninsula based on practical interests rather than ideals, and then secure support from neighboring countries and anticipate their roles.

Fourth, the *Korean Peace Process* should collaborate with other countries' regional initiatives. Every country has its own regional strategy and initiative, such as Free and Open Indo-Pacific (FOIP) of Japan and the U.S., Belt Road Initiative (BRI) of China, etc. Therefore, we need to examine closely the regional initiatives of neighboring countries, in order to get support from other countries to our regional policies.

Fifth, we should promote North Korean and regional policy as a solid national strategy, not as an agenda for each government and then acquire international trust from the other countries. As mentioned above, North Korea policy is always a 'hot potato' issue, especially in the South Korean government. It can be the identity or philosophy for each government. For that reason, it is inevitable that the North Korea policy changes whenever the regime changes in the ROK. Nevertheless, the unchanging values we must uphold in order to resolve the North Korean nuclear issue and have peace and prosperity on the Korean Peninsula and in Northeast Asia with sincerity.

References

English

Delgado, Enrique. 1978. *Economic Integration in Central America.* Washington D.C.: Brookings Institution.

Hass, Ernst B. 1975. *The Obsolescence of Regional Integration Theory.* Berkeley: Institute of International Studies.

Hemmer, Christopher and Katzenstein, Pete.J. 2002. "Why is there No NATO in Asia? Collective Identity, Regionalism, and the Origins of Multilateralism," *International Organization* 56(3), pp. 575-607.

Kahler, Miles. 1993. "Multilateralism with Small and Large Numbers," John Gerard Ruggie, ed. *Multilateralism Matters: The Theory and Praxis of an Institutional Form.* New York: Columbia University Press.

Kim, Heajin. "Northeast Asia, Trust and the NAPCI" *The Diplomat.* (2015.12.18.)

Reiterer, Michael. 2015. "The NAPCI in the Volatile Security Environment of North-East Asia: Which Role for the European Union?" *European Foreign Affairs Review* 20(4), pp. 573-589.

Snyder, Scott. "How South Korea's NAPCI Could Complement The 'Rebalance' To Asia," *Forbes.* (2015.10.1.)

Vershbow, Alexander. 2014. "NAPCI: Solving the Asian Paradox," *NATO.* (2014.10.28.)

Korean

Choi, Eunmi. 2018. "The task of promoting the Northeast Asia Peace and Cooperation Platform," *IFANS Focus* 2018-54. The Institute of Foreign Affairs and National Security of Korea National Diplomatic Academy.

__________. 2020. "South Korea's Diplomacy in the New Security Era – Suggestions for the Establishment of Multilateral Cooperation Order in Northeast Asia," *ISSUE BRIEF.* 2020-25. The Asan Institute for Policy Studies.

Kim, Chi-Wook. 2016. "Assessing the Northeast Asia Peace and Cooperation Initiative (NAPCI): A Middle-Power Diplomacy Perspective," *East Asian Studies* 71, pp.1-27.

Kim, Yong-Woo. 2004. "A comparative study of the applicable international situations of functionalism and Neo-functionalism," *Korean Policy Sciences* 8(3), pp.2-22.

Northeast Asia Peace and Cooperation Initiative Team. 2014. *Northeast Asia Peace and Cooperation Initiative.* Orem

Park, Jae-Young. 2007. *UN and International Organization.* Bobmunsa.

Seo, Bo-hyeok. 2009. "The Path of the Institutionalization of Multilateral Security Cooperation: A Study of the Application of C/OSCE Case into Northeast Asia," *Korean Journal of International Relations.* 49(2), pp. 7-31.

Song, Byung Rok. 2002. "The Applicability and Problems of OSCE to East Asia," *The Journal of Contemporary European Studies* 16, pp. 41-70.

The Sejong Institute. 2015. *Final Report on Northeast Peace and Cooperation Forum 2015*. The Sejong Institute.

________________. 2016. *Final Report of Public-Private Network Building Project 2016*. The Sejong Institute.

________________. 2017. *The White Paper of Multilateral Cooperation in Northeast Asia (2013.2-2017.4): The Progress and Challenges of Northeast Asia Peace and Cooperation Initiative*. Ministry of Foreign Affairs.

Hong, Yong-pyo. 2005. "Rethinking the June 15 North–South Joint Declaration: Theoretical Background and Meaning," Hong Yong-pyo and Cho Han-beom. *Review of the June 15 North–South Joint Declaration: Theory and Practice*. KINU Study Series 2005-03. Korea Institute for National Unification

Hwang, Ki-Sik and Yu, Jae-Eui. 2010. "The Challenge and Frustration in East Asian Regional Cooperation: the Paradox of Regional Cooperation for Hegemonic Rivalry," *New Asia*. 17(4), pp. 55-73.

Website

Cheong Wa Dae of the Republic of Korea. https://www1.president.go.kr/

Inter-Korean Summit. http://koreasummit.kr/

The Institute of Foreign Affairs and National Security, Korea National Diplomatic Academy http://www.ifans.go.kr/

Ministry of Unification. https://www.unikorea.go.kr

Ministry of Foreign Affairs. www.mofa.go.kr

Policy Briefing of the Republic of Korea. https://www.korea.kr/

The National Unification Advisory Council. https://nuac.go.kr/

United Nations Development Programme. https://www.undp.org

Authors' Bios

Sang-Hwan Lee is a professor of international relations at Hankuk University of Foreign Studies (HUFS) who was a Dean of Student Affairs and a President of Research & Industry-University Foundation. He was a Director of Global Politics Institute at HUFS, a Vice-President of Korean Political Science Association and a President of Korean Association of Political Science & Communication. Also, he was a Dean of Graduate School of Politics, Government & Communication at HUFS. Dr. Lee was an advisory committee member of the Presidential Office and joined in an advisory committee of the Ministry of Unification. Also, he has worked as an associate editor of International Area Studies Review published by Sage Publication in cooperation with HUFS and PRIO (Peace Research Institute Oslo, Norway) since 2012. He received his Ph.D. from Michigan State University in the US, and has taught at Changwon National University and HUFS since 1997. He was a President of Korean Association of International Studies (KAIS) in 2020. He has published his research papers in Korea Observer, Pacific Focus, International Area Studies Review, Journal of East Asian Affairs, Korean Journal of Area Studies, Journal of American Studies, and etc.

Scott Gates (PhD, University of Michigan, 1989) is Professor of Political Science at the University of Oslo and Research Professor at the Peace Research Institute Oslo (PRIO). He is the President of the Peace Science Society (International), 2020-2021. He is the Editor of the Journal of Peace Research and Editor of International Area Studies Review. He was Director of the Center for the Study of Civil War (CSCW) at PRIO, 2002-2013, which was designated by the Research Council of Norway as a Center of Excellence. Gates has published over thirty peer-reviewed articles and twelve books including: Fragile Bargains: Civil Conflict and Power Sharing in Africa, coauthored with Kaare Strøm (Cambridge University Press, forthcoming) and Limited War in South Asia with Kaushik Roy (Routledge, 2018). His articles have appeared in APSR, AJPS, JOP, JCR, JPR, inter alia. Gates' current research interests include bureaucratic politics, applied game theory, the consequences of warfare, democratization, regime stability, and the organizational basis of rebellion and non-violent resistance.

Soohwan Hwang is a senior researcher at Kangwon Institute for Unification Studies(KIUS), Kangwon National University. He received his M.A., and Ph.D. in the Department of Political Science from Hankuk University of Foreign Studies (Seoul, Korea). His research interests include inter-Korean relations, Korean unification and peace studies.

Sukhoon Hong is a Research Fellow at the Korea Institute for National Unification. His research area includes the US-North Korea relations and North Korean foreign policy as well as the Asian "peace regime." He received his Ph.D. in Political Science from the University of Georgia (USA). Hong's existing works in this area have been published in KINU's policy reports, International Area Studies Review, the Korean Journal of International Studies, National Security and Strategy, the Journal of Peace Studies, and in various book chapters. Recently, he authored "North Korea's Transition of Its Economic Development Strategy: Its Significance and the Political Environment surrounding the Korean Peninsula" published in the Korean Journal of Defense Analysis, December 2018 issue.

Håvard Mokleiv Nygård (PhD, University of Oslo, 2014) is Research Director at the Peace

Research Institute Oslo (PRIO). Nygård's main research interests are related to understanding the causes, consequences and dynamics of armed conflict, contentious action, peacebuilding, and social order. His research has a been published in inter alia the American Journal of Political Science, Journal of Politics, World Politics, Journal of Peace Research, Journal of Conflict Resolution, and World Development. Nygård regularly consults for various international organizations such as the World Bank, the United Nations Development Program, the Community of Democracies, the EU External Action Services, and the Human Security Report.

Dongsoo Kim is currently Associate Professor at the Division of International and Area Studies at Pukyong National University in Busan, South Korea. Before joining Pukyong National University, He worked as research fellow at Korea Institute for National Unification, Seoul, South Korea. He also taught at the University of Southern Mississippi, Hattiesburg, Mississippi and West Liberty University, West Liberty, West Virginia in the United States. Dr. Kim received his Ph.D. in political science and international affairs from the University of Georgia, Athens, Georgia. His research interest include, but are not limited to, international conflict, US foreign policy, and US-North Korea relations, and inter-Korean relations. His publication include "The Struggle between Security and Democracy: An Alternative Explanation of the Democratization of South Korea," Pacific Focus (April 2010); Risk-Taking or Risk-Aversive: Understanding North Korea's Foreign Policy of Brinkmanship (co-authored with Yongseok Choy), Korea Observer (Autumn 2011).

Wonjae Hwang (Ph.D. in Political Science, Michigan State University) is an associate professor of the department of political science at the University of Tennessee. His research focuses on how globalization affects domestic politics and international relations, and Korean/Asian politics. His work has been published in numerous journals including American Journal of Political Science, Journal of Politics, International Studies Quarterly, and Asian Survey. His book, South Korea's Changing Foreign Policy: The Impact of Democratization and Globalization, explores how democratization and economic globalization have changed domestic politics in South Korea and reshaped its foreign policies.

Inhan Kim (Ph.D. in Political Science from University of Virginia) is an associate professor of the Department of Political Science and International Relations at Ewha Womans University. His research focuses on inter-Korean relations and U.S. foreign policy in East Asia. His research works have been published in the Pacific Review, the Washington Quarterly and other academic journals.

Jiyoun Park (Ph.D. in North Korean Studies, Ewha Womans University) is an assistant professor at the School of International Studies, Jeonbuk National University. Her research interests are in the field of North Korea, foreign aid, and economic sanctions. Her research works have been published in several journals, including International Political Science Review, Journal of the Asia Pacific Economy, International Journal of Conflict and Violence and etc.

Hyun Jin Choi (Ph.D. in political science, Michigan State University) is an associate professor of political science at Kyung Hee University, Seoul. His research interests fall within the field of civil war, Sub-Saharan Africa, and international development. Prior to joining Kyung Hee University, Professor Choi was a Postdoctoral Research Fellow of the European Research Council at the University of Sussex, England. His articles have been published in numerous refereed journals, including Global Environmental Change, International Studies Quarterly, Comparative Politics, Journal of Conflict Resolution, and International Political Science Review.

Youngwan Kim (Ph.D. in political science, University of Iowa) is Professor at the Division of

Language and Diplomacy, Hankuk University of Foreign Studies. His research interests include NGOs, foreign aid, international development cooperation, international organizations, and international law. With co-authored book, International Organizations, his representative works have been published in several journals like World Development, Development and Change, Foreign Policy Analysis, Disasters, etc

Jaeyoung Hur is an Assistant Professor at the Global Leaders College, Yonsei University. He received his M.A., and Ph.D. in the Department of Political Science from Yonsei University (Seoul, Korea). His current areas of research include unification of the Korean Peninsula, inter-Korean relations, political and media discourse analysis, public opinion. He can be reached at jyounghur@yonsei.ac.kr.

Sanghoon Park is a Ph.D. student of the Department of Political Science at the University of South Carolina, Columbia. He received a bachelor's degree in political science and international relations and a master's degree in political science from Hankuk University of Foreign Studies in Seoul, Republic of Korea. His research interest includes how and under what conditions autocrats use their power to perpetuate their rule.

Atsushi Tago is a professor of International Relations at the School of Political Science and Economics, Waseda University (Ph.D., University of Tokyo, 2007). He is specialized in a scientific study of international politics. More specifically, he publishes articles on American use of force and its coalition of the willing. Currently, he is working on scientific study of Public Diplomacy. His recent study with co-authors appeared in Political Communication, which also turned into a Washington Post Monkey Cage article. He has been a PRIO Global Fellow since 2017.

Mason Richey is Associate Professor of international politics at Hankuk University of Foreign Studies (Seoul, South Korea). Dr. Richey has also held positions as a POSCO Visiting Research Fellow at the East-West Center (Honolulu, HI) and a DAAD Scholar at the University of Potsdam. His research focuses on U.S. and European foreign and security policy as applied to the Asia-Pacific. Recent scholarly articles have appeared (inter alia) in Pacific Review, Asian Security, Global Governance, and Foreign Policy Analysis. Shorter analyses and opinion pieces have been published in 38North, War on the Rocks, Le Monde, the Sueddeutsche Zeitung, and Forbes, among other venues.

Daewon Ohn is Professor of International Relations and European Union (EU) Studies at the Graduate School of International and Area Studies, Hankuk University of Foreign Studies. He received his MA from Georgetown University and a PhD from the London School of Economics and Political Science. Professor Ohn has written numerous books and articles on European security and defence policy and the foreign and security policies of the great powers in the modern period. His recent research topics have included the foreign, security and defence policy of the EU and the prospects of transatlantic security cooperation.

Jangho Kim is Associate Professor at, and was formerly the Dean of, the Division of Language & Diplomacy, Hankuk University of Foreign Studies. He currently serves on numerous committees in the university, including the Admissions Committee and the Committee for Future and Vision. Previously, he was a Research Fellow at the Korea Institute for National Unification (KINU). While at KINU, he was in charge of its External Affairs which included the tasks of dealing with the media, all activities abroad, and organizing and over-seeing the proceedings of all international conferences. He also served as a member of the Presidential National Unification Advisory Council. He is an Associate Editor of the International Area Studies Review. His main research interests are on international relations theory, Sino-American Relations, Korean Foreign Policy, and middle power diplomacy. He has published in books, policy papers, government funded research and white papers, as well as articles in academic journals.

Jae Jeok Park (Ph.D. in International Relations, Australian National University) is Associate Professor at Hankuk University of Foreign Studies in Seoul. Previously, he worked as a visiting professor at Institute of Foreign Affairs and National Security(IFANS) and a research fellow at Korea Institute for National Unification(KINU). His research interests include alliance politics, US security policy in Indo-Pacific, the US-ROK alliance, and the US-Australia alliance.

Eunmi Choi (Ph.D. in political science, Korea University) is a Research Fellow at the Asan Institute for Policy Studies (AIPS). Her main area of research interests is Korea-Japan Relations, Japanese politics and diplomacy, and multilateral cooperation in Northeast Asia. Her recent publications include National Identity and China-Japan-Korea Relations (2020, co-authored), "Historical Development and Structural Transformation of Conflict Management Mechanism between Korea and Japan(2020, The Journal of Asiatic Studies), "Where is NAPCI?: The Challenges and Limitations of the (Neo-)Functionalist Approach for Multilateral Cooperation in Northeast Asia" (2020, National Strategy), etc.

Issues and Perspectives in The Korean Peace Process

The Korean Association of International Studies · Sang-Hwan Lee

First Printed	2021.2.22
First Published	2021.2.25
Director	Seongwoo Yun
Executive Contents Creator	Sunho Shin
Contents Creator	Haejung Jang
	Keunyoung Lee
Designer	Seungmin Woo
Published by	HANKUK UNIVERSITY OF FOREIGN STUDIES
	KNOWLEDGE CONTENTS & PRESS
	107, Imun-ro, Dongdaemun-gu, Seoul 02450, Korea
	Tel.) 82-2-2173-2497 Fax.) 82-2-2173-3363
	E-mail) press@hufs.ac.kr
	Online) http://press.hufs.ac.kr
Printed by	K·PRINTEC Tel.) 053-313-3673
ISBN	979-11-5901-852-7 [93340]
Price	22,000 Won